Java™ 5

A Beginner's Tutorial

Budi Kurniawan

Java^{TM} 5 : A Beginner's Tutorial
Copyright © 2006 by Budi Kurniawan
First Edition: March 2006

International Standard Book Number: 0-9752128-5-0

Printed in the United States of America
Book and Cover Designer: Mona Setiadi

Technical Reviewer: Paul Deck
Indexer: Chris Mayle

Warning and Disclaimer

Table of Contents

Introduction

Welcome to *Java 5: A Beginner's Tutorial*. Java is a mature programming language that is easy to learn. At the same time it is also a vast collection of technologies that are so diverse that beginners often don't know where to start. If you are one of them, then this book is for you because it has been designed as a tutorial for novices.

As a beginner's tutorial, this book does not teach you every Java technology there is. (It is impossible to cram everything into a single volume anyway, and that's why most Java titles are focused on one technology.) Rather, this book covers the most important Java programming topics that you need to master to be able to learn other technologies yourself. Nonetheless this book is comprehensive that by fully understanding all the chapters and doing the exercises you'll be able to perform an intermediate Java programmer's daily tasks quite well.

This book offers all the three subjects that a professional Java programmer must be proficient in:

- Java as a programming language;
- Object-oriented programming (OOP) with Java;
- Java core libraries.

What makes structuring an effective Java course difficult is the fact that the three subjects mentioned above are interdependent. On the one hand, Java is an OOP language, so its syntax is easier to learn if you already know about OOP. On the other hand, OOP features such as inheritance, polymorphism, and data encapsulation, are best taught if accompanied by real-world examples. Unfortunately, understanding real-world Java programs requires knowledge of the Java core libraries.

Because of such interdependence, the three main topics are not grouped into three isolated parts. Instead, chapters discussing a major topic and chapters teaching another are interwoven. For example, before explaining polymorphism, this book makes sure that you are familiar with certain Java classes so that real-world examples can be given. In addition, because a language feature such as generics cannot be explained effectively without the comprehension of a certain set of classes, it is covered after the discussion of the supporting classes.

There are also situations whereby a topic can be found in two or more places. For instance, the **for** statement is a basic language feature that should be discussed in an early chapter. However, **for** can also be used to iterate over a collection of objects, a feature that should only be given after the Collections Framework is taught. Therefore, **for** is first presented in Chapter 3, "Statements" and then revisited in Chapter 11, "The Collections Framework."

The rest of this introduction presents a high-level overview of Java, an introduction to OOP, a brief description of each chapter, and instructions for installing the Java software.

Java, the Language and the Technology

Java is not only a object-oriented programming language, it is also a set of technologies that make software development more rapid and resulting applications more robust and secure. For years Java has been the technology of choice because of the benefits it offers:

- platform independence
- ease of use
- complete libraries that speed up application development
- security
- scalability
- extensive industry support

Sun Microsystems introduced Java in 1995 and Java—even though it had been a general-purpose language right from the start—was soon well known as the language for writing applets, small programs that run inside Web browsers and add interactivity to static Web sites. The growth of the Internet had much to contribute to the early success of Java.

Having said that, applets were not the only factor that made Java shine. The other most appealing feature of Java was its platform-independence promise, hence the slogan "Write Once, Run Anywhere." What this means is the very same program you write will run on Windows, Unix, Mac, Linux, and other operating systems. This was something no other programming language could do. At that time, C and C++ were the two most commonly used languages for developing serious applications. Java seemed to have stolen their thunder since its first birthday.

That was Java version 1.0.

In 1997, Java 1.1 was released, adding significant features such as a better event model, Java Beans, and internationalization to the original.

Java 1.2 was launched in December 1998. Three days afterwards, the version number was changed to 2, marking the beginning of a huge marketing campaign that started in 1999 to sell Java as the "next generation" technology. Java 2 was sold in four flavors: the Standard Edition (J2SE), the Enterprise Edition (J2EE), the Micro Edition (J2ME), and Java Card (that never adopted "2" in its brand name).

The next version released in 2000 was 1.3, hence J2SE 1.3. 1.4 came two years later to make J2SE 1.4. J2SE version 1.5 was released in 2004. However, the name Java 2 version 1.5 was then changed to Java 5.

Note

See http://www.java.com/en/javahistory/ and http://java.sun.com/features/1998/05/birthday.html for more detail on the history of Java. Java naming is also discussed in the article "Building and Strengthening the Java Brand" that can be found at http://java.sun.com/developer/technicalArticles/JavaOne2005/naming.html.

What Makes Java Platform Independent?

You must have heard of the terms "platform-independent" or "cross-platform," which means your program can run on multiple operating systems. This is one major factor that made Java popular. But, what makes Java platform independent?

In traditional programming, source code is compiled into executable code. This executable code can run only on the platform it is intended to run. In other words, code written and compiled for Windows will only run on Windows, code written in Linux will only run on Linux, and so on. This is depicted in Figure I.1.

Figure I.1: Traditional programming paradigm

A Java program, on the other hand, is compiled to bytecode. You cannot run bytecode by itself because it is not native code. Bytecode can only run on a Java Virtual Machine (JVM). A JVM is a native application that interprets bytecode. By making the JVM available in many platforms, Sun transformed Java into a cross-platform language. As shown in Figure I.2, the very same bytecode can run on any operating system for which a JVM has been developed.

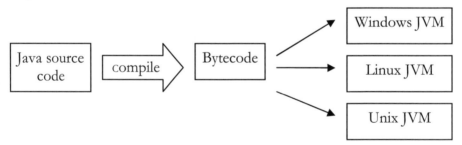

Figure I.2: Java programming model

Currently JVMs are available for Windows, Unix, Linux, Free BSD, Macintosh, and practically all other operating systems in the world.

JDK, JRE, JVM, What's the Difference?

I mentioned previously that Java programs must be compiled. In fact, any programming language will need a compiler to be really useful. A compiler is a program that converts program source code to an executable format, either a bytecode, native code, or something else. Before you can start programming

Java, you need to download a Java compiler. The Java compiler is a program named **javac**, which is short for Java compiler.

While **javac** can compile Java sources to bytecode, to run bytecode you need a Java Virtual Machine. In addition, because you will invariably use classes in the Java core libraries, you also need to download these libraries. The Java Runtime Environment (JRE) contains both a JVM and class libraries. As you may suspect, the JRE for Windows is different from that for Linux, which is different from the one for yet another operating system.

The Java software is available in two distributions:

- The JRE, which includes a JVM and the core libraries. This is good for running bytecode.
- The JDK, which includes the JRE plus a compiler and other tools. This is required software to write and compile Java programs.

To summarize, a JVM is a native application that runs bytecode. The JRE is an environment that includes a JVM and Java class libraries. The JDK includes the JRE plus other tools including a Java compiler. You can download the JRE and the JDK from Sun's Web site:

```
http://java.sun.com/j2se/1.5.0/download.jsp
```

Even though both the JRE and the JDK are free to use, the distribution licensing is different. Generally, you can distribute the JRE but must pay to distribute the JDK.

The first version of the JDK is 1.0. The versions after that are 1.1, 1.2, 1.3, 1.4, and 1.5. For minor releases, add another number to the version number. For instance, 1.5.1 is the first minor upgrade to version 1.5.

JDK 1.5 (code-named Tiger) is the latest release of the JDK and is better known as JDK 5. The version of the JRE included in a JDK is the same as the JDK. Therefore, JDK 1.5 contains JRE 1.5. The JDK is also often called the SDK (Software Development Kit).

In addition to the JDK, a Java programmer needs to download Java documentation that explains classes in the core libraries. You can download the documentation from the same URL that provides the JRE and the JDK.

Java 2, J2SE, J2EE, J2ME, Java 5, What Are They?

Sun Microsystems has done a lot to promote Java. Part of its marketing strategy was to coin the name Java 2, which was basically JDK 1.2. There were three editions of Java 2:

- Java 2 Platform, Standard Edition (J2SE). J2SE is basically the JDK. It also serves as the foundation for technologies defined in J2EE.
- Java 2 Platform, Enterprise Edition (J2EE). It defines the standard for developing component-based multi-tier enterprise applications. Features include Web services support and development tools (SDK).
- Java 2 Platform, Micro Edition (J2ME). It provides an environment for applications that run on consumer devices, such as mobile phones, personal digital assistants (PDAs), and TV set-top boxes. J2ME includes a JVM and a limited set of class libraries.

Name changes occurred in version 5. J2SE became *Java Platform, Standard Edition 5* (Java SE 5). Also, the 2 in J2EE and J2ME has been dropped. The next version of the enterprise edition is *Java Platform, Enterprise Edition 5* (Java EE 5). J2ME is now called *Java Platform, Micro Edition* (Java ME, without a version number). In this book, Java 5 is used to refer to Java SE 5.

Note that while Java SE 5 is a product (a JDK), J2EE and Java EE 5 are sets of specifications that include technologies such as servlets, JavaServer Pages, JavaServer Faces, Java Messaging Service, etc. To develop and run J2EE and Java EE 5 applications, you will need a J2EE/Java EE 5 application server. Anyone can implement a J2EE/Java EE 5 application server. This explains the availability of various application servers in the market, including some open source ones. Here are examples of J2EE/Java EE 5 application servers:

- BEA's WebLogic
- IBM's WebSphere
- Sun Microsystems' Sun Java Application Server
- Oracle's 10g Application Server
- GlassFish
- JBoss
- Jonas
- Apache Geronimo

JBoss, Jonas, and Geronimo are open source application servers. They have different licenses, though, so make sure you read them before using the products.

The Java Community Process (JCP) Program

Java's continuous dominance as the technology of choice owes much to Sun's strategy to include other industry players in determining the future of Java. This way, many people feel that they also own Java. Many large corporations, such as IBM, BEA, Oracle, Nokia, Fujitsu, etc, invest heavily in Java because they too can propose a specification for a technology and put forward what they want to see in the next version of a Java technology. This collaborative effort takes the form of the JCP Program. The URL of its Web site is http://www.jcp.org.

An Overview of Object-Oriented Programming

Object-oriented programming (OOP) works by modeling applications on real-world objects. Three principles of OOP are encapsulation, inheritance, and polymorphism. They are given thorough coverage in this book.

The benefits of OOP are real. These are the reason why most modern programming languages, including Java, are object-oriented (OO). I can even cite two well-known examples of language transformation to support OOP: The C language evolved into C++ and Visual Basic was upgraded into Visual Basic.NET.

This section explains the benefits of OOP and provides an assessment of how easy or hard it is to learn OOP.

The Benefits of OOP

The benefits of OOP include easy code maintenance, code reuse, and extendibility. These benefits are presented in more detail below.

1. **Ease of maintenance**. Modern software applications tend to be very large. Once upon a time, a "large" system comprised a few thousand

lines of code. Now, even those consisting of one million lines are not considered that large. When a system gets larger, it starts giving its developers problems. Bjarne Stroustrup, the father of C++, once said something like this. A small program can be written in anything, anyhow. If you don't quit easily, you'll make it work, at the end. But a large program is a different story. If you don't use techniques of "good programming," new errors will emerge as fast as you fix the old ones. The reason for this is there is interdependency among different parts of a large program. When you change something in some part of the program, you may not realize how the change might affect other parts. OOP makes it easy to make applications modular, and modularity makes maintenance less of a headache. Modularity is inherent in OOP because a class, which is a template for objects, is a module by itself. A good design should allow a class to contain similar functionality and related data. An important and related term that is used often in OOP is coupling, which means the degree of interaction between two modules. Loosely coupling among parts make code reuse—another benefit of OOP—easier to achieve.

2. **Reusability**. Reusability means that code that has previously been written can be reused by the code writer and others who need the same functionality provided by the original code. It is not surprising, then, that an OOP language often comes with a set of ready-to-use libraries. In the case of Java, the language is accompanied by hundreds of class libraries or Application Programming Interfaces (APIs) that have been carefully designed and tested. It is also easy to write and distribute your own library. Support for reusability in a programming platform is very attractive, because it shortens the time taken to develop an application. One of the main challenges to class reusability is creating good documentation for the class library. How fast can a programmer find a class that provides the functionality he/she is looking for? Is it faster to find such a class or write a new one from scratch? Fortunately, Java core and extended APIs come with extensive documentation.

Reusability does not only apply to the coding phase through the reuse of classes and other types; when designing an application in an OO system, solutions to OO design problems can also be reused. These solutions are called design patterns. To make it easier to refer to each solution, ach pattern is given a name. The early catalog of reusable design pattern can be found in the classic book *Design Patterns: Elements of Reusable Object-*

Oriented Software, by Erich Gamma, Richard Helm, Ralph Johnson, and John Vlissides.

3. **Extendibility**

   Every application is unique. It has its own requirements and specifications. In terms of reusability, sometimes you cannot find an existing class that provides the exact functionality that your application requires. However, you will probably find one or two that provide part of the functionality. Extendibility means that you can still use those classes by extending them so that they suit your need. You still save time, because you don't have to write code from scratch.

   In OOP, extendibility is achieved through inheritance. You can extend an existing class, add some methods or data to it, or change the behavior of methods you don't like. If you know the basic functionality that will be used in many cases, but you don't want your class to provide very specific functions, you can provide a generic class that can be extended later to provide functionality specific to an application.

Is OOP Hard?

Java programmers need to master OOP. As it happens, it does make a difference if you have had programmed using a procedural language, such as C or Pascal. In the light of this, there is bad news and good news.

First the bad news.

Researchers have been debating the best way to teach OOP at school; some argue that it is best to teach procedural programming before OOP is introduced. In many curricula, we see that a OOP course can be taken when a student is nearing the final year of his/her university term.

More recent studies, however, argue that someone with procedural programming skill thinks in a paradigm very different from how OO programmers view and try to solve problems. When this person needs to learn OOP, the greatest struggle he/she faces is having to go through a paradigm shift. It is said that it takes six to 18 months to switch your mindset from procedural to object-oriented paradigms. Another study shows that students who have not learned procedural programming do not find OOP that difficult.

Now the good news.

Java qualifies as one of the easiest OOP languages to learn. For example, you do not need to worry about pointers, don't have to spend precious time solving memory leaks caused by forgetting to destroy unused objects, etc. On top of that, Java comes with very comprehensive class libraries with relatively very few bugs in their early versions. Once you know the nuts and bolts of OOP, programming with Java is really easy.

New Features in Java 5

If you have used Java before and now want to upgrade your skills, you might be interested in learning the new features in Java 5, all of which are covered in this book. If you are an absolute beginner, feel free to skip this section.

- **Generics**. Provides compile-time type safety while still allowing a type or method to operate on objects of various types.
- **Enhanced for Loop**. The **for** statement can now be used to iterate over an array and a collection.
- **Autoboxing/unboxing**. Automatic conversion of primitives to wrapper types and vice versa.
- **Enum type**. A new enumeration type in Java.
- **Varargs**. Allows a method to accept a variable number of arguments.
- **Static import**. Eliminates the need to qualify static members with class names.
- **Annotations**. A special type of interface used for annotating any program elements.

About This Book

The following presents the overview of each chapter.

Chapter 1, "Your First Taste of Java" aims at giving you the feel of working with Java. This includes writing a simple Java program, compiling it using the **javac** tool, and running it using the **java** program. In addition, some advice on code conventions and integrated development environments is also given.

Chapter 2, "Language Fundamentals", teaches you the Java language syntax. You will be introduced to topics such as character sets, primitives, variables, operators, etc.

Chapter 3, "Statements", explains Java statements **for, while, do-while, if, if-else, switch, break,** and **continue**.

Chapter 4, "Objects and Classes," is the first OOP lesson in this book. It starts by explaining what a Java object is an how it is stored in memory. It then continues with a discussion of classes, class members, and two OOP concepts (abstraction and encapsulation). Some related topics, such as garbage collection and object comparison, are briefly discussed.

Chapter 5, "Core Classes" covers important classes in the Java core libraries: **java.lang.Object, java.lang.String, java.lang.StringBuffer** and **java.lang.StringBuilder**, wrapper classes, and **java.util.Scanner**. The concepts of boxing/unboxing and varargs are also taught. This is an important chapter because the classes explained in this chapter are some of the most commonly used classes in the Java programming language.

Chapter 6, "Inheritance" discusses the OOP feature that enables code extendibility. This chapter teaches you how to extend a class, affect the visibility of a subclass, override a method, and so forth.

Undoubtedly, error handling is an important feature of any programming language. As a mature language, Java has a very robust error handling mechanism that can help prevent bugs from creeping in. Chapter 7, "Error Handling" is a detailed discussion of this mechanism.

Chapter 8, "Numbers and Dates" deals with three issues when working with numbers and dates: parsing, formatting, and manipulation. This chapter introduces Java classes that can help you with these tasks.

Chapter 9, "Interfaces and Abstract Classes", explains that an interface is more than a class without implementation. An interface defines a contract between a service provider and a client. This chapter explains how to work with interfaces and abstract classes.

Chapter 10, "Enums" covers enum, a new type in Java 5.

Chapter 11, "The Collections Framework" shows how you can use the members of the **java.util** package to group objects and manipulate them.

Generics are the most important feature in Java 5 and Chapter 12, "Generics" adequately explains this feature.

Chapter 13, "Input Output" introduces the concept of streams and explains how you can use the four stream types in the **java.io** package to perform input-output operations. In addition, object serialization and deserialization are discussed.

Chapter 14, "Nested and Inner Classes" explains how you can write a class within another class and why this OOP feature can be very useful.

Chapter 15, "Swing Basics" is the first installment of the two chapters on Swing. It briefly discusses the AWT components and thoroughly explains some basic Swing components.

Chapter 16, "Swinging Higher" is the second chapter on Swing. It covers more advanced techniques such as layout management, event handling, and Swing's look and feel.

Polymorphism is one of the main pillars of OOP. It is incredibly useful in situations whereby the type of an object in not known at compile time. Chapter 17, "Polymorphism" explains this feature and provides useful examples.

Chapter 18, "Annotations" talks about one of the new features in Java 5. It explains the standard annotations that come with the JDK, meta-annotations, and custom annotations.

Today it is common for software applications to be deployable to different countries and regions. Such applications need to be designed with internationalization in mind. Chapter 19, "Internationalization" explores related techniques that can be used in Java.

Applets are small programs that run on the Web browser. Chapter 20, "Applets" explains the lifecycle of an applet, security restrictions, and **JApplet**.

Chapter 21, "Java Networking" deals with classes that can be used in network programming. A simple Web server application is presented to illustrate how to use these classes.

Accessing databases and manipulating data are some of the most important tasks when writing business applications. There are many flavors of database servers and access to different databases requires different skills. Fortunately for Java programmers, the Java Database Connectivity (JDBC) technology provides a uniform way of accessing databases. JDBC is discussed in Chapter 22, "Java Database Connectivity."

A thread is a basic processing unit to which an operating system allocates processor time, and more than one thread can be executing code inside a process. Chapter 23, "Java Threads," shows that in Java multithreaded programming is not only the domain of expert programmers.

Chapter 24, "Security" is a tutorial on how Java application users can restrict running Java applications and how you can use cryptography to secure your application and data.

Chapter 25, "Java Web Applications" explores the Servlet technology and the Servlet API and presents several examples.

Chapter 26, "JavaServer Pages" explains another Web development technology and shows how to write JSP pages.

Chapter 27, "Generating Java Doc" discusses the **javadoc** tool that Java programmers can use to generate documentation for their APIs.

Chapter 28, "Application Deployment," talks about Java Web Start and how to use it to deploy Java applications over the Internet, across a local network, and from a CD.

Appendix A, "javac", Appendix B, "java", and Appendix C, "jar" explain the **javac**, **java**, and **jar** tools, respectively.

Appendix D, "NetBeans" and Appendix E, "Eclipse" provide brief tutorials on NetBeans and Eclipse, respectively.

Downloading and Installing Java 5

Before you can start compiling and running Java programs, you need to download and install the JDK as well as configure some system environment variables. It is also recommended that you download the API documentation.

Downloading and Installing the JDK

The JDKs for Windows, Linux, and UNIX can be downloaded from this URL:

```
http://java.sun.com/j2se/1.5.0/download.jsp
```

Once you click the link, you'll be redirected to a page that lets you select an installation for your platform: Windows, Linux, or Unix. The 64 bit versions for certain platforms are available. Also, note that the same link also provides the JRE. However, you need the JDK, and the JDK includes the JRE.

For Macintosh, download the JDK from this URL:

```
http://developer.apple.com/java/download/
```

After obtaining the JDK, you need to install it. Installation varies from one operating system to another. These subsections detail the installation process.

Installation on Windows

Installation on Windows is easy. Simply double-click the icon of the executable file you downloaded and follow the instructions.

Installation on UNIX and Linux

On these platforms, the JDK is available in two installation formats.

- Self-extracting binary file. This format can be used to install the JDK in a location you choose and you do not need to be a root user.
- Packages. A compressed file containing packages to be installed.

If you are using the self-extracting binary installation, follow these steps.

1. Use **chmod** to give the file the execute permissions:

   ```
   chmod +x shFile
   ```

   Here, *shFile* is the downloaded sh file for your platform.
2. Change directory to the location where you would like the files to be installed.
3. Run the self-extracting binary. Execute the downloaded file with the path prepended to it. For example, if the file is in the current directory, prepend it with "./" (necessary if "." is not in the PATH environment variable):

   ```
   ./shFile
   ```

If you downloaded the JDK in the package format, see the following URLs:

```
http://java.sun.com/j2se/1.5.0/install-linux.html
http://java.sun.com/j2se/1.5.0/install-solaris.html
```

Configuring System Environment Variables

After you install the JDK, you can start compiling and running Java programs. However, you can only invoke the compiler and the JRE from the location of the **javac** and **java** programs or by including the installation path in your command. To make compiling and running programs easier, it is important that you set the **PATH** environment variable on your computer so that you can invoke **javac** and **java** from any directory.

Setting the Path Environment Variable on Windows

To set the **PATH** environment variable on Windows NT, Windows 2000, and Windows XP, do these steps:

1. Click **Start**, **Settings**, **Control Panel**.
2. Double-click **System**.
3. on Windows NT, select the **Environment** tab. On Windows 2000 and Windows XP select the **Advanced** tab and then click on **Environment Variables**.
4. Locate the **Path** environment variable in the **User Variables** or **System Variables** panes. The value of **Path** is a series of directories separated by semicolons. Now, add the full path to the **bin** directory of your Java installation directory to the end of the existing value of **Path**. The directory looks something like:

   ```
   C:\Program Files\Java\jdk1.5.0_<version>\bin
   ```

5. Click **Set**, **OK**, or **Apply**.

Setting the Path Environment Variable on UNIX and Linux

Set the path environment variable on these operating systems depends on the shell you use.

For the C shell, add the following to the end of your ~/.cshrc file:

```
set path=(path/to/jdk/bin $path)
```

where *path/to/jdk/bin* is the bin directory under your JDK installation directory.

For the Bourne Again shell, add this line to the end of your **~/.bashrc** or **~/.bash_profile** file:

```
export PATH=/path/to/jdk/bin:$PATH
```

Here, *path/to/jdk/bin* is the **bin** directory under your JDK installation directory.

Testing the Installation

To confirm that you have installed the JDK correctly, type **javac** on the command line from any directory on your machine. If you see instructions on how to correctly run **javac**, then you have successfully installed it. On the other hand, if you can only run **javac** from the **bin** directory of the JDK installation directory, your **PATH** environment variable was not configured properly.

Installing Java API Documentation

When programming Java, you will invariably use classes from the core libraries. Even seasoned programmers look up the documentation for those libraries when they are coding. Therefore, it is also recommended to download and install the documentation.

You can download the documentation from this site:

```
http://java.sun.com/j2se/1.5.0/download.jsp
```

Downloading Program Examples and Answers

The program examples accompanying this book and answers to the questions in each chapter can be downloaded from this URL:

```
http://books.brainysoftware.com/download/jdk5Samples.zip
```

Chapter 1
Your First Taste of Java

Developing a Java program involves writing code, compiling it into bytecode, and running the bytecode. This is a process you will repeat again and again during your career as a Java programmer, and it is crucial that you feel comfortable with it. The main objective of this chapter therefore is to give you the opportunity to experience the process of software development in Java.

As it is important to write code that not only works but that is also easy to read and maintain, this chapter introduces you to Java code conventions. And, since smart developers use an integrated development environments (IDEs) to make their lives easier, the last section of this chapter provides some advice on Java IDEs.

Your First Java Program

This section highlights steps in Java development: writing the program, compiling it into bytecode, and running the bytecode.

Writing a Java Program

You can use any text editor to write a Java program. Open a text editor and write the code in Listing 1.1. Alternatively, if you have downloaded the program examples accompanying this book, you can simply copy it to your text editor.

Listing 1.1: A simple Java program

```java
class MyFirstJava {
    public static void main(String[] args) {
        System.out.println("Java rocks.");
    }
```

}

For now, suffice it to say that Java code must reside in a class. Also, make sure you save the code in Listing 1.1 as the **MyFirstJava.java** file. All Java source files must have the **java** extension.

Compiling Your Java Program

You use the **javac** program in the **bin** directory of your JDK installation directory to compile Java programs. Assuming you have edited the **PATH** environment variable in your computer (if not, see the section "Downloading and Installing Java 5" in Introduction), you should be able to invoke **javac** from any directory. To compile the **MyFirstJava** class in Listing 1.1, do the following:

1. Open a command prompt and change directory to the directory where the **MyFirstProgram.java** file was saved in.
2. Type the following command.

```
javac MyFirstJava.java
```

If everything goes well, **javac** will create a file named **MyFirstJava.class** in your working directory.

Note
The **javac** tool has more features that you can use by passing options. For example, you can tell it where you want the generated class file to be created. Appendix A, "javac" discusses **javac** in clear detail.

Running Your Java Program

To run your Java program, use the **java** program that is part of the JDK. Again, having added the **PATH** environment variable, you should be able to invoke **java** from any directory. From your working directory, type the following and press Enter.

```
java MyFirstJava
```

Note that you do not include the **class** extension when running a Java program.

You will see the following on your console.

```
Java rocks.
```

Congratulations. You have successfully written your first Java program. Since the sole aim of this chapter is to familiarize yourself with the writing and compiling process, I will not be attempting to explain how the program works.

Note

The **java** tool is an advanced application that you can configure by passing options. For instance, you can set the amount of memory allocated to it. Appendix B, "java" explains these options.

Note

The **java** tool can also be used to run a Java class that is packaged in a jar file. Check the section "Setting an Application's Entry Point" in Appendix C, "jar."

Java Code Conventions

It is important to write correct Java programs that run. However, it is also crucial to write programs that are easy to read and maintain. It is believed that eighty percent of the lifetime cost of a piece of software is spent on maintenance. Also, the turnover of programmers is high, thus it is very likely that someone other than you will maintain your code during its lifetime. Whoever inherits your code will appreciate clear and easy-to-read program sources.

Using consistent code conventions is one way to make your code easier to read. (Other ways include proper code organization and sufficient commenting.) Code conventions include filenames, file organization, indentation, comments, declaration, statements, white space, and naming conventions. Consider the following example.

A class declaration starts with the keyword **class** followed by a class name and the opening brace {. You can place the opening brace on the same line as the class name, as shown in Listing 1.1, or you can write it on the next line, as demonstrated in Listing 1.2.

Listing 1.2: MyFirstJava written using a different code convention

```
class MyFirstJava
{
    public static void main(String[] args)
    {
        System.out.println("Java rocks.");
    }
}
```

The code in Listing 1.2 is as good as the one in Listing 1.1. It is just that the class has been written using a different convention. You should adopt a consistent style for all your program elements. It is up to you to define your own code conventions, however Sun Microsystems has published a document that outlines standards that its employees should follow. The document can be viewed here.

```
http://java.sun.com/docs/codeconv/
```

Program samples in this book will follow the recommended conventions outlined in this document. I'd also like to encourage you to develop the habit of following these conventions since the first day of your programming career, so that writing clear code comes naturally at a later stage.

Your first lesson on styles is about indentation. The unit of indentation must be four spaces. If tabs are used in place of spaces, they must be set every eight spaces (not four).

Integrated Development Environments (IDEs)

It is true that you can write Java programs using a text editor. However, an IDE will help. Not only will it check the syntax of your code, an IDE can also auto complete code, debug, and trace your programs. In addition, compilation can happen automatically as you type, and running a Java program is simply a matter of clicking a button. As a result, you will develop in much shorter time.

There are dozens of Java IDEs out there, and, fortunately, the best of them are free. Here is a brief list.

- NetBeans (free and open source)
- Eclipse (free and open source)

- Sun's Java Studio Enterprise (free)
- Sun's Java Studio Creator (free)
- Oracle JDeveloper (free)
- Borland JBuilder
- IBM's WebSphere Studio Application Developer
- BEA WebLogic Workshop
- IntelliJ IDEA

The two most popular are NetBeans and Eclipse and the past few years have seen a war between the two to become the number one. NetBeans and Eclipse are both open source with strong backers. Sun Microsystems launched NetBeans in 2000 after buying the Czech company Netbeans Ceska Republika and is still heavily investing in it. Eclipse was originated by IBM to compete with NetBeans.

Which one is better depends on who you ask, but their popularity has become the impetus that propelled other software makers to give away their IDEs too. Even Microsoft, whose .NET technology is Java's most fierce competitor, followed suit by no longer charging for the Express Edition of its Visual Studio.NET.

This book provides a brief tutorial of NetBeans and Eclipse in Appendix D and Appendix E, respectively. Do consider using an IDE because it helps a lot.

Summary

This chapter helped you write your first Java program. You used a text editor to write the program, used **javac** to compile it to a class file, and ran the class file with the **java** tool.

As programs grow in complexity and projects get larger, an IDE will help expedite application development. Two tutorials on open source IDEs are given in Appendix C and Appendix D.

Questions

1. If you had saved the code in Listing 1.1 using a different name, such as **whatever.java**, would it have compiled?
2. If you had used a file extension other than java when saving the code in Listing 1.1, for example as **MyFirstJava.txt**, would it have compiled?

Chapter 2
Language Fundamentals

Java is an object-oriented programming (OOP) language, therefore an understanding of OOP is of utmost importance. You can find the first lesson of OOP in Chapter 4, "Objects and Classes." However, before you explore many features and techniques in OOP, make sure you study the prerequisite: basic programming concepts discussed in this chapter. The topics covered are as follows.

- Encoding Sets. Java supports the Unicode character encoding set and program element names are not restricted to ASCII (American Standard Code for Information Interchange) characters. Text can be written using characters in practically any human language in use today.
- Primitives. Java is an OOP language and Java programs deal with objects most of the time. However, there are also non-object elements that represent numbers and simple values such as true and false. These simple non-object programming elements are called primitives.
- Variables. Variables are place holders whose contents can change. There are many types of variables.
- Constants. Place holders whose values cannot be changed.
- Literals. Literals are representations of data values that are understood by the Java compiler.
- Primitive conversion. Changing the type of a primitive to another type.
- Operators. Operators are notations indicating that certain operations are to be performed.

Note

If you have programmed with C or C++, two popular languages at the time Java was invented, you should feel at home learning Java because Java syntax is very similar to that of C and C++. However, the creator of Java added a number of features not available in C and C++ and excluded a few aspects of them.

ASCII and Unicode

Traditionally, computers in English speaking countries only used the ASCII (American Standard Code for Information Interchange) character set to represent alphanumeric characters. Each character in the ASCII is represented by 7 bits. There are therefore 128 characters in this character set. These include the lower case and upper case Latin letters, numbers, and punctuation marks.

The ASCII character set was later extended to include another 128 characters, such as the German characters ä, ö, ü, and the British currency symbol £. This character set is called extended ASCII and each character is represented by 8 bits.

ASCII and the extended ASCII are only two of the many character sets available. Another popular one is the character set standardized by the ISO (International Standards Organization), ISO-8859-1, also known as Latin-1. Each character in ISO-8859-1 is represented by 8 bits as well. This character set contains all the characters required for writing text in many of the western European languages, such as German, Danish, Dutch, French, Italian, Spanish, Portuguese, and, of course, English. An eight-bit-per-character character set is convenient because a byte is also 8 bits long. As such, storing and transmitting text written in an 8-bit character set is most efficient.

However, not every language uses Latin letters. Chinese, Korean, and Thai are examples of languages that use different character sets. For example, each character in the Chinese language represents a word, not a letter. There are thousands of these characters and 8 bit is not enough to represent all the characters in the character set. The Japanese use a different character set for their language too. In total, there are hundreds of different character sets for all languages in the world. This is confusing, because a code that represents a particular character in a character set represents a different character in another character set.

Unicode is a character set developed by the non-profit organization called the Unicode Consortium (www.unicode.org). This body attempts to include all characters in all languages in the world into one single character set. A unique number in Unicode represents exactly one character. Currently at version 4.0, Unicode is used in Java, XML, ECMAScript, LDAP, etc. It has also been adopted by industry leaders such as IBM, Microsoft, Oracle, Sun, HP, Apple, and others.

Initially, a Unicode character was represented by 16 bits, which were enough to represent more than 65,000 different characters. 65,000 characters are sufficient for encoding most of the characters in major languages in the world. However, the Unicode consortium planned to allow for encoding for as many as a million more characters. With this amount, you then need more than 16 bits to represent each character. In fact, a 32 bit system is considered a convenient way of storing Unicode characters.

Now, you see a problem already. While Unicode provides enough space for all the characters used in all languages, storing and transmitting Unicode text is not as efficient as storing and transmitting ASCII or Latin-1 characters. In the Internet world, this is a huge problem. Imagine having to transfer 4 times as much data as ASCII text!

Fortunately, character encoding can make it more efficient to store and transmit Unicode text. You can think of character encoding as analogous to data compression. And, there are many types of character encodings available today. The Unicode Consortium endorses three of them:

- UTF-8. This is popular for HTML and for protocols whereby Unicode characters are transformed into a variable length encoding of bytes. It has the advantages that the Unicode characters corresponding to the familiar ASCII set have the same byte values as ASCII, and that Unicode characters transformed into UTF-8 can be used with much existing software. Most browsers support the UTF-8 character encoding.
- UTF-16. In this character encoding, all the more commonly used characters fit into a single 16-bit code unit, and other less commonly use characters are accessible via pairs of 16-bit code units.
- UTF-32. This character encoding uses 32 bits for every single character. This is clearly not a choice for Internet applications. At least, not at present.

ASCII characters still play a dominant role in software programming. Java too uses ASCII for almost all input elements, except comments, identifiers, and the contents of characters and strings. For the latter, Java supports Unicode characters. This means, you can write comments, identifiers, and strings in languages other than English. For example, if you are a Chinese speaker living in Beijing, you can use Chinese characters for variable names. As a comparison, here is a piece of Java code that declares an identifier named **password**, which consists of ASCII characters:

```
String password = "secret";
```

By contrast, the following identifier is in simplified Chinese characters.

```
String 密码 = "secret";
```

Separators

There are several characters Java uses as separators. These special characters are presented in Table 2.1.

Symbol	Name	Description
( )	Parentheses	Used in: 1. method signatures to contain lists of arguments. 2. expressions to raise operator precedence. 3. narrowing conversions. 4. loops to contain expressions to be evaluated
{ }	Braces	Used in: 1. declaration of types. 2. blocks of statements 3. array initialization.
[]	Brackets	Used in: 1. array declaration. 2. array value dereferencing
< >	Angle brackets	Used to pass parameter to parameterized types.
;	Semicolon	Used to terminate statements and in the **for** statement to separate the initialization code, the expression, and the update code.
:	Colon	Used in the **for** statement that iterates over an array or a collection.
,	Comma	Used to separate arguments in method declarations.
.	Period	Used to separate package names from subpackages and type names, and to separate a field or method from a reference variable.

Table 2.1: Java separators

It is very important that you familiarize yourself with the symbols and the names. Don't worry if you don't understand the terms in the Description column after reading it.

Primitives

As mentioned in Introduction, when writing an object-oriented (OO) application, you create an object model that resembles the real world. For example, a payroll application would have **Employee** objects, **Tax** objects, **Company** objects, etc. In Java, however, objects are not the only data type. There is another data type called *primitive*. There are eight primitive types in Java, each with a specific format and size. Table 2.2 lists Java primitives.

Primitive	Description	Range
byte	Byte-length integer (8 bits)	-128 (-2^7) to 127 (2^7-1)
short	Short integer (16 bits)	-32,768 (-2^{15}) to 32,767 (-2^{15}-1)
int	Integer (32 bits)	-2,147,483,648 (-2^{31}) to 2,147,483,647 (-2^{31}-1)
long	Long integer (64 bits)	-9,223,372,036,854,775,808 (-2^{63}) to 9,223,372,036,854,775,807 (2^{63}-1)
float	Single-precision floating point (32-bit IEEE 754[1])	Smallest positive nonzero: $14e^{-45}$ Largest positive nonzero: $3.4028234e^{38}$
double	Double-precision floating point (64-bit IEEE 754)	Smallest positive nonzero: $4.9e^{-324}$ Largest positive nonzero: $1.7976931348623157e^{308}$
char	A Unicode character	[See Unicode 4.0 specification]
boolean	A boolean value	true or false

Table 2.2: Java primitives

The first six primitives (**byte, short, int, long, float, double**) represent numbers. Each of these has a different size. For example, a **byte** can contain any whole number between -128 and 127. To understand how the smallest and largest numbers for an integer were obtained, take a look at its size in bits. A byte is 8 bits long so there are 2^8 or 256 possible values. The first 128 values

---

[1] Standard 754 by the Institute of Electrical and Electronics Engineers (IEEE)

are reserved for -128 to -1, then 0 takes one place, leaving 127 positive values. Therefore, the range of a byte is -128 to 127.

If you need a placeholder to contain number 1000000, you need an **int**. A **long** is even larger, and you might ask, if a **long** can contain a larger set of numbers than a **byte** and an **int**, why not always use a **long**? It is because a **long** takes 64 bits and therefore consume more memory space than **byte**s and **int**s. Thus, to save space, you want to use the primitive with the smallest possible data size.

The primitives **byte**, **short**, **int**, and **long** can only hold integers or whole numbers, for numbers with decimal points you need either a **float** or a **double**.

A **char** type can contain a single Unicode character, such as 'a', '9', and '&'. The use of Unicode allows **char**s to also contain characters that do not exist in the English alphabet, such as this Japanese character ' の '. A **boolean** can contain one of two possible states (**false** or **true**).

Note
The reason why in Java not everything is an object is speed. Objects are more expensive to create and operate on than primitives. In programming an operation is said to be 'expensive' if it is resource intensive or consumes a lot of CPU cycles to complete.

Now that you're aware that there are two types of data in Java (primitives and objects), let's continue by studying how to use primitives. (Objects are discussed in Chapter 4, "Objects and Classes.") We will start the discussion by introducing variables.

Variables

Variables are data placeholders. Java is a strongly typed language, therefore every variable must have a declared type. There are two data types in Java:

- reference types. A variable of reference type provides a reference to an object.
- primitive types. A variable of primitive type holds a primitive.

How Java Stores Integer Values

You must have heard that computers work with binary numbers, which are numbers that consists of only zeros and ones. This section provides an overview that may come in useful when you learn mathematical operators.

A byte takes 8 bits, meaning there are eight bits allocated to store a byte. The leftmost bit is the sign bit. 0 indicates a positive number, and 1 denotes a negative number. 0000 0000 is the binary representation of 0, 0000 0001 of 1, 0000 0010 of 2, 0000 0011 of 3, and 0111 1111 of 127, which is the largest positive number that a byte can contain.

Now, how do you get the binary representation of a negative number? It's easy. Get the binary representation of its positive equivalent, and reverse all the bits and add 1. For example, to get the binary representation of -3 you start with 3, which is 0000 0011. Reversing the bits results in

```
1111 1100
```

Adding 1 gives you

```
1111 1101
```

which is -3 in binary.

For **int**s, the rule is the same, i.e. the leftmost bit is the sign bit. The only difference is an **int** takes 32 bits. To calculate the binary form of -1 in an **int**, we start from 1, which is

```
0000 0000 0000 0000 0000 0000 0000 0001
```

Reversing all the bits results in:

```
1111 1111 1111 1111 1111 1111 1111 1110
```

Adding 1 gives us the number we want (-1).

```
1111 1111 1111 1111 1111 1111 1111 1111
```

In addition to the data type, a Java variable also has a name or an identifier. There are a few ground rules in choosing identifiers.

1. An identifier is an unlimited-length sequence of Java letters and Java digits. An identifier must begin with a Java letter.

2. An identifier must not be a Java keyword (given in Table 2.3), a **boolean** literal, or the **null** literal.
3. It must be unique within its scope. Scopes are discussed in Chapter 4, "Objects and Classes."

Java Letters and Java Digits

The Java letters include uppercase and lowercase ASCII Latin letters A to Z (\u0041-\u005a—note that \u denotes a Unicode character) and a to z (\u0061-\u007a), and, for historical reasons, the ASCII underscore (_ or \u005f) and the dollar sign ($, or \u0024). The $ character should be used only in mechanically generated source code or, rarely, to access preexisting names on legacy systems. Java digits include the ASCII digits 0-9 (\u0030-\u0039).

abstract	continue	for	new	switch
assert	default	if	package	synchronized
boolean	do	goto	private	this
break	double	implements	protected	throw
byte	else	import	public	throws
case	enum	instanceof	return	transient
catch	extends	int	short	try
char	final	interface	static	void
class	finally	long	strictfp	volatile
const	float	native	super	while

Table 2.3: Java keywords

Here are some legal identifiers:

```
salary
x2
_x3
row_count
密码
```

Here are some invalid variables:

```
2x
java+variable
```

2x is invalid because it starts with a number. **java+variable** is invalid because it contains a plus sign.

Also note that names are case-sensitive. **x2** and **X2** are two different identifiers.

You declare a variable by writing the type first, followed by the name plus a semicolon. Here are some examples of variable declarations.

```
byte x;
int rowCount;
char c;
```

In the examples above you declare three variables:

- The variable **x** of type **byte**
- The variable **rowCount** of type **int**
- The variable **c** of type **char**

x, **rowCount**, and **c** are variable names or identifiers.

It is also possible to declare multiple variables having the same type on the same line, separating two variables with a comma. For instance:

```
int a, b;
```

which is the same as

```
int a;
int b;
```

However, writing multiple declarations on the same line is not recommended as it reduces readability.

Finally, it is possible to assign a value to a variable at the same time the variable is declared:

```
byte x = 12;
int rowCount = 1000;
char c = 'x';
```

Sun's Naming Conventions for Variables

Variable names should be short yet meaningful. They should be in mixed case with a lowercase first letter. Subsequent words start with capital letters. Variable names should not start with underscore _ or dollar sign $ characters. For example, here are some examples of variable names that are in compliance with Sun's code conventions: **userName, count, firstTimeLogin**.

Constants

In Java constants are variables whose values, once assigned, cannot be changed. You declare a constant by using the keyword **final**. By convention, constant names are all in upper case with words separated by underscores.

Here are examples of constants or final variables.

```
final int ROW_COUNT = 50;
final boolean ALLOW_USER_ACCESS = true;
```

Literals

From time to time you will need to assign values to variables in your program, such as number 2 to an **int** or the character 'c' to a **char**. For this, you need to write the value representation in a format that the Java compiler understands. This source code representation of a value is called *literal*. There are three types of literals: literals of primitive types, string literals, and the **null** literal. Only literals of primitive types are discussed in this chapter. The **null** literal is discussed in Chapter 4, "Objects and Classes" and string literals in Chapter 5, "Core Classes."

Literals of primitive types have four subtypes: integer literals, floating-point literals, character literals, and boolean literals. Each of these subtypes is explained below.

Integer Literals

Integer literals may be written in decimal (base 10, something we are used to), hexadecimal (base 16), or octal (base 8). For example, one hundred can be expressed as **100**. The following are integer literals in decimal:

```
2
123456
```

As another example, the following code assigns 10 to variable **x** of type **int**.

```
int x = 10;
```

Hexadecimal integers are written by using the prefixes **0x** or **0X**. For example, the hexadecimal number 9E is written as 0X9E or 0x9E. Octal integers are written by prefixing the numbers with 0. For instance, the following is an octal number 567:

```
0567
```

Integer literals are used to assign values to variables of types **byte**, **short**, **int**, and **long**. Note, however, you must not assign a value that exceeds the capacity of a variable. For example, the highest number for a **byte** is 127. Therefore, the following code generates a compile error because 200 is too big for a **byte**.

```
byte b = 200;
```

To assign a value to a **long**, suffix the number with the letter **L** or **l**. L is preferable because it is easily distinguishable from digit 1. A **long** can contain values between -9223372036854775808L and 9223372036854775807L (2^{63}).

Beginners of Java often ask why we need to use the suffix l or L, because even without it, such as in the following, the program still compiles.

```
long a = 123;
```

This is only partly true. An integer literal without a suffix L or l is regarded as an int. Therefore, the following will generate a compile error because 9876543210 is larger than the capacity for an **int**:

```
long a = 9876543210;
```

To rectify the problem, add an L or l at the end of the number, such as this:

```
long a = 9876543210L;
```

Floating-Point Literals

Numbers such as 0.4, 1.23, $0.5e^{10}$ are floating point numbers. A floating point number has the following parts:

- a whole number part
- a decimal point
- a fractional part
- an optional exponent

Take 1.23 as an example. For this floating point, the whole number part is 1, the fractional part is 23, and there is no optional exponent. In $0.5e^{10}$, 0 is the whole number part, 5 the fractional part, and 10 is the exponent.

In Java, there are two types of floating points:

- **float**. 32 bits in size. The largest positive float is 3.40282347e+38 and the smallest positive finite nonzero float is 1.40239846e-45.
- **double**. 64 bits in size. The largest positive double is 1.79769313486231570e+308 and the smallest positive finite nonzero double is 4.94065645841246544e-324.

In both **float**s and **double**s, a whole number part of 0 is optional. In other words, 0.5 can be written as .5. Also, the exponent can be represented by either e or E.

To express float literals, you use one of the following formats.

```
Digits . [Digits] [ExponentPart] f_or_F
. Digits [ExponentPart] f_or_F
Digits ExponentPart f_or_F
Digits [ExponentPart] f_or_F
```

Note that the part in brackets is optional.

The *f_or_F* part makes a floating point literal a **float**. The absence of this part makes a float literal a **double**. To explicitly express a double literal, you can suffix it with D or d.

To write double literals, use one of these formats.

```
Digits . [Digits] [ExponentPart] [d_or_D]
. Digits [ExponentPart] [d_or_D]
Digits ExponentPart [d_or_D]
Digits [ExponentPart] [d_or_D]
```

In both floats and doubles, *ExponentPart* is defined as follows.

```
ExponentIndicator SignedInteger
```

where *ExponentIndicator* is either **e** or **E** and *SignedInteger* is .

```
Sign_opt Digits
```

and *Sign* is either **+** or **-** and a plus sign is optional.

Examples of **float** literals include the following:

```
2e1f
8.f
.5f
0f
3.14f
9.0001e+12f
```

Here are examples of **double** literals:

```
2e1
8.
.5
0.0D
3.14
9e-9d
7e123D
```

Boolean Literals

The **boolean** type has two values, represented by literals **true** and **false**. For example, the following code declares a **boolean** variable **includeSign** and assigns it the value of **true**.

```
boolean includeSign = true;
```

Character Literals

A character literal is a Unicode character or an escape sequence enclosed in single quotes. An escape sequence is the representation of a Unicode character that cannot be entered using the keyboard or that has a special function in Java. For example, the carriage return and linefeed characters are used to terminate a line and do not have visual representation. To express a linefeed character, you need to escape it, i.e. write its character representation. Also, single quote characters need to be escaped because single quotes are used to enclosed characters.

Here are some examples of character literals:

```
'a'
'z'
'A'
'Z'
```

```
'0'
'ü'
'%'
```
'我'

Here are character literals that are escape sequences:

```
'\b'    the backspace character
'\t'    the tab character
'\\'    the backslash
'\''    single quote
'\"'    double quote
'\n'    linefeed
'\r'    carriage return
```

In addition, Java allows you to escape a Unicode character so that you can express a Unicode character using a sequence of ASCII characters. For example, the Unicode code for the character ☉ is 2299. You can write the following character literal to express this character:

'☉'

However, if you do not have the tool to produce that character using your keyboard, you can escape it this way:

```
'\u2299'
```

Primitive Conversions

When dealing with different data types, you often need to perform conversions. For example, assigning the value of a variable to another variable involves a conversion. If both variables have the same type, the assignment will always succeed. Conversion from a type to the same type is called identity conversion. For example, the following operation is guaranteed to be successful:

```
int a = 90;
int b = a;
```

However, conversion to a different type is not guaranteed to be successful or even possible. There are two other kinds of primitive conversions, the widening conversion and the narrowing conversion.

The Widening Conversion

The primitive widening conversion occurs from a type to another type whose size is the same or larger than that of the first type, such as from **int** (32 bits) to **long** (64 bits). The widening conversion is permitted in the following cases:

- **byte** to **short, int, long, float,** or **double**
- **short** to **int, long, float,** or **double**
- **char** to **int, long, float,** or **double**
- **int** to **long, float,** or **double**
- **long** to **float** or **double**
- **float** to **double**

The widening primitive conversion from an integer type to another integer type will not risk information loss. At the same token, a conversion from **float** to **double** preserves all the information. However, a conversion from an **int** or a **long** to a **float** may result in loss of precision.

The widening primitive conversion occurs implicitly. You do not need to do anything in your code. For example:

```
int a = 10;
long b = a; // widening conversion
```

The Narrowing Conversion

The narrowing conversion occurs from a type to a different type that has a smaller size, such as from a **long** (64 bits) to an **int** (32 bits). In general, the narrowing primitive conversion can occur in these cases:

- **short** to **byte** or **char**
- **char** to **byte** or **short**
- **int** to **byte, short,** or **char**
- **long** to **byte, short,** or **char**
- **float** to **byte, short, char, int,** or **long**
- **double** to **byte, short, char, int, long,** or **float**

Unlike the widening primitive conversion, the narrowing primitive conversion must be explicit. You need to specify the target type in parentheses. For example, here is an example of a narrowing conversion from **long** to **int**.

```
long a = 10;
int b = (int) a; // narrowing conversion
```

The **(int)** on the second line tells the compiler that a narrowing conversion should occur.

Narrowing conversion may incur information loss, if the converted value is larger than the capacity of the target type. The preceding example did not cause information loss because 10 is small enough for an **int**. However, in the following conversion, there is some information loss because 9876543210L is too big for an **int**.

```
long a = 9876543210L;
int b = (int) a; // the value of b is now 1286608618
```

Operators

A computer program is a collection of operations that together achieve a certain function. There are many types of operations, including addition, subtraction, multiplication, division, and bit shifting. In this section you will learn various Java operations.

An operator performs an operation on one, two, or three operands. Operands are the objects of an operation and the operator is a symbol representing the action. For example, here is an additive operation:

```
x + 4
```

In this case, **x** and 4 and the operands and + is the operator.

An operator may or may not return a result.

Note

Any legal combination of operators and operands are called an expression. For example, **x + 4** is an expression. A boolean expression results in either **true** or **false**. An integer expression produces an integer. And, the result of a floating-point expression is a floating point number.

Operators that require only one operand are called unary operators. There are a few unary operators in Java. Binary operators, the most common type of Java operator, take two operands. There is also one ternary operator, the **? :** operator, that requires three operands.

Table 2.4 list Java operators.

=	>	<	!	~	?	:			
==	<=	>=	!=	&&	||	++	--		
+	-	*	/	&	|	^	%	<<	>>	>>>
+=	-=	*=	/=	&=	|=	^=	%=	<<=	>>=	>>>=

Table 2.4: Java operators

In Java, there are six categories of operators.

- Unary operators
- Arithmetic operators
- Relational and conditional operators
- Shift and logical operators
- Assignment operators
- Other operators

Each of these operators is discussed in the following sections.

Unary Operators

Unary operators operate on one operand. There are six unary operators, all discussed in this section.

Unary Minus Operator –

The unary minus operator returns the negative of its operand. The operand must be a numeric primitive or a variable of a numeric primitive type. For example, in the following code, the value of y is -4.5;

```
float x = 4.5f;
float y = -x;
```

Unary Plus Operator +

This operator returns the value of its operand. The operand must be a numeric primitive or a variable of a numeric primitive type. For example, in the following code, the value of **y** is 4.5.

```
float x = 4.5f;
float y = +x;
```

This operator does not have much significance since its absence makes no difference.

Increment Operator ++

This operator increments the value of its operand by one. The operand must be a variable of a numeric primitive type. The operator can appear before or after the operand. If the operator appears before the operand, it is called the prefix increment operator. If it is written after the operand, it becomes the postfix increment operator.

As an example, here is a prefix increment operator in action:

```
int x = 4;
++x;
```

After **++x**, the value of **x** is 5. The preceding code is the same as

```
int x = 4;
x++;
```

After **x++**, the value of **x** is 5.

However, if the result of an increment operator is assigned to another variable in the same expression, there is a difference between the prefix operator and its postfix twin. Consider this example.

```
int x = 4;
int y = ++x;
// y = 5, x = 5
```

The prefix increment operator is applied *before* the assignment. **x** is incremented to 5, and then its value is copied to **y**.

However, check the use of the postfix increment operator here.

```
int x = 4;
int y = x++;
// y = 4, x = 5
```

With the postfix increment operator, the value of the operand (**x**) is incremented *after* the value of the operand is assigned to another variable (**y**).

Note that the increment operator is most often applied to **int**s. However, it also works with other types of numeric primitives, such as **float** and **long**.

Decrement Operator --

This operator decrements the value of its operand by one. The operand must be a variable of a numeric primitive type. Like the increment operator, there are also the prefix decrement operator and the postfix decrement operator. For instance, the following code decrements **x** and assigns the value to **y**.

```
int x = 4;
int y = --x;
// x = 3; y = 3
```

In the following example, the postfix decrement operator is used:

```
int x = 4;
int y = x--;
// x = 3; y = 4
```

Logical Complement Operator !

This operator can only be applied to a **boolean** primitive or an instance of **java.lang.Boolean**. The value of this operator is **true** if the operand is **false**, and **false** if the operand is **true**. For example:

```
boolean x = false;
boolean y = !x;
// at this point, y is true and x is false
```

Bitwise Complement Operator ~

The operand of this operator must be an integer primitive or a variable of an integer primitive type. The result is the bitwise complement of the operand. For example:

```
int j = 2;
int k = ~j; // k = -3; j = 2
```

To understand how this operator works, you need to convert the operand to a binary number and reverse all the bits. The binary form of 2 in an integer is:

```
0000 0000 0000 0000 0000 0000 0000 0010
```

Its bitwise complement is

```
1111 1111 1111 1111 1111 1111 1111 1101
```

which is the representation of -3 in an integer.

Arithmetic Operators

There are four types of arithmetic operations: addition, subtraction, multiplication, division, and modulus. Each arithmetic operator is discussed here.

Addition Operator +

The addition operator adds two operands. The types of the operands must be convertible to a numeric primitive. For example:

```
byte x = 3;
int y = x + 5; // y = 8
```

Make sure the variable that accepts the addition result has a big enough capacity. For example, in the following code the value of **k** is -294967296 and not 4 billion.

```
int j = 2000000000; // 2 billion
int k = j + j; // not enough capacity
```

On the other hand, the following works as expected:

```
long j = 2000000000; // 2 billion
long k = j + j; // the value of k is 4 billion
```

Subtraction Operator –

This operator performs subtraction between two operands. The types of the operands must be convertible to a numeric primitive type. As an example:

```
int x = 2;
int y = x - 1;        // y = 1
```

Multiplication Operator *

This operator perform multiplication between two operands. The type of the operands must be convertible to a numeric primitive type. As an example:

```
int x = 4;
int y = x * 4;      // y = 16
```

Division Operator /

This operator perform division between two operands. The left hand operand is the dividend and the right hand operand the divisor. Both the dividend and the divisor must be of a type convertible to a numeric primitive type. As an example:

```
int x = 4;
int y = x / 2;      // y = 2
```

Note that at runtime a division operation raises an error if the divisor is zero.

The result of a division using the / operator is always an integer. If the divisor does not divide the dividends equally, the remainder will be ignored. For example

```
int x = 4;
int y = x / 3;      // y = 1
```

The **java.lang.Math** class, explained in Chapter 5, "Core Classes," can perform more sophisticated division operations.

Modulus Operator %

This operator perform division between two operands and returns the remainder. The left hand operand is the dividend and the right hand operand the divisor. Both the dividend and the divisor must be of a type that is convertible to a numeric primitive type. For example the result of the following operation is 2.

```
8 % 3
```

Equality Operators

There are two equality operators, **==** (equal to) and **!=** (not equal to), both operating on two operands that can be integers, floating points, characters, or **boolean**. The outcome of equality operators is a **boolean**.

For example, the value of **c** is **true** after the comparison.

```
int a = 5;
int b = 5;
boolean c = a == b;
```

As another example,.

```
boolean x = true;
boolean y = true;
boolean z = x != y;
```

The value of **z** is **false** after comparison because **x** is equal to **y**.

Relational Operators

There are five relational operators: **<**, **>**, **<=**, and **>=**, and **instanceof**. The last one is discussed in Chapter 4, "Objects and Classes." Each of the first four operators is explained in this section.

The **<**, **>**, **<=**, and **>=** operators operate on two operands whose types must be convertible to a numeric primitive type. Relational operations return a **boolean**.

The **<** operator evaluates if the value of the left-hand operand is less than the value of the right-hand operand. For example, the following operation returns **false**:

```
9 < 6
```

The **>** operator evaluates if the value of the left-hand operand is greater than the value of the right-hand operand. For example, this operation returns **true**:

```
9 > 6
```

The **<=** operator tests if the value of the left-hand operand is less than or equal to the value of the right-hand operand. For example, the following operation evaluates to **false**:

```
9 <= 6
```

The **>=** operator tests if the value of the left-hand operand is greater than or equal to the value of the right-hand operand. For example, this operation returns **true**:

```
9 >= 9
```

Conditional Operators

There are three conditional operators: the AND operator **&&**, the OR operator **||**, and the **? :** operator. Each of these is detailed below.

The && operator

This operator takes two expressions as operands and both expressions must return a value that must be convertible to **boolean**. It returns **true** if both operands evaluate to **true**. Otherwise, it returns **false**. If the left-hand operand evaluates to **false**, the right-hand operand will not be evaluated. For example, the following returns **false**.

```
(5 < 3) && (6 < 9)
```

The || Operator

This operator takes two expressions as operands and both expressions must return a value that must be convertible to **boolean**. **||** returns **true** if one of the operands evaluates to **true**. If the left-hand operand evaluates to **true**, the right-hand operand will not be evaluated. For instance, the following returns **true**.

```
(5 < 3) || (6 < 9)
```

The ? : Operator

This operator operates on three operands. The syntax is

```
expression1 ? expression2 : expression3
```

Here, *expression1* must return a value convertible to **boolean**. If *expression1* evaluates to **true**, *expression2* is returned. Otherwise, *expression3* is returned.

For example, the following expression returns 4.

```
(8 < 4) ? 2 : 4
```

Shift Operators

A shift operator takes two operands whose type must be convertible to an integer primitive. The left-hand operand is the value to be shifted, the right-hand operand indicates the shift distance. There are three types of shift operators:

- the left shift operator **<<**
- the right shift operator **>>**
- the unsigned right shift operator **>>>**

The Left Shift Operator <<

The left shift operator bit-shifts a number to the left, padding the right bits with 0. The value of **n << s** is **n** left-shifted **s** bit positions. This is the same as multiplication by two to the power of s.

For example, left-shifting an **int** whose value is 1 with a shift distance of 3 (1 << 3) results in 8. Again, to figure this out, you convert the operand to a binary number.

```
0000 0000 0000 0000 0000 0000 0000 0001
```

Shifting to the left 3 shift units results in:

```
0000 0000 0000 0000 0000 0000 0000 1000
```

which is equivalent to 8 (the same as $1 * 2^3$).

Another rule is this. If the left-hand operand is an **int**, only the first five bits of the shift distance will be used. In other words, the shift distance must be within the range 0 and 31. If you pass an number greater than 31, only the first five bits will be used. This is to say, if **x** is an **int, x << 32** is the same as **x << 0; x << 33** is the same as **x << 1**.

If the left-hand operand is a **long**, only the first six bits of the shift distance will be used. In other words, the shift distance actually used is within the range 0 and 63.

The Right Shift Operator >>

The right shift operator **>>** bit-shifts the left-hand operand to the right. The value of **n >> s** is **n** right-shifted **s** bit positions. The resulting value is **n/2^s**.

As an example, **16 >> 1** is equal to 8. To prove this, write the binary representation of 16.

```
0000 0000 0000 0000 0000 0000 0001 0000
```

Then, shifting it to the right by 1 bit results in.

```
0000 0000 0000 0000 0000 0000 0000 1000
```

which is equal to 8.

The Unsigned Right Shift Operator >>>

The value of **n >>> s** depends on whether **n** is positive or negative. For a positive **n**, the value is the same as **n >> s**.

If **n** is negative, the value depends on the type of **n**. If **n** is an **int**, the value is **(n>>s)+(2<<~s)**. If **n** is a **long**, the value is **(n>>s)+(2L<<~s)**.

Assignment Operators

There are twelve assignment operators:

```
=   +=   -=   *=   /=   %=   <<=   >>=   >>>=   &=   ^=   |=
```

Assignment operators take two operands whose type must be of an integral primitive. The left-hand operand must be a variable. For instance:

```
int x = 5;
```

Except for the assignment operator **=**, the rest work the same way and you should see each of them as consisting of two operators. For example, **+=** is actually **+** and **=**. The assignment operator **<<=** has two operators, **<<** and **=**.

The two-part assignment operators work by applying the first operator to both operands and then assign the result to the left-hand operand. For example **x += 5** is the same as **x = x + 5**.

x -= 5 is the same as **x = x - 5**.

x <<= 5 is equivalent to **x = x << 5**.

x &= 5 produces the same result as **x = x &= 5**.

Integer Bitwise Operators & | ^

The bitwise operators **& | ^** perform a bit to bit operation on two operands whose types must be convertible to **int**. **&** indicates an AND operation, **|** an OR operation, and **^** an exclusive OR operation. For example,

```
0xFFFF & 0x0000 = 0x0000
0xF0F0 & 0xFFFF = 0xF0F0
0xFFFF | 0x000F = 0xFFFF
0xFFF0 ^ 0x00FF = 0xFF0F
```

Logical Operators & | ^

The logical operators **& | ^** perform a logical operation on two operands that are convertible to **boolean**. **&** indicates an AND operation, **|** an OR operation, and **^** an exclusive OR operation. For example,

```
true & true  = true
true & false = false
true | false = true
false | false = false
true ^ true = false
false ^ false = false
false ^ true = true
```

Operator Precedence

In most programs, multiple operators often appear in an expression, such as.

```
int a = 1;
int b = 2;
int c = 3;
int d = a + b * c;
```

What is the value of **d** after the code is executed? If you say 9, you're wrong. It's actually 7.

Multiplication operator ***** takes precedence over addition operator **+**. As a result, multiplication will be performed before addition. However, if you want the addition to be executed first, you can use parentheses.

```
int d = (a + b) * c;
```

The latter will assign 9 to **d**.

Table 2.5 lists all the operators in the order of precedence. Operators in the same column have equal precedence.

Operator	
postfix operators	[ ] . (params) expr++ expr--
unary operators	++expr --expr +expr -expr ~ !
creation or cast	new (type)expr
multiplicative	* / %
additive	+ -
shift	<< >> >>>
relational	< > <= >= instanceof
equality	== !=
bitwise AND	&
bitwise exclusive OR	^
bitwise inclusive OR	|
logical AND	&&
logical OR	||
conditional	? :
assignment	= += -= *= /= %= &= ^= |= <<= >>= >>>=

Table 2.5: The precedence of operators

Note that parentheses have the highest precedence. Parentheses can also make expressions clearer. For example, consider the following code:

```
int x = 5;
int y = 5;
boolean z = x * 5 == y + 20;
```

The value of **z** after comparison is **true**. However, the expression is far from clear.

You can rewrite the last line using parentheses.

```
boolean z = (x * 5) == (y + 20);
```

which does not change the result because ***** and **+** have higher precedence than **==**, but this makes the expression much clearer.

Promotion

Some unary operators (such as **+**, **-**, and **~**) and binary operators (such as **+**, **-**, *****, **/**) cause automatic promotion, i.e. elevation to a wider type such as from **byte** to **int**. Consider the following code:

```
byte x = 5;
byte y = -x; // error
```

The second line surprisingly causes an error even though a byte can accommodate -5. The reason for this is the unary operator - causes the result of **-x** to be promoted to **int**. To rectify the problem, either change **y** to **int** or perform an explicit narrowing conversion like this.

```
byte x = 5;
byte y = (byte) -x;
```

For unary operators, if the type of the operand is **byte**, **short**, or **char**, the outcome is promoted to **int**.

For binary operators, the promotion rules are as follows.

- If any of the operands is of type **byte** or **short**, then both operands will be converted to **int** and the outcome will be an **int**.
- If any of the operands is of type **double**, then the other operand is converted to **double** and the outcome will be a **double**.
- If any of the operands is of type **float**, then the other operand is converted to **float** and the outcome will be a **float**.
- If any of the operands is of type **long**, then the other operand is converted to **long** and the outcome will be a **long**.

For example, the following code causes a compile error:

```
short x = 200;
short y = 400;
short z = x + y;
```

You can fix this by changing **z** to **int** or perform an explicit narrowing conversion of **x + y**, such as

```
short z = (short) (x + y);
```

Note that the parentheses around **x + y** is required, otherwise only **x** would be converted to **int** and the result of addition of a **short** and an **int** will be an **int**.

Comments

It is good practice to write comments throughout your code, sufficiently explaining what functionality a class provides, what a method does, what a field contains, and so forth.

There are two types of comments in Java, both with syntax similar to comments in C and C++.

- Traditional comments. Enclose a traditional comment in **/*** and ***/**.
- End-of-line comments. Use double slashes (//) which causes the rest of the line after // to be ignored by the compiler.

For example, here is a comment that describes a method

```
/*
  toUpperCase capitalizes the characters of in a String object
*/
public void toUpperCase(String s) {
```

Here is an end-of-line comment:

```
public int rowCount; //the number of rows returned from the database
```

Traditional comments do not nest, which means

```
/*
  /* comment 1 */
  comment 2 */
```

is invalid because the first ***/** after the first **/*** will terminate the comment. As such, the comment above will have the extra **comment 2 */**, which will generate a compiler error.

On the other hand, end-of-line comments can contain anything, including the sequences of characters **/*** and ***/**, such as this:

```
// /* this comment is okay */
```

Summary

This chapter presents Java language fundamentals, the basic concepts and topics that you should master before proceeding to more advanced subjects. Topics of discussion include character sets, variables, primitives, literals, operators, operator precedence, and comments.

Chapter 3 continues with statements, another important topic of the Java language.

Questions

1. What does ASCII stand for?
2. Does Java use ASCII characters or Unicode characters?
3. What are reference type variables, and what are primitive type variables?
4. How are constants implemented in Java?
5. What is an expression?
6. Name at least ten operators in Java.
7. What is the ternary operator in Java?
8. What is operator precedence?
9. Name two types of Java comments.

Chapter 3
Statements

A computer program is a compilation of instructions, and each of these instructions is called a statement. There are many types of statements in Java and some—such as **if**, **while**, **for**, and **switch**—are conditional statements that determine the flow of the program. Even though statements are not features specific to object-oriented programming, they are vital parts of the language fundamentals. This chapter discusses Java statements, starting with an overview and then providing details of each of them. The **return** statement, which is the statement to exit a method, is discussed in Chapter 4, "Objects and Classes."

An Overview of Java Statements

In programming, a statement is an instruction to do something. Statements control the sequence of execution of a program. Assigning a value to a variable is an example of a statement.

```
x = z + 5;
```

Even a variable declaration is a statement.

```
long secondsElapsed;
```

By contrast, an *expression* is a combination of operators and operands that gets evaluated. For example, **z + 5** is an expression.

In Java a statement is terminated with a semicolon and multiple statements can be written on a single line.

```
x = y + 1; z = y + 2;
```

However, writing multiple statements on a single line is not recommended as it obscures code readability.

Note

In Java, an empty statement is legal and does nothing:

```
;
```

Some expressions can be made statements by terminating them with a semicolon. For example, **x++** is an expression. However, this is a statement:

```
x++;
```

Statements can be grouped in a block. By definition, a block is a sequence of the following programming elements within braces:

- statements
- local class declarations
- local variable declaration statements

A statement and a statement block can be labeled. Label names follow the same rule as Java identifiers and are terminated with a colon. For example, the following statement is labeled **sectionA**.

```
sectionA: x = y + 1;
```

And, here is an example of labeling a block:

```
start: {
    // statements
}
```

The purpose of labeling a statement or a block is so that it can be referenced by the **break** and **continue** statements.

The if Statement

The **if** statement is a conditional branch statement. The syntax of the **if** statement is either one of these two:

```
if (booleanExpression) {
    statement(s)
}
```

```
if (booleanExpression) {
    statement(s)
} else {
    statement(s)
}
```

If *booleanExpression* evaluates to **true**, the statements in the block following the **if** statement are executed. If it evaluates to **false**, the statements in the **if** block are not executed. If *booleanExpression* evaluates to **false** and there is an **else** block, the statements in the **else** block are executed.

For example, in the following **if** statement, the **if** block will be executed if **x** is greater than 4.

```
if (x > 4) {
    // statements
}
```

In the following example, the **if** block will be executed if **a** is greater than 3. Otherwise, the **else** block will be executed.

```
if (a > 3) {
    // statements
} else {
    // statements
}
```

Note that the good coding style suggests that statements in a block be indented.

If the expression to be evaluated is too long to be written in a single line, it is recommended that you use two units of indentation for subsequent lines. For example.

```
if (numberOfLoginAttempts < numberOfMaximumLoginAttempts
        || numberOfMinimumLoginAttempts > y) {
    y++;
}
```

If there is only one statement in an **if** or **else** block, the braces are optional.

```
if (a > 3)
    a++;
else
    a = 3;
```

However, this may pose what is called the dangling else problem. Consider the following example:

```
if (a > 0 || b < 5)
    if (a > 2)
        System.out.println("a > 2");
    else
        System.out.println("a < 2");
```

The **else** statement is dangling because it is not clear which **if** statement the **else** statement is associated with. An **else** statement is always associated with the immediately preceding **if**. Using braces makes your code clearer.

```
if (a > 0 || b < 5) {
    if (a > 2) {
        System.out.println("a > 2");
    } else {
        System.out.println("a < 2");
    }
}
```

If there are multiple selections, you can also use **if** with a series of **else** statements.

```
if (booleanExpression1) {
    // statements
} else if (booleanExpression2) {
    // statements
}
...
else {
    // statements
}
```

For example

```
if (a == 1) {
    System.out.println("one");
} else if (a == 2) {
    System.out.println("two");
} else if (a == 3) {
    System.out.println("three");
} else {
    System.out.println("invalid");
}
```

In this case, the **else** statements that are immediately followed by an **if** do not use braces. See also the discussion of the **switch** statement in the section, "The switch Statement" later in this chapter.

The while Statement

In many occasions, you may want to perform the same action several times in a row. In other words, you have a block of code that you want executed repeatedly. Intuitively, this can be done by repeating the lines of code. For instance, a beep can be achieved using this line of code:[2]

```
java.awt.Toolkit.getDefaultToolkit().beep();
```

And, to wait for half a second you use these lines of code.

```
try {
    Thread.currentThread().sleep(500);
} catch (Exception e) {
}
```

Therefore, to produce three beeps with a 500 milliseconds interval between two beeps, you can simply repeat the same code:

```
java.awt.Toolkit.getDefaultToolkit().beep();
try {
    Thread.currentThread().sleep(500);
} catch (Exception e) {
}
java.awt.Toolkit.getDefaultToolkit().beep();
try {
    Thread.currentThread().sleep(500);
} catch (Exception e) {
}
java.awt.Toolkit.getDefaultToolkit().beep();
```

However, there are circumstances where repeating code does not work. Here are some of those:

---

[2] What this line of code and the following lines of code do will become clear after you finish reading Chapter 4.

- The number of repetition is higher than 5, which means the number of lines of code increases five fold. If there is a line that you need to fix in the block, copies of the same line must also be modified.
- If the number of repetitions is not known in advance.

A much cleverer way is to put the repeated code in a loop. This way, you only write the code once but you can instruct Java to execute the code any number of times. One way to create a loop is by using the **while** statement, which is the topic of discussion of this section. Another way is to use the **for** statement, which is explained in the next section.

The **while** statement has the following syntax.

```
while (booleanExpression) {
    statement(s)
}
```

Here, *statement(s)* will be executed as long as *booleanExpression* evaluates to **true**. If there is only a single statement inside the braces, you may omit the braces. For clarity, however, you should always use braces even when there is only one statement.

As an example of the **while** statement, the following code prints integer numbers that are less than three.

```
int i = 0;
while (i < 3) {
    System.out.println(i);
    i++;
}
```

Note that the execution of the code in the loop is dependent on the value of **i**, which is incremented with each iteration until it reaches 3.

To produce three beeps with an interval of 500 milliseconds, use this code:

```
int j = 0;
while (j < 3) {
    java.awt.Toolkit.getDefaultToolkit().beep();
    try {
        Thread.currentThread().sleep(500);
    } catch (Exception e) {
    }
    j++;
}
```

Sometimes, you use an expression that always evaluates to **true** (such as the **boolean** literal **true**) but relies on the **break** statement to escape from the loop.

```
int k = 0;
while (true) {
    System.out.println(k);
    k++;
    if (k > 2) {
        break;
    }
}
```

You will learn about the **break** statement in the section, "The break Statement" later in this chapter.

The do-while Statement

The **do-while** statement is like the **while** statement, except that the associated block always gets executed at least once. Its syntax is as follows:

```
do {
    statement(s)
} while (booleanExpression);
```

With **do-while**, you put the statement(s) to be executed after the **do** keyword. Just like the **while** statement, you can omit the braces if there is only one statement within them. However, always use braces for the sake of clarity.

For example, here is an example of the **do-while** statement:

```
int i = 0;
do {
    System.out.println(i);
    i++;
} while (i < 3);
```

This prints the following to the console:

```
0
1
2
```

The following **do-while** demonstrates that at least the code in the **do** block will be executed once even though the initial value of **j** used to test the expression **j < 3** evaluates to **false**.

```
int j = 4;
do {
    System.out.println(j);
    j++;
} while (j < 3);
```

This prints the following on the console.

```
4
```

The for Statement

The **for** statement is like the **while** statement, i.e. you use it to enclose code that needs to be executed several times. However, **for** is more complex than **while**.

The **for** statement starts with an initialization, followed by an expression evaluation for each iteration and the execution of a statement block if the expression evaluates to **true**. An update statement will also be executed after the execution of the statement block for each iteration.

The **for** statement has following syntax:

```
for ( init ; booleanExpression ; update ) {
    statement(s)
}
```

Here, *init* is an initialization that will be performed before the first iteration, *booleanExpression* is a boolean expression which will cause the execution of *statement(s)* if it evaluates to **true**, and *update* is a statement that will be executed *after* the execution of the statement block. *init*, *expression*, and *update* are optional.

The **for** statement will stop only if one of the following conditions is met:

- *booleanEpression* evaluates to **false**
- A **break** or **continue** statement is executed
- A runtime error occurs.

It is common to declare a variable and assign a value to it in the initialization part. The variable declared will be visible to the *expression* and *update* parts as well as to the statement block.

For example, the following **for** statement loops five times and each time prints the value of **i**.

```
for (int i = 0; i < 3; i++) {
    System.out.println(i + "   ");
}
```

The **for** statement starts by declaring an **int** named **i** and assigning 0 to it:

```
int i = 0;
```

It then evaluates the expression **i < 3**, which evaluates to **true** since **i** equals 0. As a result, the statement block is executed, and the value of **i** is printed. It then performs the update statement **i++**, which increments **i** to 1. That concludes the first loop.

The **for** statement then evaluates the value of **i < 3** again. The result is again **true** because **i** equals 1. This causes the statement block to be executed and **1** is printed on the console. Afterwards, the update statement **i++** is executed, incrementing **i** to 2. That concludes the second loop.

Next, the expression **i < 3** is evaluated and the result is **true** because **i** equals 2. This causes the statement block to be run and 2 is printed on the console. Afterwards, the update statement **i++** is executed, causing **i** to be equal to 3. This concludes the second loop.

Next, the expression **i < 3** is evaluated again, and the result is **false**. This stops the **for** loop.

This is what you see on the console:

```
0
1
2
```

Note that the variable **i** is not visible anywhere else since it is declared within the **for** loop.

Note also that if the statement block within **for** only consists of one statement, you can remove the braces, so in this case the above **for** statement can be rewritten as:

```
for (int i = 0; i < 3; i++)
    System.out.println(i);
```

However, using braces even if there is only one statement makes your code clearer.

Here is another example of the **for** statement.

```
for (int i = 0; i < 3; i++) {
    if (i % 2 == 0) {
        System.out.println(i);
    }
}
```

This one loops three times. For each iteration the value of **i** is tested. If **i** is even, its value is printed. The result of the **for** loop is as follows:

```
0
2
```

The following **for** loop is similar to the previous case, but uses **i += 2** as the update statement. As a result, it only loops twice, when **i** equals 0 and when it is 2.

```
for (int i = 0; i < 3; i += 2) {
    System.out.println(i);
}
```

The result is

```
0
2
```

A statement that decrements a variable is often used too. Consider the following **for** loop:

```
for (int i = 3; i > 0; i--) {
    System.out.println(i);
}
```

which prints:

```
3
2
1
```

The initialization part of the **for** statement is optional. In the following **for** loop, the variable **j** is declared outside the loop, so potentially **j** can be used from other points in the code outside the **for** statement block.

```
int j = 0;
for ( ; j < 3; j++) {
    System.out.println(j);
}
// j is visible here
```

As mentioned previously, the update statement is optional. The following **for** statement moves the update statement to the end of the statement block. The result is the same.

```
int k = 0;
for ( ; k < 3; ) {
    System.out.println(k);
    k++;
}
```

In theory, you can even omit the *booleanExpression* part. For example, the following **for** statement does not have one, and the loop is only terminated with the **break** statement. See the section, "The break Statement" for more information.

```
int m = 0;
for ( ; ; ) {
    System.out.println(m);
    m++;
    if (m > 4) {
        break;
    }
}
```

If you compare **for** and **while**, you'll see that you can always replace the **while** statement with **for**. This is to say that

```
while (expression) {
    ...
}
```

can always be written as

```
for ( ; expression; ) {
    ...
}
```

Note

In addition, in Java 5 **for** has been enhanced so that it can iterate over an array or a collection. See Chapters 5, "Core Classes" and Chapter 11, "The Collections Framework" for the discussions of the enhanced **for**.

The break Statement

The **break** statement is used to break from an enclosing **do, while, for,** or **switch** statement. It is a compile error to use **break** anywhere else.

For example, consider the following code

```
int i = 0;
while (true) {
    System.out.println(i);
    i++;
    if (i > 3) {
        break;
    }
}
```

The result is

```
0
1
2
3
```

Note that **break** breaks the loop without executing the rest of the statements in the block.

Here is another example of break, this time in a **for** loop.

```
int m = 0;
for ( ; ; ) {
    System.out.println(m);
    m++;
    if (m > 4) {
        break;
    }
}
```

The **break** statement can be followed by a label. The presence of a label will transfer control to the start of the code identified by the label. For example, consider this code.

```
start:
for (int i = 0; i < 3; i++) {
    for (int j = 0; j < 4; j++) {
        if (j == 2) {
            break start;
        }
        System.out.println(i + ":" + j);
    }
}
```

The use of label start identifies the first **for** loop. The statement **break start;** therefore breaks from the first loop. The result of running the preceding code is as follows.

```
0:0
0:1
```

Java does not have a goto statement like in C or C++, and labels are meant as a form of goto. However, just as using goto in C/C++ may obscure your code, the use of labels in Java may make your code unstructured. The general advice is to avoid labels if possible and to always use them with caution.

The continue Statement

The **continue** statement is like **break** but it only stops the execution of the current iteration and causes control to begin with the next iteration.

For example, the following code prints the number 0 to 9, except 5.

```
for (int i = 0; i < 10; i++) {
    if (i == 5) {
        continue;
    }
    System.out.println(i);
}
```

When **i** is equals to 5, the expression of the **if** statement evaluates to **true** and causes the **continue** statement to be called. As a result, the statement below it that prints the value of **i** is not executed and control continues with the next loop, i.e. for **i** equals 6.

As with **break**, **continue** may be followed by a label to identify which enclosing loop to continue to. As with labels with **break**, employ **continue label** with caution and avoid it if you can.

Here is an example of **continue** with a label.

```
start:
for (int i = 0; i < 3; i++) {
    for (int j = 0; j < 4; j++) {
        if (j == 2) {
            continue start;
        }
        System.out.println(i + ":" + j);
    }
}
```

The result of running this code is as follows:

```
0:0
0:1
1:0
1:1
2:0
2:1
```

The switch Statement

An alternative to a series of **else if**, as discussed in the last part of the section, "The if Statement," is the **switch** statement. The **switch** statement allows you to choose a block of statements to run from a selection of code, based on the return value of an expression. The expression used in the **switch** statement must return an **int** or an enumerated value.

Note
Java 5 enum is discussed in Chapter 10, "Enums."

The syntax of the **switch** statement is as follows.

```
switch(expression) {
case value_1 :
```

```
    statement(s);
    break;
case value_2 :
    statement(s);
    break;

  .

  .

  .

case value_n :
    statement(s);
    break;
default:
    statement(s);
}
```

Failure to add a **break** statement after a case will not generate a compile error but may have more serious consequences because the statements on the next case will be executed.

Here is an example of the **switch** statement. If the value of **i** is 1, "One player is playing this game." is printed. If the value is 2, "Two players are playing this game is printed." If the value is 3, "Three players are playing this game is printed. For any other value, "You did not enter a valid value." will be printed.

```
int i = ...;
switch (i) {
case 1 :
    System.out.println("One player is playing this game.");
    break;
case 2 :
    System.out.println("Two players are playing this game.");
    break;
case 3 :
    System.out.println("Three players are playing this game.");
    break;
default:
    System.out.println("You did not enter a valid value.");
}
```

Summary

The sequence of execution of a Java program is controlled by statements. In this chapter, you have learned the following Java control statements: **if, while, do-while, for, break, continue,** and **switch.** Understanding how to use these statements is crucial to writing correct programs.

Questions

1. What is the difference between an expression and a statement?
2. How do you escape from the following while loop?

```
while (true) {
    // statements
}
```

3. Is there any difference between using the postfix increment operator and the prefix increment operator as the update statement of a **for** loop?

```
for (int x = 0; x < length; x++)
for (int x = 0; x < length; ++x)
```

4. What will be printed on the console if the code below is executed:

```
int i = 1;
switch (i) {
case 1 :
    System.out.println("One player is playing this game.");
case 2 :
    System.out.println("Two players are playing this game.");
    break;
default:
    System.out.println("You did not enter a valid value.");
}
```

Hint: no **break** after case 1.

Chapter 4
Objects and Classes

Object-oriented programming (OOP) works by modeling applications on real-world objects. The benefits of OOP, which were discussed in Introduction, are real, which explains why OOP is the paradigm of choice today and why OOP languages like Java are popular. This chapter introduces you to objects and classes, the template to make objects. If you are new to OOP, you may want to read this chapter carefully. A good understanding of OOP is the key to writing quality programs.

This chapter starts by explaining what an object is and what constitutes a class. It then teaches you how to create objects in Java using the **new** keyword, how objects are stored in memory, how classes can be organized into packages, how to use access control to achieve encapsulation, how the Java Virtual Machine (JVM) loads and link your objects, and how Java manages unused objects. In addition, method overloading and static class members are explained.

What Is a Java Object?

When developing an application in an OOP language, you create a model that resembles a real-life situation to solve your problem. Take for example a company payroll application, which can calculate the take home pay of an employee and the amount of income tax to be paid. An application like this would have a **Company** object to represent the company using the application, **Employee** objects that represent the employees in the company, **Tax** objects to represent the tax details of each employee, and so on. Before you can start programming such applications, however, you need to understand what Java objects are and how to create them.

Let's begin with a look at objects in life. Objects are everywhere, living (persons, pets, etc) and otherwise (cars, houses, streets, etc); concrete (books, televisions, etc) and abstract (love, knowledge, tax rate, regulations, and so forth). Every object has two features: attributes and actions the object is able to perform. For example, the following are some of a car's attributes:

- color
- number of tires
- plate number
- number of valves

Additionally, a car can perform these actions:

- run
- brake

As another example, a dog has the following attributes: color, age, type, weight, etc. And it also can bark, run, urinate, sniff, etc.

A Java object also has attribute(s) and can perform action(s). In Java, attributes are called fields and actions are called methods. In other programming languages these may be known differently. For example, methods are often called functions.

Both fields and methods are optional, meaning some Java objects may not have fields but have methods and some others may have fields but not methods. Some, of course, have both attributes and methods and some have neither.

How do you create Java objects? This is the same as asking, "How do you make cars?" Cars are expensive objects that need careful design that takes into account many things, such as safety and cost-effectiveness. You need a good blueprint to make good cars. To create Java objects, you need similar blueprints: classes.

Java Classes

A class is a blueprint or a template to create objects of identical type. If you have an **Employee** class, you can create any number of **Employee** objects. To create **Street** objects, you need a **Street** class. A class determines what kind of objects you get. For example, if you create an **Employee** class that has **age** and **position** fields, all **Employee** objects created out of this **Employee** class will have **age** and **position** fields as well. No more no less. The class determines the object.

In summary, classes are an OOP tool that enable programmers to create the abstraction of a problem. In OOP, abstraction is the act of using programming objects to represent real-world objects. As such, programming objects do not need to have the details of real-world objects. For instance, if an **Employee** object in a payroll application needs only be able to work and receive a salary, then the **Employee** class needs only two methods, **work** and **receiveSalary**. OOP abstraction ignores the fact that a real-world employee can do many other things including eat, run, kiss, and kick.

Classes are the fundamental building blocks of a Java program. All program elements in Java must reside in a class, even if you are writing a simple program that does not require Java's object-oriented features. A Java beginner needs to consider three things when writing a class:

- the class name
- the fields
- the methods

There are other things that can be present in a class, but they can be discussed later.

A class declaration must use the keyword **class** followed by a class name. Also, a class has a body within braces. Here is a general syntax for a class:

```
class className {
    [class body]
}
```

For example, Listing 4.1 shows a Java class named **Employee**, where the lines in bold are the class body.

Listing 4.1: The Employee class

```
class Employee {
    int age;
    double salary;
}
```

Note

By convention, class names capitalize the initial of each word. For example, here are some names that follow the convention: **Employee, Boss, DateUtility, PostOffice, RegularRateCalculator**. This type of naming convention is known as Pascal naming convention. The other convention, the camel naming convention, capitalize the initial of each word, except the first word. Method and field names use the camel naming convention.

A class definition must be saved in a file that has the same name as the class name. The file name must also have the **java** extension. For instance, the **Employee** class in Listing 4.1 must be saved as **Employee.java**.

Note

In UML class diagrams, a class is represented by a rectangle that consists of three parts: the topmost part is the class name, the middle part is the list of fields, and the bottom part is the list of methods. (See Figure 4.1) The fields and methods can be hidden if showing them is not important.

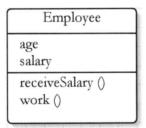

Figure 4.1: The Employee class in the UML class diagram

Fields

Fields are variables. They can be primitives or references to objects. For example, the **Employee** class in Listing 4.1 has two fields, **age** and **salary**. In Chapter 2 we have learned how to declare and initialize variables of primitive types.

However, a field can also refer to another object. For instance, an **Empoyee** class may have an **address** field of type **Address**, which is a class that represents a street address:

```
Address address;
```

In other words, an object can contain other objects, that is if the class of the former contains variables that reference to the latter.

Field names should follow the camel naming convention. The initial of each word in the field, except for the first word, is written with a capital letter. For example, here are some "good" field names: **age**, **maxAge**, **address**, **validAddress**, **numberOfRows**.

Methods

Methods define actions that a class's objects (or instances) can do. A method has a declaration part and a body. The declaration part consists of a return value, the method name, and a list of arguments. The body contains code that perform the action.

To declare a method, use the following syntax:

```
returnType methodName (listOfArguments)
```

The return type of a method can be a primitive, an object, or void. The return type **void** means that the method returns nothing. The declaration part of a method is also called the signature of the method.

For example, here is the **getSalary** method that returns a **double**.

```
double getSalary()
```

The **getSalary** method does not accept arguments.

As another example, here is a method that returns an **Address** object.

```
Address getAddress()
```

And, here is a method that accepts an argument:

```
int negate(int number)
```

If a method takes more than one argument, two arguments are separated by a comma. For example, the following **add** method takes two **int**s and return an **int**.

```
int add(int a, int b)
```

Also note that Java 5 adds a new feature that allows a method to have a variable number of arguments. For details, see the section, "Varargs" in Chapter 5, "Core Classes."

The Method main

A special method called **main** provides the entry point to an application. An application normally has many classes and only one of the classes needs to have the method **main**. This method allows the class containing it to be invoked.

The signature of the method **main** is as follows.

```
public static void main(String[] args)
```

If you ask why there is "public static void" before **main**, you will get the answer towards the end of this chapter.

In addition, you can pass arguments to **main** when using **java** to run a class. To pass arguments, type them after the class name. Two arguments are separated by a space.

```
java className arg1 arg2 arg3 ...
```

All arguments must be passed as strings. For instance, to pass two arguments, "1" and "safeMode" when running the **Test** class, you type this:

```
java Test 1 safeMode
```

Strings are discussed in Chapter 5, "Core Classes."

Constructors

Every class must have at least one constructor. Otherwise, no objects could be created out of the class and the class would be useless. As such, if your class does not explicitly define a constructor, the compiler adds one for you.

A constructor is used to construct an object. A constructor looks like a method and is sometimes called a constructor method. However, unlike a method, a constructor does not have a return value, not even **void**. Additionally, a constructor must have the same name as the class.

The syntax for a constructor is as follows.

```
constructorName (listOfArguments) {
    [constructor body]
}
```

A constructor may have zero argument, in which case it is called a no-argument (or no-arg, for short) constructor. Constructor arguments can be used to initialize the fields in the object.

If the Java compiler adds a no-arg constructor to a class because the class has none, the addition will be implicit, i.e. it will not be displayed in the source file. However, if there is a constructor, regardless of the number of arguments it accepts, no constructor will be added to the class by the compiler.

As an example, Listing 4.2 adds two constructors to the **Employee** class in Listing 4.1.

Listing 4.2: The Employee class with constructors

```
public class Employee {
    public int age;
    public double salary;
    public Employee() {
    }
    public Employee(int ageValue, double salaryValue) {
        age = ageValue;
        salary = salaryValue;
    }
}
```

The second constructor is particularly useful. Without it, to assign values to age and position, you would need to write extra lines of code to initialize the fields:

```
employee.age = 20;
employee.salary = 90000.00;
```

With the second constructor, you can pass the values at the same time you create an object.

```
new Employee(20, 90000.00);
```

The **new** keyword is new to you, but you will learn how to use it in the next section.

Class Members in UML Class Diagrams

Figure 4.1 depicts a class in a UML class diagram. The diagram provides a quick summary of all fields and methods. You could do more in UML. UML allows you to include field types and method signatures. For example, Figure 4.2 presents the **Book** class with five fields and one method.

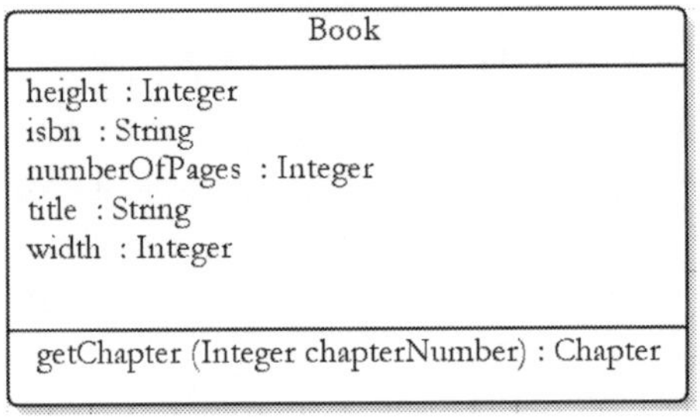

```
                          Book
    height  : Integer
    isbn  : String
    numberOfPages  : Integer
    title  : String
    width  : Integer

    getChapter (Integer chapterNumber) : Chapter
```

Figure 4.2: Including class member information in a class diagram

Note that in a UML class diagram a field and its type is separated by a colon. A method's argument list is presented in parentheses and its return type is written after a colon.

Creating Objects

Now that you know how to write a class, it is time to learn how to create an object from a class. An object is also called an instance. The word construct is often used in lieu of create, thus constructing an **Employee** object. Another term commonly used is *instantiate*. Instantiating the **Employee** class is the same as creating an instance of **Employee**.

There are a number of ways to create an object, but the most common one is by using the **new** keyword. **new** is always followed by the constructor of the class to be instantiated. For example, to create an **Employee** object, you write:

```
new Employee();
```

Most of the time, you will want to assign the created object to an object variable (or a reference variable), so that you can manipulate the object later. To achieve this, you just need to declare an object reference with the same type as the object. For instance:

```
Employee employee = new Employee();
```

Here, **employee** is an object reference of type **Employee**.

Once you have an object, you can call its methods and access its fields, by using the object reference that was assigned the object. You use a period (.) to call a method or a field. For example:

```
objectReference.methodName
objectReference.fieldName
```

The following code, for instance, creates an **Employee** object and assigns values to its **age** and **salary** fields:

```
Employee employee = new Employee();
employee.age = 24;
employee.salary = 50000;
```

When an object is created, the JVM also performs initialization that assign default values to fields. This will be discussed further in the section, "Object Creation Initialization" later in this chapter.

The null Keyword

A reference variable refers to an object. There are times, however, when a reference variable does not have a value (it is not referencing an object). Such a reference variable is said to have a null value. For example, the following class level reference variable is of type **Book** but has not been assigned a value;

```
Book book; // book is null
```

If you declare a local reference variable within a method but do not assign an object to it, you will need to assign null to it to satisfy the compiler:

```
Book book = null;
```

Class-level reference variables will be initialized when an instance is created, therefore you do not need to assign **null** to them.

Trying to access the field or method of a null variable reference raises an error, such as in the following code:

```
Book book = null;
```

```
System.out.println(book.title); // error because book is null
```

You can test if a reference variable is **null** by using the **==** operator. For instance.

```
if (book == null) {
    book = new Book();
}
System.out.println(book.title);
```

Objects in Memory

When you declare a variable in your class, either in the class level or in the method level, you allocate memory space for data that will be assigned to the variable. For primitives, it is easy to calculate the amount of memory taken. For example, declaring an **int** costs you four bytes and declaring a **long** sets you back eight bytes. However, calculation for reference variables is different.

When a program runs, some memory space is allocated for data. This data space is logically divided into two, the stack and the heap. Primitives are allocated in the stack and Java objects reside in the heap.

When you declare a primitive, a few bytes are allocated in the stack. When you declare a reference variable, some bytes are also set aside in the stack, but the memory does not contain an object's data, it contains the address of the object in the heap. In other words, when you declare

```
Book book;
```

Some bytes are set aside for the reference variable **book**. The initial value of **book** is **null** because there is not yet object assigned to it. When you write

```
Book book = new Book();
```

you create an instance of **Book**, which is stored in the heap, and assign the address of the instance to the reference variable **book**. A Java reference variable is like a C++ pointer except that you cannot manipulate a reference variable. In Java, a reference variable is used to access the member of the object it is referring to. Therefore, if the **Book** class has the public **review** method, you can call the method by using this syntax:

```
book.review();
```

An object can be referenced by more than one reference variable. For example,

```
Book myBook = new Book();
Book yourBook = myBook;
```

The second line copies the value of **myBook** to **yourBook**. As a result, **yourBook** is now referencing the same **Book** object as **myBook**.

Figure 4.3 illustrates memory allocation for a **Book** object referenced by **myBook** and **yourBook**.

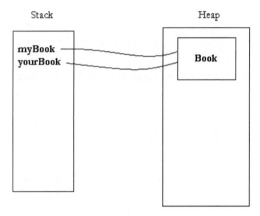

Figure 4.3: An object referenced by two variables

On the other hand, the following code creates two different **Book** objects:

```
Book myBook = new Book();
Book yourBook = new Book();
```

The memory allocation for this code is illustrated in Figure 4.4.

Now, how about an object that contains another object? For example, consider the code in Listing 4.3 that shows the **Employee** class that contains an **Address** class.

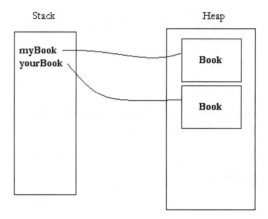

Figure 4.4: Two objects referenced by two variables

Listing 4.3: The Employee class that contains another class

```
package app04;
public class Employee {
    Address address = new Address();
}
```

When you create an **Employee** object using the following code, an **Address** object is also created.

```
Employee employee = new Employee();
```

Figure 4.5 depicts the position of each object in the heap.

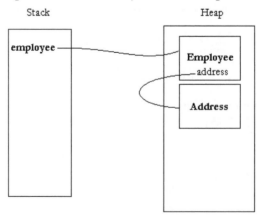

Figure 4.5: An object "within" another object

It turns out that the **Address** object is not really inside the **Employee** object. However, the **address** field within the **Employee** object has a reference to the **Address** object, thus allowing the **Employee** object to manipulate the **Address** object. Because in Java there is no way of accessing an object except through a reference variable assigned the object's address, no one else can access the **Address** object 'within' the **Employee** object.

The Concept of Packages

If you are developing an application that consists of different parts, you may want to organize your classes to retain maintainability. With Java, you can group related classes or classes with similar functionality in packages. For example, standard Java classes come in packages. Java core classes are in the **java.lang** package. All classes for performing input and output operations are members of the **java.io** package, and so on. If a package needs to be organized in more detail, you can create packages that share part of the name of the former. For example, the Java class library comes with the **java.lang.annotation** and **java.lang.reflect** packages. However, mind you that sharing part of the name does not make two packages related. The **java.lang** package and the **java.lang.reflect** package are different packages.

Package names that start with **java** are reserved for the core libraries. Consequently, you cannot create a package that starts with the word **java**. You can compile classes that belong to such a package, but you cannot run them.

In addition, packages starting with **javax** are meant for extension libraries that come with the core libraries. You should not create packages that start with **javax** either.

In addition to class organization, packaging can avoid naming conflict. For example, an application may use the **MathUtil** class from company A and an identically named class from another company if both classes belong to different packages. For this purpose, by convention your package names should be based on your domain name in reverse. Therefore, Sun's package names start with **com.sun**. My domain name is **brainysoftware.com**, so it's appropriate for me to start my package name with **com.brainysoftware**. For example, I would place all my applets in the **com.brainysoftware.applet** package and my servlets in **com.brainysoftware.servlet**.

A package is not a physical object, and therefore you do not need to create one. To group a class in a package, use the keyword **package** followed by the package name. For example, the following **MathUtil** class is part of the **com.brainysoftware.common** package:

```
package com.brainysoftware.common;
public class MathUtil {
    ...
}
```

Java also introduced the term *fully qualified name*, which refers to a class name that carries with it its package name. The fully qualified name of a class is its package name followed by a period and the class name. Therefore, the fully qualified name of the **MathUtil** class that belongs to package **com.sun.common** is **com.sun.common.MathUtil**.

A class that has no package declaration is said to belong to the default package. For example, the **Employee** class in Listing 4.1 belongs to the default package.

Even though a package is not a physical object, package names have a bearing on the physical location of their class source files. A package name represents a directory structure in which a period in a package name indicates a subfolder. For example, all Java source files in the **com.brainysoftware.common** package must reside in the **common** directory that is a subdirectory of the **brainysoftware** directory. In turn, the latter must be a subdirectory of the **com** directory. Figure 4.6 depicts a folder structure for the **com.brainysoftware.common.MathUtil** class.

Figure 4.6: The physical location of a class in a package

Compiling a class in a non-default package presents a challenge for beginners. To compile such a class, you need to include the package name, replacing the dot (.) with /. For example, to compile the **com.brainysoftware.common.MathUtil** class, change directory to the working directory (the directory which is the parent directory of **com**) and type

```
javac com/brainysoftware/common/MathUtil.java
```

By default, **javac** will place the result in the same directory structure as the source. In this case, the **MathUtil.class** file will be created in the **com/brainysoftware/common** directory.

Running a class that belongs to a package follows a similar rule: you must include the package name, replacing . with /. For example, to run the **com.brainysoftware.common.MathUtil** class, type the following from your working directory.

```
java com/brainysoftware/common/MathUtil
```

The packaging of your classes also affects the visibility of your classes, as will be witnessed in the next section.

Note
Code samples accompanying this book are grouped into packages too. The packages are named **com.brainysoftware.jdk5.app*XX***, where ***XX*** is the chapter number.

Encapsulation and Access Control

An OOP principle, encapsulation is a mechanism that protects parts of an object that need to be secure and exposes only parts that are safe to be exposed. A television is a good example of encapsulation. Inside it are thousands of electronic components that together form the parts that can receive signals and decode them into images and sound. These components are not to be exposed to users, however, so Sony and other manufacturers wrap them in a strong metallic cover that does not break easily. For a television to be easy to use, it exposes buttons that the user can touch to turn on and off the set, adjust brightness, turn up and down the volume, and so on.

Back to encapsulation in OOP, let's take as an example a class that can encode and decode messages. The class exposes two methods called **encode** and **decode**, that users of the class can access. Internally, there are dozens of variables used to store temporary values and other methods that perform supporting tasks. The author of the class hides these variables and other methods because allowing access to them may compromise the security of the encoding/decoding algorithms. Besides, exposing too many things makes the class harder to use. As you can see later, encapsulation is a powerful feature.

Java supports encapsulation through access control. Access control is governed by access control modifiers. There are four access control modifiers in Java: **public**, **protected**, **private**, and the default access level. Access control modifiers can be applied to classes or class members. We'll look at them in the following subsections.

Class Access Control Modifiers

In an application with many classes, a class will be instantiated and used from other classes that are members of the same package as the former or that are members of other packages. You can control from which packages your class can be "seen" by employing an access control modifier at the beginning of the class declaration.

A class can have either the public or the default access control level. You make a class public by using the **public** access control modifier. A class whose declaration bears no access control modifier has default access. A public class is visible from anywhere. Listing 4.4 shows a public class named **Book**.

Listing 4.4: The public Book class

```
package app04;
public class Book {
    String isbn;
    String title;
    int width;
    int height;
    int numberOfPages;
}
```

The **Book** class is a member of the **app04** package and has five fields. Since **Book** is public, it can be instantiated from any other classes. In fact, most classes in the Java core libraries are public classes. For example, here is the declaration of the **java.io.File** class:

```
public class File
```

A public class must be saved in a file that has the same name as the class, and the extension must be **java**. The **Book** class in Listing 4.4 must be saved in the

Book.java file. Also, because **Book** belongs to package **app04**, the **Book.java** file must reside inside the **app04** directory.

Note

A Java source file can only contain one public class. However, it can contain other classes that are not public.

When there is no access control modifier preceding a class declaration, the class has the default access level. For example, Listing 4.5 presents the **Chapter** class that has the default access level.

Listing 4.5: The Chapter class, with the default access level

```
package app04;
class Chapter {
    String title;
    int numberOfPages;

    public void review() {
        Page page = new Page();
        int sentenceCount = page.numberOfSentences;
        int pageNumber = page.getPageNumber();
    }
}
```

Classes with the default access level can only be used by other classes that belong to the same package. For instance, the **Chapter** class can be instantiated from inside the **Book** class because **Book** belongs to the same package as **Chapter**. However, **Chapter** is not visible from other packages.

For example, you can add the following **getChapter** method inside the **Book** class:

```
Chapter getChapter() {
    return new Chapter();
}
```

On the other hand, if you try to add the same **getChapter** method to a class that does not belong to the **app04** package, a compile error will be raised.

Class Member Access Control Modifiers

Class members (methods, fields, constructors, etc) can have one of four access control levels: public, protected, private, and default access. The **public** access control modifier is used to make a class member public, the **protected** modifier to make a class member public, and the **private** modifier to make a class member private. Without an access control modifier, a class member will have the default access level.

Table 4.1 shows the visibility of each access level.

Access Level	From classes in other packages	From classes in the same package	From child classes	From the same class
public	yes	yes	yes	yes
protected	no	yes	yes	yes
default	no	yes	no	yes
private	no	no	no	yes

Table 4.1: Class member access levels

Note

The default access is sometimes called package private. To avoid confusion, this book will only use the term default access.

A public class member can be accessed by any other classes that can access the class containing the class member. For example, the **toString** method of the **java.lang.Object** class is public. Here is the method signature:

```
public String toString()
```

Once you instantiate an **Object** object, you can call its **toString** method because **toString** is public.

```
Object obj = new Object();
obj.toString();
```

Recall that you access a class member by using this syntax:

```
referenceVariable.memberName
```

In the preceding code, **obj** is a reference variable to an instance of **java.lang.Object** and **toString** is the method defined in the **java.lang.Object** class.

A protected class member has a more restricted access level. It can be accessed only from

- any class in the same package as the class containing the member
- a child class of the class containing the member

Note

A child class is a class that extends another class. Chapter 6, "Inheritance" explains this concept.

For instance, consider the public **Page** class in Listing 4.6.

Listing 4.6: The Page class

```
package app04;
public class Page {
    int numberOfSentences = 10;
    private int pageNumber = 5;
    protected int getPageNumber() {
        return pageNumber;
    }
}
```

Page has two fields (**numberOfSentences** and **pageNumber**) and one method (**getPageNumber**). First of all, because the **Page** class is public, it can be instantiated from any other class. However, even if you can instantiate it, there is no guarantee you can access its members by using the *referenceVariable.memberName* syntax. It depends on from which class you are accessing the **Page** class's members.

Its **getPageNumber** method is protected, so it can be accessed from any classes that belong to **app04**, the package that houses the **Page** class. For example, consider the **review** method in the **Chapter** class (given in Listing 4.5).

```
public void review() {
    Page page = new Page();
    int sentenceCount = page.numberOfSentences;
    int pageNumber = page.getPageNumber();
}
```

The **Chapter** class can access the **getPageNumber** method because **Chapter** belongs to the same package as the **Page** class. Therefore, **Chapter** can access all protected members of the **Page** class.

The default access allows classes in the same package access a class member. For instance, the **Chapter** class can access the **Page** class's **numberOfSentences** field because the **Page** and **Chapter** classes belong to the same package. However, **numberOfSentences** is not accessible from a subclass of **Page** if the subclass belongs to a different package. This differentiates the protected and default access levels and will be explained in detail in Chapter 6, "Inheritance."

A class's private members can only be accessed from inside the same class. For example, there is no way you can access the **Page** class's private **pageNumber** field from anywhere other than the **Page** class itself. However, look at the following code from the **Page** class definition.

```
private int pageNumber = 5;
protected int getPageNumber() {
    return pageNumber;
}
```

The **pageNumber** field is private, so it can be accessed from the **getPageNumber** method, which is defined in the same class. The return value of **getPageNumber** is **pageNumber**, which is private. Beginners are often confused by this kind of code. If **pageNumber** is private, why do we use it as a return value of a protected method (**getPageNumber**)? Note that access to **pageNumber** is still private, so other classes cannot modify this field. However, using it as a return value of a non-private method is allowed.

How about constructors? Access levels to constructors are the same as those for fields and methods. Therefore, constructors can have public, protected, default, and private access levels. You may think that all constructors must be public because the intention of having a constructor is to make the class instantiable. However, to your surprise, this is not so. Some constructors are made private so that their classes cannot be instantiated by using the **new** keyword. Private constructors are normally used in singleton classes. If you are interested in this topic, there are articles on this topic that you can find easily on the Internet.

Note
In a UML class diagram, you can include information on class member access level. Prefix a public member with +, a protected member with # and a private member with -. Members with no prefix are regarded as

having the default access level. Figure 4.7 shows the **Manager** class
with members having various access levels.

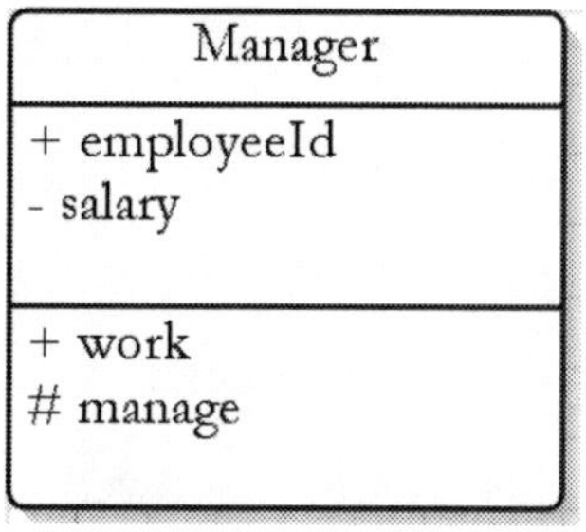

Figure 4.7: Including class member access level in a UML class diagram

The this Keyword

You use the **this** keyword from any method or constructor to refer to the
current object. For example, if you have a class-level field having the same
name as a local variable, you can use this syntax to refer to the former:

`this.field`

A common use is in the constructor that accepts values used to initialize fields.
Consider the **Box** class in Listing 4.7.

Listing 4.7: The Box class

```
package com.brainysoftware.jdk5.app04;
public class Box {
    int length;
    int width;
    int height;
    public Box(int length, int width, int height) {
        this.length = length;
        this.width = width;
        this.height = height;
    }
}
```

The **Box** class has three fields, **length**, **width**, and **height**. Its constructor
accepts three arguments used to initialize the fields. It is very convenient to use
length, **width**, and **height** as the parameter names because they reflect what

they are. Inside the constructor, **length** refers to the **length** argument, not the **length** field. **this.length** refers to the class-level **length** field.

It is of course possible to change the argument names, such as this.

```
public Box (int lengthArg, int widthArg, int heightArg) {
    length = lengthArg;
    width = widthArg;
    height = heightArg;
}
```

This way, the class-level fields are not shadowed by local variables and you do not need to use the **this** keyword to refer to the class-level fields However, using the **this** keyword spares you from having to think of different names for your method or constructor arguments.

Using Other Classes

It is common to use other classes from the class you are writing. Using classes in the same package as your current class is allowed by default. However, to use classes in other packages, you must first import the packages or the classes you want to use.

Java provides the keyword **import** to indicate that you want to use a package or a class from a package. For example, to use the **java.io.File** class from your code, you must have the following **import** statement:

```
package app04;
import java.io.File;

public class Demo {
    ...
}
```

Note that **import** statements must come after the **package** statement but before the class declaration. The **import** keyword can appear multiple times in a class.

```
package app04;
import java.io.File;
import java.util.List;

public class Demo {
```

```
    . . .
}
```

Sometimes you need many classes in the same package. You can import all classes in the same package by using the wild character *. For example, the following code imports all members of the **java.io** package.

```
package app04;
import java.io.*;
public class Demo {
    . . .
}
```

Now, not only can you use the **java.io.File** class, but you can use other members in the **java.io** package too. However, to make your code more readable, it is recommended that you import a package member one at a time. In other words, if you need to use both the **java.io.File** class and the **java.io.FileReader** class, it is better to have two **import** statements like the following than to use the * character.

```
import java.io.File;
import java.io.FileReader;
```

Note
Members of the **java.lang** package are imported automatically. Thus, to use the **java.lang.String**, for example, you do not need to explicitly import the class.

The only way to use classes that belong to other packages without importing them is to use the fully qualified names of the classes in your code. For example, the following code declares the **java.io.File** class using its fully qualified name.

```
java.io.File file = new java.io.File(filename);
```

If you class import identically-named classes from different packages, you must use the fully qualified names when declaring the classes. For example, the Java core libraries contain the classes **java.sql.Date** and **java.util.Date**. Importing both upsets the compiler. In this case, you must write the fully qualified names of **java.sql.Date** and **java.util.Date** in your class to use them.

Note

Java classes can be deployed in a jar file. See Appendix A details how to compile a class that uses other classes in a jar file. Appendix B shows how to run a Java class in a jar file. Appendix C provides instructions on the **jar** tool, a program that comes with the JDK to package your Java classes and related resources.

A class that uses another class depends on the latter. A UML diagram that depicts this dependency is shown in Figure 4.8.

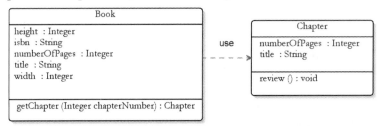

Figure 4.8: Dependency in the UML class diagram

A dependency relationship is represented by a dashed line with an arrow. In Figure 4.8 the **Book** class is dependent on **Chapter** because the **getChapter** method returns a **Chapter** object.

Final Variables

Java does not reserve the keyword constant to create constants. However, in Java you can prefix a variable declaration with the keyword **final** to make its value unchangeable. You can make both local variables and class fields final.

For example, the number of months in a year never changes, so you can write:

```
final int numberOfMonths = 12;
```

As another example, in a class that performs mathematical calculation, you can declare the variable **pi** whose value is equal to 22/7 (the circumference of a circle divided by its diameter, in math represented by the Greek letter π).

```
final float pi = (float) 22 / 7;
```

Once assigned a value, the value cannot change. Attempting to change it will result in a compile error.

Note that the casting **(float)** after **22 / 7** is needed to convert the value of division to **float**. Otherwise, an **int** will be returned and the **pi** variable will have a value of 3.0, instead of 3.1428.

Also note that since Java uses Unicode characters, you can simply define the variable **pi** as π if you don't think typing it is harder than typing **pi**.

```
final float π = (float) 22 / 7;
```

Note
You can also make a method final, thus prohibiting it from being overridden in a subclass. This will be discussed in Chapter 6, "Inheritance."

Static Members

You have learned that to access a public field or method of an object, you use a period after the object reference, such as:

```
// Create an instance of Book
Book book = new Book();
// access the review method
book.review();
```

This implies that you must create an object first before you can access its members. However, in previous chapters, you've seen examples that used **System.out.print** to print values to the console. You may have noticed that you could call the **out** field without first having to construct a **System** object. How come you did not have to do something like this?

```
System ref = new System();
ref.out;
```

Rather, you use a period after the class name:

```
System.out
```

Java (and many OOP languages) supports the notion of static members, which are class members that can be called without first instantiating the class. The

out field in **java.lang.System** is static, which explains why you can write **System.out**.

Static members are not tied to class instances. Rather, they can be called without having an instance. In fact, the method **main**, which acts as the entry point to a class, is static because it must be called before any object is created.

To create a static member, you use the keyword **static** in front of a field or method declaration. If there is an access modifier, the **static** keyword may come before or after the access modifier. These two are correct:

```
public static int a;
static public int b;
```

However, the first form is more often used.

For example, Listing 4.8 shows the **MathUtil** class with a static method:

Listing 4.8: The MathUtil class

```
package com.brainysoftware.jdk5.app04;
public class MathUtil {
    public static int add(int a, int b) {
        return a + b;
    }
}
```

To use the **add** method, you can simply call it this way:

```
MathUtil.add(a, b)
```

The term instance methods/fields are used to refer to non-static methods and fields.

From inside a static method, you cannot call instance methods or instance fields because they only exist after you create an object. You can access other static methods or fields from a static method, however.

A common confusion that a beginner often encounter is when they cannot compile their class because they are calling instance members from the **main** method. Listing 4.9 shows such a class.

Listing 4.9: Calling non-static members from a static method

```
package com.brainysoftware.jdk5.app04;
public class StaticDemo {
    public int b = 8;
```

```
public static void main(String[] args) {
    System.out.println(b);
}
}
```

The line in bold causes a compile error because it tries to access non-static field **b** from the **main** static method. There are two solutions to this.

1. Make **b** static
2. Create an instance of the class, then access **b** by using the object reference.

Which solution is appropriate depends on the situation. It often takes years of OOP experience to come up with a good decision that you're comfortable with.

Note

You can only declare a static variable in a class level. You cannot declare local static variables even if the method is static.

How about static reference variables? You can declare static reference variables. The variable will contain an address, but the object referenced is stored in the heap. For instance

```
static Book book = new Book();
```

Static reference variables provide a good way of exposing the same object that needs to be shared among other different objects.

Note

In UML class diagrams, static members are underlined. For example, Figure 4.9 shows the **MathUtil** class with the static method **add**.

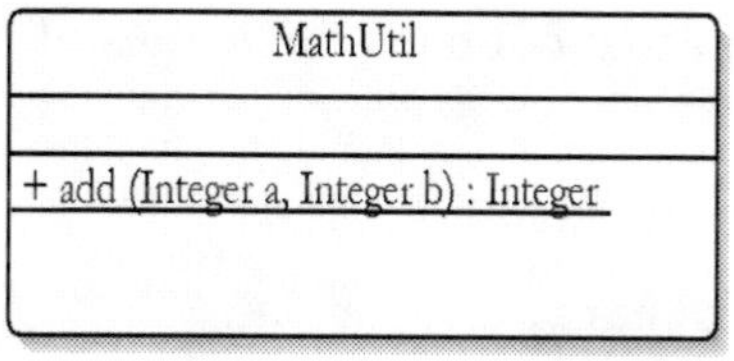

MathUtil
+ add (Integer a, Integer b) : Integer

Figure 4.9: Static members in UML class diagrams

Static Final Variables

In the section, "Final Variables" previously in the chapter, you learned that you could create a final variable by using the keyword **final**. However, final variables at a class level or local variables will always have the same value when the program is run. If you have multiple objects of the same class with final variables, the value of the final variables in those objects will have the same values. It is more common (and also more prudent) to make a final variable static too. This way, all objects share the same value.

The naming convention for static final variables is to have them in upper case and separate two words with an underscore. For example

```
static final int NUMBER_OF_MONTHS = 12;
static final float PI = (float) 22 / 7;
```

The positions of **static** and **final** are interchangeable, but it is more common to use "static final" than "final static."

If you want to make a static final variable accessible from outside the class, you can make it public too:

```
public static final int NUMBER_OF_MONTHS = 12;
public static final float PI = (float) 22 / 7;
```

To better organize your constants, sometimes you want to put all your static final variables in a class. This class most often does not have a method or other fields and is never instantiated.

For example, sometimes you want to represent a month as an **int**, therefore January is 1, February is 2, and so on. Then, you use the word January instead of number 1 because it's easier to remember. Listing 4.10 shows the **Months** class that contains the names of months and its representation.

Listing 4.10: The Months class

```
package com.brainysoftware.jdk5.app04;
public class Months {
    public static final int JANUARY = 1;
    public static final int FEBRUARY = 2;
    public static final int MARCH = 3;
    public static final int APRIL = 4;
    public static final int MAY = 5;
```

```
    public static final int JUNE = 6;
    public static final int JULY = 7;
    public static final int AUGUST = 8;
    public static final int SEPTEMBER = 9;
    public static final int OCTOBER = 10;
    public static final int NOVEMBER = 11;
    public static final int DECEMBER = 12;
}
```

In your code, you can get the representation of January by writing.

```
int thisMonth = Months.JANUARY;
```

Classes similar to **Months** are very common prior to Java 5. However, Java 5 offers the new type **enum** that can eliminate the need for public static final variables. **enum** is explain in Chapter 10, "Enums."

Static final reference variables are also possible. However, note that only the variable is final, which means once it is assigned an address to an instance, it cannot be assigned another object of the same type. However, the fields in the referenced object itself can be changed.

In the following line of code

```
public static final Book book = new Book();
```

book always refer to this particular instance of **Book**. Reassigning it to another **Book** object raises a compile error:

```
book = new Book(); // compile error
```

However, you can change the **Book** object's field value.

```
book.title = "No Excuses";  // assuming the title field is public
```

Static import

There are a number of classes in the Java core libraries that contain static final fields. One of them is the **java.util.Calendar** class, that has the static final fields representing days of the week (**MONDAY, TUESDAY**, etc). To use a static final field in the **Calendar** class, you must first import the **Calendar** class.

```
import java.util.Calendar;
```

Then, you can use it by using the notation *className.staticField*.

```
if (today == Calendar.SATURDAY)
```

However, in Java 5 you can import static fields using the **import static** keywords. For example, you can do

```
import static java.util.Calendar.SATURDAY;
```

Then, to use the imported static field, you do not need the class name:

```
if (today == SATURDAY)
```

> **Note**
> The **java.util.Calendar** class is discussed in more detail in Chapter 5, "Core Classes."

Variable Scope

You have seen that you can declare variables in several different places:

- In a class body as class fields. Variables declared here are referred to as class-level variables.
- As parameters of a method or constructor.
- In a method's body or a constructor's body.
- Within a statement block, such as inside a **while** or **for** block.

Now it's time to learn the scope of variables.

Variable scope refers to the accessibility of a variable. The rule is that variables defined in a block are only accessible from within the block. The scope of the variable is the block in which it is defined. For example, consider the following **for** statement.

```
for (int x = 0; x < 5; x++) {
    System.out.println(x);
}
```

The variable **x** is declared within the **for** statement. As a result, **x** is only available from within this **for** block. It is not accessible or visible from anywhere else. When the JVM executes the **for** statement, it creates **x**. When it is finished executing the **for** block, it destroys **x**. After **x** is destroyed, **x** is said to be out of scope.

Rule number 2 is a nested block can access variables declared in the outer block. Consider this code.

```
for (int x = 0; x < 5; x++) {
    for (int y = 0; y < 3; y++) {
        System.out.println(x);
        System.out.println(y);
    }
}
```

The preceding code is valid because the inner **for** block can access **x**, which is declared in the outer **for** block.

Following the rules, variables declared as method parameters can be accessed from within the method body. Also, class-level variables are accessible from anywhere in the class.

If a method declares a local variable that has the same name as a class-level variable, the former will 'shadow' the latter. To access the class-level variable from inside the method body, use the **this** keyword.

Method Overloading

Method names are very important and should reflect what the methods do. In many circumstances, you may want to use the same name for multiple methods because they have similar functionality. For instance, the method **printString** may take a **String** argument and prints the string. However, the same class may also provide a method that prints part of a **String** and accepts two arguments, the **String** to be printed and the character position to start printing from. You want to call the latter method **printString** too because it does print a **String**, but that would be the same as the first **printString** method.

Thankfully, Java allows you to have multiple methods having the same name, as long as each method accept different sets of argument types. In other words, in our example, it is legal to have these two methods in the same class.

```
public String printString(String string)
public String printString(String string, int offset)
```

This technique is called method overloading.

The return value of the method is not taken into consideration. As such, these two methods must not exist in the same class:

```
public int countRows(int number);
public String countRows(int number);
```

This is because a method can be called without assigning its return value to a variable. In such situations, having the above **countRows** methods would confuse the compiler as it would not know which method is being called when you write

```
System.out.println(countRows(3));.
```

A trickier situation is depicted in the following methods whose signatures are very similar.

```
public int printNumber(int i) {
    return i*2;
}
public long printNumber(long l) {
    return l*3;
}
```

It is legal to have these two methods in the same class. However, you might wonder, which method is being called if you write **printNumber(3)**?

The key is to recall from Chapter 2, "Language Fundamentals" that a numeric literal will be translated into an **int** unless it is suffixed **L** or **l**.. Therefore, **printNumber(3)** will invoke this method:

```
public int printNumber(int i)
```

To call the second, pass a **long**:

```
printNumber(3L);
```

Note
Static methods can also be overloaded.

By Value or By Reference?

You can pass primitive variables or reference variables to a method. Primitive variables are passed by value and reference variables are passed by reference. What this means is when you pass a primitive variable, the JVM will copy the value of the passed-in variable to a new local variable. If you change the value of the local variable, the change will not affect the passed in primitive variable.

If you pass a reference variable, the local variable will refer to the same object as the passed in reference variable. If you change the object referenced within your method, the change will also be reflected in the calling code. Listing 4.11 shows the **ReferencePassingTest** class that demonstrates this.

Listing 4.11: The ReferencePassingTest class

```
package com.brainysoftware.jdk5.app04;
class Point {
    public int x;
    public int y;
}
public class ReferencePassingTest {
    public static void increment(int x) {
        x++;
    }
    public static void reset(Point point) {
        point.x = 0;
        point.y = 0;
    }
    public static void main(String[] args) {
        int a = 9;
        increment(a);
        System.out.println(a); // prints 9
        Point p = new Point();
        p.x = 400;
        p.y = 600;
        reset(p);
        System.out.println(p.x); // prints 0
    }
}
```

There are two methods in **ReferencePassingTest**, **increment** and **reset**. The **increment** method takes an **int** and increments it. The **reset** method accepts a **Point** object and resets its **x** and **y** fields.

Now pay attention to the **main** method. We passed **a** (whose value is 9) to the **increment** method. After the method invocation, we printed the value of **a** and you get 9, which means that the value of **a** did not change.

Afterwards, you create a **Point** object and assign the reference to **p**. You then initialize its fields and pass it to the **reset** method. The changes in the **reset** method affects the **Point** object because objects are passed by reference. As a result, when you print the value of **p.x**, you get 0.

Loading, Linking, and Initialization

Now that you've learned how to create classes and objects, let's take a look at what happens when the JVM executes a class.

You run a Java program by using the **java** tool. For example, you use the following command to run the **DemoTest** class.

```
java DemoTest
```

After the JVM is loaded into memory, it starts its job by invoking the **DemoTest** class's **main** method. There are three things the JVM will do next in the specified order: loading, linking, and initialization.

Loading

The JVM loads the binary representation of the Java class (in this case, the **DemoTest** class) to memory and may cache it in memory, just in case the class is used again in the future. If the specified class is not found, an error will be thrown and the process stops here.

Linking

There are three things that need to be done in this phase: verification, preparation, and resolution (optional). Verification means the JVM checks that the binary representation complies with the semantic requirements of the Java programming language and the JVM. If, for example, you tamper with a class file created as a result of compilation, the class file may no longer work.

Preparation prepares the specified class for execution. This involves allocating memory space for static variables and other data structured for that class.

Resolution checks if the specified class references other classes/interfaces and if the other classes/interfaces can also be found and loaded. Checks will be done recursively to the referenced classes/interfaces.

For example, if the specified class contains the following code:

```
MathUtil.add(4, 3)
```

the JVM will load, link, and initialize the **MathUtil** class before calling the static **add** method.

Or, if the following code is found in the **DemoTest** class:

```
Book book = new Book();
```

the JVM will load, link, and initialize the **Book** class before an instance of **Book** is created.

Note that a JVM implementation may choose to perform resolution at a later stage, i.e. when the executing code actually requires the use of the referenced class/interface.

Initialization

In this last step, the JVM initializes static variables with assigned or default values and executes static initializers (code in **static** blocks). Initialization occurs just before the **main** method is executed. However, before the specified class can be initialized, its parent class will have to be initialized. If the parent class has not been loaded and linked, the JVM will first load and link the parent class. Again, when the parent class is about to be initialized, the parent's parent will be treated the same. This process occurs recursively until the initialized class is the topmost class in the hierarchy.

For example, if a class contains the following declaration

```
public static int z = 5;
```

the variable **z** will be assigned the value 5. If no initialization code is found, a static variable is given a default value. Table 4.2 lists default values for Java primitives and reference variables.

Type	Default Value
boolean	false
byte	0
short	0
int	0
long	0L
char	\u0000
float	0.0f
double	0.0d
object reference	null

Table 4.2: Default values for primitives and references

In addition, code in **static** blocks will be executed. For example, Listing 4.12 shows the **StaticCodeTest** class with static code that gets executed when the class is loaded. Like static members, you can only access static members from static code.

Listing 4.12: StaticCodeTest

```
package com.brainysoftware.jdk5.app04;
public class StaticInitializationTest {
    public static int a = 5;
    public static int b = a * 2;
    static {
        System.out.println("static");
        System.out.println(b);
    }
    public static void main(String[] args) {
        System.out.println("main method");
    }
}
```

If you run this class, you will see the following on your console:

```
static
10
main method
```

Object Creation Initialization

Initialization happens when a class is loaded, as described in the section "Linking, Loading, and Initialization" earlier in this chapter. However, you can also write code that performs initialization every time an instance of a class is created.

When the JVM encounters code that instantiates a class, the JVM does the following.

1. Allocates memory space for a new object, with room for the instance variables declared in the class plus room for instance variables declared in its parent classes.
2. Processes the invoked constructor. If the constructor has parameters, the JVM creates variables for these parameter and assigns them values passed to the constructor.
3. If the invoked constructor begins with a call to another constructor (using the **this** keyword), the JVM processes the called constructor.
4. Performs instance initialization and instance variable initialization for this class. Instance variables that are not assigned a value will be assigned default values (See Table 4.2). Instance initialization applies to code in braces:

```
{
    // code
}
```

5. Executes the rest of the body of the invoked constructor.
6. Returns a reference variable that refers to the new object.

Note that instance initialization is different from static initialization. The latter occurs when a class is loaded and has nothing to do with instantiation. Instance initialization, by contrast, is performed when an object is created. In addition, unlike static initializers, instance initialization may access instance variables.

For example, Listing 4.13 presents a class named **InitTest1** that has the initialization section. There is also some static initialization code to give you the idea of what is being run.

Listing 4.13: The InitTest1 class

```java
package com.brainysoftware.jdk5.app04;

public class InitTest1 {
    int x = 3;
    int y;
    // instance initialization code
    {
        y = x * 2;
        System.out.println(y);
    }

    // static initialization code
    static {
        System.out.println("Static initialization");
    }
    public static void main(String[] args) {
        InitTest1 test = new InitTest1();
        InitTest1 moreTest = new InitTest1();
    }
}
```

When run, the **InitTest** class will print the following on the console:

```
Static initialization
6
6
```

The static initialization is performed first, before any instantiation takes place. This is where the JVM prints the "Static initialization" message. Afterwards, the **InitTest1** class is instantiated twice, explaining why you see "6" twice.

The problem with having instance initialization code is this. As your class grows bigger it becomes harder to notice that there exists initialization code.

Another way to write initialization code is in the constructor. In fact, initialization code in a constructor is more noticeable and hence preferable. Listing 4.14 shows the **InitTest2** class that puts initialization code in the constructor.

Listing 4.14: The InitTest2 class

```java
package com.brainysoftware.jdk5.app04;
public class InitTest2 {
    int x = 3;
    int y;
```

```
    // instance initialization code
    public InitTest2() {
        y = x * 2;
        System.out.println(y);
    }
    // static initialization code
    static {
        System.out.println("Static initialization");
    }
    public static void main(String[] args) {
        InitTest2 test = new InitTest2();
        InitTest2 moreTest = new InitTest2();
    }
}
```

The problem with this is when you have more than one constructor and each of them must call the same code. The solution is to wrap the initialization code in a method and let the constructors call them. Listing 4.15 shows this

Listing 4.15: The InitTest3 class

```
package com.brainysoftware.jdk5.app04;

public class InitTest3 {
    int x = 3;
    int y;
    // instance initialization code
    public InitTest3() {
        init();
    }
    public InitTest3(int x) {
        this.x = x;
        init();
    }
    private void init() {
        y = x * 2;
        System.out.println(y);
    }
    // static initialization code
    static {
        System.out.println("Static initialization");
    }
    public static void main(String[] args) {
        InitTest3 test = new InitTest3();
        InitTest3 moreTest = new InitTest3();
    }
```

```
}
```

Note that the **InitTest3** class is preferable because the calls to the **init** method from the constructors make the initialization code more obvious than if it is in an initialization block.

Comparing Objects

In real life, when I say "My car is the same as your car" I mean my car is of the same type as yours, as new as your car, has the same color, etc.

In Java, you manipulate objects by using the variables that reference them. Bear in mind that reference variables do not contain objects but rather contain addresses to the objects in the memory. Therefore, when you compare two reference variables **a** and **b**, such as in this code

```
if (a == b)
```

you are actually asking if **a** and **b** are referencing the same object, and not whether or not the objects referenced by **a** and **b** are identical.

Consider this example.

```
Object a = new Object();
Object b = new Object();
```

The type of object **a** references is identical to the type of object **b** references. However, **a** and **b** reference two different instances and **a** and **b** contains different memory addresses. Therefore, **(a == b)** returns **false**.

Comparing object references this way is hardly useful because most of the time you are more concerned with the objects, not the addresses of the objects. If what you want is compare objects, you need to look for methods specifically provided by the class to compare objects. For example, to compare two **String** objects, you can call its **equals** method. (See Chapter 5, "Core Classes") Whether or not comparing the contents of two objects is possible depends on whether or not the corresponding class supports it. A class can support object comparison by implementing the **equals** method it inherits from **java.lang.Object**. (See the section "java.lang.Object" in Chapter 5)

In addition, there are utility classes you can use to compare objects. See the discussion of **java.lang.Comparable** and **java.util.Comparator** in the section

"Making Your Objects Comparable and Sortable" in Chapter 11, "The Collections Framework."

The Garbage Collector

In several examples so far, I have shown you how to create objects using the **new** keyword, but you have never seen code that explicitly destroys unused objects to release memory space. If you are a C++ programmer you may have wondered if I had shown flawed code, because in C++ you must discipline yourself to destroy objects after use.

Java comes equipped with a feature called the garbage collector, which destroys unused objects and frees the memory. Unused objects are defined as objects that are no longer referenced or objects whose references are already out of scope.

With this feature, Java becomes much easier than C++ because Java programmers do not need to worry about reclaiming memory space. This, however, does not entail that you may create objects as many as you want because memory is (still) limited and it takes some time for the garbage collector to start. That's right, you can still run out of memory.

Summary

OOP models applications on real-world objects. Since Java is an OOP language, objects play a central role in Java programming. Objects are created based on a template called a class. In this chapter you've learned how to write a class and class members. There are many types of class members, including three that were discussed in this chapter: fields, methods, and constructors. There are other types of Java members such as enum and inner classes, which will be covered in other chapters.

In this chapter you have also learned two powerful OOP features, abstraction and encapsulation. Abstraction in OOP is the act of using programming objects to represent real-world objects. Encapsulation is a mechanism that protects parts of an object that need to be secure and exposes only parts that are safe to be exposed. Another feature discussed in this chapter is method overloading. Method overloading allows a class to have methods with the same name as long as their signatures are sufficiently different.

Java also comes with a garbage collector that eliminates to manually destroy unused objects. Objects are garbage collected when they are out of scope or no longer referenced.

Questions

1. Name at least three element types that a class can contain.
2. What are the differences between a method and a constructor?
3. Does a class in a class diagram display its constructors?
4. What does **null** mean?
5. What do you use the **this** keyword for?
6. When you use the **==** operator to compare two object references, do you actually compare the contents of the objects? Why?
7. What is the scope of variables?
8. What does "out of scope" mean?
9. How does the garbage collector decide which objects to destroy?
10. What is method overloading?

Chapter 5
Core Classes

Before we study other features of object-oriented programming (OOP), let's examine several important classes that are commonly used in Java. These classes are included in the Java core libraries that come with the JDK. Mastering them will help you understand the examples that accompany the next OOP lessons.

The most prominent class of all is definitely **java.lang.Object**. However, it is hard to talk about this class without first covering inheritance, which we will do in Chapter 6, "Inheritance." Therefore, **java.lang.Object** is only discussed briefly in this chapter. Right now we will concentrate on classes that you can use in your programs. We'll start with **java.lang.String** and other types of strings: **java.lang.StringBuffer** and **java.lang.StringBuilder**. Then, we'll discuss arrays and the **java.lang.System** class. The **java.util.Scanner** class is also included here because it provides a convenient way to take user input.

There are also two concepts explained at the end of the chapter, boxing/unboxing and varargs. They are explained after the core classes because the latter are the prerequisite for these concepts.

Note

When describing a method in a Java class, presenting the method signature is always helpful. A method often takes as parameters objects whose classes belong to different packages than the method's class. Or, it may return a type from a different package than its class. For clarity, fully qualified names will be used for classes from different packages. For example, here is the signature of the **toString** method of **java.lang.Object**:

```
public String toString()
```

A fully qualified name for the return type is not necessary because the return type **String** is part of the same package as **java.lang.Object**. On the other hand, the signature of the **toString** method in **java.util.Scanner** uses a fully qualified name because the **Scanner** class is part of a different package (**java.util**).

```
public java.lang.String toString()
```

java.lang.Object

The **java.lang.Object** class represents a Java object. In fact, all classes are direct or indirect descendants of this class. Since we have not learned inheritance (which is only given in Chapter 6, "Inheritance"), the word descendant probably makes no sense to you. Therefore, we will briefly discuss the method in this class and revisit this class in Chapter 6.

Here are the methods in the **Object** class.

```
protected Object clone()
```
Creates and returns a copy of this object. A class implements this method to support object cloning.

```
public boolean equals(Object obj)
```
Compares this object with the passed-in object. A class must implement this method to provide a means to compare the contents of its instances.

```
protected void finalize()
```
Called by the garbage collector on an object that is about to be garbage-collected. In theory a subclass can override this method to dispose of system resources or to perform other cleanup. However, performing the aforesaid operations should be done somewhere else and you should not touch this method.

```
public final Class getClass()
```
Returns a **java.lang.Class** object of this object. See the section "java.lang.Class" for more information on the **Class** class.

```
public int hashCode()
```
Returns a hash code value for this object.

```
public String toString()
```
Returns the description of this object.

In addition, there are also the **wait, notify**, and **notifyAll** methods that you use when writing multithreaded applications. These methods are discussed in Chapter 23, "Java Threads."

java.lang.String

I have not seen a serious Java program that does not use the **java.lang.String** class. **String** is one of the most often used classes and definitely one of the most important.

A **String** object represents a string, i.e. a piece of text. You can also think of a **String** as a sequence of Unicode characters. A **String** object can consists of any number of characters. A **String** that has zero character is called an empty **String**. **String** objects are constant. Once they are created, their values cannot be changed. Because of this, **String** instances are said to be immutable. And, because they are immutable, they can be safely shared.

You could construct a **String** object by using the **new** keyword, but this is not a common way to create a **String**. Most often, you assign a string literal to a **String** reference variable. Here is an example:

```
String s = "Java is cool";
```

This produces a **String** object containing "Java is cool" and assigns a reference to it to **s**. It is the same as the following.

```
String message = new String("Java is cool");
```

However, assigning a string literal to a reference variable works differently from using the **new** keyword. If you use the **new** keyword, the JVM will always create a new instance of **String**. With the string literal, you get an identical **String** object, but the object is not always new. It may come from a pool if the string "Java is cool" has been created before.

Thus, using a string literal is better because the JVM can save some CPU cycles for constructing a new instance. Because of this, we seldom use the **new** keyword when creating a **String** object. The **String** class's constructors can be used if we have specific needs, such as converting a character array into a **String**.

Comparing Two Strings

String comparison is one of the most useful operations in Java programming. Consider the following code.

```
String s1 = "Java";
String s2 = "Java";
if (s1 == s2) {
    ...
}
```

Here, **(s1 == s2)** evaluates to **true** because **s1** and **s2** reference the same instance. On the other hand, in the following code **(s1 == s2)** evaluates to **false** because **s1** and **s2** reference different instances:

```
String s1 = new String("Java");
String s2 = new String("Java");
if (s1 == s2) {
    ...
}
```

This shows the difference between creating **String** objects by writing a string literal and by using the **new** keyword.

Comparing two **String** objects by using the **==** operator is of little use because you are comparing the addresses referenced by two variables. Most of the time, when comparing two **String** objects, you want to know whether the values of the two objects are the same. In this case, you need to use the **String** class's **equals** method.

```
String s1 = "Java";
if (s1.equals("Java")) // returns true.
```

And, sometimes you see this style.

```
if ("Java".equals(s1))
```

In **(s1.equals("Java"))**, the **equals** method on **s1** is called. If **s1** is null, this expression will generate a runtime error. To be safe, you have to make sure that **s1** is not null, by first checking if the reference variable is null.

In the following code, if **s1** is null, the **if** statement will return **false** without evaluating the second expression.

```
if (s1 != null && s1.equals("Java"))
```

This is because the AND operator **&&** will not evaluate the right hand operand if the left hand operand evaluates to **false**.

In **("Java".equals(s1))**, the JVM creates or takes from the pool a **String** object containing "Java" and calls its **equals** method. No nullity checking is required here. If **s1** is null, the expression simply returns **false**.

String Literals

Because you always work with **String** objects, it is important to understand the rules for working with string literals.

First of all, a string literal starts and ends with a double quote ("). Second, it is a compile error to change line before the closing ". For example, this will generate a compile-time error.

```
String s2 = "This is an important
        point to note";
```

You can compose long string literals by using the plus sign to concatenate two string literals.

```
String s1 = "Java strings " + "are important";
String s2 = "This is an important " +
        "point to note";
```

Escaping Certain Characters

You sometimes need to use special characters in your strings such as carriage return (CR) and linefeed (LF). In other times, you may want to have a double quote character in your string. In the case of CR and LF, it is not possible to input these characters because pressing Enter changes lines. A way to include special characters is to escape them, i.e. use the character replacement for them.

Here are some escape sequences:

```
\u          /* a Unicode character
\b          /* \u0008: backspace BS */
\t          /* \u0009: horizontal tab HT */
\n          /* \u000a: linefeed LF */
\f          /* \u000c: form feed FF */
\r          /* \u000d: carriage return CR */
```

```
\"              /* \u0022: double quote " */
\'              /* \u0027: single quote ' */
\\              /* \u005c: backslash \ */
```

For example, the following code includes the Unicode character 0122 at the end of the string.

```
String s = "Please enter this character \u0122";
```

To obtain a **String** object whose value is John "The Great" Monroe, you escape the double quotes:

```
String s = "John \"The Great\" Monroe";
```

The String Class's Constructors

The **String** class provides a number of constructors. These constructors allow you to create an empty string, a copy of another string, and a **String** from an array of chars or bytes. Use the constructors with caution as they always create a new instance of **String**.

Note
Arrays are discussed in the section "Arrays."

```
public String()
```
> Creates an empty string.

```
public String(String original)
```
> Creates a copy of the original string.

```
public String(char[] value)
```
> Creates a **String** object from an array of chars.

```
public String(byte[] bytes)
```
> Creates a **String** object by decoding the bytes in the array using the computer's default encoding.

```
public String(byte[] bytes, String encoding)
```
> Creates a **String** object by decoding the bytes in the array using the specified encoding.

The String Class's Methods

The **String** class provides methods to manipulate the value of a **String**. However, since **String** objects are immutable, the result of the manipulation is always a new **String** object.

Here are some of the more useful methods.

```
public char charAt(int index)
```
Returns the char at the specified index. For example, the following code returns 'J'.

```
"Java is cool".charAt(0)
```

```
public String concate(String s)
```
Concatenates the specified string to the end of this **String** and return the new **String**. For example, **"Java ".concat("is cool")** returns "Java is cool".

```
public boolean equals(String anotherString)
```
Compares the value of this **String** and *anotherString* and returns **true** if the values match.

```
public boolean endsWith(String suffix)
```
Tests if this **String** ends with the specified suffix.

```
public int indexOf(String substring)
```
Returns the index of the first occurrence of the specified substring. If no match is found, returns -1. For instance, the following code returns 8.

```
"Java is cool".indexOf("cool")
```

```
public int indexOf(String substring, int fromIndex)
```
Returns the index of the first occurrence of the specified substring starting from the specified index. If no match is found, returns -1.

```
public int lastIndexOf(String substring)
```
Returns the index of the last occurrence of the specified substring. If no match is found, returns -1.

```
public int lastIndexOf(String substring, int fromIndex)
```
Returns the index of the last occurrence of the specified substring starting from the specified index. If no match is found, returns -1. For example, the following expression returns 3.

```
"Java is cool".lastIndexOf("a")
```

```
public String substring(int beginIndex)
```

Returns a substring of the current string starting from the specified index. For instance, **"Java is cool".substring(8)** returns "cool".

```
public String substring(int beginIndex, int endIndex)
```
Returns a substring of the current string starting from *beginIndex* to *endIndex*. For example, the following code returns "is":

```
"Java is cool".substring(5, 7)
```

```
public String replace(char oldChar, char newChar)
```
Replaces every occurrence of *oldChar* with *newChar* in the current string and returns the new **String**. For instance, **"dingdong".replace('d', 'k')** returns "kingkong".

```
public int length()
```
Returns the number of characters in this **String**. For example, **"Java is cool".length()** returns 12.

```
public String[] split(String regEx)
```
Splits this **String** around matches of the specified regular expression. For example, **"Java is cool".split(" ")** returns an array of three **String**s. The first array element is "Java", the second "is", and the third "cool".

```
public boolean startsWith(String prefix)
```
Tests if the current string starts with the specified prefix.

```
public char[] toCharArray()
```
Converts this string to an array of chars.

```
public String toLowerCase()
```
Converts all the characters in the current string to lower case. For instance, **"Java is cool".toLowerCase()** returns "java is cool".

```
public String toUpperCase()
```
Converts all the characters in the current string to upper case. For instance, **"Java is cool".toUpperCase()** returns "JAVA IS COOL".

```
public String trim()
```
Trims the trailing and leading white spaces and returns a new string. For example, **" Java ".trim()** returns "Java".

In addition, there are two static methods, **valueOf** and **format**. The **valueOf** method converts a primitive, a char array, or an instance of **Object** into a string representation and there are nine overloads of this method.

```
public static String valueOf(boolean value)
```

```
public static String valueOf(char value)
public static String valueOf(char[] value)
public static String valueOf(char[] value, int offset, int length)
public static String valueOf(double value)
public static String valueOf(float value)
public static String valueOf(int value)
public static String valueOf(long value)
public static String valueOf(Object value)
```

For example, the following code returns the string "23"

```
String.valueOf(23);
```

The **format** method is a new method in Java 5 and allows you to pass an arbitrary number of parameters. Here is its signature.

```
public static String format(String format, Object... args)
```

However, I will hold off discussing the **format** method here because to understand it, you need to understand arrays and variable arguments. It will be explained in the section "Varargs" later in this chapter.

java.lang.StringBuffer and java.lang.StringBuilder

String objects are immutable and are not suitable to use if you need to append or insert characters into them because string operations on **String** always create a new String object. For append and insert, you'd be better off using the **java.lang.StringBuffer** class or the **java.lang.StringBuilder** class. Once you're finished manipulating the string, you can convert a **StringBuffer** or **StringBuilder** object to a **String**.

Until JDK 1.4, the **StringBuffer** class was solely used for mutable strings. Methods in **StringBuffer** are synchronized, making **StringBuffer** suitable for use in multithreaded environments. However, the price for synchronization is performance. JDK 5 adds the **StringBuilder** class, which is the unsynchronized version of **StringBuffer**. **StringBuilder** should be chosen over **StringBuffer** if you do not need synchronization.

Note
Synchronization and thread safety are discussed in Chapter 23, "Java Threads."

The rest of this section will use the **StringBuilder** class. However, the discussion is also applicable to **StringBuffer** as both **StringBuilder** and **StringBuffer** shares similar constructors and methods.

StringBuilder Class's Constructors

The **StringBuilder** class has four constructors. You can pass a **java.lang.CharSequence**, a **String**, or an **int**.

```
public StringBuilder()
public StringBuilder(CharSequence seq)
public StringBuilder(int capacity)
public StringBuilder(String string)
```

If you create a **StringBuilder** object without specifying the capacity, the object will have a capacity of 16 characters. If its content exceeds 16 characters, it will grow automatically. If you know that your string will be longer than 16 characters, it is a good idea to allocate enough capacity as it takes time to grow a **StringBuilder**'s capacity.

StringBuilder Class's Methods

The **StringBuilder** class has several methods. The main ones are **capacity**, **length**, **append**, and **insert**.

```
public int capacity()
```
> Returns the capacity of the **StringBuilder** object.

```
public int length()
```
> Returns the length of the string the **StringBuilder** object stores. The value is less than or equal to the capacity of the **StringBuilder**.

```
public StringBuilder append(String string)
```
> Appends the specified **String** to the end of the contained string. In addition, **append** has various overloads that allow you to pass a primitive, a char array, and an **java.lang.Object** instance.
>
> For example, examine the following code.
>
> ```
> StringBuilder sb = new StringBuilder(100);
> sb.append("Matrix ");
> sb.append(2);
> ```

After the last line, the content of **sb** is "Matrix 2".

One important point to note is that the **append** methods return the **StringBuilder** object itself, the same object on which **append** is invoked. As a result, you can chain calls to the **append** methods.

```
sb.append("Matrix ").append(2);
```

`public StringBuilder insert(int offset, String string)`

Inserts the specified string at the position indicated by *offset*. In addition, **insert** has various overloads that allow you to pass primitives and a **java.lang.Object** instance. For example,

```
StringBuilder sb2 = new StringBuilder(100);
sb2.append("night");
sb2.insert(0, 'k'); // value = "knight"
```

Like **append**, **insert** also returns the current **StringBuilder** object, so chaining **insert** is also permitted.

`public String toString()`

Returns a **String** object representing the value of the **StringBuilder**.

Primitive Wrappers

For the sake of performance, not everything in Java is an object. There are also primitives, such as **int**, **long**, **float**, **double**, etc. When working with both primitives and objects, there are often circumstances that necessitate primitive to object conversions and vice versa. For example, a **java.util.Collection** object (discussed in Chapter 11, "The Collections Framework") requires that you pass objects to it. If you want to store primitive values in a **Collection**, they must be converted to objects first.

The **java.lang** package has several classes that function as primitive wrappers. They are **Boolean**, **Character**, **Byte**, **Double**, **Float**, **Integer**, **Long**, and **Short**. **Byte**, **Double**, **Float**, **Integer**, **Long**, and **Short** share similar methods, therefore only **Integer** will be discussed here. You should consult the Javadoc for information on the others.

Note

In Java 5, conversions from primitives to objects and vice versa are easier than in previous Java releases, thanks to the boxing and unboxing mechanisms. Boxing and unboxing are discussed in the section "Boxing and Unboxing" later in this chapter.

The following sections discuss the wrapper classes in detail.

java.lang.Integer

The **java.lang.Integer** class wraps an **int**. The **Integer** class has two static final fields of type **int**: **MIN_VALUE** and **MAX_VALUE**. **MIN_VALUE** contains the minimum possible value for an **int** (-2^{31}) and **MAX_VALUE** the maximum possible value for an **int** (2^{31} - 1).

The **Integer** class has two constructors:

```
public Integer(int value)
public Integer(String value)
```

For example, this code constructs two **Integer** objects.

```
Integer i1 = new Integer(12);
Integer i2 = new Integer("123");
```

Integer has the no-arg **byteValue, doubleValue, floatValue, intValue, longValue,** and **shortValue** methods that convert the wrapped value to a **byte, double, float, int, long,** and **short,** respectively. In addition, the **toString** method converts the value to a **String**.

There are also static methods that you can use to parse a **String** to an **int** (**parseInt**) and convert an **int** to a **String** (**toString**). The signatures of the methods are as follows.

```
public static int parsetInt(String string)
public static String toString(int i)
```

java.lang.Boolean

The **java.lang.Boolean** class wraps a **boolean**. Its static final fields **FALSE** and **TRUE** represents a **Boolean** object that wraps the primitive value **false** and a **Boolean** object wrapping the primitive value **true**, respectively.

You can construct a **Boolean** object from a **boolean** or a **String**, using one of these constructors.

```
public Boolean(boolean value)
public Boolean(String value)
```

For example:

```
Boolean b1 = new Boolean(false);
Boolean b2 = new Boolean("true");
```

To convert a **Boolean** to a **boolean**, use its **booleanValue** method:

```
public boolean booleanValue()
```

In addition, the static method **valueOf** parses a **String** to a **Boolean** object.

```
public static Boolean valueOf(String string)
```

And, the static method **toString** returns the string representation of a **boolean**.

```
public static String toString(boolean boolean)
```

java.lang.Character

The **Character** class wraps a **char**. There is only one constructor in this class:

```
public Character(char value)
```

To convert a **Character** object to a **char**, use its **charValue** method.

```
public char charValue()
```

There are also a number of static methods that can be used to manipulate characters.

```
public static boolean isDigit(char ch)
```
Determines if the specified argument is one of these: '1', '2', '3', '4', '5', '6', '7', '8', '9', '0'.

```
public static char toLowerCase(char ch)
```
Converts the specified char argument to its lower case.

```
public static char toUpperCase(char ch)
```
Converts the specified char argument to its upper case.

Arrays

In Java you can use arrays to group primitives of the same type or group objects of the same type. The entities belonging to an array is called the components of the array. In the background, every time you create an array, the compiler creates an object which allows you to:

- get the number of components in the array through the **length** field. The length of an array is the number of components in it.
- access each component by specifying an index. This indexing is zero-based. Index 0 refers to the first component, 1 to the second component, etc.

All the components of an array have the same type, called the *component type* of the array. An array is not resizable and an array with zero component is called an empty array.

An array is a Java object. Therefore, you treat a variable that refers to an array like other reference variables. For one, you can compare it with **null**.

```
String[] names;
if (names == null)   // evaluates to true
```

If an array is a Java object, then there must be a class that gets instantiated when you create an array. May be something like **java.lang.Array**? The truth is, no. Arrays are indeed special Java objects whose class is never documented and is not meant to be extended.

Note
An array can also contain other arrays, creating an array of arrays.

To use an array, first you need to declare one. You can use this syntax to declare an array:

```
type[] arrayName;
```

or

```
type arrayName[]
```

For example, the following declares an array of **long**s named **numbers**:

```
long[] numbers;
```

Declaring an array does not create an array or allocate space for its components, the compiler simply creates an object reference. One way to create an array is by using the **new** keyword. You must specify the size of the array you are creating.

```
new type[size]
```

As an example, the following code creates an array of four **int**s:

```
new int[4]
```

Alternatively, you can declare and create an array in the same line.

```
int[] ints = new int[4];
```

To reference the components of an array, use an index after the variable name. For example, the following snippet creates an array of four **String** objects and initializes its first member.

```
String[] names = new String[4];
names[0] = "Hello World";
```

> **Note**
>
> Referencing an out of bound member will raise a runtime error. To be precise, a **java.lang.ArrayIndexOutOfBoundsException** will be thrown. See Chapter 7, "Error Handling" for information on exceptions.

> **Note**
>
> When an array is created, its components are either **null** (if the component type is an object type) or the default value of the component type (if the array contains primitives). For example, an array of **int**s contain zeros by default.

You can also create and initialize an array without using the **new** keyword. Java allows you to create an array by grouping values within a pair of braces. For example, the following code creates an array of three **String** objects.

```
String[] names = { "John", "Mary", "Paul" };
```

The following code creates an array of four **int**s and assign the array to the variable **matrix**.

```
int[] matrix = { 1, 2, 3, 10 };
```

Iterating over an Array

Prior to Java 5, the only way to iterate the members of an array was to use a **for** loop and the array's indices. For example, the following code iterates over a **String** array referenced by the variable **names**:

```
for (int i = 0; i < 3; i++) {
    System.out.println("\t- " + names[i]);
}
```

Java 5 has enhanced the **for** statement. You can now use it to iterate over an array or a collection without the index. Use this syntax to iterate over an array:

```
for (componentType variable : arrayName)
```

Where *arrayName* is the reference to the array, *componentType* is the component type of the array, and *variable* is a variable that references each component of the array.

For example, the following code iterates over an array of **String**s.

```
String[] names = { "John", "Mary", "Paul" };
for (String name : names) {
    System.out.println(name);
}
```

The code prints the following on the console.

```
John
Mary
Paul
```

Changing an Array Size

Once an array is created, its size cannot be changed. For example, the following code creates an array of three **int**s:

```
int numbers[] = new int[3];
```

If you want to change the size, you must create a new array and populates it using the values of the old array. For instance, the following code increases the size of **numbers**, an array of three **int**s, to 4.

```
int[] numbers = { 1, 2, 3 };
```

```
int[] temp = new int[4];
int length = numbers.length;
for (int j = 0; j < length; j++) {
    temp[j] = numbers[j];
}
numbers = temp;
```

Passing a String Array to main

The static void method **main** is invoked to run a Java class. Here is the signature of the **main** method:

```
public static void main(String[] args)
```

You can pass arguments to the **main** method by feeding them to the **java** tool. The arguments should appear after the class name and two arguments are separated by a space. To be precise, you should use the following syntax:

```
java className arg1 arg2 arg3 ... arg-n
```

Listing 5.1 shows a class that iterates over the **main** method's **String** array argument.

Listing 5.1: Accessing the main method's arguments

```
package com.brainysoftware.jdk5.app05;
public class MainMethodTest {
    public static void main(String[] args) {
        for (String arg : args) {
            System.out.println(arg);
        }
    }
}
```

The following command invokes the class and passes two arguments to the **main** method.

```
java com/brainysoftware/jdk5/app05/MainMethodTest john mary
```

The **main** method will then print the arguments to the console.

```
john
mary
```

java.lang.Class

One of the members of the **java.lang** package is a class named **Class**. Every time the JVM creates an object, it also creates a **java.lang.Class** object that describes the type of the object. All instances of the same class share the same **Class** object. You can obtain the **Class** object by calling the **getClass** method of the object. This method is inherited from **java.lang.Object**.

For example, the following code creates a **String** object, invokes the **getClass** method on the **String** instance, and then invokes the **getName** method on the **Class** object.

```
String country = "Fiji";
Class myClass = country.getClass();
System.out.println(myClass.getName()); // prints java.lang.String
```

As it turns out, the **getName** method returns the fully qualified name of the class represented by a **Class** object.

The **Class** class also brings the possibility of creating an object without using the **new** keyword. You achieve this by using the two methods of the **Class** class, **forName** and **newInstance**.

```
public static Class forName(String className)
public Object newInstance()
```

The static **forName** method creates a **Class** object of the given class name. The **newInstance** method creates a new instance of a class.

The following example uses **forName** to create a **Class** object of the **com.brainysoftware.jdk.app05.Test** class and create an instance of the **Test** class. Since **newInstance** returns a **java.lang.Object** object, you need to downcast it to its original type.

```
Class klass = null;
try {
    klass = Class.forName("com.brainysoftware.jdk5.app05.Test");
} catch (ClassNotFoundException e) {
}

if (klass != null) {
try {
    // create an instance of the Test class
    Test test = (Test) klass.newInstance();
```

```
} catch (IllegalAccessException e) {
} catch (InstantiationException e) {
}
```

Do not worry about the **try ... catch** blocks as they will be explained in Chapter 7, "Error Handling."

You might want to ask this question, though. Why would you want to create an instance of a class using **forName** and **newInstance**, when using the **new** keyword is shorter and easier? You would do that because there are circumstances whereby the name of the class is not known when you are writing the program.

java.lang.System

The **System** class is a final class that exposes useful static fields and static methods that can help you with common tasks.

The three fields of the **System** class are **out, in**, and **err**:

```
public static final java.io.PrintStream out;
public static final java.io.InputStream in;
public static final java.io.PrintStream err;
```

The **out** field represents the standard output stream which by default is the same console used to run the running Java application. We will learn more about **PrintStream** in Chapter 13, "Input Output," but for now know that you can use the **out** field to write messages to the console. You will often write the following line of code:

```
System.out.print(message);
```

where *message* is a **String** object. However, **PrintStream** has many **print** method overloads that accept different types, so you can pass any primitive type to the **print** method:

```
System.out.print(12);
System.out.print('g');
```

In addition, there are **println** methods that are equivalent to **print**, except that **println** adds a line terminator at the end of the argument.

Note also that because **out** is static, you can access it by using this notation: **System.out**, which returns a **java.io.PrintStream** object. You then access the many methods on the **PrintStream** object as you would methods of other objects: **System.out.print**, **System.out.format**, etc.

The **err** field also represents a **PrintStream** object, and by default the output is channeled to the console from where the current Java program was invoked. However, its purpose is to display error messages that should get immediate attention of the user.

For example, here is how you can use **err**:

```
System.err.println("You have a runtime error.");
```

The **in** field represents the standard input stream. You can use it to accept user keyboard input. For example, the **getUserInput** method in Listing 5.2 accepts the user input and returns it as a String:

Listing 5.2: The getUserInput method

```
public String getUserInput() {
    StringBuilder sb = new StringBuilder();
    try {
        char c = (char) System.in.read();
        while (c != '\r') {
            sb.append(c);
            c = (char) System.in.read();
        }
    } catch (IOException e) {
    }
    return sb.toString();
}
```

However, in Java 5 there is a utility class, **java.util.Scanner**, that you can use to receive keyboard input. This class is discussed in the next section "java.util.Scanner" later in this chapter.

The **System** class has many useful methods, all of which are static. Some of the more important ones are listed here.

```
public static void arraycopy(Object source, int sourcePos,
        Object destination, int destPos, int length)
```
This method copies the content of an array (source) to another array (destination), beginning at the specified position, to the specified

position of the destination array. For example, the following code uses **arraycopy** to copy the contents of **array1** to **array2**.

```
int[] array1 = {1, 2, 3, 4};
int[] array2 = new int[array1.length];
System.arraycopy(array1, 0, array2, 0, array1.length);
```

`public static void exit(int status)`

Terminates the running program and the current JVM. You normally pass 0 to indicate that a normal exit and a nonzero to indicate there has been an error in the program prior to calling this method.

`public static long currentTimeMillis()`

Returns the computer time in milliseconds. The value represents the number of milliseconds that has elapsed since January 1, 1970 UTC. To get the string representation of the current computer time, use this:

```
System.out.println(new java.util.Date());
```

The **Date** class is discussed in Chapter 8, Numbers and Date." However, **currentTimeMillis** is useful if you want to time an operation. For instance, the following code measure the time it takes to perform a block of code:

```
long start = System.currentTimeMillis();
// block of code to time
long end = System.currentTimeMillis();
System.out.println("It took " + (end - start) +
        " milliseconds");
```

`public static long nanoTime()`

New to Java 5, this method is similar to **currentTimeMillis**, but provide more precision, i.e. in nanoseconds.

```
long start = System.nanoTime();
// block of code to time
long end = System.nanoTime();
System.out.println("It took " + (end - start) +
        " nanoseconds");
```

`public static String getProperty(String key)`

This method returns the value of the specified property. It returns **null** if the specified property does not exist. There are system properties and there are user-defined properties. When a Java program runs, the JVM provides values that may be used by the program as properties.

Each property comes as a key/value pair. For example, the **os.name** system property provides the name of the operating system running the JVM. Also, the directory name from which the application was invoked is provided by the JVM as a property named **user.dir**. To get the value of the **user.dir** property, you use:

```
System.getProperty("user.dir");
```

Table 5.1 lists the system properties.

System property	Description
java.version	Java Runtime Environment version
java.vendor	Java Runtime Environment vendor
java.vendor.url	Java vendor URL
java.home	Java installation directory
java.vm.specification.version	Java Virtual Machine specification version
java.vm.specification.vendor	Java Virtual Machine specification vendor
java.vm.specification.name	Java Virtual Machine specification name
java.vm.version	Java Virtual Machine implementation version
java.vm.vendor	Java Virtual Machine implementation vendor
java.vm.name	Java Virtual Machine implementation name
java.specification.version	Java Runtime Environment specification version
java.specification.vendor	Java Runtime Environment specification vendor
java.specification.name	Java Runtime Environment specification name
java.class.version	Java class format version number
java.class.path	Java class path
java.library.path	List of paths to search when loading libraries
java.io.tmpdir	Default temp file path
java.compiler	Name of JIT compiler to use
java.ext.dirs	Path of extension directory or directories
os.name	Operating system name
os.arch	Operating system architecture
os.version	Operating system version
file.separator	File separator ("/" on UNIX)
path.separator	Path separator (":" on UNIX)
line.separator	Line separator ("\n" on UNIX)
user.name	User's account name
user.home	User's home directory
user.dir	User's current working directory

Table 5.1: Java system properties

```
public static void setProperty(String property, String newValue)
```
You use **setProperty** to create a user-defined property or change the value of the current property. For instance, you can use this code to create a property named **password**:

```
System.setProperty("password", "tarzan");
```

And, you can retrieve it by using **getProperty**:

```
System.getProperty("password")
```

For instance, here is how you change the **user.name** property.

```
System.setProperty("user.name", "tarzan");
```

Note
A Java program can be run with a security manager, in order to restrict the running program. If this is the case, you may not be able to read the system properties or some of them. For more information, see Chapter 24, "Security."

```
public static String getProperty(String key, String default)
```
This method is similar to the single argument **getProperty** method, but returns a default value if the specified property does not exist.

```
public static java.util.Properties getProperties()
```
This method returns all system properties. The return value is a **java.util.Properties** object. The **Properties** class is a subclass of **java.util.Hashtable** (discussed in Chapter 11, "The Collections Framework").
For example, the following code uses the **list** method of the **Properties** class to iterate and display all system properties on the console.

```
java.util.Properties properties = System.getProperties();
properties.list(System.out);
```

java.util.Scanner

Java 5 adds the **java.util.Scanner** class. You use a **Scanner** object to scan a piece of text. In this chapter, we will only concentrate on its use to receive keyboard input.

Receiving keyboard input with **Scanner** is easy. All you need to do is instantiate the **Scanner** class by passing **System.in**. Then, to receive user input, call the **next** method on the instance. The **next** method buffers the characters the user input from the keyboard or other devices until the user presses Enter. It then returns a **String** containing the characters the user entered excluding the carriage-return character sequence. Listing 5.3 demonstrates the use of **Scanner** to receive user input.

Listing 5.3: Using Scanner to receive user input

```
Scanner scanner = new Scanner(System.in);
String s = scanner.next();
```

Compared to the code in Listing 5.2, using **Scanner** is much simpler.

Boxing and Unboxing

Conversion from primitive types to corresponding wrapper objects and vice versa can happen automatically in Java 5. In prior releases, you had to use methods in wrapper classes to do this. Boxing refers to the conversion of a primitive to a corresponding wrapper instance, such as from an **int** to a **java.lang.Integer**. Unboxing is the conversion of a wrapper instance to a primitive type, such as from **Byte** to **byte**.

For example, the following code is legal in Java 5.

```
Integer number = new Integer(100);
int[] ints = new int[2];
ints[0] = number;
```

ints is an **int** array and in the last line you assign an **Integer** object to its first member. Prior to Java 5, this would raise an exception, because an array must have components of the same type. In Java 5, however, the compiler will unbox **number** before assigning it to the first member of **ints**.

Varargs

Varargs is a new feature in Java 5 that allows methods to have a variable length of argument list.

In Chapter 4, you learned that every method has a signature. For example, here is the signature of the **getInteger** method of the **java.lang.Integer** class.

```
public static Integer getInteger(String nm, Integer val)
```

There are two parameters in the argument list, indicating that you must pass two arguments when invoking the method.

Prior to Java 5, if you want the flexibility of passing a variable number of arguments to a method, you had to wrap the arguments in an array. The **main** method is a good example of this technique, and this was discussed in the section "Arrays" earlier in this chapter. The signature of the **main** method is reprinted here.

```
public static void main(String[] args)
```

If you understand arrays well, varargs is also easy to comprehend. Basically, instead of an array, you use a type with ellipses in the signature. Therefore, using the varargs version, the **main** method can be written this way.

```
public static void main(String... args)
```

The ellipsis says that there is zero or more arguments of this type.

If an argument list contains both fixed arguments (arguments that must exist) and variable arguments, the variable arguments must come last.

In the background, the variable arguments are still passed in as an array, therefore the type of each variable argument must be the same. Also, since varargs are passed as an array, inside your method you will get an array. The code in Listing 5.4 is a rewrite of the code in Listing 5.3.

Listing 5.4: Using varargs

```
package com.brainysoftware.jdk5.app05;
public class MainMethodTest {
    public static void main(String... args) {
        for (String arg : args) {
            System.out.println(arg);
        }
    }
}
```

Note that if the user passes no argument, you get an array with a size of zero. There is no need to check if the array is null.

For users of your class, using varargs is easier because they can simply list the arguments, there is no need to create an array and populate it with the arguments.

Read also the section "The format and printf Methods" that illustrates some practical uses of varargs.

The format and printf Methods

A popular example of varargs can be found in the **format** method of the **java.lang.String** and **java.io.PrintStream** classes. Here is its signature.

```
public static String format(String formatString, Object... args)
```

This method returns a **String** formatted using the specified format string and arguments. The format pattern must follow the rules specified in the **java.util.Formatter** class and you can read them in the JavaDoc for the **Formatter** class. A brief description of these rules are as follows.

To specify an argument, use the notation **$s**, which denotes the next argument in the array. For example, the following is a method call to the **printf** method.

```
String firstName = "John";
String lastName = "Adams";
System.out.format("First name: %s. Last name: %s",
        firstName, lastName);
```

This prints the following string to the console:

```
First name: John. Last name: Adams
```

Without varargs, you have to do it in a more cumbersome way.

```
String firstName = "John";
String lastName = "Adams";
System.out.println("First name: " + firstName +
        ". Last name: " + lastName);
```

Note
The **printf** method in **java.io.PrintStream** is an alias for **format**.

The formatting example described here is only the tip of the iceberg. The formatting feature is much more powerful than that and you are encourage to explore it by reading the Javadoc for the **Formatter** class.

Summary

In this chapter you have examined several important classes such as **java.lang.String**, arrays, **java.lang.System**, and **java.util.Scanner**. You have also learned two concepts: boxing/unboxing and variable arguments. The last section covered the implementation of varargs in **java.lang.String** and **java.io.PrintStream**.

Questions

1. What does it mean when we say that **Strings** are immutable objects?
2. How did you receive user input in prior releases of Java, and how would you do it in Java 5?
3. Now that Java 5 supports boxing and unboxing, are wrapper classes still useful?
4. How do you resize an array?
5. What is varargs?

Chapter 6
Inheritance

Inheritance is a very important feature of object-oriented programming (OOP). It is what makes code extensible in any OOP language. Extending a class is also called inheriting or subclassing. In Java, by default all classes are extendible, even though you can use the **final** keyword to prevent classes from being subclassed. This chapter explains all you need to know about inheritance in the Java programming language and provides some examples.

An Overview of Inheritance

You extend a class by creating a new class. The former and the latter will then have a parent-child relationship. The original class is the parent class or the base class or the superclass. The new class is called a child class or a subclass or a derived class of the parent. The process of extending a class in object-oriented programming is called inheritance. In a subclass you can add new methods and new fields as well as override existing methods in the parent class to change their behaviors.

Figure 6.1 presents a UML class diagram that depicts a parent-child relationship between a class and its child class.

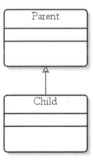

Figure 6.1: The UML class diagram for a parent class and a child class

Note that a line with an arrow is used to depict generalization, e.g. the parent-child relationship.

A child class can in turn be extended, unless you specifically make it inextensible by making them final. Final classes are discussed in the section, "Final Classes" later in this chapter.

The benefits of inheritance are obvious. Inheritance gives you the opportunity to add some functionality that does not exist in the original class. It also gives you the chance to change the behaviors of the existing class to better suit your needs.

Note

All Java classes automatically extend the **java.lang.Object**. **Object** is the ultimate superclass in Java.

The extends Keyword

You extend a class by using the **extends** keyword in a class declaration, after the class name and before the parent class. Listing 6.1 presents a class named **Parent** and Listing 6.2 a class named **Child** that extends **Parent**.

Listing 6.1: The Parent class

```
public class Parent {
}
```

Listing 6.2: The Child class

```
public class Child extends Parent {
}
```

Extending a class is as simple as that.

Note

In Java a class can only extend one class. This is unlike C++ where multiple inheritance is allowed. However, the notion of multiple inheritance can be achieved by using interfaces in Java, as discussed in Chapter 9, "Interfaces and Abstract Classes."

The is-a Relationship

There is a special relationship that is formed when you create a new class by inheritance. The subclass and the superclass has an "is-a" relationship.

For example, **Animal** is a class that represents animals. There are many types of animals, including birds, fish, and dogs, so you can create subclasses of **Animal** that represent specific types of animals. Figure 6.2 features the **Animal** class with three subclasses, **Bird**, **Fish**, and **Dog**.

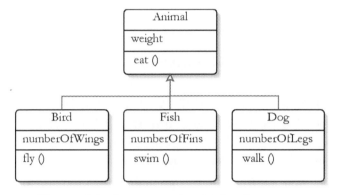

Figure 6.2: An example of inheritance

The is-a relationship between the subclasses and the superclass **Animal** is very apparent. A bird "is an" animal, a dog is an animal, and a fish is an animal. And, the subclasses are special types of the superclass. For example, a bird is a special type of animal. The is-a relationship does not go the other way, however. An animal is not necessarily a bird or a dog.

Listing 6.3 presents the classes in question.

Listing 6.3: The Animal class and its subclasses

```
package com.brainysoftware.jdk5.app06;
class Animal {
    public float weight;
    public void eat() {
    }
}

class Bird extends Animal {
    public int numberOfWings = 2;
    public void fly() {
```

```
    }
}
class Fish extends Animal {
    public int numberOfFins = 2;
    public void swim() {
    }
}
class Dog extends Animal {
    public int numberOfLegs = 4;
    public void walk() {
    }
}
```

In this example, the **Animal** class defines the **weight** field that applies to all animals. It also declares the **eat** method because animals eat.

The **Bird** class is a special type of **Animal**, it inherits the **eat** method and the **weight** field. **Bird** also adds the **numberOfWings** field and the **fly** method. This shows that the more specific **Bird** class extends the functionality and behavior of the more generic **Animal** class.

A subclass inherits all public methods and fields of its superclass. For example, you can create a **Dog** object and call its **eat** method:

```
Dog dog = new Dog();
dog.eat();
```

The **eat** method is declared in the **Animal** class; the **Dog** class simply inherits it.

A consequence of the is-a relationship is that it is legal to assign a subclass's instance to a reference variable of the parent type. For example, the following code is valid because **Bird** is a subclass of **Animal**, and a **Bird** is always an **Animal**.

```
Animal animal = new Bird();
```

However, the following is illegal because there is no guarantee that an **Animal** is always a **Dog**.:

```
Dog dog = new Animal();
```

Accessibility

From within a subclass you can access its superclass's public and protected methods and fields, but not the superclass's private methods. If the subclass and the superclass are in the same package, you can also access the superclass's default methods and fields.

Consider the **P** and **C** classes in Listing 6.4.

Listing 6.4: Showing accessibility

```
package com.brainysoftware.jdk5.app06;
public class P {
    public void publicMethod() {
    }
    protected void protectedMethod() {
    }
    void defaultMethod() {
    }
}
class C extends P {
    public void testMethods() {
        publicMethod();
        protectedMethod();
        defaultMethod();
    }
}
```

P has three methods, one public, one protected, and one with the default access level. **C** is a subclass of **P**. As you can see in the **C** class's **testMethods** method, **C** can access its parent's public and protected method. In addition, because **C** and **P** are in the same package, **C** can also access **P**'s default method.

However, it does not mean you can expose **P**'s non-public methods through its subclass. For example, the following code will not compile:

```
package test;
import com.brainysoftware.jdk5.app06.C;
public class AccessibilityTest {
    public static void main(String[] args) {
        C c = new C();
        c.protectedMethod();
    }
```

```
}
```

protectedMethod is **P**'s protected method. It is not accessible from outside **P**, except from a subclass. Since **AccessibilityTest** is not a subclass of **P**, you cannot access **P**'s protected method through its subclass **C**.

Method Overriding

When you extends a class, you can change the behavior of a method in the parent class. This is called method overriding, and this happens when you write in a subclass a method that has the same signature as a method in the parent class. If only the name is the same but the list of arguments is not, then it is method overloading. (See Chapter 4, "Objects and Classes")

You override a method to change its behavior. To override a method, you simply have to write the new method in the subclass, without having to change anything in the parent class. You can override the superclass's public and protected methods. If the subclass and superclass are in the same package, you can also override method with the default access level.

An example of method overriding is demonstrated by the **Box** class in Listing 6.5.

Listing 6.5: The Box class

```
package com.brainysoftware.jdk5.app06;
public class Box {
    public int length;
    public int width;
    public int height;

    public Box(int length, int width, int height) {
        this.length = length;
        this.width = width;
        this.height = height;
    }

    public String toString() {
        return "I am a Box.";
    }

    public Object clone() {
```

```
        return new Box(1, 1, 1);
    }
}
```

The **Box** class extends the **java.lang.Object** class. It is an implicit extension since the **extends** keyword is not used. **Box** overrides the public **toString** method and the protected **clone** method. Note that the **clone** method in **Box** is public whereas in **Object** it is protected. Increasing visibility of a superclass's method from protected to public is allowed. However, reducing visibility is illegal.

What if you create a method that has the same signature as a private method in the superclass? It is not method overriding, since private methods are not visible from outside the class.

Note
You cannot override a final method. To make a method final, use the **final** keyword in the method declaration. For example:

```
public final java.lang.String toUpperCase(java.lang.String s)
```

Calling the Superclass's Constructors

A subclass is just like another class, you use the **new** keyword to create an instance of a child class. If you do not explicitly write a constructor in your subclass, the compiler will implicitly add a no-arg constructor.

When you instantiate a child class by invoking one of its constructors, the first thing the constructor does is call the no-argument constructor of the direct parent class. In the parent class, the constructor also calls the constructor of its direct parent class. This process repeats itself until the constructor of the **java.lang.Object** class is reached. The conclusion is, if you create a child object, all its parent classes are also instantiated.

This process is illustrated in the **Base** and **Sub** classes in Listing 6.6.

Listing 6.6: Calling a superclass's no-arg constructor

```
package com.brainysoftware.jdk5.app06;

class Base {
    public Base() {
```

```
        System.out.println("Base");
    }
    public Base(String s) {
        System.out.println("Base." + s);
    }
}
public class Sub extends Base {
    public Sub(String s) {
        System.out.println(s);
    }
    public static void main(String[] args) {
        Sub sub = new Sub("Start");
    }
}
```

When the **Sub** class is run, you will see the following on the console:

```
Base
Start
```

This proves that the first thing that the **Sub** class's constructor does is invoke the **Base** class's no-arg constructor.

At compilation, the compiler has implicitly changed **Sub**'s constructor to

```
public Sub(String s) {
    super();
    System.out.println(s);
}
```

The keyword **super** represents an instance of the direct superclass of the current object. Since **super** is called from an instance of **Sub**, **super** represents an instance of **Base**, its direct superclass.

You can explicitly call the parent's constructor from a subclass's constructor by using the **super** keyword, but **super** must be the first statement in the constructor. Using the **super** keyword is handy if you want another constructor in the superclass to be invoked. For example, you can modify the constructor in **Sub** to the following.

```
public Sub(String s) {
    super(s);
    System.out.println(s);
}
```

This constructor calls the single argument constructor of the parent class, by using **super(s)**. As a result, if you run the class you will see the following on the console.

```
Base.Start
Start
```

Now, what if the superclass does not have a no-arg constructor and you do not make an explicit call to another constructor from a subclass? This is illustrated in the **Parent** and **Child** classes in listing 6.7.

Listing 6.7: Implicit calling to the parent's constructor that does not exist

```
package com.brainysoftware.jdk5.app06;
class Parent {
    public Parent(String s) {
        System.out.println("Parent(String)");
    }
}

public class Child extends Parent {
    public Child() {
    }
}
```

This will generate a compile error because the compiler adds an implicit call to the no-argument constructor in **Parent**, while the **Parent** class has only one constructor, the one that accepts a **String**. You can remedy this situation by explicitly calling the parent's constructor from the **Child** class's constructor:

```
public Child() {
    super(null);
}
```

Note

It actually makes sense for a child class to call its parent's constructor from its own constructor because an instance of a subclass must always be accompanied by instances of each of its parents. This way, a call to a method that is not overridden by the child class will be passed to its parent until the first in the hierarchy is found.

Calling the Superclass's Hidden Members

The **super** keyword has another purpose in life. It can be used to call a hidden member or an overridden method in the superclass. Since **super** represents an instance of the direct parent, super.*memberName* returns the specified member in the parent class. You can access any member in the superclass that is visible from the subclass. For example, Listing 6.8 shows two classes that have a parent-child relationship: **Tool** and **Pencil**.

Listing 6.8: Using super to access a hidden member

```
package com.brainysoftware.jdk5.app06;
class Tool {
    public String toString() {
        return "Generic tool";
    }
}

public class Pencil extends Tool {
    public String toString() {
        return "I am a Pencil";
    }

    public void write() {
        System.out.println(super.toString());
        System.out.println(toString());
    }

    public static void main(String[] args) {
        Pencil pencil = new Pencil();
        pencil.write();
    }
}
```

The **Pencil** class overrides the **toString** method in the **Tool** class. If you run the **Pencil** class, you will see the following on the console.

```
Generic tool
I am a Pencil
```

Unlike calling the parent's constructor, invoking the parent's member does not have to be the first statement in the calling method.

Type Casting

Like primitives, you can also cast an object to another type. With objects, you can cast an instance of a subclass to its parent class. Casting an object to a parent class is called upcasting. Here is an example, assuming that **Child** is a subclass of **Parent**.

```
Child child = new Child();
Parent parent = child;
```

To upcast a **Child** object, all you need to do is assign the object to a reference variable of type **Parent**. Note that the **parent** reference variable cannot access the members that are only available in **Child**.

Because **parent** references an object of type **Child**, you can cast it back to **Child**. This time, it is called downcasting because you are casting an object to a class down the inheritance hierarchy. Downcasting requires that you write the child type in brackets. For example:

```
Child child2 = (Child) parent;
```

Final Classes

You can prevent others from extending your class by making it final using the keyword **final** in the class declaration. The keyword final may appear after or before the access modifier. For example:

```
public final class Pencil
final public class Pen
```

The first form is more common.

Even though making a class final makes your code slightly faster, the difference is too insignificant to notice. Design consideration, and not speed, should be the reason why you want to make a class final. For example, the **java.lang.String** class is final because the designer of the class did not want us to change the behavior of the **String** class.

The instanceof Keyword

The **instanceof** keyword can be used to test if an object is of a specified type. It is normally used in an **if** statement and its syntax is.

```
if (objectReference instanceof type)
```

where *objectReference* references an object being investigated. For example, the following **if** statement returns **true**.

```
String s = "Hello";
if (s instanceof java.lang.String)
```

However, applying **instanceof** on a **null** reference variable returns **false**. For example, the following **if** statement returns **false**.

```
String s;
if (s instanceof java.lang.String)
```

Also, since a subclass "is a" type of its superclass, the following **if** statement, where **Child** is a subclass of **Parent**, returns **true**.

```
Child child = new Child();
if (child instanceof Parent)     // evaluates to true
```

Summary

Inheritance is one of the fundamental principles in object-oriented programming. Inheritance makes code extensible. In Java all classes by default extend the **java.lang.Object** class. To extend a class, use the **extends** keyword. Method overriding is another OOP feature directly related to inheritance. It enables you to change the behavior of a method in the parent class. You can prevent your class from being subclassed by using the **final** keyword.

Questions

1. Does a subclass inherit its superclass's constructors?
2. Why is it legal to assign an instance of subclass to a superclass variable?

3. What is the difference between method overriding and method overloading?
4. Why is it necessary for an instance of a subclass to be accompanied by an instance of each parent?

Chapter 7
Error Handling

Error handling is an important feature in any programming language. A good error handling mechanism makes it easier for programmers to write robust applications and prevent bugs from creeping in. Programmers of some languages have to use many **if** statements to detect all possible conditions that might lead to an error. This could make your code excessively complex. In a larger program, this practice could easily lead to spaghetti like code.

Java has a very nice approach to error handling by using the **try** statement. With this strategy, part of the code that could potentially lead to an error is isolated in a block. Should an error occur, this error is caught and resolved locally. This chapter teaches you how.

Catching Exceptions

You can isolate code that may cause a runtime error using the **try** statement, which normally is accompanied by the **catch** and the **finally** statements. Such isolation typically occurs in a method body. If an error is encountered, Java stops the processing of the **try** block and jump to the **catch** block. Here you can gracefully handle the error or notify the user by 'throwing' a **java.lang.Exception** object. Another scenario is to re-throw the exception or a new **Exception** object back to the code that called the method. It is then the client's call to handle the error. If a thrown exception is not caught, the application will stop abruptly.

This is the syntax of the **try** statement.

```
try {
    [code that may throw an exception]
} catch (ExceptionType-1 e) {
    [code that is executed when ExceptionType-1 is thrown]
} [catch (ExceptionType-2 e) {
```

```
    [code that is executed when ExceptionType-2 is thrown]
}]
  ...
} [catch (ExceptionType-n e) {
    [code that is executed when ExceptionType-n is thrown]
}]
[finally {
    [code that runs regardless of whether an exception was thrown]]
}]
```

The steps for error handling can be summarized as follows:

1. Isolate code that could lead to an error in the **try** block.
2. For each individual **catch** block, you write code that is to be executed if an exception of that particular type occurs in the **try** block.
3. In the **finally** block, you write code that will be run whether or not an error has occurred.

Note that the **finally** block is optional.

The previous syntax shows that you can have more than one **catch** block. This is because the code can throw different types of exceptions. When an exception is thrown from the **try** block, control is passed to the first **catch** block. If the type of exception thrown matches or is a subclass of the exception in the first **catch** block, the code in the **catch** block is executed and then control goes to the **finally** block, if one exists.

If the type of exception thrown does not match the exception type in the first **catch** block, the JVM goes to the next **catch** block and does the same thing until it finds a match. If no match is found, the exception object will be thrown to the method caller. If the caller does not put the offending code that calls the method in a **try** block, the program crashes.

To illustrate the use of this error handling, consider the **NumberDoubler** class in Listing 7.1. When the class is run, it will prompt you for input. You can type anything, including non-digits. If your input is successfully converted to a number, it will double it and print the result. If your input is invalid, the program will print an "Invalid input" message.

Listing 7.1: The NumberDoubler class

```
package com.brainysoftware.jdk5.app07;
import java.util.Scanner;
public class NumberDoubler {
```

```
public static void main(String[] args) {
    Scanner scanner = new Scanner(System.in);
    String input = scanner.next();
    try {
        double number = Double.parseDouble(input);
        System.out.printf("Result: %s", number);
    }
    catch (NumberFormatException e) {
        System.out.println("Invalid input.");
    }
}
}
```

The **NumberDoubler** class uses the **java.util.Scanner** class to take user input (discussed in Chapter 5, "Core Classes").

```
Scanner scanner = new Scanner(System.in);
String input = scanner.next();
```

It then uses the static **parseDouble** method of the **java.lang.Double** class to convert the string input to a **double**. Note that the code that calls **parseDouble** resides in a **try** block. This is necessary because the **parseDouble** method may throw a **java.lang.NumberFormatException**, as indicated by the signature of the **parseDouble** method.

```
public static double parseDouble(String s)
        throws NumberFormatExcpetion
```

The **throws** statement in the method signature tells you that it could throw a **NumberFormatException** and it is the responsibility of the method caller to catch it.

Without the **try** block, invalid input will give you this embarrassing error message before the system crashes:

```
Exception in thread "main" java.lang.NumberFormatException:
```

The java.lang.Exception Class

Erroneous code can throw any type of exception. For example, an invalid argument throws a **java.lang.NumberFormatException**, and calling a method on a null reference variable throws a **java.lang.NullPointerException**. All Java exception classes derive from the

java.lang.Exception class. It is therefore worthwhile to spend some time studying this class.

Among others, the **Exception** class has the following methods:

```
public String toString()
```
> Returns the description of the exception.

```
public void printStackTrace()
```
> Prints the description of the exception followed by a stack trace for the **Exception** object. By analyzing the stack trace, you can find out which like is causing the problem. Here is an example of what **printStackTrace** may print on the console.

```
java.lang.NullPointerException
        at MathUtil.doubleNumber(MathUtil.java:45)
        at MyClass.performMath(MyClass.java: 18)
        at MyClass.main(MyClass.java: 90)
```

> This tells you that a **NullPointerException** has been thrown. The line that throws the exception is Line 45 of the **MathUtil.java** class, inside the **doubleNumber** method. The **doubleNumber** method was called by **MyClass.performMath**, which in turns was called by **MyClass.main**.

Most of the time a **try** block is accompanied by a **catch** block that catches the **java.lang.Exception** in addition to other **catch** blocks. The **catch** block that catches **Exception** must appear last. If other **catch** blocks fail to catch the exception, the last **catch** will do that. Here is an example.

```
try {
    // code
} catch (NumberFormatException e) {
    // handle NumberFormatException
} catch (Exception e) {
    // handle other exceptions
}
```

You use multiple **catch** blocks because the code in the **try** block may throw a **java.lang.NumberFormatException** or other type of exception. If the latter is thrown, it will be caught by the last **catch** block.

Be warned, though: The order of the **catch** blocks is important. You cannot, for example, put the **catch** block for handling **java.lang.Exception** before any other **catch** block. This is because the JVM tries to match the thrown exception with the argument of the **catch** blocks in the order of appearance. **java.lang.Exception** catches everything; therefore, the **catch** blocks after it would be useless.

If you have several **catch** blocks whereby the argument type of a **catch** block is derived from the argument of another **catch** block, make sure the more specific exception type appears first. For example, when trying to open a file, you need to catch the **java.io.FileNotFoundException** just in case the file cannot be found. However, you may want to make sure that you also catch **java.io.IOException** to so that other I/O-related exceptions are caught. Since **FileNotFoundException** is a child class of **IOException**, the **catch** block that handles **FileNotFoundException** must appear before the **catch** block that handles **IOException**.

Throwing an Exception from a Method

When having to catch an exception in a method, you have two options to handle the error that occurs inside the method. You can either handle the error in the method, thus quietly catching the exception without notifying the caller (this has been demonstrated in the previous examples), or you can throw the exception back to the caller and let the caller handle it. If you choose the second option, the calling code must catch the exception that is thrown back by the method.

Listing 7.2 presents the **capitalize** method that changes the first letter of a **String** to upper case.

Listing 7.2: The capitalize method

```
public String capitalize(String s) throws NullPointerException {
    if (s == null) {
        throw new NullPointerException(
                "Your passed a null argument");
    }
    Character firstChar = s.charAt(0);
    String theRest = s.substring(1);
    return firstChar.toString().toUpperCase() + theRest;
}
```

If you pass a null to the **capitalize** method, it will throw a new **NullPointerException**. Pay attention to the code that instantiates the **NullPointerException** class and throws the instance:

```
throw new NullPointerException(
        "Your passed a null argument");
```

The **throw** keyword is used to throw an exception. This is different from the **throws** statement which is used at the end of a method signature to indicate that an exception of a given type may be thrown from the method.

The following shows code that calls **capitalize**.

```
String input = null;
try {
    String capitalized = util.capitalize(input);
    System.out.println(capitalized);
} catch (NullPointerException e) {
    System.out.println(e.toString());
}
```

Note
A constructor can also throw exceptions

User-Defined Exceptions

You can create a user-defined exception by subclassing **java.lang.Exception**. There are several reasons for having user-defined exception. One of them is to create a customized error message.

For example, Listing 7.3 shows the **AlreadyCapitalizedException** class that derives from **java.lang.Exception**.

Listing 7.3: The AlreadyCapitalizedException class

```
package com.brainysoftware.jdk5.app07;
public class AlreadyCapitalizedException extends Exception {
    public String toString() {
        return "Input has already been capitalized";
    }
}
```

You can throw an **AlreadyCapitalizedException** from the **capitalize** method in Listing 7.2. The modified **capitalize** method is given in Listing 7.4.

Listing 7.4: The modified capitalize method

```
public String capitalize(String s)
      throws NullPointerException, AlreadyCapitalizedException {
    if (s == null) {
        throw new NullPointerException(
              "Your passed a null argument");
    }
    Character firstChar = s.charAt(0);
    if (Character.isUpperCase(firstChar)) {
        throw new AlreadyCapitalizedException();
    }
    String theRest = s.substring(1);
    return firstChar.toString().toUpperCase() + theRest;
}
```

Now, the **capitalize** method may throw one of two exceptions. You comma-delimit multiple exceptions in a method signature.

Clients that call **capitalize** must now catch both exceptions. This code shows a call to **capitalize**.

```
StringUtil util = new StringUtil();
String input = "Capitalize";
try {
    String capitalized = util.capitalize(input);
    System.out.println(capitalized);
} catch (NullPointerException e) {
    System.out.println(e.toString());
} catch (AlreadyCapitalizedException e) {
    e.printStackTrace();
}
```

Since **NullPointerException** and **AlreadyCapitalizedException** do not have a parent-child relationship, the order of the **catch** blocks above is not important.

When a method throws multiple exceptions, rather than catch all the exceptions, you can simply write a catch block that handles **java.lang.Exception**. Rewriting the code above:

```
StringUtil util = new StringUtil();
String input = "Capitalize";
```

```
try {
    String capitalized = util.capitalize(input);
    System.out.println(capitalized);
} catch (Exception e) {
    System.out.println(e.toString());
}
```

While it's more concise, the last code lacks specifics and does not allow you to handle each exception separately.

Final Words on Exception Handling

The **try** statement imposes some performance penalty. Therefore, do not use it over-generously. If it is not hard to test for a condition, then you should do the testing rather than depending on the **try** statement. For example, calling a method on a null object throws a **NullPointerException**. Therefore, you could always surround a method call with a **try** block:

```
try {
    ref.method();
...
```

However, it is not hard at all to check if **ref** is null prior to calling **methodA**. Therefore, the following code is better because it eliminates the **try** block.

```
if (ref != null) {
    ref.methodA();
}
```

Summary

This chapter discussed the use of structured error handling and presented examples for each case. You have also been introduced to the **java.lang.Exception** class and its properties and methods. The chapter concluded with a discussion on user-defined exceptions.

Question

1. What is the advantage of the **try** statement?

Chapter 8
Numbers and Dates

In Java numbers are represented by the primitives **byte**, **short**, **int**, **long**, **float**, **double**, and their wrapper classes, which were explained in Chapter 5, "Core Classes.". Dates can be represented by different classes, most commonly by the **java.util.Date** class. There are three issues when working with numbers and dates: parsing, formatting, and manipulation.

Parsing is to do with the conversion of a string into a number or a date. Parsing is commonplace because Java programs often require user input and user input is received as a **String**. If what the programs need is a number or a date, the string has to be converted into a number or a date. Conversion is not always straightforward. Before conversion can take place, you first need to read the **String** and check if it contains characters that make up a number or a date. For example, "123data" is not a number even though it starts with a number. "123.45" is a float, but not an integer. "12/25/2006" looks like a date, but this is only valid if the program is expecting a date in mm/dd/yyyy format. Converting a string to a number is called number parsing, and converting a string to a date is referred to as date parsing.

Once you have a number or a date, you may want to display it in a specific format. For instance, 1000000 may be displayed as 1,000,000 and 12/25/2006 as Dec 25, 2006. This is number formatting and date formatting, respectively.

This chapter discusses number and date parsing, as well as number and date formatting. These tasks are easily achieved in Java as it provides classes for this purpose. In addition, the **java.lang.Math** class, which provides methods to perform mathematical operations, is also discussed. On top of that, there is a section on the **java.util.Calendar** class, a class that can manipulate dates.

Number Parsing

A Java program may require that the user input a number that will be processed or become an argument of a method. For example, a currency converter program would need the user to type in a value to be converted. You can use the **java.util.Scanner** class to receive user input. However, the input will be a **String**, even though it represents a number. Before you can work with the number, you need to parse the string. The output of a successful parsing is a number.

Therefore, the purpose of number parsing is to convert a string into a numeric primitive type. If parsing fails, for example because the string is not a number or a number outside the specified range, your program can throw an exception.

The wrappers of primitives, the **Byte, Short, Integer, Long, Float,** and **Double** classes, provide static methods to parse strings. For example, the **Integer** class has the **parseInteger** method with the following signature.

```
public static int parseInt(String s) throws NumberFormatException
```

This method parses a **String** and returns an **int**. If the **String** does not contain a valid integer representation, a **NumberFormatException** will be thrown.

For example, the following snippet uses **parseInt** to parse the string "123" to 123.

```
int x = Integer.parseInt("123");
```

Similarly, the **Byte** class provides the **parseByte** method, the **Long** class the **parseLong** method, the **Short** class the **parseShort** method, the **Float** class the **parseFloat** method, and the **Double** class the **parseDouble** method.

For example, the **NumberTest** class in Listing 8.1 takes user input and parses it. If the user types in an invalid number, an error message will be displayed.

Listing 8.1: Parsing numbers (NumberTest.java)

```
package com.brainysoftware.jdk5.app08;
import java.util.Scanner;
public class NumberTest {
    public static void main(String[] args) {
        Scanner scanner = new Scanner(System.in);
```

```
        String userInput = scanner.next();
        try {
            int i = Integer.parseInt(userInput);
            System.out.println("The number entered: " + i);
        } catch (NumberFormatException e) {
            System.out.println("Invalid user input");
        }
    }
}
```

Number Formatting

Number formatting helps make your numbers more readable. For example, 1000000 is more readable if printed as 1,000,000 (or 1.000.000 if your locale uses . to separated the thousands). Java provides you with the **java.text.NumberFormat** class, which is an abstract class. Since it is abstract, you cannot obtain an instance by using the **new** keyword. Instead, you instantiate its subclass **java.text.DecimalFormat**, which is a concrete implementation of **NumberFormat**.

```
NumberFormat nf = new DecimalFormat();
```

However, you should not call the **DecimalFormat** class's constructor directly. Instead, use the the **NumberFormat** class's **getInstance** static method. This method may return an instance of **DecimalFormat** but might also return an instance of a subclass other than **DecimalFormat**.

Now, how do you use **NumberFormat** to format numbers, such as 1234.56? Easy, simply pass the numbers to its **format** method and you'll get a **String**. However, should number 1234.56 be formatted as 1,234.56 or 1234,56? Well, it really depends in which side of the Atlantics you live. If you are in the US, you may want 1,234.56. If you live in Germany, however, 1234,56 makes more sense. Therefore, before you start using the **format** method, you want to make sure you get the correct instance of **NumberFormat** by telling it where you live, or, actually, in what locale you want it formatted. In Java, a locale is represented by the **java.util.Locale** class, which I'll explain further in Chapter 19, "Internationalization." For now, remember that the **getInstance** method of the **NumberFormat** class also has an overload that accepts a **java.util.Locale**.

```
public NumberFormat getInstance(java.util.Locale locale)
```

If you pass **Locale.Germany** to the method, you'll get a **NumberFormat** object that formats numbers according to the German locale. If you pass **Locale.US**, you get one for the US number format. The no-argument **getInstance** method returns a **NumberFormat** object with the user computer's locale.

Listing 8.2 shows the **NumberFormatTest** class that demonstrates how to use the **NumberFormat** class to format a number.

Listing 8.2: The NumberFormatTest class

```
package com.brainysoftware.jdk5.app08;
import java.text.NumberFormat;
import java.util.Locale;
public class NumberFormatTest {
    public static void main(String[] args) {
        NumberFormat nf = NumberFormat.getInstance(Locale.US);
        System.out.println(nf.getClass().getName());
        System.out.println(nf.format(123445));
    }
}
```

When run, the output of the execution is

```
java.text.DecimalFormat
123,445
```

The first output line shows that a **java.text.DecimalFormat** object was produced upon calling **NumberFormat.getInstance**. The second shows how the **NumberFormat** formats the number 123445 into a more readable form.

Number Parsing with java.text.NumberFormat

You can also use the **parse** method of **NumberFormat** to parse numbers. One of this method's overloads has the following signature:

```
public java.lang.Number parse(java.lang.String source)
        throws ParseException
```

Note that the **parse** method returns a **java.lang.Number** object, the parent of such classes as **Integer**, **Long**, etc.

The java.lang.Math Class

The **Math** class is a utility class that provides static methods for mathematical operations. There are also two static final double fields: **E** and **PI**. **E** represents the base of natural logarithms (e). Its value is close to 2.718. **PI** is the ratio of the circumference of a circle to its diameter (pi). Its value is 22/7 or approximately 3.1428.

Some of the methods in the **Math** class are given below.

```
public static double abs(double a)
```
Returns the absolute value of the specified double..

```
public static double acos(double a)
```
Returns the arc cosine of an angle, in the range of 0.0 through pi.

```
public static double asin(double a)
```
Returns the arc sine of an angle, in the range of –pi/2 through pi/2.

```
public static double atan(double a)
```
Returns the arc tangent of an angle, in the range of –pi/2 through pi/2.

```
public static double cos(double a)
```
Returns the cosine of an angle.

```
public static double exp(double a)
```
Returns Euler's number e raised to the power of the specified double.

```
public static double log(double a)
```
Returns the natural logarithm (base e) of the specified double.

```
public static double log10(double a)
```
Returns the base 10 logarithm of the specified double.

```
public static double max(double a, double b)
```
Returns the greater of the two specified double values.

```
public static double min(double a, double b)
```
Returns the smaller of the two specified double values.

The java.util.Date Class

There are at least two classes that you use when working with dates and times. The first is **java.util.Date**, a class normally used to represent dates and times. The second is **java.util.Calendar**, often used to manipulate dates. In addition, times can also be represented as a **long**. See the discussion of the **currentTimeMillis** method of the **java.lang.System** class in Chapter 5, "Core Classes."

The **Date** class has two constructors that you can safely use (the other constructors are deprecated):

```
public Date()
public Date(long time)
```

The no-argument constructor creates a **Date** object representing the current date and time. The second constructor creates a **Date** that represents the specified number of milliseconds since January 1, 1970, 00:00:00 GMT.

The **Date** class features several useful methods, two of them are **after** and **before**.

```
public boolean after(Date when)
public boolean before(Date when)
```

The **after** method returns **true** if this date is a later time than the *when* argument. Otherwise, it returns **false**. The **before** method returns **true** if this date is before the specified date and returns **false** otherwise.

For example, the following code prints "date1 before date2" because the first date represents a time that is one millisecond earlier than the second.

```
Date date1 = new Date(1000);
Date date2 = new Date(1001);
if (date1.before(date2)) {
    System.out.println("date1 before date2");
} else {
    System.out.println("date1 not before date2");
}
```

Many of the methods in **Date**, such as **getDate, getMonth, getYear**, are deprecated. You should not use these methods. Instead, use similar methods in the **java.util.Calendar** class.

The java.util.Calendar Class

The **java.util.Date** class has methods that allow you to construct a **Date** object from date components, such as the day, month, and year. However, these methods are deprecated. First, you need to create a **java.util.Calendar** object using its static **getInstance** method. Here are two overloads:

```
public static Calendar getInstance()
public static Calendar getInstance(Locale locale)
```

The first overload returns an instance that employs the computer's locale. Therefore, to get a **Calendar** instance, do this.

```
Calendar calendar = Calendar.getInstance();
```

Once you have a **Calendar** object, there is a lot you can do. For example, you can use its **getTime** method to obtain a **Date** object. Here is its signature:

```
public final Date getTime();
```

The resulting **Date** object, needless to say, contains components you initially passed to construct the **Calendar** object. In other words, if you construct a **Calendar** object that represents May 7, 2000 00:00:00, the **Date** object obtained from its **getTime** method will also represent May 7, 2000 00:00:00.

To obtain a date part, such as the hour, the month, or the year, use the **get** method. A first glance at its signature does not reveal much on how to use this method.

```
public int get(int field)
```

To use it, pass a valid field to the **get** method. A valid field is one of the following values: **Calendar.YEAR, Calendar.MONTH, Calendar.DATE, Calendar.HOUR, Calendar.MINUTE, Calendar.SECOND,** and **Calendar.MILLISECOND**.

get(Calendar.YEAR) returns an **int** representing the year. If it is year 2006, you get 2006. **get(Calendar.MONTH)** returns a zero-based index of the month, with 0 representing January, 1 February, and 11 December. The others (**get(Calendar.DATE), get(Calendar.HOUR),** and so on) return a number representing the date/time unit.

The last thing worth mentioning: if you already have a **Date** object and want to make use of the methods in **Calendar**, you can construct a **Calendar** object by using the **setTime** method:

```
public void setTime(Date date)
```

Here is an example:

```
// myDate is a Date
Calendar calendar = Calendar.getInstance();
calendar.setTime(myDate);
```

To change a date/time component, use its **set** method:

```
public void set(int field, int value)
```

For example, to change the month component of a **Calendar** object to **December**, use this.

```
calendar.set(Calendar.MONTH, Calendar.DECEMBER)
```

There are also **set** method overloads that let you change multiple components at the same time:

```
public void set(int year, int month, int date)
public void set(int year, int month, int date,
        int hour, int minute, int second)
```

Date Parsing and Formatting with DateFormat

Java's answer to date parsing and formatting is the **java.text.DateFormat** and **java.text.SimpleDateFormat** classes. **DateFormat** is an abstract class with static **getInstance** methods that allows you to obtain an instance of a subclass. **SimpleDateFormat** is a concrete implementation of **DateFormat** that is easier to use than its parent. This section covers both classes.

DateFormat

DateFormat supports styles or patterns. There are four styles you can format a **Date** object to. Each style is represented by an **int** value. The four **int** fields that represent the styles are:

- **DateFormat.SHORT**. For example, 12/2/05
- **DateFormat.MEDIUM**. For example, Dec 2, 2005
- **DateFormat.LONG**. For example, December 2, 2005
- **DateFormat.FULL**. For example, Friday, December 2, 2005

When you create a **DateFormat** object, you need to decide which style you will be using for parsing or formatting. You cannot change a **DateFormat** object's style once you create it, but you can definitely have multiple instances of **DateFormat** that support different styles.

To obtain a **DateFormat** instance, use this static method.

```
public static DateFormat getDateInstance(int style)
```

where *style* is one of **DateFormat.SHORT**, **DateFormat.MEDIUM**, **DateFormat.Long**, or **DateFormat.FULL**. For example, the following code creates a **DateFormat** instance having the **MEDIUM** style.

```
DateFormat df = DateFormat.getDateInstance(DateFormat.MEDIUM)
```

To format a **Date** object, call its **format** method:

```
public final java.lang.String format(java.util.Date date)
```

To parse a string representation of a date, use the **parse** method. Here is the signature of the **parse** method.

```
public java.util.Date parse(java.lang.String date)
        throws ParseException
```

Note that you must compose your string according to the style of the **DateFormat**.

Listing 8.3 shows the **DateFormatTest** class that illustrates how to parse and format a date.

Listing 8.3: The DateFormatTest class

```
package com.brainysoftware.jdk5.app08;
import java.text.DateFormat;
import java.text.ParseException;
import java.util.Date;
public class DateFormatTest {
    public static void main(String[] args) {
        DateFormat shortDf =
                DateFormat.getDateInstance(DateFormat.SHORT);
```

```
        DateFormat mediumDf =
                DateFormat.getDateInstance(DateFormat.MEDIUM);
        DateFormat longDf =
                DateFormat.getDateInstance(DateFormat.LONG);
        DateFormat fullDf =
                DateFormat.getDateInstance(DateFormat.FULL);
        System.out.println(shortDf.format(new Date()));
        System.out.println(mediumDf.format(new Date()));
        System.out.println(longDf.format(new Date()));
        System.out.println(fullDf.format(new Date()));

        // parsing
        try {
            Date date = shortDf.parse("12/12/2006");
        } catch (ParseException e) {
        }
    }
}
```

Another point to note when working with **DateFormat** (and
SimpleDateFormat) is leniency. Leniency refers to whether or not a strict
rule will be applied at parsing. For example, if a **DateFormat** object is lenient,
it will accept this **String**: Jan 32, 2005, despite the fact that such a date does
not exist. In fact, it will take the liberty of converting it to Feb 1, 2006. If a
DateFormat object is not lenient, it will not accept dates that do not exist. By
default, a **DateFormat** object is lenient. The **isLenient** method and
setLenient method allow you to check a **DateFormat**'s leniency and change
its leniency.

```
public boolean isLenient()
public void setLenient(boolean value)
```

SimpleDateFormat

SimpleDateFormat is more powerful than **DateFormat** because you can use
your own date patterns that are different from the four styles found in
DateFormat. For example, you can format and parse dates in dd/mm/yyyy,
mm/dd/yyyy, yyyy-mm-dd, and so on. All you need to do is pass a pattern to a
SimpleDateFormat constructor.

From experience, **SimpleDateFormat** is a better choice than
DateFormat especially for parsing. Here is one of the constructors in
SimpleDateFormat.

```
public SimpleDateFormat(java.lang.String pattern)
        throws java.lang.NullPointerException,
        java.lang.IllegalArgumentException
```

The complete rules for a valid pattern can be read in the Javadoc for the
SimpleDateFormat class. The more commonly used patterns can be used by
a combination of y (representing a year digit), M (representing a month digit)
and d (representing a date digit). Examples of patterns are dd/MM/yyyy, dd-
MM-yyyy, MM/dd/yyyy, yyyy-MM-dd.

Listing 8.4 shows the **SimpleDateFormatTest** that demonstrates the use
of **SimpleDateFormat** for parsing and formatting.

Listing 8.4: The SimpleDateFormatTest class

```
package com.brainysoftware.jdk5.app08;
import java.text.ParseException;
import java.text.SimpleDateFormat;
import java.util.Date;
public class SimpleDateFormatTest {
    public static void main(String[] args) {
        String pattern = "MM/dd/yyyy";
        SimpleDateFormat format = new SimpleDateFormat(pattern);
        try {
            Date date = format.parse("12/31/2006");
        } catch (ParseException e) {
            e.printStackTrace();
        }
        // formatting
        System.out.println(format.format(new Date()));
    }
}
```

Summary

In Java you use primitives and wrapper classes to represent number and the
java.util.Date class to represents dates. There are three types of operations
that you frequently perform when dealing with number and dates: parsing,
formatting and manipulation. This chapter showed how to perform them.

Number parsing is achieved through the use of the **parse*XXX*** methods in wrapper classes, such as **parseInteger** in **java.lang.Integer** and **parseLong** in **java.lang.Long**. The **java.text.NumberFormat** class can be used for number parsing and number formatting. For complex mathematical operations, use the static methods in **java.lang.Math**.

Date manipulation, on the other hand, is best done with the help of the **java.util.Calendar** class. Date parsing and formatting can be performed by using the **java.text.DateFormat** and the **java.text.SimpleDateFormat** classes.

Questions

1. What can you do with the **java.lang.Math** class's static methods?
2. What do you use to represents dates?
3. What class should you use if you want to define you own date pattern?

Chapter 9
Interfaces and Abstract Classes

Java beginners often get the impression that an interface is simply a class without implementation code. While this is not technically incorrect, it obscures the real purpose of having the interface in the first place. The interface is more than that. The interface should be regarded as a contract between a service provider and its clients. This chapter therefore focuses on the concepts before explaining how to write an interface.

The second topic in this chapter is the abstract class. Technically speaking, an abstract class is a class that cannot be instantiated and must be implemented by a subclass. However, the abstract class is important because in some situations it can take the role of the interface. We'll see how to use the abstract class too in this chapter.

The Concept of the Interface

When learning the interface for the first time , novices often focus on how to write one, rather than understanding the concept behind it. They think an interface is something like a Java class declared with the **interface** keyword and whose methods have no body.

While the description is not inaccurate, treating an interface as an implementation-less class misses the big picture. A better definition of an interface is a contract. It is a contract between a service provider (server) and the user of such a service (client). Sometimes the server defines the contract, sometimes the client does.

Consider this real-world example. Microsoft Windows is the most popular operating system in the world, but Microsoft does not make printers. For printing, we still rely on those people at HP, Canon, Samsung, and the like. Each of these printer makers uses a proprietary technology. However, their products can all be used to print any document from any Windows application. How come?

This is because Microsoft said something to this effect to the printer manufacturers, "If you want your products to be useable on Windows (and we know you all do), you must implement this **Printable** interface."

The interface is as simple as this:

```
interface Printable {
    void print(Document document);
}
```

where *document* is the document to be printed.

Implementing this interface, printer makers write printer drivers. Every printer has a different driver, but they all implement **Printable**. A printer driver is an implementation of **Printable**. In this case, these printer drivers are the service provider.

The client of the printing service is all Windows applications. It is easy to print on Windows because an application just needs to call the **print** method and pass a **Document** object. Because the interface is freely available, client applications can be compiled without waiting for an implementation to be available.

The point is, printing to different printers from different applications is possible thanks to the **Printable** interface. A contract between printing service providers and printing clients.

An interface can define both fields and methods. However, the methods have no implementation. To be useful, an interface has to have an implementation class that actually performs the action.

Figure 9.1 illustrates the **Printable** interface and its implementation in an UML class diagram.

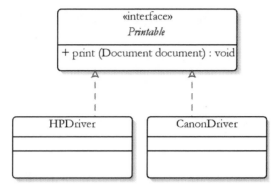

Figure 9.1: An interface and two implementation classes in a class diagram

In the class diagram, an interface has the same shape as a class, however the name is printed in italic and prefixed with <<interface>>. The **HPDriver** and **CanonDriver** classes are classes that implement the **Printable** interface. The implementations are of course different. In the **HPDriver** class, the **print** method contains code that enables printing to a HP printer. In **CanonDriver**, the code enables printing to a Canon driver. In UML class diagrams, a class and an interface are joined by a dash-line with an arrow. This type of relationship is often called realization because the class provides real implementation (code that actually works) of the abstraction provided by the interface.

Note
This case study is imaginary. However, the problem and the solution are real. I hope this provides you with more understanding of what the interface is. It is a contract.

The Interface, Technically Speaking

Now that you understand what the interface is, let's examine how you can create one. In Java, like the class, the interface is a type. (Therefore, a Java type is either a class or an interface.) Follow this format to write an interface:

```
accessModifier interface interfaceName {

}
```

Like a class, an interface has either a public or the default access level. An interface can have fields and methods. However, all interface members are implicitly public. Listing 9.1 shows an interface named **Printable**.

Listing 9.1: The Printable interface

```
package com.brainysoftware.jdk5.app09;
public interface Printable {
    void print(Object o);
}
```

The **Printable** interface has a method, **print**. Note that **print** is public even though there is no **public** keyword in front of the method declaration. You can of course use the keyword **public** before the method signature.

Just like a class, an interface is a template for creating objects. Unlike an ordinary class, however, an interface cannot be instantiated. It simply defines a set of methods that Java classes can implement.

To implement an interface, you use the **implements** keyword after the class declaration. A class can implement multiple interfaces. For example, Listing 9.2 shows the **CanonDriver** class that implements **Printable**.

Listing 9.2: An implementation of the Printable interface

```
package com.brainysoftware.jdk5.app09;
public class CanonDriver implements Printable {
    public void print(Object obj) {
        // code that does the printing
    }
}
```

An implementation class has to override all methods in the interface. The relationship between an interface and its implementing class can be likened to a parent class and a subclass. An instance of the class is also an instance of the interface. For example, the following **if** statement will evaluates to **true**.

```
CanonDriver driver = new CanonDriver();
if (driver instanceof Printable)    // evaluates to true
```

The interface supports inheritance. An interface can extend another interface. If interface **A** extends interface **B**, **A** is said to be a subinterface of **B**. **B** is the superinterface of **A**. Because **A** directly extends **B**, **B** is the direct superinterface of **A**. Any interfaces that extend **B** are indirect subinterfaces of **A**. Figure 9.2 shows an interface that extends another interface. Note that the type of the line connecting both interfaces is the same as the one used for extending a class.

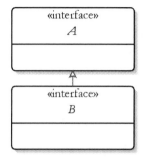

Figure 9.2: Extending an interface

Fields in an Interface

Fields in an interface must be initialized and are implicitly public, static, and final. However, you may redundantly use the modifiers **public**, **static**, and **final**. These lines of code have the same effect.

```
public int STATUS = 1;
int STATUS = 1;
public static final STATUS = 1;
```

Note that by convention field names in an interface are written in upper case.

It is a compile error to have two fields with the same name in an interface. However, an interface might inherit more than one field with the same name from its superinterfaces.

Methods

You declare methods in an interface just as you would in a class. However, methods in an interface do not have a body, they are immediately terminated by a semicolon. All methods are implicitly public and abstract, even though it is legal to have the **public** and **abstract** modifiers in front of a method declaration.

The syntax of a method in an interface is

```
[methodModifiers] ReturnType MethodName(listOfArgument)
        [ThrowClause];
```

where *methodModifiers* is **abstract** and **public**.

In addition, methods in an interface must not be declared static because static methods cannot be abstract.

Base Classes

Some interfaces have many methods, and implementing classes must override all the methods. This can be a tedious task if only some of the methods are actually used in the code. For this reason, you can create a generic implementation class that overrides the methods in the interface with default code. An implementing class then extends the generic class and overrides only methods it wants to change. This kind of generic class, often called a base class, is handy because it helps you code faster.

For example, the **javax.servlet.Servlet** interface is the interface that must be implemented by all servlet classes. This interface has five methods: **init**, **service**, **destroy**, **getServletConfig**, **getServletInfo**. Of the five, only the **service** method is always implemented by servlet classes. The **init** method is implemented occasionally, but the rest are rarely used. Despite the fact, all implementing classes must provide implementation for all five methods. What a chore this would be for servlet programmers.

To make servlet programming easier and more fun, the Servlet API also defines the **javax.servlet.GenericServlet** class, which provides default implementation for all methods in the **Servlet** interface. When you write a servlet, instead of writing a class that implements the **javax.servlet.Servlet** interface (and ending up having to implement five methods), you extend the **javax.servlet.GenericServlet** and provide only implementation for methods you need to use (most probably, only the **service** method).

Compare the **TediousServlet** class in Listing 9.7 that implements **javax.servlet.Servlet** and the one in Listing 9.8 that extends **javax.servlet.GenericServlet**. Which one is simpler?

Listing 9.7: The TediousServlet class

```
package test;
```

```
import java.io.IOException;
import javax.servlet.Servlet;
import javax.servlet.ServletConfig;
import javax.servlet.ServletException;
import javax.servlet.ServletRequest;
import javax.servlet.ServletResponse;

public class TediousServlet implements Servlet {
    public void init(ServletConfig config) throws ServletException {
    }
    public void service(ServletRequest request,
            ServletResponse response)
            throws ServletException, IOException {
        response.getWriter().print("Welcome");
    }
    public void destroy() {
    }
    public String getServletInfo() {
        return null;
    }
    public ServletConfig getServletConfig() {
        return null;
    }
}
```

Listing 9.8: The FunServlet class

```
package test;
import java.io.IOException;
import javax.servlet.GenericServlet;
import javax.servlet.ServletException;
import javax.servlet.ServletRequest;
import javax.servlet.ServletResponse;

public class FunServlet extends GenericServlet {
    public void service(ServletRequest request,
            ServletResponse response)
            throws ServletException, IOException {
        response.getWriter().print("Welcome");
    }
}
```

Note

Servlet programming is discussed in Chapter 25, "Java Web Applications."

Abstract Classes

With the interface, you have to write an implementation class that perform the actual action. If there are many methods in the interface, you risk wasting time overriding methods that you don't use. An abstract class has a similar role to an interface, i.e. provide a contract between a service provider and its clients, but at the same time an abstract class can provide implementation. Methods that must be explicitly overridden can be declared abstract. You still need to create an implementation class because you cannot instantiate an abstract class, but you don't need to override methods you don't want to use or change.

You create an abstract class by using the **abstract** modifier in the class declaration. To make an abstract method, use the **abstract** modifier in front of the method declaration. Listing 9.9 shows the **DefaultPrinter** abstract class as an example.

Listing 9.9: The DefaultPrinter class

```
package com.brainysoftware.jdk5.app09;
public abstract class DefaultPrinter {
    public String toString() {
        return "Use this to print documents.";
    }
    public abstract void print(Object document);
}
```

There are two methods in the **DefaultPrinter** abstract class, **toString** and **print**. The **toString** method has an implementation, so you do not need to override this method in an implementation class, unless you want to change its return value. The **print** method is declared abstract and does not have a body. Listing 9.10 presents the **MyPrinterClass** class that is the implementation class of **DefaultPrinter**.

Listing 9.10: An implementation of DefaultPrinter

```
package com.brainysoftware.jdk5.app09;
public class MyPrinter extends DefaultPrinter {
    public void print(Object document) {
        System.out.println("Printing document");
        // some code here
    }
```

}

A concrete implementation class such as **MyPrinter** must override all abstract methods. Otherwise, it itself must be declared abstract.

Declaring a class abstract is a way to tell the class user that you want them to extend the class. You can still declare a class abstract even if it does not have an abstract method.

In UML class diagrams, an abstract class looks similar to a concrete class, except that the name is italicized. Figure 9.3 shows an abstract class.

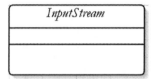

Figure 9.3: An abstract class

Summary

The interface plays an important role in Java because it defines a contract between a service provider and its clients. This chapter showed you how to use the interface. A base class provides a generic implementation of an interface and expedites program development by providing default implementation of code.

An abstract class is like an interface, but it may provide implementation of some of its methods.

Questions

1. Why is it more appropriate to regard an interface as a contract than as a implementationless class?
2. What is a base class?
3. What is an abstract class?
4. Is a base class the same as an abstract class?

Chapter 10
Enums

In Chapter 2, "Language Fundamentals," you have seen that you sometimes use static final fields as enumerated values. Java 5 adds a new type, enum, for enumerating values. This chapter presents a complete discussion of enum.

An Overview of Enum

You use enum to create a set of valid values for a field or a method. For example, in a typical application, the only possible values for the **customerType** are **Individual** or **Organization**. For the **State** field, valid values may be all the states in the US plus Canadian provinces, and some others. With **enum**, you can easily restrict your program to take only one of the valid values.

An enum type can stand alone or can be part of a class. You make it stand alone if it needs to be referenced from multiple places in your application. If it is only used from inside a class, enum is better made part of the class.

For example, suppose you have the **CustomerType** enum definition in Listing 10.1.

Listing 10.1: The CustomerType enum

```
package com.brainysoftware.jdk5.app10;
public enum CustomerType {
    INDIVIDUAL,
    ORGANIZATION
}
```

The **CustomerType** enum has two enumerated values: **INDIVIDUAL** and **ORGANIZATION**. Enum values are case sensitive and by convention are capitalized. Two enum values are separated by a comma and values can be written on a single line or multiple lines. The enum in Listing 10.1 is written in multiple lines to improve readability.

Having an enum is like having another type. For example, the **Customer** class in Listing 10.2 has three fields, one of which (the **customerField**) is of type **CustomerType**.

Listing 10.2: The Customer class that uses CustomerType

```
package com.brainysoftware.jdk5.app10;
public class Customer {
    public String customerName;
    public CustomerType customerType;
    public String address;
}
```

You can use a value in an enum just like you would a class's static member. For example, this code illustrates the use of **CustomerType**.

```
Customer customer = new Customer();
customer.customerType = CustomerType.INDIVIDUAL;
```

Notice how the **customerType** field of the **Customer** object is assigned the enumerated value **INDIVIDUAL** of the **CustomerType** enum? Because the **customerType** field is of type **CustomerType**, it can only be assigned a value of the **CustomerType** enum.

The use of enum at the first glance is no difference than the use of static finals. However, there are some basic differences between enums and classes incorporating static finals.

Static finals are not a perfect solution for something that should accept only predefined values. For example, consider the **CustomerTypeStaticFinals** class in Listing 10.3.

Listing 10.3: Using static finals

```
package com.brainysoftware.jdk5.app10;
public class CustomerTypeStaticFinals {
    public static final int INDIVIDUAL = 1;
    public static final int ORGANIZATION = 2;
}
```

Suppose you have a class named **OldFashionedCustomer** that resembles the **Customer** class in Listing 10.2, but uses **int** for its **customerType** field.

The following code creates an instance of **OldFashionedCustomer** and assigns a value to its **customerType** field:

```
OldFashionedCustomer ofCustomer = new OldFashionedCustomer();
ofCustomer.customerType = 5;
```

Notice that there is nothing preventing you from assigning any value of integer, including those that are not valid. This shows that using static finals does not restrict the value of the **customerType** field. In guaranteeing that a variable is assigned only a valid value, enums are better than static finals.

Another difference is that an enumerated value is an object. Therefore, it behaves like an object. For example, you can use it as a **Map** key. The section, "The Enum Class" discusses enums as objects in further details.

Enums in a Class

You can use enums as members of a class. You use this approach if the enum is only used internally inside the class. For example, the **Shape** class in Listing 10.4 defines a **ShapeType** enum.

Listing 10.4: Using an enum as a class member

```
package com.brainysoftware.jdk5.app10;
public class Shape {
    private enum ShapeType {
        RECTANGLE, TRIANGLE, OVAL
    };
    private ShapeType type = ShapeType.RECTANGLE;
    public String toString() {
        if (this.type == ShapeType.RECTANGLE) {
            return "Shape is rectangle";
        }
        if (this.type == ShapeType.TRIANGLE) {
            return "Shape is triangle";
        }
        return "Shape is oval";
    }
}
```

The java.lang.Enum Class

When you define an enum, the compiler creates a class definition that extends the **java.lang.Enum** class. This class is a direct descendant of **java.lang.Object**. Unlike ordinary classes, however, an enum has the following properties:

- There is no public constructor, making it impossible to instantiate.
- It is implicitly static
- There is only one instance for each enum constant.
- You can call the method values on an enum in order to iterate its enumerated values. See the next section "Iterating Enumerated Values" for more details on this.

Iterating Enumerated Values

You can iterate the values in an enum by using the **for** loop (discussed in Chapter 3, "Statements"). You first need to call the **values** method that returns an array-like object that contains all values in the specified enum. Using the **CustomerType** enum in Listing 10.1, you can use the following code to iterate over it.

```
for (CustomerType customerType : CustomerType.values() ) {
    System.out.println(customerType);
}
```

This prints all values in **CustomerType**, starting from the first value. Here is the result:

```
INDIVIDUAL
ORGANIZATION
```

Switching on Enum

In Java 5 the **switch** statement can also work on enumerated values of an enum. Here is an example using the **CustomerType** enum in Listing 10.1 and the **Customer** class in Listing 10.2:

```
Customer customer = new Customer();
customer.customerType = CustomerType.INDIVIDUAL;

switch (customer.customerType) {
case INDIVIDUAL:
    System.out.println("Customer Type: Individual");
    break;
case ORGANIZATION:
    System.out.println("Customer Type: Organization");
    break;
}
```

Note that you must *not* prefix each case with the enum type. The following
would raise a compile error:

```
case CustomerType.INDIVIDUAL:
    //
case CustomerType.ORGANIZATION:
    //
```

Summary

Java 5 supports a new type: enum. It is a special class that is a subclass of
java.lang.Enum. Enum is preferred over static finals because it is more
secure. You can switch on an enum and iterate its values by using the **values**
method in an enhanced **for** loop.

Questions

1. How do you write an enum?
2. Why are enums safer than static final fields?

Chapter 11
The Collections Framework

When writing object-oriented programs, we often work with groups of objects, either objects of the same type or of different types. In Chapter 5, "Core Classes" you have learned that arrays can be used to group objects of the same type. Unfortunately, arrays lack the flexibility you need to rapidly develop applications. They cannot be resized and they cannot hold objects of different types. Fortunately, Java comes with a set of interfaces and classes that make working with groups of objects easier: the Collections Framework. This chapter deals with the most important types in the Collections Framework that a Java beginner should know. Most of them are very easy to use and there's no need to provide extensive examples. More attention is paid to the last section of the chapter, "Making Your Objects Comparable and Sortable" where carefully designed examples are given because it is important for every Java programmer to know how to make objects comparable and sortable.

Note on Generics

Discussing the Collections Framework would not be complete without generics. On the other hand, explaining generics without previous knowledge of the Collections Framework would be difficult. Therefore, there needs to be a compromise: The Collections Framework will be explained first in this chapter and will be revisited in Chapter 12, "Generics." Since up to this point no knowledge of generics is assumed, the discussion of the Collections Framework in this chapter will have to use class and method signatures as they appear in pre-5 JDK's, instead of signatures used in Java 5 that imply the presence of generics. As long as you read both this chapter and Chapter 12, you will have up-to date knowledge of both the Collections Framework and generics.

An Overview of the Collections Framework

A collection is an object that groups other objects. Also referred to as a container, a collection provides methods to store, retrieve, and manipulate its elements. Collections help Java programmers easily manage objects.

A Java programmer should be familiar with the most important types in the Collections Framework, all of which are part of the **java.util** package. The relationships between these types are shown in Figure 11.1.

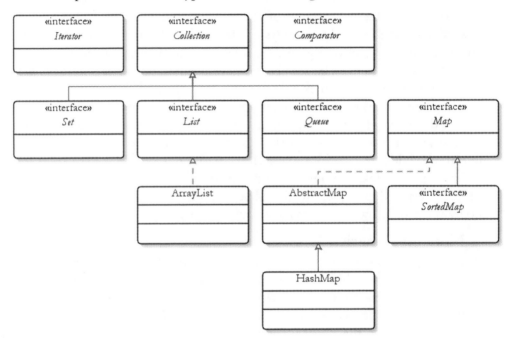

Figure 11.1: The Collections Framework

The main type in the Collections Framework is, unsurprisingly, the **Collection** interface. **Collection** has three main subinterfaces: **List**, **Set**, and **Queue**. In addition, there is the **Map** interface that can be used to store key/value pairs. A subinterface of **Map**, **SortedMap**, guarantees that the keys are in ascending order. Other implementations of **Map** are **AbstractMap** and its concrete implementation **HashMap**. Other interfaces include **Iterator** and **Comparator**. The latter is used to make your objects sortable and comparable.

Most of the interfaces in the Collections Frameworks come with implementation classes. Sometimes there are two versions of an implementation, the synchronized version and the unsynchronized version. For instance, the **java.util.Vector** class and the **ArrayList** class are implementations of the **List** interface. Both **Vector** and **ArrayList** provide similar functionality, however **Vector** is synchronized and **ArrayList** unsynchronized. Synchronized versions of an implementation were included in the first version of the JDK. Only later, Sun added the unsynchronized versions so that programmers could write better performing applications. The unsynchronized versions should thus be in preference to the synchronized ones. If you need to use an unsynchronized implementation in a multi-threaded environment, you can still synchronize it yourself.

Note
Working in a multi-threaded environment in discussed in Chapter 23, "Java Threads."

The Collection Interface

The **Collection** interface is used to group objects together. Unlike arrays that cannot be resized and can only group objects of the same type, collections allow you to add any type of object and do not force you to specify an initial size.

Collection comes with methods that are easy to use. To add an element object, you use the **add** method. To add members of another Collection, use **addAll**. To remove all elements, use **clear**. To inquire about the number of elements of a **Collection**, you call its **size** method. To test if a **Collection** contains an element, use **isEmpty**. And, to move its elements to an array, use **toArray**. As **Collection** does not have a direct concrete implementation in the Collections Framework, we'll learn how to use these methods in the implementations of its subinterfaces, such as **List**, **Set**, and **Queue**.

An important point to note is that **Collection** extends the **Iterable** interface, from which **Collection** inherits the **iterator** method. This method returns an **Iterator** object that you can use to iterate over the collection's elements. Check the section, "Iterable and Iterator" later in this chapter.

In addition, new to Java 5, you can use the **for** statement to iterate a **Collection** object's elements.

List and ArrayList

List is the most popular subinterface of **Collection**, and **ArrayList** is the most commonly used implementation of **List**. Also known as a sequence, a **List** is an ordered collection. You can access its elements by using indices and you can insert an element into an exact location. Index 0 of a **List** references the first element, index 1 the second element, and so on.

The **add** method inherited from **Collection** appends the specified element to the end of the list. It has the following signature.

```
public boolean add(java.lang.Object element)
```

This method returns **true** if the addition is successful. Otherwise, it returns **false**. Some implementations of **List**, such as **ArrayList**, allow you to add null, some don't.

List adds another **add** method with the following signature:

```
public void add(int index, java.lang.Object element)
```

With this **add**, you can insert an element at any position.

In addition, you can replace and remove an element by using the **set** and **remove** methods, respectively.

```
public java.lang.Object set(int index, java.lang.Object element)
public java.lang.Object remove(int index)
```

The **set** method replaces the element at the position specified by *index* with *element* and returns the reference to the element inserted. The **remove** method removes the element at the specified position and returns the reference to the removed element.

To create a **List**, you normally assign an **ArrayList** object to a **List** reference variable.

```
List myList = new ArrayList();
```

The no-argument constructor of **ArrayList** creates an **ArrayList** object with an initial capacity of ten elements. The size will grow automatically as you add more elements than its capacity. If you know the number of elements in your **ArrayList** will be more than its capacity, you can use the second constructor:

```
public ArrayList(int initialCapacity)
```

This will result in a slightly faster **ArrayList** because the instance does not have to grow in capacity.

List allows you to store duplicate elements in the sense that two or more references referencing the same object can be stored. Listing 11.1 demonstrates the use of **List**, **ArrayList**, and some of their methods.

Listing 11.1: Using List

```
package com.brainysoftware.jdk5.app11;
import java.util.ArrayList;
import java.util.List;

public class ListTest {
    public static void main(String[] args) {
        List myList = new ArrayList();
        String s1 = "Hello";
        String s2 = "Hello";
        myList.add(100);
        myList.add(s1);
        myList.add(s2);
        myList.add(s1);
        myList.add(1);
        myList.add(2, "World");
        myList.set(3, "Yes");
        myList.add(null);
        System.out.println("Size: " + myList.size());
        for (Object object : myList) {
            System.out.println(object);
        }
    }
}
```

When run, here is the result on the console.

```
Size: 6
100
Hello
World
```

```
Yes
Hello
1
null
```

List also adds methods to search the collection, **indexOf** and **lastIndexOf**:

```
public int indexOf(java.lang.Object obj)
public int lastIndexOf(java.lang.Object obj)
```

indexOf compares the *obj* argument with its elements by using the **equals** method starting from the first element, and returns the index of the first match. **lastIndexOf** does the same thing but comparison is done from the last element to the first. Both **indexOf** and **lastIndexOf** return -1 if no match was found.

Note
List allows duplicate elements. By contrast, **Set** does not.

Iterating Over a Collection with Iterator and for

When programming with **Collection**, iterating over it is one of the most common tasks around. There are two ways to do this: by using **Iterator** and by using **for**.

Recall that **Collection** extends **Iterable**. **Iterable** has one method: **iterator**. This method returns a **java.util.Iterator** that you can use to iterate over the **Collection**. The **Iterator** interface has the following methods:

- **hasNext**. **Iterator** employs a kind of pointer that initially points to a place before the first element. **hasNext** returns **true** if there are more element(s) after the pointer. Calling **next** moves this pointer to the next element. Calling **next** for the first time on an **Iterator** causes its pointer to point to the first element. Of course, because the pointer is only a concept, there is no way you can obtain a reference to it.
- **next**. Moves the internal pointer to the next element and returns the element. Invoking **next** after the last element is returned throws a **java.util.NoSuchElementException**. Therefore, it is safest to call **hasNext** before invoking **next** to test if there is a next element.
- **remove**. Removes the element pointed by the internal pointer.

A common way to iterate over a **Collection** using an **Iterator** is either by employing **while** or **for**. Suppose **myList** is an **ArrayList** that you want to iterate over. The following snippet uses the **while** statement to iterate over it. For each element returned, the code prints it to the console.

```
Iterator iterator = myList.iterator();
while (iterator.hasNext()) {
    String element = (String) iterator.next();
    System.out.println(element);
}
```

This is identical to:

```
for (Iterator iterator = myList.iterator(); iterator.hasNext(); ) {
    String element = (String) iterator.next();
    System.out.println(element);
}
```

The **for** statement in JDK 5 has been enhanced. It can iterate over a **Collection** without the need to call the **iterator** method. The syntax is

```
for (Type identifier : expression) {
    statement(s)
}
```

In which *expression* must be an **Iterable**. Since **Collection** extends **Iterable**, you can use enhanced **for** to iterate over any **Collection**. For example, this code shows how to use **for**.

```
for (Object object : myList) {
    System.out.println(object);
}
```

Using **for** to iterate over a collection is a shortcut for using **Iterator**. In fact, the code that uses enhanced **for** above is translated into the following by the compiler.

```
for (Iterator iterator = myList.iterator(); iterator.hasNext(); ) {
    String element = (String) iterator.next();
    System.out.println(element);
}
```

Set and HashSet

A **Set** represents a mathematical set. It is a **Collection** that, unlike **List**, does not allow duplicates. There must not be two elements of a **Set**, say **e1** and **e2**, such that **e1.equals(e2)**. The **add** method of **Set** returns **false** if you try to add a duplicate element. For example, this code prints "addition failed."

```
Set set = new HashSet();
set.add("Hello");
if (set.add("Hello")) {
    System.out.println("addition successful");
} else {
    System.out.println("addition failed");
}
```

The first time you called **add**, the string "Hello" was added. The second time around it failed because adding another "Hello" would result in duplicates in the **Set**.

Some implementations of **Set** allow at most one null element. Some do not allow nulls. For instance, **HashSet**, the most popular implementation of **Set**, allows at most one null element. When using **HashSet**, be warned that there is no guarantee the order of elements will remain unchanged. **HashSet** should be your first choice of **Set** because it is faster than other implementations of **Set**, **TreeSet** and **LinkedHashSet**.

Queue and LinkedList

Queue extends **Collection** by adding methods that support the ordering of elements in a first-in-first-out (FIFO) basis. FIFO means that the element first added will be the first you get when retrieving elements. This is in contrast to a **List** in which you can choose which element to retrieve by passing an index to its **get** method.

Queue adds the following methods.

- **offer**. This method inserts an element just like the **add** method. However, **offer** should be used if adding an element may fail. This method returns **false** upon failing to add an element and does not throw an exception. On the other hand, a failed insertion with **add** throws an exception.

- **remove**. Removes and returns the element at the head of the **Queue**. If the **Queue** is empty, it returns a **java.util.NoSuchElementException**.
- **poll**. This method is like the **remove** method. However, if the **Queue** is empty it returns null and does not throw an exception.
- **element**. Returns but does not remove the head of the **Queue**. If the **Queue** is empty, throws a **java.util.NoSuchElementException**.
- **peek**. Also returns but does not remove the head of the **Queue**. However, **peek** returns null if the **Queue** is empty, instead of throwing an exception.

When you call the **add** or **offer** methods on a **Queue**, the element is always added at the tail of the **Queue**. To retrieve an element, you can use the **remove** or **poll** methods. **remove** and **poll** always remove and return the element at the head of the **Queue**.

For example, the following code creates a **LinkedList** (an implementation of **Queue**) to show the FIFO nature of **Queue**.

```
Queue queue = new LinkedList();
queue.add("one");
queue.add("two");
queue.add("three");
System.out.println(queue.remove());
System.out.println(queue.remove());
System.out.println(queue.remove());
```

The code produces this result:

```
one
two
three
```

This demonstrates that **remove** always removes the element at the head of the **Queue**. In other words, you cannot remove "three" (the third element added to the **Queue**) before removing "one" and "two."

Note
The **java.util.Stack** class is a **Collection** that behaves in a last-in-first-out (LIFO) manner.

Collection Conversion

Implementations of the **Collection** interface normally have a constructor that accepts a **Collection** object. This enables you to convert a **Collection** to a different type of **Collection**, such as a **Queue** to a **List**, or a **List** to a **Set**, etc. Here are the constructors of some implementations:

```
public ArrayList(Collection c)
public HashSet(Collection c)
public LinkedList(Collection c)
```

As an example, the following code converts a **Queue** to a **List**.

```
Queue queue = new LinkedList();
queue.add("Hello");
queue.add("World");
List list = new ArrayList(queue);
```

And this converts a **List** to a **Set**.

```
List myList = new ArrayList();
myList.add("Hello");
myList.add("World");
myList.add("World");
Set set = new HashSet(myList);
```

The **List myList** has three elements, two of which are duplicates. Since **Set** does not allow duplicate elements, only one of the duplicates will be accepted. The resulting **Set** in the above code will only have two elements.

Map and HashMap

A **Map** is a storage that hold key to value mappings. There cannot be duplicate keys in a **Map** and each key maps to at most one value.

To add a key/value pair to a **Map**, you use the **put** method. Its signature is as follows:

```
public void put(java.lang.Object key, java.lang.Object value)
```

Note that both the key and the value must not be a primitive. However, the following code that passes primitives to both the key and the value is legal because boxing is performed before the **put** method is invoked.

```
map.put(1, 3000);
```

Alternatively, you can use **putAll** and pass a **Map**.

```
public void putAll(Map map)
```

You can remove a mapping by passing the key to the **remove** method.

```
public void remove(java.lang.Object key)
```

To remove all mappings, use **clear**. And, to know the number of mappings, use the **size** method. In addition, **isEmpty** returns **true** if the size is zero.

To obtain a value, you can pass a key to the **get** method:

```
public java.lang.Object get(java.lang.Object key)
```

In addition to the methods discussed so far, there are three no-argument methods that provide a view to a **Map**.

- **keySet**. Returns a **Set** containing all keys in the **Map**.
- **values**. Returns a **Collection** containing all values in the **Map**.
- **entrySet**. Returns a **Set** containing **Map.Entry** objects, each of which represents a key/value pair. The **Map.Entry** interface provides the **getKey** method that returns the key part and the **getValue** method that returns the value.

There are several implementations of **Map** in the **java.util** package. The most commonly used are **HashMap** and **Hashtable**. **HashMap** is unsynchronized and **Hashtable** is synchronized. Therefore, **HashMap** is the faster one between the two.

The following code demonstrates the use of **Map** and **HashMap**.

```
Map map = new HashMap();
map.put("1", "one");
map.put("2", "two");

System.out.println(map.size()); //print 2
System.out.println(map.get("1")); //print "one"

Set keys = map.keySet();
```

```
// print the keys
for (Object object : keys) {
    System.out.println(object);
}
```

Making Your Objects Comparable and Sortable

In real life, objects are comparable. Dad's car is more expensive than Mom's, this dictionary is thicker than those books, Granny is older than Auntie Mollie (well, yeah, living objects too are comparable), and so forth. In writing object-oriented programs, there are often needs to compare instances of the same class. And, once instances are comparable, they can be sorted. As an example, given two **Employee** objects, you may want to know which one has stayed in the organization longer. Or, in a search method for **Person** instances whose first name is Larry, you may want to display search results sorted by age in a descending or ascending order. You can make objects comparable by implementing the **java.lang.Comparable** and **java.util.Comparator** interfaces. We'll see how to use these interfaces in the following sections.

Using java.lang.Comparable

The **java.util.Arrays** class provides the static method **sort** that can sort any array of objects. Here is the signature.

```
public static void sort(java.lang.Object[] a)
```

Because all Java classes derive from **java.lang.Object**, all Java objects are a type of **java.lang.Object**. This means you can pass an array of any objects to the **sort** method.

However, how does the **sort** method know how to sort arbitrary objects? It's easy to sort numbers or strings, but how do you sort an array of **Elephant** objects, for example?

First, check the **Elephant** class in Listing 11.2.

Listing 11.2: The Elephant class

```
public class Elephant {
    public float weight;
    public int age;
```

```
    public float tuskLength; // in centimeters
}
```

Since you are the author of the **Elephant** class, you get to decide how you want **Elephant** objects to be sorted. Let's say that you want to sort them by their weights and ages. Now, how do you tell **Arrays.sort** of your decision?

Arrays.sort has defined a contract between itself and objects that needs its sorting service. The contract takes the form of the **java.lang.Comparable** interface. (See Listing 11.3)

Listing 11.3: The java.lang.Comparable method

```
package java.lang;
public interface Comparable {
    public int compareTo(Object obj);
}
```

Any class that needs to support sorting by **Arrays.sort** must implement the **Comparable** interface. In Listing 11.3, the argument *obj* in the **compareTo** method refers to the object being compared with this object. The code implementation for this method in the implementing class must return a positive number if this object is greater than the argument object, zero if both are equal, and a negative number if this object is less than the argument object.

Listing 11.4 presents the modified **Elephant** class that implements **Comparable**.

Listing 11.4: The Elephant class implementing Comparable

```
package com.brainysoftware.jdk5.app11;
public class Elephant implements Comparable {
    public float weight;
    public int age;
    public float tuskLength;
    public int compareTo(Object obj) {
        Elephant anotherElephant = (Elephant) obj;
        if (this.weight > anotherElephant.weight) {
            return 1;
        } else if (this.weight < anotherElephant.weight) {
            return -1;
        } else {
            // both elephants have the same weight, now
            // compare their age
            return (this.age - anotherElephant.age);
        }
```

```
        }
}
```

Now that our **Elephant** class implements **Comparable**, we can use **Arrays.sort** to sort an array of **Elephant** objects. In doing its job, the **sort** method will treat each **Elephant** object as a **Comparable** object (because **Elephant** implements **Comparable**, an **Elephant** object can be considered a type of **Comparable**) and call the **compareTo** method on the object. The **sort** method does this repeatedly until the position of the **Elephant** objects in the array has been organized correctly by their weights and ages. Listing 11.5 provides a class that tests the **sort** method on **Elephant** objects.

Listing 11.5: Sorting elephants

```
package com.brainysoftware.jdk5.app11;
import java.util.Arrays;

public class ElephantTest {
    public static void main(String[] args) {
        Elephant elephant1 = new Elephant();
        elephant1.weight = 100.12F;
        elephant1.age = 20;
        Elephant elephant2 = new Elephant();
        elephant2.weight = 120.12F;
        elephant2.age = 20;
        Elephant elephant3 = new Elephant();
        elephant3.weight = 100.12F;
        elephant3.age = 25;

        Elephant[] elephants = new Elephant[3];
        elephants[0] = elephant1;
        elephants[1] = elephant2;
        elephants[2] = elephant3;

        System.out.println("Before sorting");
        for (Elephant elephant : elephants) {
            System.out.println(elephant.weight + ":" +
                    elephant.age);
        }
        Arrays.sort(elephants);
        System.out.println("After sorting");
        for (Elephant elephant : elephants) {
            System.out.println(elephant.weight + ":" +
                    elephant.age);
        }
```

```
    }
}
```

If you run the **ElephantTest** class, you'll get the following on your console.

```
Before sorting
100.12:20
120.12:20
100.12:25
After sorting
100.12:20
100.12:25
120.12:20
```

Classes such as **java.lang.String**, **java.util.Date**, and primitive wrapper classes all implement **java.lang.Comparable**.

Using Comparable and Comparator

Implementing **java.lang.Comparable** enables you to define one way to compare instances of your class. However, objects sometimes are comparable in more ways. For example, two **Person** objects may need to be compared by age or by last/first name. In cases like this, you need to create a **Comparator** that defines how two objects should be compared. To make objects comparable in two ways, you need two comparators.

To create a comparator, you write a class that implements the **Comparator** interface. You then provide the implementation for its **compare** method. This method has the following signature.

```
public int compare(java.lang.Object o1, java.lang.Object o2)
```

compare returns zero if *o1* and *o2* are equal, a negative integer if *o1* is less than *o2*, and a positive integer if *o1* is greater than *o2*.

As an example, the **Person** class in Listing 11.6 implements **Comparable**. Listings 11.7 and 11.8 present two comparators of **Person** objects (by last name and by first name), and Listing 11.9 offers the class that instantiates the **Person** class and the two comparators.

Listing 11.6: The Person class implementing Comparable.

```
package com.brainysoftware.jdk5.app11;
```

```
public class Person implements Comparable {
    private String firstName;
    private String lastName;
    private int age;
    public String getFirstName() {
        return firstName;
    }
    public void setFirstName(String firstName) {
        this.firstName = firstName;
    }
    public String getLastName() {
        return lastName;
    }
    public void setLastName(String lastName) {
        this.lastName = lastName;
    }
    public int getAge() {
        return age;
    }
    public void setAge(int age) {
        this.age = age;
    }
    public int compareTo(Object anotherPerson)
            throws ClassCastException {
        if (!(anotherPerson instanceof Person)) {
            throw new ClassCastException(
                    "A Person object expected.");
        }
        int anotherPersonAge = ((Person) anotherPerson).getAge();
        return this.age - anotherPersonAge;
    }
}
```

Listing 11.7: The LastNameComparator class

```
package com.brainysoftware.jdk5.app11;
import java.util.Comparator;

public class LastNameComparator implements Comparator {
    public int compare(Object person, Object anotherPerson) {
        String lastName1 = ((Person)
        person).getLastName().toUpperCase();
        String firstName1 = ((Person)
        person).getFirstName().toUpperCase();
        String lastName2 = ((Person)
        anotherPerson).getLastName().toUpperCase();
        String firstName2 = ((Person) anotherPerson).getFirstName()
```

```
            .toUpperCase();
        if (lastName1.equals(lastName2)) {
            return firstName1.compareTo(firstName2);
        } else {
            return lastName1.compareTo(lastName2);
        }
    }
}
```

Listing 11.8: The FirstNameComparator class

```
package com.brainysoftware.jdk5.app11;
import java.util.Comparator;

public class FirstNameComparator implements Comparator {
    public int compare(Object person, Object anotherPerson) {
        String lastName1 = ((Person)
      person).getLastName().toUpperCase();
        String firstName1 = ((Person)
      person).getFirstName().toUpperCase();
        String lastName2 = ((Person)
      anotherPerson).getLastName().toUpperCase();
        String firstName2 = ((Person) anotherPerson).getFirstName()
                .toUpperCase();
        if (firstName1.equals(firstName2)) {
            return lastName1.compareTo(lastName2);
        } else {
            return firstName1.compareTo(firstName2);
        }
    }
}
```

Listing 11.9: The PersonTest class

```
package com.brainysoftware.jdk5.app11;
import java.util.Arrays;

public class PersonTest {
    public static void main(String[] args) {
        Person[] persons = new Person[4];
        persons[0] = new Person();
        persons[0].setFirstName("Elvis");
        persons[0].setLastName("Goodyear");
        persons[0].setAge(56);

        persons[1] = new Person();
        persons[1].setFirstName("Stanley");
```

```java
persons[1].setLastName("Clark");
persons[1].setAge(8);

persons[2] = new Person();
persons[2].setFirstName("Jane");
persons[2].setLastName("Graff");
persons[2].setAge(16);

persons[3] = new Person();
persons[3].setFirstName("Nancy");
persons[3].setLastName("Goodyear");
persons[3].setAge(69);

System.out.println("Natural Order");
for (int i = 0; i < 4; i++) {
    Person person = persons[i];
    String lastName = person.getLastName();
    String firstName = person.getFirstName();
    int age = person.getAge();
    System.out.println(lastName + ", " + firstName +
            ". Age:" + age);
}

Arrays.sort(persons, new LastNameComparator());
System.out.println();
System.out.println("Sorted by last name");
for (int i = 0; i < 4; i++) {
    Person person = persons[i];
    String lastName = person.getLastName();
    String firstName = person.getFirstName();
    int age = person.getAge();
    System.out.println(lastName + ", " + firstName +
            ". Age:" + age);
}

Arrays.sort(persons, new FirstNameComparator());
System.out.println();
System.out.println("Sorted by first name");
for (int i = 0; i < 4; i++) {
    Person person = persons[i];
    String lastName = person.getLastName();
    String firstName = person.getFirstName();
    int age = person.getAge();
    System.out.println(lastName + ", " + firstName +
            ". Age:" + age);
}
```

```
        Arrays.sort(persons);
        System.out.println();
        System.out.println("Sorted by age");
        for (int i = 0; i < 4; i++) {
            Person person = persons[i];
            String lastName = person.getLastName();
            String firstName = person.getFirstName();
            int age = person.getAge();
            System.out.println(lastName + ", " + firstName +
                    ". Age:" + age);
        }
    }
}
```

If you run the **PersonTest** class, you will get the following result.

```
Natural Order
Goodyear, Elvis. Age:56
Clark, Stanley. Age:8
Graff, Jane. Age:16
Goodyear, Nancy. Age:69

Sorted by last name
Clark, Stanley. Age:8
Goodyear, Elvis. Age:56
Goodyear, Nancy. Age:69
Graff, Jane. Age:16

Sorted by first name
Goodyear, Elvis. Age:56
Graff, Jane. Age:16
Goodyear, Nancy. Age:69
Clark, Stanley. Age:8

Sorted by age
Clark, Stanley. Age:8
Graff, Jane. Age:16
Goodyear, Elvis. Age:56
Goodyear, Nancy. Age:69
```

Summary

In this chapter you have learned how to use the core types in the Collections Framework. The main type is the **java.util.Collection** interface, which has three main subinterfaces: **List**, **Set**, and **Queue**. Each subtype comes with several implementations. There are synchronized implementations and there are unsynchronized ones. The latter are usually preferable because they are faster.

There is also the **Map** interface that can store mappings of keys to values. Two main implementations of **Map** are **HashMap** and **Hashtable**. **HashMap** is faster than **Hashtable** because it is unsynchronized.

Lastly, you have also learned the **java.lang.Comparable** and **java.util.Comparator** interfaces. Both are important because they can make your objects comparable and sortable.

Questions

1. Name at least seven types of the Collections Framework.
2. What is the different between **ArrayList** and **Vector**?
3. Why is **Comparator** more powerful than **Comparable**?

Chapter 12
Generics

Generics are the most important feature in Java 5. They enable you to write a type (a class or an interface) and create an instance of it by passing a reference type or reference types. The instance will then be restricted to only working with the type(s). For instance, the **java.util.List** interface has been made generic in Java 5. When creating a **List** object, you pass a Java type to it and produce a **List** instance that can only work with objects of that type. That is, if you pass **java.lang.String**, the **List** instance can only hold **String** objects; if you pass **java.lang.Integer**, the instance can only store **Integer** objects. In addition to parameterized types, you can create parameterized methods too.

The first benefit of generics is stricter type checking at compile time . This is most apparent in the Collections Framework. In addition, generics eliminate most type castings you had to perform when working with the Collections Framework in pre-5 Java releases.

This chapter teaches you how to use and write generic types. It starts with the section "Life without Generics", which reminds us what we missed in earlier versions of JDK's. Then, it presents some examples of generic types. After the discussions of the syntax and the use of generic types with bounds, this chapter concludes with a section that explains how to write generic types.

Life without Generics

All Java classes derive from **java.lang.Object**, which means all Java objects can be cast to **Object**. Because of this, in the JDK's prior to version 5, many methods in the Collections Framework accept an **Object** argument. This way, the collections become general-purpose utility types that can hold objects of any type. This imposes unpleasant consequences.

For example, the **add** method of **List** in pre-5 JDK's accepts an **Object** argument:

```
public boolean add(java.lang.Object element)
```

As a result, you can pass an object of any type to **add**. The use of **Object** is by design. Otherwise, it could only work with a specific type of objects and there would then have to be different **List** types, e.g. **StringList**, **EmployeeList**, **AddressList**, etc.

The use of **Object** in **add** is fine, but consider the **get** method, that returns a member element of a **List** instance. Here is its signature prior to Java 5.

```
public java.lang.Object get(int index)
        throws IndexOutOfBoundsException
```

get returns an **Object**. Here is where the unpleasant consequences start to kick in. Suppose you have stored two **String** objects in a **List**:

```
List stringList1 = new ArrayList();
stringList1.add("Java 5");
stringList1.add("with generics");
```

When retrieving a member from **stringList1**, you get an instance of **java.lang.Object**. In order to work with the original type of the member element, you must first downcast it to **String**.

```
String s1 = (String) stringList1.get(0);
```

With generic types, you can forget about type casting you do when retrieving objects from a **List**. And, there is more. Using the generic **List** interface in Java 5, you can create **List** instances with special purposes. For example, you can create a **List** instance that only accepts **String** objects, another that only accepts **Employee** objects, and so on.

Introducing Generic Types

Like a method, a generic type can accept parameters too. This is why a generic type is often called a parameterized type. Instead of passing primitives or object references in parentheses as with methods, you pass reference types in angle brackets to generic types.

Declaring a generic type is like declaring a non-generic one, except that you use angle brackets to enclose the list of type variables for the generic type.

```
MyType<typeVar1, typeVar2, ...>
```

For example, to declare a **java.util.List** in Java 5, you write

```
List<E> myList;
```

E is called a type variable, namely a variable that will be replaced by a type. The value substituting for a type variable will then be used as the argument type or the return type of a method or methods in the generic type. For the **List** interface, when an instance is created, E will be used as the argument type of **add** and other methods. E will also be used as the return type of **get** and other methods. Here are the signatures of **add** and **get**.

```
public boolean add<E o>
public E get(int index)
```

Note

A generic type that uses a type variable E allows you to pass E when declaring or instantiating the generic type. Additionally, if E is a class, you may also pass a subclass of E; if E is an interface, you may also pass a class that implements E.

If you pass **String** to a declaration of **List**, as in

```
List<String> myList;
```

the **add** method of the **List** instance referenced by **myList** will expect a **String** object as its argument and its **get** method will return a **String**. Because **get** returns a specific type of object, no downcasting is required.

Note

By convention, you use a single uppercase letter for type variable names.

To instantiate a generic type, you pass the same list of parameters as when declaring it. For instance, to create an **ArrayList** that works with **String**, you pass **String** in angle brackets.

```
List<String> myList = new ArrayList<String>();
```

As another example, **java.util.Map** is defined as

```
public interface Map<K, V>
```

K is used to denote the type of map keys and *V* the type of map values. The **put** and **values** methods have the following signatures:

```
public V put(K key, V value)
public Collection<V> values()
```

> ### Note
> A generic type must not be a direct or indirect child class of **java.lang.Throwable** because exceptions are thrown at runtime, and therefore it is not possible to check what type of exception that might be thrown at compile time.

As an example, Listing 12.1 compares **List** in JDK 1.4 and in JDK 5.

Listing 12.1: Working with generic List

```
package com.brainysoftware.jdk5.app12;
import java.util.List;
import java.util.ArrayList;

public class GenericListTest {
    public static void main(String[] args) {
        // in JDK 1.4
        List stringList1 = new ArrayList();
        stringList1.add("Java 5");
        stringList1.add("with generics");
        // cast to java.lang.String
        String s1 = (String) stringList1.get(0);
        System.out.println(s1.toUpperCase());

        // now with generics in JDK 5
        List<String> stringList2 = new ArrayList<String>();
        stringList2.add("Java 5");
        stringList2.add("with generics");
        // no need for type casting
        String s2 = stringList2.get(0);
        System.out.println(s2.toUpperCase());
    }
}
```

In Listing 12.1, **stringList2** is a generic **List**. The declaration **List<String>** tells the compiler that this instance of **List** can only hold **String** objects. Of course, in other occasions, you can create instances of **List** that work with other types of objects. Note, though, that when retrieving member elements of the **List** instance, no downcasting is necessary because its **get** method returns the intended type, namely **String**.

Note
With generic types, type checking is done at compile time.

What's interesting here is the fact that a generic type is itself a type and can be used as a type variable. For example, if you want your **List** to store lists of strings, you can declare the **List** by passing **List<String>** as its type variable, as in

```
List<List<String>> myListOfListsOfStrings;
```

To retrieve the first string from the first list in **myList**, you would use:

```
String s = myListOfListsOfStrings.get(0).get(0);
```

Listing 12.2 presents the **ListOfListsTest** class that demonstrates a **List** (named **listOfLists**) that accepts a **List** of **String** objects.

Listing 12.2: Working with List of Lists

```
package com.brainysoftware.jdk5.app12;
import java.util.ArrayList;
import java.util.List;
public class ListOfListsTest {
    public static void main(String[] args) {
        List<String> listOfStrings = new ArrayList<String>();
        listOfStrings.add("Hello again");
        List<List<String>> listOfLists =
                new ArrayList<List<String>>();
        listOfLists.add(listOfStrings);
        String s = listOfLists.get(0).get(0);
        System.out.println(s); // prints "Hello again"
    }
}
```

Additionally, a generic type can accept more than one type variables. For example, the **java.util.Map** interface has two type variables. The first defines the type of its keys and the second the type of its values. Listing 12.3 presents an example of how to use a generic **Map**.

Listing 12.3: Using the generic Map

```
package com.brainysoftware.jdk5.app12;
import java.util.HashMap;
import java.util.Map;
public class MapTest {
    public static void main(String[] args) {
        Map<String, String> map = new HashMap<String, String>();
        map.put("key1", "value1");
        map.put("key2", "value2");
        String value1 = map.get("key1");
    }
}
```

In Listing 12.3, to retrieve a value indicated by **key1**, you do not need to perform type casting.

Using Generic Types without Type Parameters

Now that the collection types in Java 5 have been made generic, what about legacy codes that used the same types? Fortunately, they will still work in Java 5 because you can use generic types without type parameters. For example, you can still use the **List** interface the old way, as demonstrated by the following part of Listing 12.1.

```
List stringList1 = new ArrayList();
stringList1.add("Java 5");
stringList1.add("with generics");
String s1 = (String) stringList1.get(0);
```

A generic type used without parameters is called a raw type. This means that code written for JDK 1.4 and earlier versions will continue working in Java 5.

One thing to note, though. The Java 5 compiler expects you to use generic types with parameters. Otherwise, the compiler will issue warnings, thinking that you may have forgotten to define type variables with the generic type. For example, compiling the code in Listing 12.1 gave you the following warning because the first **List** was used as a raw type.

```
Note: com/brainysoftware/jdk5/app12/GenericListTest.java uses
    unchecked or unsafe operations.
Note: Recompile with -Xlint:unchecked for details.
```

You have these options at your disposal if you do not want to get warnings when working with raw types:

- compile with the **–source 1.4** flag.
- use the **@SupressWarnings("unchecked")** annotation (See Chapter 18, "Annotations")
- upgrade your code to use **List<Object>**. Instances of **List<Object>** can accept any type of object and behave like a raw type **List**. However, the compiler will not complain.

Warning
Raw types are available for backward compatibility. New development should shun raw types. It is possible that future versions of Java will not allow raw types.

Using the ? Wildcard

I mentioned that if you declare a **List<aType>**, the **List** instance works with instances of *aType* and you can store objects of one of these types:

- an instance of *aType*.
- an instance of a subclass of *aType*, if *aType* is a class
- an instance of a class implementing *aType* if *aType* is an interface.

Note however that a generic type is a Java type by itself, just like **java.lang.String** or **java.io.File**. Passing different lists of type variables to a generic type result in different types. For example, **list1** and **list2** below reference to different types of objects.

```
List<Object> list1 = new ArrayList<Object>();
List<String> list2 = new ArrayList<String>();
```

list1 references a **List** of **java.lang.Object** instances and **list2** references a **List** of **String** objects. Even though **String** is a subclass of **Object**, **List<String>** has nothing to do with **List<Object>**. Therefore, passing a **List<String>** to a method that expects a **List<Object>** will raise a compile time error. Listing 12.4 shows this.

Listing 12.4: AllowedTypeTest.java

```java
package com.brainysoftware.jdk5.app12;
import java.util.ArrayList;
import java.util.List;

public class AllowedTypeTest {
    public static void doIt(List<Object> l) {
    }
    public static void main(String[] args) {
        List<String> myList = new ArrayList<String>();
        // this will generate a compile error
        doIt(myList);
    }
}
```

Listing 12.4 won't compile because you passed the wrong type to the method **doIt**. **doIt** expects an instance of **List<Object>** and you are passing an instance of **List<String>**.

The solution to this problem is the **?** wildcard. **List<?>** means a list of objects of any type. Therefore, the **doIt** method should be changed to:

```java
public static void doIt(List<?> l) {
}
```

There are circumstances where you want to use the wildcard. For example, if you have a **printList** method that prints the members of a **List**, you may want to make it accept a **List** of any type. Otherwise, you would end up writing many overloads of **printList**. Listing 12.5 shows the **printList** method that uses the **?** wildcard.

Listing 12.5: Using the ? wildcard

```java
package com.brainysoftware.jdk5.app12;
import java.util.ArrayList;
import java.util.List;

public class WildCardTest {
    public static void printList(List<?> list) {
        for (Object element : list) {
            System.out.println(element);
        }
    }
    public static void main(String[] args) {
        List<String> list1 = new ArrayList<String>();
```

```
        list1.add("Hello");
        list1.add("World");
        printList(list1);

        List<Integer> list2 = new ArrayList<Integer>();
        list2.add(100);
        list2.add(200);
        printList(list2);
    }
}
```

The code in Listing 12.4 demonstrates that **List<?>** in the **printList** method means a **List** of any type.

Note, however, it is illegal to use the wildcard when declaring or creating a generic type, such as this.

```
List<?> myList = new ArrayList<?>(); // this is illegal
```

If you want to create a **List** that can accept any type of object, use **Object** as the type variable, as in the following line of code:

```
List<Object> myList = new ArrayList<Object>();
```

Using Bounded Wildcards in Methods

In the section "Using the ? Wildcard" above, you learned that passing different type variables to a generic type creates different Java types, despite a parent-child relationship between the type variables. In many cases, you may want a method to accept a **List** of different types. For example, if you have a **getAverage** method that returns the average of numbers in a list, you may want to pass a list of integers or a list of floats or a list of another number type. However, if you write **List<Number>** as the argument type to **getAverage**, you won't be able to pass a **List<Integer>** instance or a **List<Double>** instance because **List<Number>** is a different type from **List<Integer>** or **List<Double>**. You can use **List** as a raw type or use a wildcard, but this is depriving you of type safety checking at compile time because you can also pass a list of anything, such as an instance of **List<String>**. You could use **List<Number>**, but you must always pass a **List<Number>** to the method. This would make your method less useful because you work with

List\<Integer> or **List\<Long>** probably more often than with **List\<Number>**.

Java 5 adds another rule to circumvent this restriction, i.e. by allowing you to define an upper bound of a type variable. This way, you can pass a type or its subtype. In the case of the **getAverage** method, you may be able to pass a **List\<Number>** or a **List** of instances of a **Number** subclass, such as **List\<Integer>** or **List\<Float>**.

The syntax for using an upper bound is as follows:

```
GenericType<? extends upperBoundType>
```

For example, for the **getAverage** method, you would write:

```
List<? extends Number>
```

Listing 12.6 illustrates the use of such a bound.

Listing 12.6: Using a bounded wildcard

```
package com.brainysoftware.jdk5.app12;
import java.util.ArrayList;
import java.util.List;
public class BoundedWildcardTest {
    public static double getAverage(
            List<? extends Number> numberList) {
        double total = 0.0;
        for (Number number : numberList) {
            total += number.doubleValue();
        }
        return total/numberList.size();
    }

    public static void main(String[] args) {
        List<Integer> integerList = new ArrayList<Integer>();
        integerList.add(3);
        integerList.add(30);
        integerList.add(300);
        System.out.println(getAverage(integerList)); // 111.0
        List<Double> doubleList = new ArrayList<Double>();
        doubleList.add(3.0);
        doubleList.add(33.0);
        System.out.println(getAverage(doubleList)); // 18.0
    }
}
```

Thanks to the upper bound, the **getAverage** method in Listing 12.6 allows you to pass a **List<Number>** or a **List** of instances of any subclass of **java.lang.Number**.

Lower Bounds

The **extends** keyword is used to define an upper bound of a type variable. Though useable in very few applications, it is also possible to define a lower bound of a type variable, by using the **super** keyword. For example, using **List<? super Integer>** as the type to a method argument indicates that you can pass a **List<Integer>** or a **List** of objects whose class is a superclass of **java.lang.Integer**.

Writing Generic Types

The previous sections concentrated on using generic types, notably the ones in the Collections Framework. Now it's time to learn to write your own generic types.

Basically, writing a generic type is not much different from writing other types, except for the fact that you declare a list of type variables that you intend to use somewhere in your class. These type variables come in angle brackets after the type name. For example, the **Point** class in Listing 12.7 is a generic class. A **Point** object represents a point in a coordinate system and has the X component (abscissa) and the Y component (ordinate). By making **Point** generic, you can specify the degree of accuracy of a **Point** instance. For example, if a **Point** object needs to be very accurate, you can pass **Double** as the type variable. Otherwise, **Integer** will suffice.

Listing 12.7: The Point generic class

```
package com.brainysoftware.jdk5.app12;
public class Point<T> {
    T x;
    T y;
    public Point(T x, T y) {
        this.x = x;
        this.y = y;
    }
    public T getX() {
        return x;
    }
```

```
    public T getY() {
        return y;
    }
    public void setX(T x) {
        this.x = x;
    }
    public void setY(T y) {
        this.y = y;
    }
}
```

In Listing 12.7, **T** is the type variable for the **Point** class. **T** is used as the return value of both **getX** and **getY** and as the argument type for **setX** and **setY**. In addition, the constructor also accepts two **T** type variables.

Using **Point** is just like using other generic types. For example, the following code creates two **Point** objects, **point1** and **point2**. The former passes **Integer** as the type variable, the latter **Double**.

```
Point<Integer> point1 = new Point<Integer>(4, 2);
point1.setX(7);
Point<Double> point2 = new Point<Double>(1.3, 2.6);
point2.setX(109.91);
```

Summary

Generics enable stricter type checking at compile time. Used especially in the Collections Framework, generics make two contributions. First, they add type checking to collection types at compile time, so that the type of objects that a collection can hold is restricted to the type passed to it.. For example, you can now create an instance of **java.util.List** that hold strings and will not accept **Integer** or other types. Second, generics eliminate the need for type casting when retrieving an element from a collection.

Generic types can be used without type variables, i.e. as raw types. This provision makes it possible to run pre-Java 5 codes with JRE 5. For new applications, you are advised against using raw types as future releases of Java may not support them.

In this chapter you have also learned that passing different type variables to a generic type results in different Java types. This is to say that **List<String>** is a different type from **List<Object>**. Even though **String** is a subclass of **java.lang.Object**, passing a **List<String>** to a method that expects a **List<Object>** generates a compile error. Methods that expect a **List** of anything can use the **?** wildcard. **List<?>** means a **List** of objects of any type.

Finally, you have seen that writing generic types is not that different from writing ordinary Java types. You just need to declare a list of type variables in angle brackets after the type name. You then use these type variables as the types of method return values or as the types of method arguments. By convention, a type variable name consists of a single uppercase letter.

Questions

1. What are the main benefits of generics?
2. What is the meaning of parameterized type?

Chapter 13
Input Output

Input output (IO) is one of the most common operations performed by a program. Examples of IO operations are.

- Create and delete files
- Read from and write to a file or network socket.
- Serialize (or save) objects to persistent storage and retrieve saved objects.

Java provides the **java.io** package that contains types you can use to perform IO operations. Many IO failed operations may throw a **java.io.IOException**. They may also throw a **java.lang.SecurityException** if the failure is related to the lack of permission to perform a certain function.

Learning Java IO programming by iterating the members of **java.io** may not be the best approach, considering there are 12 interfaces, 50 classes, plus 16 exception classes. This chapter therefore presents topics based on functionality and select the most important members of the **java.io** package.

The **java.io.File** class is the first topic in this chapter. It provides methods for creating and deleting files and directories, checking the existence of a file, and so on.

However, the **File** class does not provide functionality to read and write a file's content. For this, you need a stream. Streams, which are discussed in the section "The Concept of Input/Output Streams," act like water pipes that facilitate the transmission of data. There are four types of streams: **InputStream**, **OutputStream**, **Reader**, and **Writer**. For better performance, there are also classes that wrap these streams and buffer the data being read or written. The names of these classes start with **Buffered** and the classes are **BufferedInputStream**, **BufferedOutputStream**, **BufferedReader**, and **BufferedWriter**.

Reading from and writing to a stream dictate that you do so sequentially, which means to read the second unit of data, you must read the first one first. The **java.io** package provides the **RandomAccessFile** for non-sequential operations. This class is the subsequent topic of discussion.

This chapter concludes with object serialization and deserialization, using the **ObjectInputStream** and **ObjectOutputStream** classes.

The File Class

A **File** object represents a file or directory pathname, and not a physical file or a directory. Therefore, the physical file/directory that a **File** object references does not need to exist. The main advantage of **File** is that it provides a system-independent way of representing a pathname. For example, in Unix/Linux you use a forward slash (/) to separate a directory from a subdirectory or a file. The **myNotes.txt** file in the **tmp** directory can be written as **/tmp/myNotes.txt**. Windows, on the other hand, uses a backslash (****). Therefore, **C:\temp\myNotes.txt** specifies the **myNotes.txt** file in **C:\temp**. When writing Java code to manipulate files and directories, it would be tedious if you had to deal with different separators for different operating systems. Fortunately, the **File** class addresses this issue. For one, you can use its **separator** static field that returns a **String** to separate a directory and a subdirectory or a directory from a file. The value of **separator** depends on the operating system. In Unix/Linux, **separator** returns the string "/". In Windows, it returns "\". The **charSeparator** static field is similar to separator, but returns a **char**.

For instance, if you have a path to a directory named **parent** and a file called **filename**, you can join them in a system-independent way by using this code:

```
parent + File.separator + filename
```

The result will be the correct path to the physical file, regardless the operating system your application runs on.

File Constructors

The **File** class provides several constructors. The simplest one has the following signature:

```
public File(java.lang.String pathname)
```

where *pathname* is either an absolute or relative path name. If *pathname* is null, a **java.lang.NullPointerException** is thrown. For example, you can pass an absolute path to a file or directory like this:

```
File file1 = new File("C:\\temp\\myNote.txt"); // in Windows
File file2 = new File("/tmp/myNote.txt");       // in Linux/Unix
```

If passing a relative path name, the path is relative to the directory from which you run your application. For example, if you invoke the **java** program from **C:\workDir**, the variable **file3** below references a file or directory named **music** under **C:\workDir**.

```
File file3 = new File("music");
```

If you have a file located under a certain directory, you could use this constructor to refer to the file, concatenating the directory and the file using **File.separator**:

```
// userSelectedDir is a directory selected by the user at runtime
// and filename is a String containing the name of the file.
File myFile = new File(userSelectedDir + File.separator + filename);
```

However, it is shorter to use the second constructor whose signature is as follows.

```
public File(java.lang.String parent, java.lang.String child)
```

where *parent* is an absolute or relative path to a directory and *child* is the path to a file or a subdirectory. If *child* is an absolute path, then it will be converted into a relative pathname in a system-dependent way. If *parent* is an empty string, then *child* will be converted into an abstract pathname and resolved against a system-dependent default directory.

For example, the following code references a **data** directory under **userSelectedDir**.

```
File myFile = new File(userSelectedDir, data);
```

If *parent* is **null,** it is the same as passing child to the single-argument constructor: **File(*child*).**

The third constructor is similar to the second one, except that the parent is a **File** object instead of a **String:**

```
public File(File parent, String.java.lang child)
```

If *parent* is **null,** it's the same as invoking the single-argument constructor.

The last constructor of **File** accepts a URI.

```
public File(java.net.URI uri)
```

You use this to create a **File** object by converting the given **file:** URI into an abstract pathname.

File Methods

The following are the more important methods of **File.**

```
public boolean canRead()
```
> Tests if the application can read the file referenced by this **File** object.

```
public boolean canWrite()
```
> Tests if the application can write to the file referenced by this **File** object.

```
public boolean createNewFile() throws IOException
```
> Creates a new empty file in the location and using the name denoted by this File object.

```
public boolean delete()
```
> Deletes the file or directory referenced by this **File** object.

```
public boolean makeDir()
```
> Creates the directory named by this **File** object.

```
public boolean isFile()
```
> Tests if this **File** object references a file.

```
public boolean isDirectory()
```
> Tests if this **File** object references a directory.

```
public boolean exists()
```
> Tests if the file or directory denoted by this **File** object exists.

```
public File[] listFiles()
```
If this **File** object denotes a directory, this method returns an array of **File** objects referencing the subdirectories and files in the directory. Otherwise, returns **null**.

The Concept of Input/Output Streams

Java IO streams can be likened to water pipes. Just like water pipes connect city houses to a water reservoir, a Java stream connects Java code to a "data reservoir." In Java terminology, this "data reservoir" is called a sink and could be a file, a network socket, or memory. The good thing about streams is you employ a uniform way to transport data from and to different sinks, hence simplifying your code. You just need to construct the correct stream. For example, if the sink is a file you construct a file stream,.

Depending on the data direction, there are two types of streams, input stream and output stream. You use an input stream to read from a sink and an output stream to write to a sink. Because data can be classified into binary data and characters (human readable data), there are also two types of input streams and two types of output streams. These streams are represented by the following four abstract classes in the **java.io** package.

- **Reader**. A stream to read characters from a sink.
- **Writer**. A stream to write characters to a sink.
- **InputStream**. A stream to read binary data from a sink.
- **OutputStream**. A stream to write binary data to a sink.

As mentioned before, the benefit of streams is they define methods for data reading and writing that can be used regardless the data source or destination. To connect to a particular sink, you simply need to construct the correct implementation class. For example, the **Reader** class defines method for reading characters from a sink. If the sink is a file, you instantiate the **FileReader** class. In a similar token, the **FileWriter** class is the **Writer** class implementation that writes to a file, **FileInputStream** is used to read binary data from a file, and **FileOutputStream** represents a stream to write binary data to a file. A typical sequence of operations when working with a stream is as follows:

1. Create a stream. The resulting object is already open, there is no **open** method to call.
2. Perform reading/writing operations.
3. Close the stream by calling its **close** method.

These classes will be discussed in clear detail in the following sections.

Binary data is anything but human-readable information.

Reading Binary Data

You use an **InputStream** to read binary data from a sink. **InputStream** is an abstract class with a number of implementation classes, as shown in Figure 13.1.

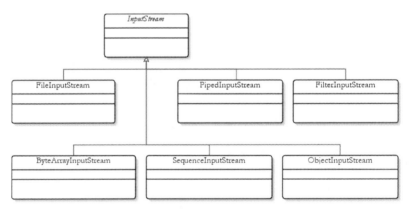

Figure 13.1: The hierarchy of InputStream

This section will discuss two child classes of **InputStream**, **FileInputStream** and **BufferedInputStream**. **FileInputStream** enables easy reading from a file and **BufferedInputStream** provides data buffering that improves performance. The **ObjectInputStream** class is used in object serialization and is discussed in the section, "Object Serialization" later in this chapter.

InputStream

At the core of the **InputStream** class are three **read** method overloads.

```
public int read()
public int read(byte[] data)
public int read(byte[] data, int offset, int length)
```

An **InputStream** employs an internal pointer that points to the starting position of the data to be read. Each of the **read** method overloads returns the number of bytes read or -1 if no data was read into the **InputStream**. This happens when the internal pointer has reached the end of file.

The no-argument **read** method is the easiest to use. It reads the next single byte from this **InputStream** and returns an **int**, which you can then cast to **byte**. Using this method to read a file, you use a **while** block that keeps looping until the **read** method returns -1:

```
int i = inputStream.read();
while (i != -1) {
    byte b = (byte) I;
    // do something with b
}
```

For speedier reading, you should use the second and third **read** method overloads, which require you to pass a byte array. The data will then be stored in this array. The size of array is a matter of compromise. If you assign a big number, the read operation will be faster because more bytes are read each time. However, this means allocating more memory space for the array. In practice, the array size should start from 1000 and up.

What if there are fewer bytes available than the size of the array? The **read** method overloads return the number of bytes read, so you always know which elements of your array contain valid data. For example, if you use an array of 1,000 bytes to read an **InputStream** and there are 1,500 bytes to read, you will need to invoke the **read** method twice. The first invocation gives you 1,000 bytes, the second 500 bytes.

You can choose to read fewer bytes than the array size using the three-argument **read** method overload:

```
public int read(byte[] data, int offset, int length)
```

This method overload reads *length* bytes into the byte array. The value of *offset* determines the position of the first byte read in the array.

In addition to the **read** methods, there are also these methods:

```
public int available() throws IOException
```

This method returns the number of bytes that can be read (or skipped over) without blocking.

```
public long skip(long n) throws IOException
```
Skips over the specified number of bytes from this **InputStream**. The actual number of bytes skipped is returned and this may be smaller than the prescribed number.

```
public void mark(int readLimit)
```
Remember the current position of the internal pointer in this **InputStream**. Calling reset afterwards will return the pointer to the marked position. The *readLimit* argument specifies the number of bytes to be read before the mark position get invalidated.

```
public void reset()
```
Repositions the internal pointer in this **InputStream** to the marked position. Its signature is as follows.

```
public void close()
```
Closes this **InputStream**. You should always call this method when you are done with this **InputStream** to release resources.

You will see an example of **InputStream** in the next section, "The FileInputStream Class."

FileInputStream

The **FileInputStream** class is a subclass of InputStream and allows you to read binary data sequentially from a file. Its constructors allow you to pass either a **File** object or a path to a file. Here are the signatures of the constructors.

```
public FileInputStream(String path)
public FileInputStream(File file)
```

As an example, the code in Listing 13.1 shows the **FileInputStreamTest** class that contains the **compareFiles** method. This method uses **FileInputStream** and methods from the **InputStream** class to compare files.

Listing 13.1: The compareFiles method that uses FileInputStream

```
package com.brainysoftware.jdk5.app13;
import java.io.File;
import java.io.FileInputStream;
```

```java
import java.io.IOException;

public class FileInputStreamTest {
    public boolean compareFiles (String filePath1,
            String filePath2) {
        boolean areFilesIdentical = true;
        File file1 = new File(filePath1);
        File file2 = new File(filePath2);
        if (!file1.exists() || !file2.exists()) {
            System.out.println("One or both files do not exist");
            return false;
        }
        System.out.println("length:" + file1.length());
        if (file1.length()!= file2.length()) {
            System.out.println("lengths not equal");
            return false;
        }
        try {
            FileInputStream fis1 = new FileInputStream(file1);
            FileInputStream fis2 = new FileInputStream(file2);
            int i1 = fis1.read();
            int i2 = fis2.read();
            while (i1 != -1) {
                if (i1 != i2) {
                    areFilesIdentical = false;
                    break;
                }
                i1 = fis1.read();
                i2 = fis2.read();
            }
            fis1.close();
            fis2.close();
        } catch (IOException e) {
            System.out.println("IO exception");
            areFilesIdentical = false;
        }
        return areFilesIdentical;
    }

    public static void main(String[] args) {
        FileInputStreamTest test = new FileInputStreamTest();
        test.compareFiles("c: \\line2.bmp","c: \\line3.bmp");
    }
}
```

The **compareFiles** method returns the **boolean areFiledIdentical**, which is **true** only if the compared files are identical. The brain of the method is this block.

```
int i1 = fis1.read();
int i2 = fis2.read();
while (i1 != -1) {
    if (i1 != i2) {
        areFilesIdentical = false;
        break;
    }
    i1 = fis1.read();
    i2 = fis2.read();
}
```

It reads the next byte from the first **FileInputStream** to **i1** and the second **FileInputStream** to **i2** and compares **i1** with **i2**. It continues reading until **i1** and **i2** are different, in which case it will break from the **while** loop.

BufferedInputStream

For better improvement you should use **BufferedInputStream** to wrap any **InputStream** you are working with. **BufferedInputStream** has two constructors that accept an **InputStream**:

```
public BufferedInputStream(InputStream in)
public BufferedInputStream(InputStream in, int bufferSize)
```

For example, the following code wraps a **FileInputStream** with a **BufferedInputStream**.

```
FileInputStream fis = new FileInputStream(aFile);
BufferedInputStream bis = new BufferedInputStream(fis);
```

Then, instead of calling the methods on *fis*, work with the **BufferedInputStream** *bis*.

Writing Binary Data

The **OutputStream** abstract class represents a stream for writing binary data to a sink. Its child classes are shown in Figure 13.2.

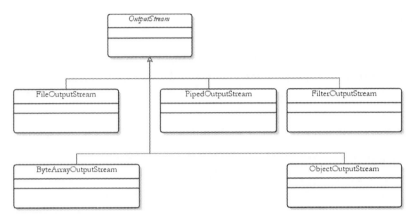

Figure 13.2: The implementation classes of OutputStream

This section discusses two implementation classes: **FileOutputStream** and **BufferedOutputStream**. **FileOutputStream** provides a convenient way to write to a file and **BufferedOutputStream** provides better performance. The **ObjectOutputStream** class plays an important role in object serialization and is discussed in the section, "Object Serialization" later in this chapter.

OutputStream

The OutputStream class defines three **write** method overloads, which are mirrors of the **read** method overloads in **InputStream**:

```
public void write(int b)
public void write(byte[] data)
public void write(byte[] data, int offset, int length)
```

The first overload writes the lowest 8 bits of the integer *b* to this **OutputStream**. The second writes the content of a byte array to this **OutputStream**. The third overload writes *length* bytes of the data starting at offset *offset*.

In addition, there are also the no-argument **close** and **flush** methods. **close** closes the **OutputStream** and **flush** forces any buffered content to be written out to the sink.

We'll look at an example in the next section, "The FileOutputStream Class."

FileOutputStream

The **FileOutputStream** class is a subclass of **OutputStream**. You use **FileOutputStream** to write binary data to a file. The most important thing to note is its constructors. They allow you to construct a **FileOutputStream** object by passing a string containing a path name or a **File** object. You can also specify whether you want to append the output to an existing file.

Here are the signatures of some of its constructors.

```
public FileOutputStream(String path)
public FileOutputStream(String path, boolean append)
public FileOutputStream(File file)
public FileOutputStream(File file, boolean append)
```

With the first and third constructors, if a file by the specified name already exists, the file will be overwritten. To append to an existing file, pass **true** to the second or fourth constructor.

As an example, Listing 13.2 shows the **FileOutputStreamTest** class that contains the **copyFile** method.

Listing 13.2: The FileOutputStreamTest class

```java
package com.brainysoftware.jdk5.app13;
import java.io.File;
import java.io.FileInputStream;
import java.io.FileOutputStream;
import java.io.IOException;

public class FileOutputStreamTest {
    public void copyFiles(String originPath, String destinationPath)
            throws IOException {
        File originFile = new File(originPath);
        File destinationFile = new File(destinationPath);
        if (!originFile.exists() || destinationFile.exists()) {
            throw new IOException(
                    "Origin file must exist and " +
                    "Destination file must not exist");
        }
        try {
            byte[] readData = new byte[1024];
            FileInputStream fis = new FileInputStream(originFile);
            FileOutputStream fos =
                    new FileOutputStream(destinationFile);
            int i = fis.read(readData);
```

```
        while (i != -1) {
            fos.write(readData, 0, i);
            i = fis.read(readData);
        }
        fis.close();
        fos.close();
    } catch (IOException e) {
        throw e;
    }
}

public static void main(String[] args) {
    FileOutputStreamTest test = new FileOutputStreamTest();
    try {
        test.copyFiles("c:\\temp\\line1.bmp",
    "c:\\temp\\line3.bmp");
        System.out.println("Copied Successfully");
    } catch (IOException e) {
    }
}
}
```

This part of the **copyFile** method does the work

```
byte[] readData = new byte[1024];
FileInputStream fis = new FileInputStream(originFile);
FileOutputStream fos = new FileOutputStream(destinationFile);
int i = fis.read(readData);
while (i != -1) {
    fos.write(readData, 0, i);
    i = fis.read(readData);
}
fis.close();
fos.close();
```

The **readData byte** array is used to store the data read from the
FileInputStream. The number of bytes read is assigned to **i**. The code then
calls the write method on the **FileOutputStream** object, passing the byte
array and **i** as the third argument.

```
fos.write(readData, 0, i);
```

BufferedOutputStream

You should always wrap your **OutputStream** with a **BufferedOutputStream** for better performance. The **BufferedOutputStream** class has two constructors that accept an **OutputStream**.

```
public BufferedOutputStream(OutputStream out)
public BufferedOutputStream(OutputStream out, int bufferSize)
```

The first constructor uses the default buffer size, the second lets you decide. For example, you'll get better performance if you wrap a **FileOutputStream** like this:

```
FileOutputStream fos = new FileOutputStream(aFile);
BufferedOutputStream bos = new BufferedOutputStream(fos);
```

Writing Text (Characters)

The abstract class **Writer** defines a stream used for writing characters. Figure 13.3 shows the implementation classes of **Writer**.

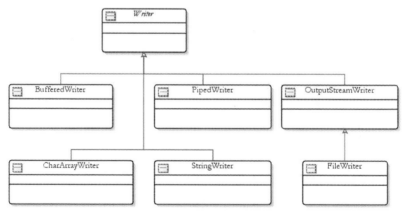

Figure 13.3: The subclasses of Writer

OutputStreamWriter facilitates the translation of characters into byte streams using a given character set. The character set guarantees that any Unicode characters you write to this **OutputStreamWriter** will be translated into the correct byte representation. FileWriter is a child class of **OutputStreamWriter**

that provides a convenient way to write characters to a file. However, **FileWriter** is not without flaws. When using **FileWriter** you are forced to output characters using the computer's encoding, which means characters outside the current character set will not be translated correctly into bytes. A better alternative to **FileWriter** is **PrintWriter**.

This section discusses the **BufferedWriter** class that buffers characters written to this **Writer** for better performance.

Writer

This class is similar to the **OutputStream** class, except that **Writer** deals with characters instead of bytes. Like **OutputStream**, the **Writer** class has three **write** method overloads:

```
public void write(int b)
public void write(char[] text)
public void write(char[] text, int offset, int length)
```

However, when working with text or characters, you ordinarily use strings. Therefore, there are two other overloads of the **write** method that accept a **String** object.

```
public void write(String text)
public void write(String text, int offset, int length)
```

The last **write** method overload allows you to pass a String and write part of the **String** to this **Writer**.

You will learn how to use several implementations of **Writer** in the following subsections.

OutputStreamWriter

An **OutputStreamWriter** is a bridge from character streams to byte streams: Characters written to an **OutputStreamWriter** are encoded into bytes using a specified character set. The latter is an important element of **OutputStreamWriter** because it enables the correct translations of Unicode characters into byte representation.

Note

The **System.getProperty("file.encoding")** method returns the default encoding of your computer.

The **OutputStreamWriter** class has four constructors:

```
public OutputStreamWriter(OutputStream out)
public OutputStreamWriter(OutputStream out,
   java.nio.charset.Charset cs)
public OutputStreamWriter(OutputStream out,
   java.nio.charset.CharsetEncoder enc)
public OutputStreamWriter(OutputStream out, String encoding)
```

All the constructors accept an **OutputStream**, to which bytes resulting from the translation of characters written to this **OutputStreamWriter** will be written. Therefore, if you want to write to a file, you can pass a **FileOutputStream** to the constructor.

The first constructor creates an instance that uses the default encoding, but the others allow you to pass the encoding that will be used when translating character streams into byte streams. The **OutputStreamWriter** class adds the **getEncoding** method that will return the name of the encoding used in this **OutputStreamWriter** as a **String**.

The **java.nio.charset.Charset** class, an argument to the second constructor, is not discussed in this book, so I will show an example that uses the last constructor. This example is given in Listing 13.3..

Listing 13.3: Using OutputStreamWriter

```
package com.brainysoftware.jdk5.app13;
import java.io.File;
import java.io.FileOutputStream;
import java.io.IOException;
import java.io.OutputStreamWriter;

public class OutputStreamWriterTest {
    public static void main(String[] args) {
        try {
            char[] chars = new char[2];
            chars[0] = '\u4F60'; // representing ?
            chars[1] = '\u597D'; // representing ?;
            String encoding = "GB18030";
            File textFile = new File("C:\\temp\\myFile.txt");
            OutputStreamWriter writer = new OutputStreamWriter(
```

```
                new FileOutputStream(textFile), encoding);
        writer.write(chars);
        writer.close();
    } catch (IOException e) {
        System.out.println(e.toString());
    }
    }
}
```

The code in Listing 13.3 creates an **OutputStreamWriter** based on a **FileOutputStream** that writes to **C:\temp\myFile.txt** on Windows. Therefore, if you are using Linux/Unix you need to change the value of **textFile**. The use of an absolute path is intentional since most readers find it easier to find if they want to open the file. The **OutputStreamWriter** uses the GB18030 encoding, the encoding the Chinese government requires all its software suppliers to use in their applications. This encoding defines the character set for Simplified Chinese characters. The use of an encoding other than English is good for showing how encoding works.

The code in Listing 13.3 passes two Chinese characters: 你 (represented by the Unicode 4F60) and 好 (Unicode 597D). 你好 means 'How are you?' in Chinese.

When executed, the **OutputStreamWriterTest** class will create the **myFile.txt** file. It is 4 bytes long. You can open it and see the Chinese characters. For the characters to be displayed correctly, you need to have the Chinese font installed in your computer.

FileWriter

FileWriter provides a convenient way of writing characters to a file. Using **FileWriter** is fine as long as you are not trying to write characters belonging to other character sets. In other words, if your computer's default language is English, writing Korean characters using **FileWriter** will not work. Unfortunately, there is no way you can change the encoding of a **FileWriter**.

FileWriter has constructors that allow you to construct an instance from a **File**, a file path, or a **FileDescriptor**. You also have the option to append to an existing file or to create a new file. Here are the constructors.

```
public FileWriter(File file)
public FileWriter(File file, boolean append)
```

```
public FileWriter(String path)
public FileWriter(String path, boolean append)
public FileWriter(FileDescriptor fileDescriptor)
```

For example, you can construct a **Writer** that writes to a file easily using **FileWriter**:

```
FileWriter writer = new FileWriter("myFile.txt");
writer.write(chars);
```

PrintWriter

PrintWriter is a better alternative to **OutputStreamWriter** and **FileWriter**. Like **OutputStreamWriter**, **PrintWriter** allows you to choose an encoding by passing the encoding information to one of its constructors. Here are some of its constructors:

```
public PrintWriter(File file)
public PrintWriter(File file, String characterSet)
public PrintWriter(String filepath)
public PrintWriter(String filepath, String ccharacterSet)
public PrintWriter(OutputStream out)
public PrintWriter(Writer out)
```

For example, using the first, second, third, and fourth constructors, you can create a **PrintWriter** that writes to a file. The two-argument constructors let you pass the name of the character set to use, so you can write any Unicode characters. In addition, you can construct a **PrintWriter** object by passing an **OutputStream** or another **Writer** object.

Also, it is easier to construct a **PrintWriter** than an **OutputStreamWriter**. For example, the following line of code

```
OutputStreamWriter writer = new OutputStreamWriter(
    new FileOutputStream(filePath), encoding);
```

can be replaced by this shorter one.

```
PrintWriter writer = new PrintWriter(filePath, encoding);
```

PrintWriter is more convenient to work with than **OutputStreamWriter** because the former adds nine **print** method overloads that allow you to output any type of Java primitives and objects. Here are the method overloads:

```
public void print(boolean b)
public void print(char c)
public void print(char[] s)
public void print(double d)
public void print(float f)
public void print(int i)
public void print(long l)
public void print(Object object)
public void print(String string)
```

There are also nine **println** method overloads, which are the same as the **print** method overloads, except that they print a new line character after printing the argument.

In addition, there are two **format** method overloads that enable you to print according to a print format. This method was covered in Chapter 5, "Core Classes."

Listing 13.4 presents an example of **PrintWriter**.

Listing 13.4: Using PrintWriter

```
package com.brainysoftware.jdk5.app13;
import java.io.IOException;
import java.io.PrintWriter;

public class PrintWriterTest {
    public static void main(String[] args) {
        try {
            PrintWriter pw = new
                    PrintWriter("c:\\temp\\printWriterOutput.txt");
            pw.println("PrintWriter is easy to use.");
            pw.println(1234);
            pw.close();
        } catch (IOException e) {
        }
    }
}
```

The nice thing about writing using a **PrinterWriter** is, when you open the resulting file, everything is human-readable. The file created by the preceding example says:

```
PrinterWriter is easy to use.
1234
```

BufferedWriter

Always wrap your Writer with a **BufferedWriter** for better performance. **BufferedWriter** has the following constructors that allow you to pass a **Writer** object.

```
public BufferedWriter(Writer writer)
public BufferedWriter(Writer writer, in bufferSize)
```

The first constructor creates a **BufferedWriter** with the default buffer size (the documentation does not say how big). The second one lets you choose the buffer size.

Therefore, if you are working with a **FileWriter**, you'll get better performance if you wrap it in a **BufferedWriter**:

```
FileWriter fw = new FileWriter(aFile);
BufferedWriter bw = new BufferedWriter(fw);
```

When working with **PrintWriter** (you'll be working mostly with this when you need to output characters to a stream), you cannot wrap it in a similar fashion, such as:

```
PrintWriter pw = new PrintWriter(aFile);
BufferedWriter bw = new BufferedWriter(pw);
```

Because then you would not be able to use the methods of the **PrintWriter**. Instead, wrap the **Writer** that is passed to a **PrintWriter**.

```
FileWriter fw = new FileWriter(aFile);
PrintWriter pw = new PrintWriter(new BufferedWriter(fw));
```

Reading Text (Characters)

You use the Reader class to read text (characters, i.e. human readable data). The hierarchy of this class is shown in Figure 13.4.

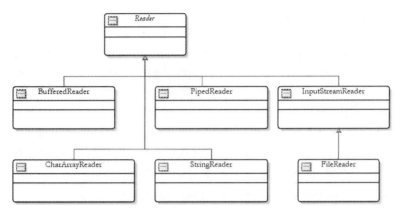

Figure 13.4: Reader and its descendents

This section discusses several child classes of **Reader**.

Note

The two more popular implementation classes of **Reader** are
InputStreamReader and **BufferedReader**.

Reader

Reader is an abstract class that represents an input stream for reading
characters. It is similar to **InputStream** except that **Reader** objects deal with
characters and not bytes. The **Reader** class has three **read** method overloads
that are similar to the **read** methods in **InputStream**:

```
public int read()
public int read(char[] data)
public int read(char[] data, int offset, int length)
```

These method overloads allow you to read a single character or multiple
characters that will be stored in a char array. Additionally, **Reader** has the
fourth read method that enables you to read characters into a
java.nio.CharBuffer.

```
public int read(java.nio.CharBuffer target)
```

In addition, **Reader** provides the following methods that are similar to those
in **InputStream**: **close**, **mark**, **reset**, and **skip**.

InputStreamReader

An **InputStreamReader** reads bytes and translates them into characters using the specified character set. Therefore, **InputStreamReader** is ideal for reading from the output of an **OutputStreamWriter** or a **PrintWriter**. The key is you must know the encoding used when writing the characters to correctly read them back.

The **InputStreamReader** class has four constructors, all of which require you to pass an **InputStream**.

```
public InputStreamReader(InputStream in)
public InputStreamReader(InputStream in,
        java.nio.charset.Charset cs)
public InputStreamReader(InputStream in,
        java.nio.charset.CharsetDecoder, dec)
public InputStreamReader(InputStream in, String charsetName)
```

For instance, to create an **InputStreamReader** that reads from a file, you can pass a **FileInputStream** to its constructor.

```
InputStreamReader reader = new InputStreamReader(
        new FileInputStream(filePath), charSet);
```

Listing 13.5 presents the **InputStreamReaderTest** class that uses a **PrintWriter** to write two Chinese characters and read them back.

Listing 13.5: Using InputStreamReader

```
package com.brainysoftware.jdk5.app13;

import java.io.File;
import java.io.FileInputStream;
import java.io.IOException;
import java.io.InputStreamReader;
import java.io.PrintWriter;

public class InputStreamReaderTest {
    public static void main(String[] args) {
        try {
            char[] chars = new char[2];
            chars[0] = '\u4F60'; // representing ?
            chars[1] = '\u597D'; // representing ?;
            String encoding = "GB18030";
            File textFile = new File("C:\\temp\\myFile.txt");
            PrintWriter writer = new PrintWriter(textFile,
```

```
                    encoding);
        writer.write(chars);
        writer.close();

        // read back
        InputStreamReader reader = new InputStreamReader(
                new FileInputStream(textFile), encoding);
        char[] chars2 = new char[2];
        reader.read(chars2);
        System.out.print(chars2[0]);
        System.out.print(chars2[1]);
        reader.close();
    } catch (IOException e) {
        System.out.println(e.toString());
    }
  }

}
```

FileReader

The **FileReader** class, a subclass of **InputStreamReader**, is a convenient class to read characters from a file. However, like the **FileWriter** class, it lacks the ability to use an encoding other than the default one. **FileWriter** cannot read the characters correctly if the encoding used for writing the file is different than the computer's current encoding.

To construct a **FileReader** object, use one of the following constructors.

```
public FileReader(File file)
public FileReader(FileDescriptor fileDescriptor)
public FileReader(String filePath)
```

BufferedReader

BufferedReader is good for two things:

1. Wraps another **Reader** and provides a buffer that will generally improve performance.
2. Provides a **readLine** method to read a line of text.

The **readLine** method has the following signature:

```
public java.lang.String readLine() throws IOException
```

It returns a line of text from this **Reader** or null if the end of the stream has been reached.

Using **BufferedReader** is very easy. For example, the following lines of code wraps an **InputStreamReader** (which is also a reader) that uses a certain encoding.

```
InputStreamReader inputStreamReader = new InputStreamReader(new
        FileInputStream(textFile), encoding  );
BufferedReader bufferedReader = new
        BufferedReader(inputStreamReader);
```

The resulting **BufferedReader** still supports the encoding of the underlying **InputStreamReader**, but at the same time it supports buffering and provides the **readLine** method.

As another example, the following code reads a text file and displays it line by line.

```
FileReader fr = new FileReader(aFile);
BufferedReader br = new BufferedReader(fr);
String line = br.readLine();
while (line != null) {
    System.out.println(line);
    line = br.readLine();
}
```

Also, prior to Java 5, you used a **BufferedReader** to read user input to the console. Listing 13.6 shows the **getUserInput** method that can take user input on the console.

Listing 13.6: The getUserInput method

```
public static String getUserInput() {
    BufferedReader br = new BufferedReader(
            new InputStreamReader(System.in));
    try {
        return br.readLine();
    } catch (IOException ioe) {
    }
    return null;
}
```

You can do this because **System.in** is of type java.io.InputStream.

Note

Java 5 has the new **java.util.Scanner** class .. that can be used to easily read user input. See Chapter 5, "Core Classes" for more detail.

Logging with PrintStream

By now you must be familiar with the print method of **System.out**. You use it especially for displaying messages and this helps you debug your code. However, by default **System.out** sends the message to the console, and this is not always preferable. For instance, if the amount of data displayed exceeds a certain lines, previous messages are no longer visible. Also, you might want to process the messages further, such as sending the messages via email.

The **PrintStream** class is an indirect subclass of **OutpuStream**. It has seven constructors:

```
public PrintStream(File file)
public PrintStream(File file, String characterSet)
public PrintStream(OutputStream out)
public PrintStream(OutputStream out, boolean autoFlush)
public PrintStream(OutputStream out, boolean autoFlush,
        String encoding)
public PrintStream(String filePath)
public PrintStream(String filePath, String characterSet)
```

You can construct a **PrintStream** by passing a **File**, an **OutputStream**, or a path to a file. Some of its constructors let you choose a character set to use.

PrintStream is very similar to **PrintWriter**. For example, both have nine **print** method overloads. Also, **PrintStream** has the **format** method similar to the **format** method of the String class. See Chapter 5, "Core Classes" for more information.

System.out is of type **java.io.PrintStream**. The **System** object lets you replace the default **PrintStream** by using the **setOut** method. Listing 13.7 presents an example that redirect the output of **System.out** to a file.

Listing 13.7: Redirecting System.out to a file

```
package com.brainysoftware.jdk5.app13;
import java.io.File;
import java.io.IOException;
```

```
import java.io.PrintStream;

public class PrintStreamTest {
    public static void main(String[] args) {
        File file = new File("C:\\temp\\debug.txt");
        try {
            PrintStream ps = new PrintStream(file);
            System.setOut(ps);
        } catch (IOException e) {
        }
        System.out.println("To File");
    }
}
```

Note

You can also replace the default **in** and **out** in the **System** object by using **setIn** and **setErr** methods.

RandomAccessFile

Using a stream to access a file dictates that the file is accessed sequentially, e.g. the first character must be read before the second, etc. Streams are ideal when the data come in a sequential fashion, for example if the medium is a tape (long time ago when the disk had not been invented) or a network socket. Streams are good for most of your applications, however sometimes you need to access a file randomly and using a stream would not be fast enough. For example, you may want to change the 1000th byte of a file without having to read the first 999 bytes. For random access like this, **RandomAccessFile** is ideal to work with.

RandomAccessFile derives directly from **java.lang.Object** and can perform both read and write operations. When opening a file using a **RandomAccessFile**, you can choose whether to open it read-only or read-write. **RandomAccessFile** has two constructors:

```
public RandomAccessFile(File file, String mode)
        throws FileNotFoundException
public RandomAccessFile(String filePath, String mode)
        throws FileNotFoundException
```

The value of **mode** can be one of these:

- "r". Open for reading only.
- "rw". Open for reading and writing. If the file does not already exist, **RandomAccessFile** creates the file.
- "rws". Open for reading and writing and require that every update to the file's content and metadata be written synchronously.
- "rwd". Open for reading and writing and require that every update to the file's content (but not metadata) be written synchronously.

A **RandomAccessFile** employs an internal pointer that points to the next byte to read. When first created, a **RandomAccessFile** points to the first byte. You can change the pointer's position by invoking the **seek** method. Its signature is as follows.

```
public void seek(long position) throws IOException
```

This pointer is zero-based which means the first byte is indicated by index 0. You can pass a number greater than the file size without throwing an exception, but this will not change the size of the file.

In addition to **seek**, the **skipBytes** method moves the pointer by the specified number of bytes. Here is its signature.

```
public int skipBytes(int offset)
```

If skipping *offset* number of bytes would pass the end of file, the internal pointer will only move to as much as the end of file. The **skipBytes** method returns the actual number of bytes skipped.

For reading from a file, **RandomAccessFile** provides a number of methods, each for reading a different data type:

```
public boolean readBoolean() throws IOException
public byte readByte() throws IOException
public char readChar() throws IOException
public double readDouble() throws IOException
public int readInt() throws IOException
public long readLong() throws IOException
public short readShort() throws IOException
```

In addition, **RandomAccessFile** can also behave like a **Reader** because it provides the **readLine** method that reads a line of text:

```
public String readLine()
```

For faster reading, **RandomAccessFile** provides the **readFully** method overloads, that read data to a byte array:

```
public void readFully(byte[] data)
public void readFully(byte[] data, int offset, int length)
```

For writing, **RandomAccessFile** provides methods that mirror the methods for reading, such as **writeBoolean**, **writeByte**, etc. Plus, there are two **write** method overloads to write the content of a byte array:

```
public void write(byte[] data)
public void write(byte[] data, int offset, int length)
```

RandomAccessFile is suitable for accessing a file that has a fixed structure randomly. For instance, you might use **RandomAccessFile** as a simple database to store fixed-length elements of data.

As an example, the code in Listing 13.8 employs **RandomAccessFile** to store **int**s and changes the value of the third **int**. An **int** takes 4 bytes, therefore the fourth **int** is pointed by the index 3-1 * 4 (3-1 because it's zero-based)

Listing 13.8: Using RandomAccessFile

```
package com.brainysoftware.jdk5.app13;

import java.io.IOException;
import java.io.RandomAccessFile;

public class RandomAccessFileTest {
    public static void main(String[] args) {
        try {
            RandomAccessFile raf = new RandomAccessFile(
                    "c:\\temp\\RAFsample.txt", "rw");
            raf.writeInt(10);
            raf.writeInt(43);
            raf.writeInt(88);
            raf.writeInt(455);

            // change the 3rd integer from 88 to 99
            raf.seek((3 - 1) * 4);
            raf.writeInt(99);
            raf.seek(0); // go to the first integer
            int i = raf.readInt();
            while (i != -1) {
                System.out.println(i);
```

```
            i = raf.readInt();
        }
        raf.close();
    } catch (IOException e) {
    }
  }
}
```

Object Serialization

When working with objects, there is sometimes a need to persist objects in memory into permanent storage so that the states of the objects can be retained and later retrieved. Java supports this through object serialization. To serialize objects, i.e. to save objects to permanent storage, you use an **ObjectOutputStream**. To deserialize objects, namely to retrieved saved objects, use **ObjectInputStream**. ObjectOutputStream is a subclass of **OutputStream** and **ObjectInputStream** is derived from **InputStream**.

The **ObjectOutputStream** class has one public constructor:

```
public ObjectOutputStream(OutputStream out)
```

Therefore, to serialize objects to a file, you can pass a **FileOutputStream** to the constructor. Once you have an **ObjectOutputStream**, you can serialize objects or primitives or the combination of both. The **ObjectOutputStream** class provides the **write*XXX*** methods for each individual type, where *XXX* denotes a type. Here is the list of the **write*XXX*** methods.

```
public void writeBoolean(boolean value)
public void writeByte(int value)
public void writeBytes(String value)
public void writeChar(int value)
public void writeChars(String value)
public void writeDouble(double value)
public void writeFloat(float value)
public void writeInt(int value)
public void writeLong(long value)
public void writeShort(short value)
public void writeObject(java.lang.Object value)
```

For objects to be serializable their classes must implement the **java.io.Serializable** interface. This interface has no method and is a marker interface. A marker interface is one that tells the JVM that an instance of an implementing class belongs to a certain type.

If a serialized object contains other objects, the contained objects' classes must also implement **Serializable** for the contained objects to be serializable.

The **ObjectInputStream** class has a public constructor:

```
public ObjectInputStream(InputStream in)
```

Therefore, to deserialize from a file, you can pass a **FileInputStream** to the constructor. The **ObjectInputStream** class has methods that are opposite of the **write**_XXX_ methods in **ObjectOutputStream**. They are as follows:

```
public boolean readBoolean()
public byte readByte()
public char readChar()
public double readDouble()
public float readFloat()
public int readInt()
public long readLong()
public short readShort()
public java.lang.Object readObject()
```

One important thing to note: object serialization is based on a last in first out method. When deserializing multiple primitives/objects, the objects that were serialized first must be deserialized last.

Listing 13.10 shows a class that serializes an **int** and a **Customer** object. Note that the **Customer** class, given in Listing 13.9, implements **Serializable**.

Listing 13.9: The Customer class

```
package com.brainysoftware.jdk5.app13;
import java.io.Serializable;

public class Customer implements Serializable {
    public int id;
    public String name;
    public String address;
    public Customer (int id, String name, String address) {
        this.id = id;
        this.name = name;
        this.address = address;
    }
}
```

Listing 13.10: Object serialization example

```java
package com.brainysoftware.jdk5.app13;
import java.io.FileInputStream;
import java.io.FileNotFoundException;
import java.io.FileOutputStream;
import java.io.IOException;
import java.io.ObjectInputStream;
import java.io.ObjectOutputStream;

public class ObjectSerializationTest {

    public static void main(String[] args) {
        // Serialize
        try {
            Customer customer = new Customer(1, "Joe Blog",
                    "12 West Cost");
            FileOutputStream fos = new FileOutputStream(
                    "c:\\temp\\objectOutput");
            ObjectOutputStream oos = new ObjectOutputStream(fos);
            // write first object
            oos.writeObject(customer);
            // write second object
            oos.writeObject("Customer Info");
            oos.close();
            fos.close();
        } catch (FileNotFoundException e) {
            System.out.print("FileNotFound");
        } catch (IOException e) {
            System.out.print("IOException");
        }

        // Deserialize
        try {
            FileInputStream fis =
                    new FileInputStream("c:\\temp\\objectOutput");
            ObjectInputStream ois = new ObjectInputStream(fis);
            // read first object
            Customer customer2 = (Customer) ois.readObject();
            System.out.println("First Object: ");
            System.out.println(customer2.id);
            System.out.println(customer2.name);
            System.out.println(customer2.address);

            // read second object
            System.out.println();
```

```
        System.out.println("Second object: ");
        String info = (String) ois.readObject();
        System.out.println(info);
        ois.close();
        fis.close();
    } catch (ClassNotFoundException ex) {
        System.out.print("ClassNotFound " + ex.getMessage());
    } catch (IOException ex2) {
        System.out.print("IOException " + ex2.getMessage());
    }
   }
 }
```

Summary

Input output operations are supported through the members of the **java.io** package. You can read and write data through streams and data is classified into binary data and text. In addition, Java support object serialization through the **Serializable** interface and the **ObjectInputStream** and **ObjectOutputStream** classes.

Questions

1. What is a stream?
2. Name four abstract classes that represent streams in the **java.io** package.
3. What is object serialization?
4. What is the requirement for a class to be serializable?

Chapter 14
Nested and Inner Classes

Nested and inner classes are often considered too confusing for beginners. However, they have some merits that make them a proper discussion topic in this book. To name a few, you can hide an implementation completely using a nested class, and it provides a shorter way of writing an event-listener.

One of the reasons nested and inner classes sometimes seem overly complex is because the terms "nested classes" and "inner classes" are often used to mean different things in different texts. This book will stick to the definitions in *The Java Language Specification, Third Edition*, which is the formal specification from Sun Microsystems (http://java.sun.com/docs/books/jls/).

This chapter starts by defining what nested classes and inner classes are and continue by explaining each type of nested classes.

An Overview of Nested Classes

Let's start this chapter by learning the correct definitions of nested and inner classes. A nested class is a class declared within the body of another class or interface. There are two types of nested classes: static inner classes and non-static nested classes. Non-static nested classes are called inner classes. There are several types of inner classes.

There are several types of inner classes:

- member inner classes
- local inner classes
- anonymous inner classes

Before we start our first discussion, let's clarify that the term "top level class" is used to refer to a class that is not defined within another class or interface. In other words, there is no class enclosing a top level class.

A nested class behaves pretty much like an ordinary (top level) class. A nested class can extend another class, implements interfaces, become the parent class of subclasses, etc. Here is an example of a simple nested class called **Nested** that is defined within a top level class named **Outer**.

```
public class Outer {
    class Nested {
    }
}
```

And, though uncommon, it is not impossible to have a nested class inside another nested class, such as this:

```
public class Outer {
    class Nested {
        class Nested2 {
        }
    }
}
```

To a top-level class, a nested class is just like other class members, such as methods and fields. For example, a nested class can have one of the four access modifiers: private, protected, default (package), and public. This is unlike a top level class that can only have either public or default.

Because nested classes are members of the enclosing classes, the behavior of static nested classes and inner classes are not exactly the same. Here are some differences.

- Static nested classes can have static members, inner classes cannot.
- Just like instance methods, inner classes can access static and non-static members of the outer class, including the private members. Static nested classes can only access the static members of the outer class.
- You can create an instance of a static nested class without first creating an instance of its outer class. By contrast, you must first create an instance of the outer class enclosing an inner class before instantiating the inner class itself.

These are the benefits of inner classes:

1. Inner classes can have access to all (including private) members of the enclosing classes.
2. Inner classes help you hide the implementation of a class completely.
2. Inner classes provides a shorter way of writing listeners in Swing and other event-based applications.

Now, let's review each type of static classes.

Static Nested Classes

A static nested class can be created without creating an instance of the outer class. Listing 14.1 shows this.

Listing 14.1: A Static Nested Class

```
package com.brainysoftware.jdk5.app14;
class Outer1 {
    private static int value = 9;
    static class Nested1 {
        int calculate() {
            return value;
        }
    }
}

public class StaticNestedTest1 {
    public static void main(String[] args) {
        Outer1.Nested1 nested = new Outer1.Nested1();
        System.out.println(nested.calculate());
    }
}
```

There are a few things to note about static nested classes:

- You refer to a nested class by using this format:

  ```
  OuterClassName.InnerClassName
  ```

- You do not need to create an instance of the enclosing class to instantiate a static nested class.
- You have access to the outer class static members from inside your static nested class

In addition, if you declare a member in a nested class that has the same name as a member in the enclosing class, the former will shadow the latter. However, you can always reference the member in the enclosing class by using this format.

```
OuterClassName.memberName
```

Note that this will still work although memberName is private. Examine the example in Listing 14.2.

Listing 14.2: Shadowing an outer class's member.

```
package com.brainysoftware.jdk5.app14;
class Outer2 {
    private static int value = 9;
    static class Nested2 {
        int value = 10;
        int calculate() {
            return value;
        }
        int getOuterValue() {
            return Outer2.value;
        }
    }
}

public class StaticNestedTest2 {
    public static void main(String[] args) {
        Outer2.Nested2 nested = new Outer2.Nested2();
        System.out.println(nested.calculate());     // returns 10
        System.out.println(nested.getOuterValue()); // returns 9
    }
}
```

Member Inner Classes

A member inner class is a class whose definition is *directly* enclosed by another class or interface declaration. An instance of a member inner class can only be created if you have a reference to an instance of its outer class. To create an instance of an inner class from within the enclosing class, you call the inner class's constructor, just as you would other ordinary classes. However, to create an instance of an inner class from outside the enclosing class, you use the following syntax:

```
EnclosingClassName.InnerClassName inner =
        enclosingClassObjectReference.new InnerClassName();
```

As usual, from within an inner class, you can use the keyword **this** to reference the current instance (the inner class's instance). To reference the enclosing class's instance you use this syntax.

```
EnclosingClassName.this
```

Listing 14.3 shows how you can create an instance of an inner class.

Listing 14.3: A member inner class

```
package com.brainysoftware.jdk5.app14;
class TopLevel {
    private int value = 9;
    class Inner {
        int calculate() {
            return value;
        }
    }
}

public class MemberInnerTest1 {
    public static void main(String[] args) {
        TopLevel topLevel = new TopLevel ();
        TopLevel.Inner inner = topLevel.new Inner();
        System.out.println(inner.calculate());
    }
}
```

Notice how you create an instance of the inner class in Listing 14.3?

A member inner class can be used to hide an implementation completely, something you cannot do without employing an inner class. The following example shows how you can use a member class to hide an implementation completely.

Listing 14.4: Hiding implementations completely

```
package com.brainysoftware.jdk5.app14;
interface Printer {
    void print(String message);
}
```

```
class PrinterImpl implements Printer {
    public void print(String message) {
        System.out.println(message);
    }
}
class SecretPrinterImpl {
    private class Inner implements Printer {
        public void print(String message) {
            System.out.println("Inner:" + message);
        }
    }
    public Printer getPrinter() {
        return new Inner();
    }
}
public class MemberInnerTest2 {
    public static void main(String[] args) {
        Printer printer = new PrinterImpl();
        printer.print("oh");
        // downcast to PrinterImpl
        PrinterImpl impl = (PrinterImpl) printer;

        Printer hiddenPrinter =
                (new SecretPrinterImpl()).getPrinter();
        hiddenPrinter.print("oh");
        // cannot downcast hiddenPrinter to Outer.Inner
        // because Inner is private
    }
}
```

The **Printer** interface has two implementations. The first is the **PrinterImpl** class, which is a normal class. It implements the **print** method as a public method. The second implementation can be found in **SecretPrinterImpl**. However, rather than implementing the **Printer** interface, the **SecretPrinterImpl** defines a private class called **Inner**, which implements **Printer**. The **getPrinter** method of **SecretPrinterImpl** returns an instance of **Inner**.

What's the difference between **PrinterImpl** and **SecretPrinterImpl**? You can see this from the main method in the test class:

```
Printer printer = new PrinterImpl();
printer.print("Hiding implementation");
// downcast to PrinterImpl
PrinterImpl impl = (PrinterImpl) printer;
```

```
Printer hiddenPrinter = (new SecretPrinterImpl()).getPrinter();
hiddenPrinter.print("Hiding implementation");
// cannot downcast hiddenPrinter to Outer.Inner
// because Inner is private
```

You assign **printer** an instance of **PrinterImpl**, and you can downcast **printer** back to **PrinterImpl**. In the second instance, you assign **Printer** with an instance of **Inner** by calling the **getPrinter** method on **SecretPrinterImpl**. However, there is no way you can downcast **hiddenPrinter** back to **SecretPrinterImpl.Inner** because **Inner** is private and therefore not visible.

Local Inner Classes

A local inner class, or local class for short, is an inner class that by definition is not a member class of any other class (because its declaration is not directly within the declaration of the outer class). Local classes have a name, as opposed to anonymous classes that do not.

A local class can be declared inside any block of code, and its scope is within the block. For example, you can declare a local class within a method, an **if** block, a **while** block, and so on. You want to write a local class if an instance of the class is only used within the scope. For example, Listing 14.4 shows an example of a local class.

Listing 14.4: Local inner class

```
package com.brainysoftware.jdk5.app14;
import java.util.Date;

interface Logger {
    public void log(String message);
}

public class LocalClassTest1 {
    String appStartTime = (new Date()).toString();
    public Logger getLogger() {
        class LoggerImpl implements Logger {
            public void log(String message) {
                System.out.println(appStartTime + " : " + message);
            }
        }
```

```
        return new LoggerImpl();
    }

    public static void main(String[] args) {
        LocalClassTest1 test = new LocalClassTest1();
        Logger logger = test.getLogger();
        logger.log("Local class example");
    }
}
```

The class in Listing 14.4 has a local class named **LoggerImpl** that resides inside the **getLogger** method. The **getLogger** method must return an implementation of the **Logger** interface and this implementation will not be used anywhere else. Therefore, it is a good idea to make an implementation that is local to the **getLogger** method. Note also that the **log** method within the local class has access to the instance field **appStartTime** of the outer class.

However, there is more. Not only does a local class have access to the members of its outer class, it also has access to local variables. However, you can only access final local variables. The compiler will generate a compile error if you try to access a local variable that is not final.

Listing 14.5 modifies the code in Listing 14.4. The **getLogger** method in Listing 14.5 allows you to pass a **String** that will become the prefix of each line logged.

Listing 14.5: PrefixLogger test

```
package com.brainysoftware.jdk5.app14;
import java.util.Date;

interface PrefixLogger {
    public void log(String message);
}

public class LocalClassTest2 {
    public PrefixLogger getLogger(final String prefix) {
        class LoggerImpl implements PrefixLogger {
            public void log(String message) {
                System.out.println(prefix + " : " + message);
            }
        }
        return new LoggerImpl();
    }
```

```
public static void main(String[] args) {
    LocalClassTest2 test = new LocalClassTest2();
    PrefixLogger logger = test.getLogger("DEBUG");
    logger.log("Local class example");
}
}
```

Anonymous Inner Classes

An anonymous inner class does not have a name. A use of this type of nested class is for writing an interface implementation. For example, the **AnonymousInnerClassTest** class in Listing 14.6 creates an anonymous inner class which is an implementation of **Printable**.

Listing 14.6: Using an anonymous inner class

```
interface Printable {
    void print(String message);
}

public class AnonymousInnerClassTest 1{
    public static void main(String[] args) {

        Printable printer = new Printable() {
            public void print(String message) {
                System.out.println(message);
            }
        }; // this is a semicolon

        printer.print("Beach Music");
    }
}
```

The interesting thing here is that you create an anonymous inner class by using the **new** keyword followed by what looks like a class's constructor (in this case **Printable()**). However, note that **Printable** is an interface and does not have a constructor. **Printable()** is followed by the implementation of the **print** method. Also, note that after the closing brace, we use a semicolon to terminate the statement that instantiates the anonymous inner class.

In addition, you can also create an anonymous inner class by extending an abstract class, like demonstrated in Listing 14.7.:

Listing 14.7: Using an anonymous inner class with an abstract class

```
abstract class Printable {
    void print(String message) {
    }
}

public class AnonymousInnerClassTest 1{
    public static void main(String[] args) {
        Printable printer = new Printable() {
            public void print(String message) {
                System.out.println(message);
            }
        }; // this is a semicolon

        printer.print("Beach Music");
    }
}
```

Of course, you can also do this even if **Printable** is not abstract.

Note
Anonymous classes are often used in Swing applications. See Chapter 16, "Swinging Higher" for details.

Behind Nested and Inner Classes

The JVM does not know the notion of nested classes. It is the compiler that works hard to compile an inner class into a top level class incorporating the outer class name and the inner class name as the name, both separated by a dollar sign. That is, the code that employs an inner class called **Inner** that resides inside **Outer** like this

```
public class Outer {
    class Inner {
    }
}
```

will be compiled into two classes: **Outer.class** and **Outer$Inner.class**.

What about anonymous inner classes? For anonymous classes, the compiler takes the liberty of generating a name for them, using numbers. Therefore, you'll see something like **Outer$1.class**, **Outer$2.class**, etc.

When a nested class is instantiated, the instance live as a separate object in the heap. It does not actually live inside the outer class object.

However, with inner class objects, they have an automatic reference to the outer class object as shown. This reference does not exist in an instance of static nested class, because a static nested class does not have access to its outer class's instance members.

How does an inner class object obtain a reference to its outer class object? Again, this happens because the compiler changes the constructor of the inner class a bit when the inner class is compiled, namely it adds an argument to every constructor. This argument is of type the outer class.

For example, a constructor like this:

```
public Inner()
```

is changed to this.

```
public Inner(Outer outer)
```

And, this

```
public Inner(int value)
```

to

```
public Inner(Outer outer, int value)
```

Note

Remember that the compiler has the discretion to change the code it compiles. For example, if a class (top level or nested) does not have a constructor, it adds a no-arg constructor to it.

The code that instantiates an inner class is also modified, with the compiler passing a reference to the outer class object to the inner class constructor. If you code:

```
Outer outer = new Outer();
Outer.Inner inner = outer.new Inner();
```

the compiler changes it to

```
Outer outer = new Outer();
Outer.Inner inner = outer.new Inner(outer);
```

When an inner class is instantiated inside the outer class, of course, the compiler passes the current instance of the outer class object using the keyword **this**.

```
// inside the Outer class
Inner inner = new Inner();
```

becomes

```
// inside the Outer class
Inner inner = new Inner(this);
```

Now, here is another piece of the puzzle. How does a nested class access its outer class's private members? No object is allowed to access another object's private members. Again, the compiler changes your code, creating a method that accesses the private member in the outer class definition. Therefore,

```
class TopLevel {
    private int value = 9;
    class Inner {
        int calculate() {
            return value;
        }
    }
}
```

is changed to two classes like this:

```
class TopLevel {
    private int value = 9;
    TopLevel() {
    }
    // added by the compiler
    static int access$0(TopLevel toplevel) {
        return toplevel.value;
    }
}
class TopLevel$Inner {
    final TopLevel this$0;
    TopLevel$Inner(TopLevel toplevel) {
        super();
        this$0 = toplevel;
    }
    int calculate() {
        // modified by the compiler
```

```
        return TopLevel.access$0(this$0);
    }
}
```

The addition happens in the background so you will not see it in your code. The compiler adds the **access$0** method that returns the private member value so that the inner class can access the private member.

Summary

A nested class is a class whose declaration is within another class. There are four types of nested class:

- Static nested classes
- Member inner classes
- Local inner classes
- Anonymous inner classes

Benefits of using nested classes include hiding the implementation of a class completely and as a shorter way of writing a class whose instance will only live within a certain context.

Questions

1. What is a nested class and what is an inner class?
2. What can you use nested classes for?
3. What is an anonymous class?

Chapter 15
Swing Basics

There are two technologies you use when developing desktop user-interface: the Abstract Window Toolkit (AWT) and Swing. You may have heard that the AWT is an old technology—having been in existence since Java 1.0—that has been replaced by Swing. It is true, but it's not time yet to toss the AWT because it's still useful.

Swing is preferred because it has a better collection of ready-to-use components. Swing components are also much more powerful than their AWT counterparts. For one, some Swing components can render HTML tags, something AWT developers would not even dare to dream about. Nonetheless, the AWT is still relevant because Swing relies on the AWT event handling mechanism and layout managers as well as its various classes; therefore you still need to know about those classes. Moreover, when developing applets (See Chapter 20, "Applets"), your knowledge of AWT will be very helpful too.

Note

Swing itself is part of the Java Foundation Classes (JFC), a collection of features for building graphical user interfaces (GUIs) and adding interactivity to Java applications. The JFC was launched at the 1997 JavaOne conference and also includes the following technologies: the Java 2D API, Drag-and-Drop support, internationalization, pluggable Look-and-Feel support, and the Accessibility API.

There are three things you need to learn to become an effective UI programmers:

- UI components. These include top-level containers (JFrame, JDialog, etc) and components that can be added to a container.
- Layout managers. How to lay out your components in a container.

- Event handling. How to write code that responds to an event, such as a button click, a mouse move, window resize, etc.

This chapter starts with AWT components, which will be only briefly discussed. Following it are sections on simple Swing components, such as **JFrame, JButton, JLabel, JTextArea, JOptionPane,** and **JDialog.** Chapter 16, "Swinging Higher" focuses on layout management and event handling.

Note

The main difference between AWT and Swing lies in how both technologies draw graphic components. AWT calls the native GUI functions of the operating system to do that. This means, programs that use AWT will look different on Windows and on Unix. The term 'peer' is often used when describing this approach. When you invoke an AWT method to draw a button, AWT will in turn delegate the task to a 'peer' native function. However, writing high-quality drawing methods that rely on native functions proves to be difficult because the native operating system does not always have a necessary function that can be used to perform certain functionality. As a result, Sun Microsystems created a new technology called Swing. Swing, on the other hand, draws all its UI components itself, hence eliminating dependence on native peers. With Swing, a GUI program will look the same everywhere, be in on Linux, Mac, or Windows. In older machines, the side-effect of having to draw everything itself is that Swing programs look a little sluggish, because of course it takes more time than if the same graphics were displayed using native functions. However, in today's computers, it is no longer a problem.

AWT Components

AWT components are grouped into the **java.awt** package. At its core is the **Component** class, which is a direct subclass of **java.lang.Object**. This is described in Figure 15.1.

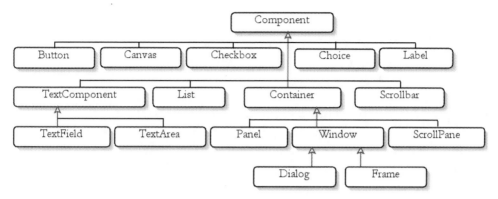

Figure 15.1: AWT components

The **Component** class has subclasses that represent components that you can draw on your UI program:

- **Button**. Represents a clickable button.
- **Canvas**. Represents a blank screen you can draw custom paintings on.
- **Checkbox**. Represents a check box.
- **Choice**. Represents a radio button.
- **Container**. Represents a component that can contain other components.
- **Label**. Represents a non-editable piece of text.
- **List**. Represents a list of options.
- **Scrollbar**. Represents horizontal and vertical scrollbars.
- **TextComponent**. A parent class of two concrete classes: **TextArea** and **TextField**. **TextField** can contain a single line of text and **TextArea** multiple lines of text.

Of special interest is the **Container** class. You can add components to a **Container** using one of its **add** methods. A concrete implementation of **Container** is **Window**, which is the parent of the **Frame** class. Even though you can instantiate **Window**, more often you will use a **Frame** or **Dialog** to contain other components because they have more functionality that make them easier to use than their parent. **Frame** and **Dialog** are similar, except for the fact that **Dialog** is often used to take user input. Almost all AWT applications will have at least one **Frame**.

The **Frame** class has the following methods:

- **setTitle**. Sets the frame's title.
- **add**. Adds an AWT component on to the frame.
- **remove**. Removes an AWT component from the frame.
- **show**. Displays this **Frame**.

In a typical AWT application, you normally start your program by constructing an instance of **Frame**, then add components to it. The code in Listing 15.1 features the **AWTFrameTest** class that adds various AWT components to a **Frame**.

Listing 15.1: Using AWT components

```
package com.brainysoftware.jdk5.app15;
import java.awt.Button;
import java.awt.Checkbox;
import java.awt.FlowLayout;
import java.awt.Frame;
import java.awt.Label;
import java.awt.TextField;

public class AWTFrameTest extends Frame {
    public static void main(String[] args) {
        AWTFrameTest frame = new AWTFrameTest();
        frame.setTitle("My AWT Frame");
        frame.setSize(300, 100);
        frame.setLayout(new FlowLayout());
        // add components
        Label label = new Label("Name");
        frame.add(label);
        TextField textField = new TextField();
        frame.add(textField);
        Button button = new Button("Register");
        frame.add(button);
        Checkbox checkbox = new Checkbox();
        frame.add(checkbox);
        frame.setVisible(true);
    }
}
```

The **AWTFrameTest** class extends the **java.awt.Frame** class. After you create a **Frame** object, you can call its **setTitle** method and pass a **String** for its title. You can also invoke the **setSize** method to set the width and height of the frame in pixels.

The line in bold is a call to the **setLayout** method. You pass a **LayoutManager** object to this method and this object determines how child components added to a frame are laid out. We will discuss **LayoutManager** further in Chapter 16, "Swinging Higher."

You can add components to a frame by using the **add** method of the **Frame** class. In the code in Listing 15.1, we added four components, a **Label**, a **TextField**, a **Checkbox**, and a **Button**. Finally, the **setVisible** method is invoked to make the frame visible.

If you run the **AWTFrameTest** class, you will see something like Figure 15.2. Its actual appearance depends on the operating system the program is running on.

Figure 15.2: An AWT Frame and some components

The frame in Figure 15.2 has a size of 300 by 100 pixels. Its title says "My AWT Frame." There are four components added to it.

Note

The close button (indicated by X) does not close the frame. In fact, making an AWT frame closeable by a single click is not straightforward. This has been remedied in Swing, which is why Swing is better and easier to program.

The GUI application in Figure 15.2 looks good enough for introduction, but there is more that you can do with the AWT library. You can add menu and submenus, you can write code that responds to an event (such as a button click or window resize), you can use a layout manager to lay out your components more properly, and so on. We will not delve into AWT components deeper because we want to focus on Swing. However, Swing also uses the AWT event handling and layout manager, topics that will be in Chapter 16, "Swinging Higher."

Useful AWT Classes

In addition to AWT classes that are parents to Swing components, there are other classes that are often used in Swing applications. These classes are discussed in this section.

java.awt.Color

A **Color** object represents a color. Creating a **Color** object is supereasy because the **Color** class provides static fields that return a specific **Color** object. The names of these fields are the same as the colors they represent. Here are some of the static final fields in the **Color** class: **BLACK, BLUE, GREEN, RED, CYAN, ORANGE, YELLOW**.

For example, to obtain a **Color** object that represents green, use this code:

```
Color color = Color.GREEN;
```

You can also create a custom color by passing red-green-blue (RGB) values to the **Color** class's constructor. For example:

```
Color myColor = new Color (246, 27, 27);
```

To change a component's color, call the **setForeGround** and **setBackGround** methods of the component.

```
component.setForeGround(Color.YELLOW) ;
component.setBackGround(Color.RED);
```

java.awt.Font

A **Font** object represents a font. Here is a constructor of the **Font** class.

```
public Font(java.lang.String name, int style, int size)
```

Here, *name* is the font name (such as "Verdana", "Arial", etc) and *size* is the point size of the font. The *style* argument takes an integer bitmask that may be **PLAIN** or a bitwise union of **BOLD** and/or **ITALIC**.

For example, the following code construct a **Font** object.

```
int style = Font.BOLD | Font.ITALIC;
```

```
Font font = new Font("Garamond", style , 11);
```

java.awt.Point

A **Point** object represents a point in a coordinate system. It has two **int** fields, **x** and **y**. You can construct a **Point** object by using one of its constructors.

```
public Point()
public Point(int x, int y)
public Point(Point anotherPoint)
```

The **Point** class's **getX** and **getY** methods return the value of the **x** and **y** fields in **double**, respectively.

java.awt.Dimension

A **Dimension** object represents a width and a height in **int**. It is meant to represent the dimension of an AWT or Swing component. There are two **int** fields, **width** and **height**. The **getWidth** and **getHeight** methods return a **double**, not an **int**. You can construct a **Dimension** object by using one of its constructors:

```
public Dimension()
public Dimension(Dimension d)
public Dimension(int width, int height)
```

The no-arg constructor create a **Dimension** with a width and a height of zero.

java.awt.Rectangle

A **Rectange** object specifies a rectangular area in the coordinate system. Its **x** and **y** fields specify the top-left corner coordinate. Its **width** and **height** fields specify the width and height of the rectangle, respectively.

Here are some of the constructors of the **Rectangle** class.

```
public Rectangle()
public Rectangle(Dimension d)
public Rectangle(int width, int height)
public Rectangle(int x, int y, int width, int height)
```

A zero value for a field is assumed if the field is missing from a constructor's argument list.

java.awt.Graphics

The **Graphics** class is an abstract class that allows the rendering of AWT and Swing components. You need to work with a **Graphics** object is you want to change the appearance of a component, create a custom component, and so on. To do this, you override a component's **paint** method:

```
public void paint(Graphics graphics)
```

The overridden method receives a **Graphics** object that you can use to paint your component. After you obtain a **Graphics** object, you can call various methods on it to draw on the **Graphics**. Here are some of the methods in the **Graphics** class: **drawArc**, **drawChars**, **drawImage**, **drawLine**, **drawOval**, **drawPolygon**, **drawPolyline**, **drawRect**, **drawString**, **fillArc**, **fillOval**, etc.

java.awt.Toolkit

The **Toolkit** abstract class has the following methods that make it interesting.

```
public static Toolkit getDefaultToolkit()
```
Returns the default implementation of the **Toolkit** class.

```
public abstract void beep()
```
Produces a beep sound.

```
public abstract Dimension getScreenSize()
```
Returns a **java.awt.Dimension** object containing the width and the height of the screen.

Basic Swing Components

Swing is the Java technology used for developing desktop applications that need graphical user interface (GUI), replacing AWT but still using the AWT event model. As a technology, Swing is mature and complete, its rich set of classes and interfaces spanning across 17 packages. Swing components are contained in the **javax.swing** package. Figure 15.3 depicts the class hierarchy of Swing components. All classes whose package is omitted belong to the **javax.swing** package.

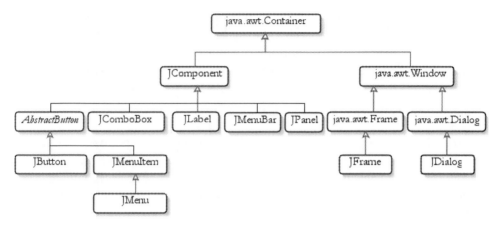

Figure 15.3: Swing components

Except for the three top-level containers **JFrame**, **JDialog**, and **JApplet**, all Swing components must reside in a container. You normally use **JFrame** as the main container of your Swing application. A **JDialog** object represents a dialog, a window used to interact with the user. A **JDialog** is like a **JFrame**, but it normally lives within a **JFrame** or another **JDialog**. There are also other dialogs that are not made from **JDialog**, for example **JOptionPane** and **JColorChooser**. **JApplet** is a subclass of the **java.applet.Applet** class. It allows applet developers to use Swing components on applets. You will learn more about applets in Chapter 20, "Applets." To differentiate Swing components from AWT components, the names of Swing components are normally prefixed with **J**.

Note that the **javax.swing.JFrame** class derives from the **java.awt.Frame** class and other Swing components from **javax.swing.JComponent**, which in turn extends **java.awt.Container**.

The following sections discuss the more important Swing components.

JFrame

A **JFrame** represents a frame container. **JFrame** is one of the three Swing top-level containers (the other two are **JDialog** and **JApplet**). Only top-level containers can appear onscreen without having to be added to another container. Other Swing components must be child components of a container.

Just like **java.awt.Frame**, you can add components to a **JFrame** by calling one of its **add** methods. However, **JFrame** has only one child component, **JRootPane**, that manages a **java.awt.Container** called the content pane. The rule is you can only add non-menu components to this content pane, not to the **JFrame** itself. Therefore, you use this code to add a component:

```
jFrame.getContentPane().add(component)
```

One thing that differentiates **JFrame** in JDK 5 and pre-5 versions is that in JDK 5 you can add a component directly to a **JFrame**. It still has the content pane and you still can only add components to its content pane. However, convenient methods have been added to **JFrame** that reroute calls to the **add** methods in the content pane. In Java 5 the preceding code is still valid, but now you can simply write:

```
jFrame.add(component)
```

And the same holds true for the **remove** and **setLayout** methods.

A Swing component can only be added to one container. Adding a component that is already in a container to another container will automatically remove the component from the first container.

In addition, **JFrame** has the **setDefaultCloseOperation** method that you can call to control what the **JFrame**'s close button does. The **setDefaultCloseOperation** method can take one of these static finals defined in the **JFrame** class:

- **WindowConstants.DO_NOTHING_ON_CLOSE**. Don't do anything.
- **WindowConstants.HIDE_ON_CLOSE** (the default). Hides the frame after invoking any registered **WindowListener** objects.
- **WindowConstants.DISPOSE_ON_CLOSE**. Hides and disposes the frame after invoking any registered WindowListener objects.
- **JFrame.EXIT_ON_CLOSE**. Exits the application using the System.exit method.

Note that the **JFrame** class implements the **javax.swing.WindowConstants** interface, so you can use the static finals above without the name **WindowConstants** from inside a **JFrame**.

As an example, to make a **JFrame** exit when the user clicks the close button, write this:

```
jFrame.setDefaultCloseOperation(JFrame.EXIT_ON_CLOSE)
```

The **JFrame** class has two methods that you call to display a **JFrame** instance, **pack** and **setVisible**.

```
public void pack()
public void setVisible(boolean visible)
```

The **pack** method resizes the **JFrame** to fit the sizes and layout of its child components. After calling **pack**, you would want to invoke **setVisible(true)** to display the **JFrame**. Two alternatives to **pack** are **setSize** and **setBounds**, which will be discussed in the subsection "Resizing and Positioning."

Listing 15.2 presents the **JFrameTest1** class that creates a simple **JFrame** object.

Listing 15.2: The JFrameTest1 class

```
package com.brainysoftware.jdk5.app15;
import javax.swing.JFrame;
import javax.swing.JLabel;
import javax.swing.SwingUtilities;
import javax.swing.UIManager;

public class JFrameTest1 {
    private static void constructGUI() {
        JFrame.setDefaultLookAndFeelDecorated(true);
        JFrame frame = new JFrame();
        frame.setTitle("My First Swing Application");
        frame.setDefaultCloseOperation(JFrame.EXIT_ON_CLOSE);
        // add a JLabel that says Welcome
        JLabel label = new JLabel("Welcome");
        frame.add(label);
        frame.pack();
        frame.setVisible(true);
    }

    public static void main(String[] args) {
        SwingUtilities.invokeLater(new Runnable() {
```

```
        public void run() {
            constructGUI();
        }
    });
    }
}
```

The JFrameTest1 in Listing 15.2 displays a **JFrame** that looks like the screenshot in Figure 15.4.

Figure 15.4: A JFrame

Notice that the window in the **JFrame** consists of two areas, the title bar and the content pane. The window has an icon on the left side of the title bar. There are also three buttons (minimize, restore, close) to the right of the title bar. The content pane is another object that gets created for each **JFrame**.

How does the code in Listing 15.2 work?

First, let's talk about the **main** method.

```
public static void main(String[] args) {
    SwingUtilities.invokeLater(new Runnable() {
        public void run() {
            constructGUI();
        }
    });
}
```

Sun recommends that you call the static **invokeLater** method of the **javax.swing.SwingUtilities** class to make sure that a special thread called the event-dispatching thread will take care of the creation of the GUI. The use of this method makes your code a bit more complex, but this ensures that your Swing applications will be displayed correctly. If you do not understand this part, that's fine. Just make sure that the code in the **main** method become your standard way of creating Swing GUI. Read the Javadoc for the **SwingUtilities** class's **invokeLater** method for more information. See also the sidebar "An Older Style Swing Invocation" that discussed how Java programmers used to show their **JFrame**s.

An Older Style Swing invocation

In older Java books, you'll find that a Swing application can be invoked from the main thread. For example, the following is how the code in Listing 15.2 would be written in older style.

```
package com.brainysoftware.jdk5.app15;
import javax.swing.JFrame;
import javax.swing.JLabel;

public class JFrameTest1 {
    public static void main(String[] args) {
        JFrame frame = new JFrame();
        frame.setTitle("My First Swing Application");
        frame.setDefaultCloseOperation(JFrame.EXIT_ON_CLOSE);
        // add a JLabel that says Welcome
        JLabel label = new JLabel("Welcome");
        frame.add(label);
        frame.pack();
        frame.setVisible(true);
    }
}
```

While the older style works for most Swing applications, for new applications you should follow the way experts at Sun Microsystems recommend, i.e. by using **SwingUtilities.invokeLater** to construct your GUI, as show in Listing 15.2.

The **constructGUI** method constructs a **JFrame** object, and you pass a **String** to its **setTitle** method. You then call the **JFrame**'s **setDefaultCloseOperation** method, passing **JFrame.EXIT_ON_CLOSE**. This line is useful because by default clicking the close button on a **JFrame** does not stop the JVM. Assigning **JFrame.EXIT_ON_CLOSE** to the **setDefaultCloseOperation** method allows you to exit the application when you click the close button.

```
JFrame frame = new JFrame();
frame.setTitle("My First Swing Application");
frame.setDefaultCloseOperation(JFrame.EXIT_ON_CLOSE);
```

The **constructGUI** method then creates a **JLabel** control and adds it to the **JFrame**'s content pane.

```
JLabel label = new JLabel("Welcome");
frame.getContentPane().add(label);
```

Finally, it calls the **pack** method of the **JFrame** to size it to fit the preferred size and layout of its subcomponents. Lastly, it calls the **setVisible** method to make the **JFrame** visible.

```
frame.pack();
frame.setVisible(true);
```

The static **setDefaultLookAndFeelDecorated** method makes your **JFrame** decorated. Without this method, your **JFrame** would look like that in Figure 15.5.

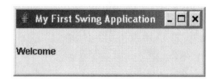

Figure 15.5: An undecorated JFrame

Resizing and Positioning

The **pack** method resizes a **JFrame** to a default width and height. Alternatively, you can resize a **JFrame** by calling the **setSize** and **setBounds** methods. If you choose to do this, **setSize** and **setBound** should be called just before the **setVisible** method. If you call **setSize**, you don't need to call **pack**.

JFrame inherits **setSize** from **java.awt.Component** and this method has two overloads:

```
public void setSize(int width, int height)
public void setSize(java.awt.Dimension d)
```

The **setBounds** method allows you to set the size as well as the new top-left corner of the **JFrame**, relative to the screen's top-left corner. Here is its signature.

```
public void setBounds(int x, int y, int width, int height)
```

JFrame inherits **setBounds** from **java.awt.Window**.

In addition, the **setLocationRelativeTo** method allows you to set your Swing component's location relative to another component.

```
public void setLocationRelativeTo(java.awt.Component component)
```

If the component is not visible or if you pass **null**, your **JFrame** will be display on the screen center.

Listing 15.3 presents another JFrame that is manually resized and positioned at the top-right corner of the screen.

Listing 15.3: Resizing and positioning a JFrame

```java
package com.brainysoftware.jdk5.app15;
import java.awt.Dimension;
import java.awt.GridLayout;
import java.awt.Toolkit;
import javax.swing.JButton;
import javax.swing.JFrame;
import javax.swing.JLabel;
import javax.swing.JTextField;
import javax.swing.SwingUtilities;

public class JFrameTest2 {
    private static void constructGUI() {
        JFrame.setDefaultLookAndFeelDecorated(true);
        JFrame frame = new JFrame();
        frame.setDefaultCloseOperation(JFrame.EXIT_ON_CLOSE);
        frame.setTitle("JFrame Test");
        frame.setLayout(new GridLayout(3, 2));
        frame.add(new JLabel("First Name:"));
        frame.add(new JTextField());
        frame.add(new JLabel("Last Name:"));
        frame.add(new JTextField());
        frame.add(new JButton("Register"));

        int frameWidth = 200;
        int frameHeight = 100;
        Dimension screenSize =
                Toolkit.getDefaultToolkit().getScreenSize();
        frame.setBounds((int) screenSize.getWidth() - frameWidth, 0,
                frameWidth, frameHeight);
        frame.setVisible(true);
    }

    public static void main(String[] args) {
        SwingUtilities.invokeLater(new Runnable() {
```

```
            public void run() {
                constructGUI();
            }
        });
    }
}
```

Running **JFrameTest2** will dislay a **JFrame** like the one in Figure 15.6

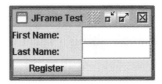

Figure 15.6: A JFrame that has been resized and repositioned.

Extending JFrame

As your Swing applications grow more complex, it is often easier to extend the **JFrame** class and construct your GUI from inside the subclass than from within a static **constructGUI** method. Listing 15.4 rewrites the **JFrameTest2** class to extend **JFrame**. You still construct your GUI using the event-dispatching thread,. however the complexity of constructing your GUI has been moved to a subclass.

Listing 15.4: Extending JFrame

```
package com.brainysoftware.jdk5.app15;
import java.awt.Dimension;
import java.awt.GridLayout;
import java.awt.Toolkit;
import javax.swing.JButton;
import javax.swing.JFrame;
import javax.swing.JLabel;
import javax.swing.JTextField;
import javax.swing.SwingUtilities;

class MyFrame extends JFrame {
    public MyFrame() {
        super();
        init();
    }

    public MyFrame(String title) {
```

```
        super(title);
        init();
    }

    private void init() {
        this.setDefaultCloseOperation(JFrame.EXIT_ON_CLOSE);
        this.setTitle("JFrame Test");
        this.setLayout(new GridLayout(3, 2));
        this.add(new JLabel("First Name:"));
        this.add(new JTextField());
        this.add(new JLabel("Last Name:"));
        this.add(new JTextField());
        this.add(new JButton("Register"));
        int frameWidth = 200;
        int frameHeight = 100;
        Dimension screenSize =
                Toolkit.getDefaultToolkit().getScreenSize();
        this.setBounds((int) screenSize.getWidth() - frameWidth, 0,
                frameWidth, frameHeight);
    }
}

public class JFrameTest3 {
    private static void constructGUI() {
        JFrame.setDefaultLookAndFeelDecorated(true);
        MyFrame frame = new MyFrame();
        frame.setVisible(true);
    }

    public static void main(String[] args) {
        SwingUtilities.invokeLater(new Runnable() {
            public void run() {
                constructGUI();
            }
        });
    }
}
```

When run, the **JFrameTest3** class produces the same result as the
JFrameTest2 class in Listing 15.3.

JComponent

All Swing components derive from the abstract **javax.swing.JComponent** class. The following are the **JComponent** class's methods to manipulate the appearance of the component.

```
public int getWidth()
```
Returns the current width of this component in pixel.

```
public int getHeight()
```
Returns the current height of this component in pixel.

```
public int getX()
```
Returns the current x coordinate of the component's top-left corner.

```
public int getY()
```
Returns the current y coordinate of the component's top-left corner.

```
public java.awt.Graphics getGraphics()
```
Returns this component's **Graphics** object you can draw on. This is useful if you want to change the appearance of a component.

```
public void setBackground(java.awt.Color bg)
```
Sets this component's background color.

```
public void setEnabled(boolean enabled)
```
Sets whether or not this component is enabled.

```
public void setFont(java.awt.Font font)
```
Set the font used to print text on this component.

```
public void setForeground(java.awt.Color fg)
```
Set this component's foreground color.

```
public void setToolTipText(java.lang.String text)
```
Sets the tool tip text.

```
public void setVisible(boolean visible)
```
Sets whether or not this component is visible.

We will discuss other methods as we progress along this chapter.

Icon and ImageIcon

The **javax.swing.Icon** interface is a template for small images used to decorate Swing components. **Icon** is discussed before other Swing components because we often use icons to decorate Swing components. Components that can use an **Icon** object include **JLabel** and **JButton**. The **Icon** interface defines the **getWidth** and **getHeight** methods that return the Icon's width and height (in pixels), respectively.

```
public int getWidth()
public int getHeight()
```

The **javax.swing.ImageIcon** class is an implementation of the **Icon** interface. The easiest constructor to use is the one that accepts a filename.

```
public ImageIcon(java.lang.String filename)
```

The *filename* argument can be a file name or the path to a file. Use a forward slash as a separator of a directory from a subdirectory. Formats supported include GIF, JPEG, and PNG.

Constructing an **Icon** by creating an instance of **ImageIcon** is as easy as this.

```
Icon icon = new ImageIcon("images/logo.gif");
```

You will see examples that create an **Icon** to decorate a Swing component, such as the ones in the sections "JLabel" and "JButton."

JLabel

A **JLabel** represents a label, i.e. a display area for non-editable text. A **JLabel** can display both text and images. It can even render HTML tags so that you can create a **JLabel** that displays multicolors or multiline text. The **javax.swing.JLabel** class has the following constructors.

```
public JLabel()
public JLabel(java.lang.String text)
public JLabel(java.lang.String text, int horizontalAlignment)
public JLabel(Icon image)
public JLabel(Icon image, int horizontalAlignment)
public JLabel(java.lang.String text, Icon icon,
        int horizontalAlignment)
```

The value of *horizontalAlignment* is one of the following:

- **SwingConstants.LEFT**
- **SwingConstants.CENTER**

- **SwingConstants.RIGHT**
- **SwingConstants.LEADING**
- **SwingConstants.TRAILING**

The **JLabel** class has the **setText** method that you can pass a **String** to. It also has the **setFont** method to set the font. Alternatively, if you want to use multifonts or multicolors in a **JLabel**, you can pass HTML tags, as demonstrated in the example in Listing 15.5

Listing 15.5: Using JLabel

```
package com.brainysoftware.jdk5.app15;
import java.awt.Color;
import java.awt.FlowLayout;
import java.awt.Font;
import javax.swing.ImageIcon;
import javax.swing.JFrame;
import javax.swing.JLabel;
import javax.swing.SwingConstants;
import javax.swing.SwingUtilities;

public class JLabelTest extends JFrame {
    private static void constructGUI() {
        JFrame.setDefaultLookAndFeelDecorated(true);
        JFrame frame = new JFrame();
        frame.setTitle("JLabel Test");
        frame.setLayout(new FlowLayout());
        frame.setDefaultCloseOperation(JFrame.EXIT_ON_CLOSE);
        JLabel label1 = new JLabel("First Name");
        label1.setFont(new Font("Courier New", Font.ITALIC, 12));
        label1.setForeground(Color.GRAY);

        JLabel label2 = new JLabel();
        label2.setText("<html>Last Name<br><font face='courier new'"
                + " color=red>(mandatory)</font></html>");
        JLabel label3 = new JLabel();
        label3.setText("<html>Last Name<br><font face=garamond "
                + "color=red>(mandatory)</font></html>");
        ImageIcon imageIcon = new ImageIcon("triangle.jpg");
        JLabel label4 = new JLabel(imageIcon);
        JLabel label5 = new JLabel("Mixed", imageIcon,
                SwingConstants.RIGHT);
        frame.add(label1);
        frame.add(label2);
        frame.add(label3);
```

```
        frame.add(label4);
        frame.add(label5);
        frame.pack();
        frame.setVisible(true);
    }

    public static void main(String[] args) {
        SwingUtilities.invokeLater(new Runnable() {
            public void run() {
                constructGUI();
            }
        });
    }
}
```

If you pass HTML tags to the **setText** method on a **JLabel**, the tags must start with "<html>" and end with "</html>".

Figure 15.7 shows the result from running the code in Listing 15.5.

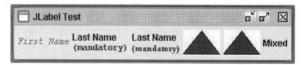

Figure 15.7: The JLabel example

JButton

A **JButton** object represents a clickable button. In a typical Swing application, a **JButton** is connected to an event listener that provides code that gets executed when the **JButton** is clicked. You will see how to achieve this in Chapter 16, "Swinging Higher."

The **JButton** class has several constructors. Here are some of them.

```
public JButton()
public JButton(Icon icon)
public JButton(java.lang.String text)
public JButton(java.lang.String text, Icon icon)
```

You can create a **JButton** that has text on it or an **Icon** or text and an icon. The **setText** and **getText** methods allows you to assign text and retrieve a **JButton**'s text, respectively.

The code in Listing 15.6 shows a **JButton** example. The **JButton** contains both text and an icon.

Listing 15.6: Using JButton

```
package com.brainysoftware.jdk5.app15;
import javax.swing.ImageIcon;
import javax.swing.JFrame;
import javax.swing.JButton;
import javax.swing.SwingUtilities;

public class JButtonTest extends JFrame {
    private static void constructGUI() {
        JFrame.setDefaultLookAndFeelDecorated(true);
        JFrame frame = new JFrame();
        frame.setDefaultCloseOperation(JFrame.EXIT_ON_CLOSE);
        frame.setTitle("JButton Test");
        ImageIcon imageIcon = new ImageIcon("triangle.jpg");
        JButton loginButton = new JButton("Login", imageIcon);
        frame.add(loginButton);
        frame.pack();
        frame.setVisible(true);
    }

    public static void main(String[] args) {
        SwingUtilities.invokeLater(new Runnable() {
            public void run() {
                constructGUI();
            }
        });
    }
}
```

Figure 15.8 shows how a **JButton** looks like when the code in Listing 15.6 is run. Note that in this example the **JButton** occupies the whole area of the **JFrame**'s content pane.

Figure 15.8: Using JButton

JTextField and JPasswordField

A **JTextField** object represents a text field. The **JTextField** class derives from **JTextComponent**, which is also the direct parent of **JTextArea** and **JEditorPane**. Some of the subclasses of **JTextField** are **JFormattedTextField** and **JPasswordField**.

A **JTextField** represents a component that allows you to enter and edit a single line of text. By contrast, a **JTextArea** enables you to manipulate multiline text.

Here are two of the **JTextField** class's constructors you can call to instantiate **JTextField**:

```
public JTextField()
public JTextField(java.lang.String text)
```

The second constructor allows you to pass a **String** that will be used as the text of the constructed **JTextField**. If you use the first constructor, you can call the **setText** method to set the text:

```
public void setText(java.lang.String text)
```

To get the text, use the **getText** method.

```
public java.lang.String getText()
```

Both **setText** and **getText** are inherited from **JTextComponent**.

A descendant of **JTextField**, **JPasswordField**, is similar to **JTextField**, except that each character of the text is displayed as an echo character, which by default is an asterisk. Here are two constructors of **JPasswordField**

```
public void JPasswordField()
public void JPasswordField(java.lang.String initialPassword)
```

To set a password, use the **setText** method inherited from the **JComponentText** class. **JPasswordField** overrides the **getText** method which is now deprecated. To obtain the contents of a **JPasswordField**, use the **getPassword** method instead.

```
public char[] getPassword()
```

You can set the echo character used for displaying each character of the password, using the **setEchoChar** method:

```
public void setEchoChar(char c)
```

Passing 0 to **setEchoChar** tells the **JPasswordField** to display the characters unmasked. The **getEchoChar** method allows you to obtain the echo character.

Listing 15.7 shows an example of **JTextField** and **JPasswordField**.

Listing 15.7: Using JTextField and JPasswordField

```
package com.brainysoftware.jdk5.app15;
import java.awt.GridLayout;
import javax.swing.JFrame;
import javax.swing.JLabel;
import javax.swing.JPasswordField;
import javax.swing.JTextField;
import javax.swing.SwingConstants;
import javax.swing.SwingUtilities;

public class JTextFieldTest extends JFrame {
    private static void constructGUI() {
        JFrame.setDefaultLookAndFeelDecorated(true);
        JFrame frame = new JFrame();
        frame.setDefaultCloseOperation(JFrame.EXIT_ON_CLOSE);
        frame.setTitle("JTextField Test");
        frame.setLayout(new GridLayout(2, 2));
        JLabel label1 = new JLabel("User Name:",
        SwingConstants.RIGHT);
        JLabel label2 = new JLabel("Password:",
        SwingConstants.RIGHT);
        JTextField userNameField = new JTextField(20);
        JPasswordField passwordField = new JPasswordField();
        frame.add(label1);
        frame.add(userNameField);
        frame.add(label2);
        frame.add(passwordField);
        frame.setSize(200, 70);
        frame.setVisible(true);
    }

    public static void main(String[] args) {
        SwingUtilities.invokeLater(new Runnable() {
            public void run() {
                constructGUI();
            }
        });
```

```
    }
}
```

The result of running the code in Listing 15.7 is shown in Figure 15.9.

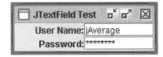

Figure 15.9: Using JTextField and JPasswordField

JTextArea

A **JTextArea** represents a multiline area for displaying text. You can change the number of lines that can be displayed at a time, as well as the number of columns. You can wrap lines and words too. You can also put your **JTextArea** in a **JScrollPane** to make it scrollable.

Here are some of the JTextArea class's constructors:

```
public JTextArea()
public JTextArea(int rows, int columns)
public JTextArea(java.lang.String text)
public JTextArea(java.lang.String text, int rows, int columns)
```

And, here are some of the more important methods in **JTextArea**.

```
public void append(java.lang.String str)
```
Appends a String to the end of the text.

```
public int getColumns()
```
Returns the number of columns in the JTextArea.

```
public int getRows()
```
Returns the number of rows in the JTextArea.

```
public void setColumns(int columns)
```
Sets the number of columns in the JTextArea.

```
public void setRows(int rows)
```
Sets the number of rows in the JTextArea.

The code in Listing 15.8 creates a **JFrame** with two **JTextArea** components. The second one is displayed in a **JScrollPane**.

Listing 15.8: Using JTextArea

```java
package com.brainysoftware.jdk5.app15;
import java.awt.Dimension;
import java.awt.FlowLayout;
import javax.swing.JFrame;
import javax.swing.JTextArea;
import javax.swing.JScrollPane;
import javax.swing.SwingUtilities;

public class JTextAreaTest {

    private static void constructGUI() {
        JFrame.setDefaultLookAndFeelDecorated(true);
        JFrame frame = new JFrame("JTextArea Test");
        frame.setLayout(new FlowLayout());
        frame.setDefaultCloseOperation(JFrame.EXIT_ON_CLOSE);
        String text = "A JTextArea object represents" +
                "a multiline area for displaying text. " +
                "You can change the number of lines " +
                "that can be displayed at a time, " +
                "as well as the number of columns. " +
                "You can wrap lines and words too. " +
                "You can also put your JTextArea in a " +
                "JScrollPane to make it scrollable.";
        JTextArea textArea1 = new JTextArea(text, 5, 10);
        textArea1.setPreferredSize(new Dimension(100, 100));
        JTextArea textArea2 = new JTextArea(text, 5, 10);
        textArea2.setPreferredSize(new Dimension(100, 100));
        JScrollPane scrollPane = new JScrollPane(textArea2,
                JScrollPane.VERTICAL_SCROLLBAR_ALWAYS,
                JScrollPane.HORIZONTAL_SCROLLBAR_ALWAYS);
        textArea1.setLineWrap(true);
        textArea2.setLineWrap(true);
        frame.add(textArea1);
        frame.add(scrollPane);
        frame.pack();
        frame.setVisible(true);
    }

    public static void main(String[] args) {
        SwingUtilities.invokeLater(new Runnable() {
            public void run() {
                constructGUI();
            }
        });
```

```
    }
}
```

When run, the class will display something similar to Figure 15.10.

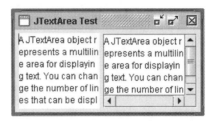

Figure 15.10: Using JTextArea

JCheckbox

JCheckBox represents a check box that the user can check and uncheck. You can construct a **JCheckBox** by passing a **String**, an icon, or a **String** and an icon. Here are some of the constructors in the **JCheckBox** class.

```
public JCheckBox(java.lang.String text)
public JCheckBox(Icon icon)
public JCheckBox(java.lang.String text, Icon icon)
```

You can programmatically check a **JCheckBox** by passing **true** to its **setSelected** method. However, there is no **getSelected** method that you can use to check if a **JCheckBox** is checked. For this, you need to use an event listener. See Chapter 16, "Swinging Higher" for information about writing event listeners.

As an example, the code in Listing 15.9 demonstrates how to use **JCheckBox**. If you run the class, you'll see something similar to Figure 15.11

Listing 15.9: Using JCheckBox

```
package com.brainysoftware.jdk5.app15;
import javax.swing.JFrame;
import javax.swing.JCheckBox;
import java.awt.FlowLayout;
import javax.swing.JLabel;
import javax.swing.SwingUtilities;

public class JCheckBoxTest {
```

```
private static void constructGUI() {
    JFrame.setDefaultLookAndFeelDecorated(true);
    JFrame frame = new JFrame("JCheckBox Test");
    frame.setLayout(new FlowLayout());
    frame.setDefaultCloseOperation(JFrame.EXIT_ON_CLOSE);
    JCheckBox ac = new JCheckBox("A/C");
    ac.setSelected(true);
    JCheckBox cdPlayer = new JCheckBox("CD Player");
    JCheckBox cruiseControl = new JCheckBox("Cruise Control");
    JCheckBox keylessEntry = new JCheckBox("Keyless Entry");
    JCheckBox antiTheft = new JCheckBox("Anti-Theft Alarm");
    JCheckBox centralLock = new JCheckBox("Central Lock");

    frame.add(new JLabel("Car Features"));
    frame.add(ac);
    frame.add(cdPlayer);
    frame.add(cruiseControl);
    frame.add(keylessEntry);
    frame.add(antiTheft);
    frame.add(centralLock);
    frame.pack();
    frame.setVisible(true);
}

public static void main(String[] args) {
    SwingUtilities.invokeLater(new Runnable() {
        public void run() {
            constructGUI();
        }
    });
}
}
```

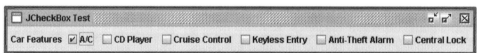

Figure 15.11: Using JCheckBox

JRadioButton

A **JRadioButton** represents a radio button. You can use multiple
JRadioButtons to represents a selection from which only one item can be

selected. To indicate a logical grouping of radio buttons, you use a **javax.swing.ButtonGroup** object.

Like **JCheckBox**, you can pass a **String**, an icon, or a **String** and an icon to construct a **JRadioButton** object. Here are some of the constructors in **JRadioButton**.

```
public JRadioButton(java.lang.String text)
public JRadioButton (Icon icon)
public JRadioButton (java.lang.String text, Icon icon)
```

To programmatically select a **JRadioButton**, you pass **true** to its **setSelected** method. However, to detect which radio button in a button group is selected, you need to use a listener. Read Chapter 16, "Swinging Higher" to learn how to achieve this.

As an example, Listing 15.10 shows code that displays three radio buttons in a button group.

Listing 15.10: Using JRadioButton

```
package com.brainysoftware.jdk5.app15;
import java.awt.FlowLayout;
import javax.swing.ButtonGroup;
import javax.swing.JFrame;
import javax.swing.JLabel;
import javax.swing.JRadioButton;
import javax.swing.SwingUtilities;

public class JRadioButtonTest {
    private static void constructGUI() {
        JFrame.setDefaultLookAndFeelDecorated(true);
        JFrame frame = new JFrame("JRadioButton Test");
        frame.setLayout(new FlowLayout());
        frame.setDefaultCloseOperation(JFrame.EXIT_ON_CLOSE);
        JRadioButton button1 = new JRadioButton("Red");
        JRadioButton button2 = new JRadioButton("Green");
        JRadioButton button3 = new JRadioButton("Blue");
        ButtonGroup colorButtonGroup = new ButtonGroup();
        colorButtonGroup.add(button1);
        colorButtonGroup.add(button2);
        colorButtonGroup.add(button3);
        button1.setSelected(true);
        frame.add(new JLabel("Color:"));
        frame.add(button1);
        frame.add(button2);
```

```
        frame.add(button3);
        frame.pack();
        frame.setVisible(true);
    }

    public static void main(String[] args) {
        SwingUtilities.invokeLater(new Runnable() {
            public void run() {
                constructGUI();
            }
        });
    }
}
```

If you run the class in Listing 15.10, you will see a **JFrame** that looks similar to Figure 15.12.

Figure 15.12: Using JRadioButton

JList

A **JList** displays a selection of objects from which the user can choose one or more options. The easiest way to construct a **JList** is to pass an array of **java.lang.Object** to its constructor:

```
public JList(java.lang.Object[] selections)
```

You can determine if the user can select a single item or multiple items from a **JList** by using the **setSelectionMode** method.

```
public void setSelectionMode(int selectionMode)
```

The possible values for *selectionMode* are

- **ListSelectionModel.SINGLE_SELECTION**. Allows a single item selection.
- **ListSelectionModel.SINGLE_INTERVAL_SELECTION**. Allows multiple item selection, but the selected items must be contiguous.

- **ListSelectionModel.SINGLE_INTERVAL_SELECTION**. Allows multiple items and the selected items may or may not be contiguous.

You can set an initial selection(s) by using the **setSelectedIndex** and **setSelectedIndices** methods (the indexing is zero-based, so index 0 refers to the first option in the **JList**).

```
public void setSelectedIndex(int index)
public void setSelectedIndices(int[] indices)
```

And, you can get the selected item(s) by using one of these methods:

```
public int getSelectedIndex()
```
> Returns the first selected index or -1 if there is no selected item.

```
public int[] getSelectedIndices()
```
> Returns an array of the selected indices.

```
public java.lang.Object getSelectedValue()
```
> Returns the first selected value, or null if no item is being selected.

```
public java.lang.Object[] getSelectedValues()
```
> Returns all the selected items as an array of Objects.

Listing 15.11 shows code that uses **JList**.

Listing 15.11: Using JList

```java
package com.brainysoftware.jdk5.app15;
import java.awt.FlowLayout;
import javax.swing.JFrame;
import javax.swing.JList;
import javax.swing.SwingUtilities;

public class JListTest {
    private static void constructGUI() {
        JFrame.setDefaultLookAndFeelDecorated(true);
        JFrame frame = new JFrame("JList Test");
        frame.setLayout(new FlowLayout());
        frame.setDefaultCloseOperation(JFrame.EXIT_ON_CLOSE);
        String[] selections = { "green", "red", "orange",
                "dark blue" };
        JList list = new JList(selections);
        list.setSelectedIndex(1);
        System.out.println(list.getSelectedValue());
        frame.add(list);
        frame.pack();
```

```
        frame.setVisible(true);
    }

    public static void main(String[] args) {
        SwingUtilities.invokeLater(new Runnable() {
            public void run() {
                constructGUI();
            }
        });
    }
}
```

When run, you should see something like Figure 15.13.

Figure 15.13: Using JList

JComboBox

JComboBox is very similar to **JList**, except that only one item can be selected. On top of that, **JComboBox** does not show all the options but only the selected item and an arrow that the user can click to see other options and select from them.

Like **JList**, you can pass an array of selection objects to **JComboBox**:

```
public JComboBox(java.lang.Object[] selection)
```

Also, the **JComboBox** class has the **getSelectedIndex**, **getSelectedItem**, and **getSelectedObjects** methods that return the selected item(s). Here are the signatures of the methods:

```
public int getSelectedIndex()
```
    Returns the selected first item or -1 if there is no selected item.

```
public java.lang.Object getSelectedItem()
```
    Returns the first value in the selection or null if there is item currently being selected.

```
public java.lang.Object[] getSelectedObjects()
```
Returns the selected item as an array of objects.

Note that the **getSelectedObjects** method returns an array that contains a maximum of one element because you cannot make multiple item selection on a **JComboBox**.

Listing 15.12 shows a **JFrame** that contains a **JComboBox**.

Listing 15.12: Using **JComboBox**

```java
package com.brainysoftware.jdk5.app15;
import java.awt.FlowLayout;
import javax.swing.JComboBox;
import javax.swing.JFrame;
import javax.swing.SwingUtilities;

public class JComboBoxTest {
    private static void constructGUI() {
        JFrame.setDefaultLookAndFeelDecorated(true);
        JFrame frame = new JFrame("JComboBox Test");
        frame.setLayout(new FlowLayout());
        frame.setDefaultCloseOperation(JFrame.EXIT_ON_CLOSE);
        String[] selections = { "green", "red", "orange",
                "dark blue" };
        JComboBox comboBox = new JComboBox(selections);
        comboBox.setSelectedIndex(1);
        System.out.println(comboBox.getSelectedItem());
        frame.add(comboBox);
        frame.pack();
        frame.setVisible(true);
    }

    public static void main(String[] args) {
        SwingUtilities.invokeLater(new Runnable() {
            public void run() {
                constructGUI();
            }
        });
    }

}
```

When run, you'll see a **JFrame** that looks like the one in Figure 15.14.

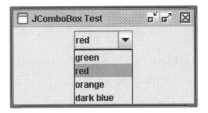

Figure 15.14: A JComboBox

JDialog

A **JDialog** represents a dialog, a top-level container that you can extend to create a window to interact with the user. You can use it to display messages, receive user input, etc. A dialog can be either modal or modeless. A modal dialog blocks user input to all other windows in the same application when it is visible. In other words, you have to close a modal dialog before other windows in the same application can get focus. A modeless one does not block user input. A dialog can belong to another dialog or a frame. Or, it can stand alone like a **JFrame**. However, most of the time you want to use a dialog that is part of a frame. For a stand alone top level container, you normally use a **JFrame**. When a dialog is part of another dialog or a frame, it will be destroyed when the owner is destroyed.

Note
The **JOptionPane** class, discussed in the section, "JOptionPane" is handy for creating simple modal dialogs.

Like **JFrame**, **JDialog** has a **JRootPane** as its only child. This means, you only add components to its content pane. However, the **add**, **remove**, and **setLayout** methods have been overridden to call the appropriate methods in the content pane. In other words, like **JFrame**, you can add a component to a **JDialog** just like this:

```
jDialog.add(component)
```

Here are some of the constructors of **JDialog**.

```
public JDialog
public JDialog(java.awt.Dialog owner)
public JDialog(java.awt.Frame owner)
public JDialog(java.awt.Dialog owner, boolean modal)
```

```
public JDialog(java.awt.Frame owner, boolean modal)
```

The last two constructors allow you to create a modal **JDialog**.

As an example, Listing 15.13 shows the **AddressDialog** class that is used to prompt for the user's address.

Listing 15.13: AddressDialog

```
package com.brainysoftware.jdk5.app15;
import java.awt.Frame;
import java.awt.GridLayout;
import javax.swing.JDialog;
import javax.swing.JLabel;
import javax.swing.JTextField;

public class AddressDialog extends JDialog {
    JLabel label1 = new JLabel("Address");
    JLabel label2 = new JLabel("City");
    JLabel label3 = new JLabel("State");
    JLabel label4 = new JLabel("Zip Code");
    JTextField addressField = new JTextField();
    JTextField cityField = new JTextField();
    JTextField stateField = new JTextField();
    JTextField zipCodeField = new JTextField();
    String[] address = new String[4];

    public AddressDialog(Frame owner, boolean modal) {
        super(owner, modal);
        init();
    }

    private void init() {
        this.setTitle("Address Dialog");
        this.setLayout(new GridLayout(4, 2));
        this.add(label1);
        this.add(addressField);
        this.add(label2);
        this.add(cityField);
        this.add(label3);
        this.add(stateField);
        this.add(label4);
        this.add(zipCodeField);
    }

    public String[] getAddress() {
        address[0] = addressField.getText();
```

```
            address[1] = cityField.getText();
            address[2] = stateField.getText();
            address[3] = zipCodeField.getText();
            return address;
        }
    }
```

Note that clients of **AddressDialog** can call its **getAddress** method to obtain the user's address information. When displayed, an **AddressDialog** looks like the one in Figure 15.15.

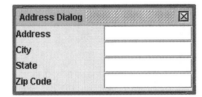

Figure 15.15: The AddressDialog

The **JDialogTest** clas in Listing 15.14 demonstrates a class that uses the **AddressDialog** class.

Listing 15.14 shows the **ComplexFrame** class, a subclass of **JFrame**. Its **main** method is used to instantiate itself.

Listing 15.14: The JDialogTest class

```
package com.brainysoftware.jdk5.app15;
import java.awt.FlowLayout;
import java.awt.event.ActionEvent;
import java.awt.event.ActionListener;
import javax.swing.JButton;
import javax.swing.JDialog;
import javax.swing.JFrame;
import javax.swing.SwingUtilities;

public class JDialogTest extends JFrame {
    AddressDialog dialog = new AddressDialog(this, false);
    public JDialogTest(String title) {
        super(title);
        init();
    }
    public JDialogTest() {
        super();
        init();
```

```
    }
    private void init() {
        this.getContentPane().setLayout(new FlowLayout());
        this.setDefaultCloseOperation(JFrame.EXIT_ON_CLOSE);
        AddressDialog dialog = new AddressDialog(this, false);
        JButton button = new JButton("Show Dialog");
        button.addActionListener(new ActionListener() {
            public void actionPerformed(ActionEvent ae) {
                displayDialog();
            }
        });
        this.getContentPane().add(button);
    }

    private void displayDialog() {
        dialog.setSize(250, 120);
        dialog.setVisible(true);
    }
    private static void constructGUI() {
        JFrame.setDefaultLookAndFeelDecorated(true);
        JDialog.setDefaultLookAndFeelDecorated(true);
        JDialogTest frame = new JDialogTest();
        frame.pack();
        frame.setVisible(true);
    }

    public static void main(String[] args) {
        SwingUtilities.invokeLater(new Runnable() {
          public void run() {
            constructGUI();
          }
        });
    }
}
```

The **JDialogTest** class displays a **JButton** you can click to display the
AddressDialog. To achieve this **JDialogTest** uses an **ActionListener**, a type
that will be discussed in Chapter 16, "Swinging Higher."

JOptionPane

A **JOptionPane** object represents a dialog box that you can use for several
purposes:

- Display a message (through the use of the **showMessageDialog** method)
- Ask for user's confirmation (using the **showConfirmDialog** method)
- Obtain the user's input (using the **showInputDialog** method)
- Do the combined three above (using the **showOptionDialog** method)

Most methods in the **JOptionPane** class are static, so you can create a dialog with a single line of code. You can use **JOptionPane** as a dialog of a frame or independently. You can pass a message, a visual component, or an icon to be displayed in the dialog. In addition, **JOptionPane** provides four default icons that are ready for use. You can even use **JOptionPane** in non-Swing applications as an easy way to interact with the user.

The following sections discuss the four main functions you can achieve using **JOptionPane**.

Using JOptionPane to Display a Message

You use the **JOptionPane** class's **showMessageDialog** method to display a message. There are three overloads of this method.

```
public static void showMessageDialog(java.awt.Component parent,
        java.lang.Object message)

public static void showMessageDialog(java.awt.Component parent,
        java.lang.Object message, java.lang.String title,
        int messageType)

public static void showMessageDialog(java.awt.Component parent,
        java.lang.Object message, java.lang.String title,
        int messageType, Icon icon)
```

The *parent* argument specified the **java.awt.Component** in which the **JOptionPane** is displayed. If the value of *component* is **null** or if the component does not have a frame, the default frame will be used.

The *message* argument specifies the message to display. The *title* argument specifies the title for the dialog window. If the first overload is used, the title is "Message."

The *messageType* argument can be assigned one of these static finals:

- **JOptionPane.ERROR_MESSAGE**
- **JOptionPane.INFORMATION_MESSAGE**

- **JOptionPane.WARNING_MESSAGE**
- **JOptionPane.QUESTION_MESSAGE**
- **JOptionPane.PLAIN_MESSAGE** (no icon will be used)

Each value of **messageType** implies the use of a different default icon. No icon is used when the messageType argument is assigned **JOptionPane.PLAIN_MESSAGE**.

For example, the following code displays four different **JOptionPane** dialogs.

```
JDialog.setDefaultLookAndFeelDecorated(true); //decorate JOptionPane
JOptionPane.showMessageDialog(null,
        "Thank you for visiting our store", "Thank You",
        JOptionPane.INFORMATION_MESSAGE);

JOptionPane.showMessageDialog(null,
        "You have not saved this document", "Warning",
        JOptionPane.WARNING_MESSAGE);

JOptionPane.showMessageDialog(null, "First Name must have a value",
        "Error", JOptionPane.ERROR_MESSAGE);
```

Figures 15.16, 15.17, and 15.18 show an information message dialog, a warning message dialog, and error message dialog, respectively.

Figure 15.16: An information message dialog

Figure 15.17: A warning message dialog

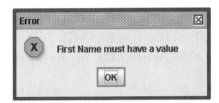

Figure 15.18: An error message dialog

Using JOptionPane to Prompt User Confirmation

You can use the **showConfirmDialog** static method to ask for user confirmation. This method displays a dialog with buttons on it, such as a Yes button, a No button, a Cancel button, or an OK button. You can select which buttons to appear or you can create your own buttons. Upon the user clicking a button, **JOptionPane** returns one of the following predefined ints:

- **JOptionPane.YES_OPTION**
- **JOptionPane.NO_OPTION**
- **JOptionPane.CANCEL_OPTION**
- **JOptionPane.OK_OPTION**

In addition, if the user closes a **JOptionPane** by clicking the close button at the top right hand corner of the dialog, the **JOptionPane.CLOSED_OPTION int** is returned.

The **showConfirmDialog** method has four overloads whose signatures are as follows.

```
public static int showConfirmDialog(java.awt.Component parent,
        java.lang.Object message)

public static int showConfirmDialog(java.awt.Component parent,
        java.lang.Object message, java.lang.String title,
        int optionType)

public static int showConfirmDialog(java.awt.Component parent,
        java.lang.Object message, java.lang.String title,
        int optionType, int messageType)

public static int showConfirmDialog(java.awt.Component parent,
        java.lang.Object message, java.lang.String title,
        int optionType, int messageType, Icon icon)
```

The *parent* argument specifies the **java.awt.Frame** in which this **JOptionPane** will be displayed. If **null** is passed to this argument or if the parent component does not have a frame, the default frame will be used.

The *message* argument specifies the message to be displayed. The title argument specifies the title that will be printed on the dialog title bar.

The *optionType* argument specifies the buttons that will be displayed. The possible values are as follows:

- **JOptionPanel.YES_NO_OPTION**, which causes the Yes and No button to be displayed.
- **JOptionPane.YES_NO_CANCEL_OPTION**, which causes the Yes, No, and Cancel buttons to be displayed.

If the first overload is used where there is no argument *optionType* is required, **JOptionPane.YES_NO_CANCEL_OPTION** is assumed.

For example, the **JOptionPaneTest2** class in Listing 15.15 shows how you can use the **JOptionPane** class to prompt user confirmation.

Listing 15.15: Using JOptionPane to prompt user confirmation

```
package com.brainysoftware.jdk5.app15;
import javax.swing.JOptionPane;

public class JOptionPaneTest2 {
    public static void main(String[] args) {
        JDialog.setDefaultLookAndFeelDecorated(true);
        int response = JOptionPane.showConfirmDialog(null,
                "Do you want to continue?", "Confirm",
                JOptionPane.YES_NO_OPTION,
        JOptionPane.QUESTION_MESSAGE);
        if (response == JOptionPane.NO_OPTION) {
            System.out.println("No button clicked");
        } else if (response == JOptionPane.YES_OPTION) {
            System.out.println("Yes button clicked");
        } else if (response == JOptionPane.CLOSED_OPTION) {
            System.out.println("JOptionPane closed");
        }
    }
}
```

When the program is run, you can see a JOptionPane dialog like the one shown in Figure 15.19.

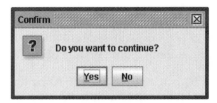

Figure 15.19: Asking user confirmation

Using JOptionPane to Obtain User Input

The third use of **JOptionPane** is to obtain user input, by using the **showInputDialog** method. This method displays a **JOptionPane** with a box for the user to type in a value. **showInputDialog** can return one of these:

- The string entered by the user if the OK button is clicked after the user types in a value.
- An empty string is the user clicks the OK button without entering a value and there is no initial value displayed.
- null if the **JOptionPane** is closed by clicking the close button or the Cancel button.
- A **java.lang.Object** if the user selects one of the predefined options displayed by the **JOptionPane**.

The **showInputDialog** method has six overloads whose signatures are as follows.

```
public static java.lang.String showInputDialog(
        java.awt.Component parent, java.lang.Object message)

public static java.lang.String showInputDialog(
        java.awt.Component parent, java.lang.Object message,
        java.lang.Object initialSelectionValue)

public static java.lang.String showInputDialog(
        java.awt.Component parent, java.lang.Object message,
        java.lang.String title, int messageType)

public static java.lang.String showInputDialog(
        java.awt.Component parent, java.lang.Object message,
        java.lang.String title, int messageType, Icon icon,
        java.lang.Object[] selectionValues,
        java.lang.Object initialSelectionValue)

public static java.lang.String showInputDialog(
```

```
            java.lang.Object message)
public static java.lang.Object showInputDialog(
        java.lang.Object message,
        java.lang.Object intialSelectionValue)
```

The *parent* argument specifies the **java.awt.Frame** in which this **JOptionPane** will be displayed. If **null** is passed to this argument or if the parent component does not have a frame, the default frame is used.

The *message* argument specifies the message to be displayed.

The *title* argument specifies the title that will be printed on the dialog title bar. If no title argument is present, the string "Input" is displayed on the title bar.

The *messageType* argument specifies the type of the message, and its values is one of the following:

- **JOptionPane.INFORMATION_MESSAGE**
- **JOptionPane.ERROR_MESSAGE**
- **JOptionPane.WARNING_MESSAGE**
- **JOptionPane.QUESTION_MESSAGE**
- **JOptionPane.PLAIN_MESSAGE**

The **JOptionPane.QUESTION_MESSAGE** value is assumed if no *messageType* argument is present.

The *selectionValues* argument specifies an array of objects that provides possible selections and the *initialSelectionValue* argument specifies the initial value in the input field.

For example, the following line of code displays an input data shown in Figure 15.20.

```
String input = JOptionPane.showInputDialog(null,
        "Enter Your Name", "John Average");
```

Figure 15.20: The Input data

As another example, consider the **JOptionPaneTest3** class in Listing 15.16.

Listing 15.16: Using JOptionPane with a predefined selections

```
package com.brainysoftware.jdk5.app15;
import javax.swing.JDialog;
import javax.swing.JOptionPane;

public class JOptionPaneTest3 {
    public static void main(String[] args) {
        JDialog.setDefaultLookAndFeelDecorated(true);
        Object[] selectionValues = { "Pandas", "Dogs", "Horses" };
        String initialSelection = "Dogs";
        Object selection = JOptionPane.showInputDialog(null,
                "What are your favorite animals?", "Zoo Quiz",
                JOptionPane.QUESTION_MESSAGE, null, selectionValues,
                initialSelection);
        System.out.println(selection);
    }
}
```

The **JOptionPaneTest3** class displays a predefined selections. Here the there are three values predefined, "Pandas", "Dogs", and "Horses." The value for the initialSelection argument is "Dogs," so this is the initial selected value. When run, the **JOptionPaneTest3** class displays something that looks like Figure 15.21

Figure 15.21: Using JOptionPane with predefined values

JFileChooser

A **JFileChooser** is a dialog specifically designed to enable users to easily select a file or files. You can create a **JFileChooser** that allows multiple selection by passing **true** to its **setMultiSelectionEnabled** method.

After you create an instance of **JFileChooser**, you can call its **show*XXX*** method to make it visible. There are three methods you can use for this purpose.

```
public int showDialog(java.awt.Component parent,
        java.lang.String approveButtonText)
```
   Displays the **JFileChooser** with a custom Approve button.

```
public int showOpenDialog(java.awt.Component parent)
```
   Displays the **JFileChooser** in the "Open File" mode.

```
public int showSaveDialog(java.awt.Component parent)
```
   Displays the **JFileChooser** in the "Save File" mode.

The return value of the three methods is one of the following:

- **JFileChooser.CANCEL_OPTION**, if the user clicks Cancel.
- **JFileChooser.APPROVE_OPTION**, if the user click an OK/Open/Save button.
- **JFileCHooser.ERROR_OPTION**, if the user closes the dialog

A return value of **JFileChooser.APPROVE_OPTION** indicates that you can call its **getSelectedFile** or **getSelectedFiles** methods. Here are the signatures of the methods.

```
public java.io.File getSelectedFile()
public java.io.File[] getSelectedFiles()
```

The **JFileChooserTest** class in Listing 15.17 presents a **JFrame** with a button. Clicking the button brings up a **JFileChooser** dialog. The name of the selected file will be displayed after you click the Open button.

Listing 15.17: Using JFileChooser

```
package com.brainysoftware.jdk5.app15;
import java.awt.FlowLayout;
import java.awt.event.ActionEvent;
import java.awt.event.ActionListener;
import java.io.File;
```

```java
import javax.swing.JButton;
import javax.swing.JDialog;
import javax.swing.JFileChooser;
import javax.swing.JFrame;
import javax.swing.SwingUtilities;

public class JFileChooserTest extends JFrame {
    private static void constructGUI() {
        JFrame.setDefaultLookAndFeelDecorated(true);
        JDialog.setDefaultLookAndFeelDecorated(true);
        JFrame frame = new JFrame("JComboBox Test");
        frame.setLayout(new FlowLayout());
        frame.setDefaultCloseOperation(JFrame.EXIT_ON_CLOSE);
        JButton button = new JButton("Select File");
        button.addActionListener(new ActionListener() {
            public void actionPerformed(ActionEvent ae) {
                JFileChooser fileChooser = new JFileChooser();
                int returnValue = fileChooser.showOpenDialog(null);
                if (returnValue == JFileChooser.APPROVE_OPTION) {
                    File selectedFile =
                            fileChooser.getSelectedFile();
                    System.out.println(selectedFile.getName());
                }
            }
        });
        frame.add(button);
        frame.pack();
        frame.setVisible(true);
    }

    public static void main(String[] args) {
        SwingUtilities.invokeLater(new Runnable() {
            public void run() {
                constructGUI();
            }
        });
    }
}
```

Figure 15.22 displays a **JFileChooser**.

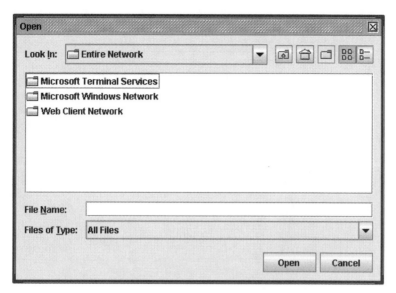

Figure 15.22: A JFileChooser

Summary

This chapter is the first of two installments on the Swing technology. You've learned the AWT basic components as well as some in the Swing collection. This chapter covered **JFrame, JButton, JLabel, JList, JComboBox, JDialog, JOptionPane,** and **JFileChooser.** Chapter 16, "Swinging Higher" presents the second part of the Swing topic. It explains the layout management and event handling.

Questions

1. Why is studying AWT still relevant today?
2. What is the AWT class that represents a component?
3. What is the easiest way to construct a **Color** object?
4. What is the only non-menu child component that can be added to a **JFrame**?
5. What is the significance of using **SwingUtilities.invokeLater** to construct Swing GUI?

6. What are the three top-level Swing containers?

Chapter 16
Swinging Higher

In Chapter 15, "Swing Basics" you examined the AWT and simple Swing components. This chapter now discusses related topics that you invariably use in Swing programming: layout management and event handling. In addition, there is also discussion about menus and the look and feel towards the end of the chapter.

Layout Managers

A container, such as a **JFrame** or a **JDialog**, needs a **java.awt.LayoutManager** object that lays out child components. The **LayoutManager** resizes the components and positions all child components, as well as rearranges the components when the container is resized. The **java.awt.Container** class has the **setLayout** method you use to add a layout manager. Since **javax.swing.JComponent** also extends the **Container** class, you can add a **LayoutManager** to a Swing component as well. For example, it is not uncommon to add a **LayoutManager** to a **JLabel** if the latter has components added to it.

In some components, you can pass a **LayoutManager** to the component class. This is the case for **JPanel**.

```
JPanel panel = new JPanel(layoutManager);
```

As for **JFrame**, you add a **LayoutManager** to its content pane:

```
jFrame.getContentPane().setLayoutManager(layoutManager)
```

In Java 5, there is a **setLayoutManager** method in **JFrame** that adds a **LayoutManager** to its content pane:

```
jFrame.setLayoutManager(layoutManager)
```

To tell the layout manager the preferred size of a component, pass a **java.awt.Dimension** object to the **setPreferredSize** method on the component. For example:

```
button.setPreferredSize(new Dimension(300, 300));
```

The **LayoutManager** interface defines the methods that a layout manager has to implement. There are a few default implementations of this interface in both **java.awt** and **javax.swing** packages. Unless you are writing a **LayoutManager** implementation, you seldom have to call the **LayoutManager** interface's methods in your code. In most scenarios, these default implementations are sufficient.

Figure 16.1 displays the **LayoutManager** interface and some of its implementations.

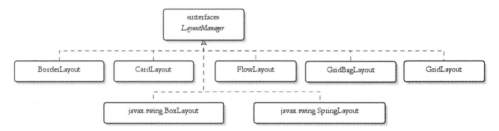

Figure 16.1: The LayoutManager interface and its implementations

In Figure 16.1 implementations without package information are part of the **java.awt** package. Two implementations in Figure 16.1, **BoxLayout** and **SpringLayout**, belong to the **javax.swing** package.

Some of the **LayoutManager** implementations are discussed in the following sections.

BorderLayout

The **BorderLayout** arranges components to fit in five regions: north, south, east, west, and center. There are five static final fields of type **java.lang.String** in the BorderLayout class that indicate these regions: **NORTH**, **SOUTH**, **EAST**, **WEST**, and **CENTER**. Each region may not contain more than one component. If you add multiple components to a region, only the last one will be displayed.

To add a component to a container employing a **BorderLayout**, you call the container's **add** method passing the component and the region field. For example, the following code adds a **JButton** to a **JFrame**.

```
jFrame.add(new JButton("Register"), BorderLayout.NORTH);
```

The absence of a region field will place the component at the center.

BorderLayout is the default layout manager. If you do not specifically add a **LayoutManager** to a container, a **BorderLayout** will be responsible for laying out child components in the container.

Listing 16.1 presents the **BorderLayoutTest1** class that shows how to use **BorderLayout**.

Listing 16.1: Using BorderLayout

```
package com.brainysoftware.jdk5.app16;
import java.awt.BorderLayout;
import javax.swing.JButton;
import javax.swing.JFrame;
import javax.swing.JTextField;
import javax.swing.SwingUtilities;

public class BorderLayoutTest1 extends JFrame {
    private static void constructGUI() {
        JFrame.setDefaultLookAndFeelDecorated(true);
        JFrame frame = new JFrame("BorderLayout Test");
        frame.setDefaultCloseOperation(JFrame.EXIT_ON_CLOSE);
        frame.setLayout(new BorderLayout());
        JTextField textField = new JTextField("<your name>");
        frame.add(textField, BorderLayout.WEST);
        JButton button =
                new JButton("<html>R<b>e</b>gister</html>");
        frame.add(button, BorderLayout.EAST);
        frame.pack();
        frame.setVisible(true);
    }

    public static void main(String[] args) {
        SwingUtilities.invokeLater(new Runnable() {
            public void run() {
                constructGUI();
            }
```

```
        });
    }
}
```

The result of running the **BorderLayoutTest1** class is shown in Figure 16.2.

Figure 16.2: A JFrame that uses a BorderLayout (left) and the same JFrame resized (right)

Note that the **JTextField** and **JButton** are placed in the west and east regions of the **JFrame**. If you resize the **JFrame**, the components maintain their positions. The size of each component adjusts accordingly, and setting the size of the components (by using **setSize**) does not have effect. It is clear the **BorderLayout** has the final say with regard to the components' sizes and positions.

Listing 16.2 shows another example of **BorderLayout**.

Listing 16.2: Another example of BorderLayout

```java
package com.brainysoftware.jdk5.app16;
import java.awt.BorderLayout;
import javax.swing.JButton;
import javax.swing.JFrame;
import javax.swing.JLabel;
import javax.swing.JTextField;
import javax.swing.SwingUtilities;

public class BorderLayoutTest2 extends JFrame {
    private static void constructGUI() {
        JFrame.setDefaultLookAndFeelDecorated(true);
        JFrame frame = new JFrame("BorderLayout Test");
        frame.setDefaultCloseOperation(JFrame.EXIT_ON_CLOSE);
        frame.setLayout(new BorderLayout());
        JLabel label1 = new JLabel("Registration Form");
        label1.setHorizontalAlignment(JLabel.CENTER);
        frame.add(label1, BorderLayout.NORTH);
        JLabel label2 = new JLabel("Name:");
        frame.add(label2, BorderLayout.WEST);
        JTextField textField = new JTextField("<your name>");
```

```
        frame.add(textField, BorderLayout.CENTER);
        JButton button1 = new JButton("Register");
        frame.add(button1, BorderLayout.EAST);
        JButton button2 = new JButton("Clear Form");
        frame.add(button2, BorderLayout.SOUTH);
        frame.setSize(300, 150);
        frame.setVisible(true);
    }

    public static void main(String[] args) {
        SwingUtilities.invokeLater(new Runnable() {
            public void run() {
                constructGUI();
            }
        });
    }
}
```

If you run the code in Listing 16.2, you'll see a **JFrame** like the one in Figure 16.3.

Figure 16.3: Another example of using BorderLayout

BorderLayout is also appropriate for containers with a single component. In this case, you add the component to the center region to make it occupy the whole area of the container.

FlowLayout

The **FlowLayout** manager arranges components in a horizontal line. By default, the flow goes from the left to the right, which means components added first will be on the left side of components added later. Components will be added to the same line until there is no more room for a component, then the next line will be used. You can change the direction of the flow by changing the **componentOrientation** property of the container:

```
frame.setComponentOrientation(java.awt.ComponentOrientation.LEFT)
```

There are three constructors in the **FlowLayout** class.

```
public FlowLayout()
public FlowLayout(int align)
public FlowLayout(int align, int horizontalGap, int verticalGap)
```

The *align* argument indicates the alignment of each row of components. The possible values are these.

- **FlowLayout.LEFT**. Left-justify component rows.
- **FlowLayout.RIGHT**. Right-justify component rows.
- **FlowLayout.CENTER**. Center component rows.
- **FlowLayout.LEADING**. Justify component rows to the leading edge of the container's orientation, e.g. to the left in the left-to-right orientation.
- **FlowLayout.TRAILING**. Justify component rows to the trailing edge of the container's orientation, e.g. to the right in the left-to-right orientation.

In the absence of the *align* argument, the default **FlowLayout.LEFT** will be used.

The *horizontalGap* argument determines the distance between two components in the same row and between the components and the container border. The *verticalGap* argument determines the distance between components in adjacent rows and the components and the container border. The default for both *horizontalGap* and *verticalGap* is 5 unit.

The code in Listing 16.3 shows a **JFrame** that uses a **FlowLayout**.

Listing 16.3: Using FlowLayout

```
package com.brainysoftware.jdk5.app16;
import java.awt.Dimension;
import java.awt.FlowLayout;
import javax.swing.JFrame;
import javax.swing.JScrollPane;
import javax.swing.JTextArea;
import javax.swing.SwingUtilities;
```

```
public class FlowLayoutTest {
    private static void constructGUI() {
        JFrame.setDefaultLookAndFeelDecorated(true);
        JFrame frame = new JFrame("FlowLayout Test");
        frame.setLayout(new FlowLayout());
        frame.setDefaultCloseOperation(JFrame.EXIT_ON_CLOSE);
        String text = "A JTextArea object represents "
                + "a multiline area for displaying text. "
                + "You can change the number of lines "
                + "that can be displayed at a time. ";
        JTextArea textArea1 = new JTextArea(text, 5, 10);
        textArea1.setPreferredSize(new Dimension(100, 100));
        JTextArea textArea2 = new JTextArea(text, 5, 10);
        textArea2.setPreferredSize(new Dimension(100, 100));
        JScrollPane scrollPane = new JScrollPane(textArea2,
                JScrollPane.VERTICAL_SCROLLBAR_ALWAYS,
                JScrollPane.HORIZONTAL_SCROLLBAR_ALWAYS);
        textArea1.setLineWrap(true);
        textArea2.setLineWrap(true);
        frame.add(textArea1);
        frame.add(scrollPane);
        frame.pack();
        frame.setVisible(true);
    }

    public static void main(String[] args) {
        SwingUtilities.invokeLater(new Runnable() {
            public void run() {
                constructGUI();
            }
        });
    }
}
```

If you run this program, you will see something similar to Figure 16.4.

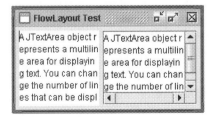

Figure 16.4: Using FlowLayout

BoxLayout

If you've been using **FlowLayout** for a while, you might be wondering if it was possible to change the direction of the flow from top to bottom or bottom to top. While you cannot do it with **FlowLayout**, **javax.swing.BoxLayout** is there to take up the challenge.

The **BoxLayout** class has only one constructor:

```
public BoxLayout(java.awt.Container target, int axis)
```

The *target* argument specifies the container that needs to be laid out and *axis* specifies the axis to lay out components along. The value of axis can be one of the following:

- **BoxLayout.X_AXIS**
- **BoxLayout.Y_AXIS**
- **BoxLayout.LINE_AXIS**
- **BoxLayout.PAGE_AXIS**

As an example, examine the code in Listing 16.4.

Listing 16.4: Using BoxLayout

```
package com.brainysoftware.jdk5.app16;
import javax.swing.BoxLayout;
import javax.swing.JButton;
import javax.swing.JFrame;
import javax.swing.SwingUtilities;

public class BoxLayoutTest {
    private static void constructGUI() {
        JFrame.setDefaultLookAndFeelDecorated(true);
        JFrame frame = new JFrame("BoxLayout Test");
        frame.setDefaultCloseOperation(JFrame.EXIT_ON_CLOSE);
        BoxLayout boxLayout = new BoxLayout(frame.getContentPane(),
                BoxLayout.Y_AXIS); // top to bottom
        frame.setLayout(boxLayout);
        frame.add(new JButton("Button 1"));
        frame.add(new JButton("Button 2"));
        frame.add(new JButton("Button 3"));
        frame.pack();
```

```
        frame.setVisible(true);
    }

    public static void main(String[] args) {
        SwingUtilities.invokeLater(new Runnable() {
            public void run() {
                constructGUI();
            }
        });
    }
}
```

When you run it, you'll get a **JFrame** like the one in Figure 16.5.

Figure 16.5: Using BoxLayout

GridLayout

As the name implies, the **GridLayout** arranges components in a grid of cells. You decide the number of cells per row and how many cells per column when you call the **GridLayout** class's constructor. Here are two of its three constructors:

```
public GridLayout(int rows, int columns)
```

```
public GridLayout(int rows, int columns,
        int horizontalGap, int verticalGap)
```

At least one of the rows and columns arguments must be nonzero.

Listing 16.5 shows an example of **GridLayout**.

Listing 16.5: Using GridLayout

```
package com.brainysoftware.jdk5.app16;
import java.awt.GridLayout;
import javax.swing.JButton;
import javax.swing.JFrame;
import javax.swing.SwingUtilities;
```

```java
public class GridLayoutTest {
    private static void constructGUI() {
        JFrame.setDefaultLookAndFeelDecorated(true);
        JFrame frame = new JFrame("GridLayout Test");
        frame.setDefaultCloseOperation(JFrame.EXIT_ON_CLOSE);
        frame.setLayout(new GridLayout(3, 2));
        frame.add(new JButton("Button 1"));
        frame.add(new JButton("Button 2"));
        frame.add(new JButton("Button 3"));
        frame.add(new JButton("Button 4"));
        frame.add(new JButton("Button 5"));
        frame.add(new JButton("Button 6"));
        frame.add(new JButton("Button 7"));
        frame.add(new JButton("Button 8"));
        frame.pack();
        frame.setVisible(true);
    }

    public static void main(String[] args) {
        SwingUtilities.invokeLater(new Runnable() {
            public void run() {
                constructGUI();
            }
        });
    }
}
```

The **GridLayoutTest** class in Listing 16.5 produces something like Figure 16.6.

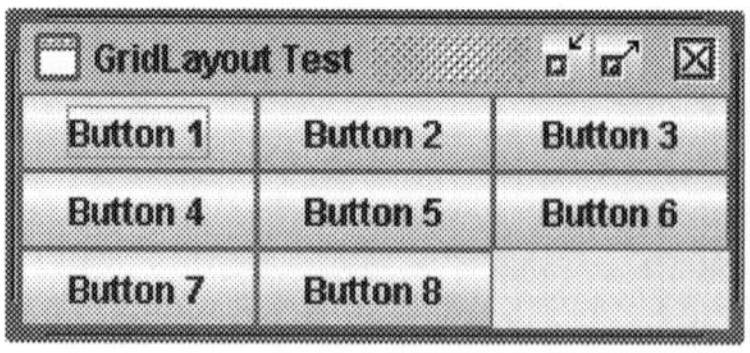

Figure 16.6: Using GridLayout

No LayoutManager

If none of the default layout manager suits your need, you can try absolute positioning by passing **null** to the **setLayout** method of a container. This means, you want to arrange your components yourself. This is the most flexible layout manager out there, but use it with care because you have to rearrange your components when your container is resized.

For each component added to a container with no layout manager, you specify its size and its position in the container. The **setBounds** method of a component can help you achieve both with a single line. As an example, Listing 16.6 features a **JFrame** that utilizes no layout manager.

Listing 16.6: Absolute positioning

```
package com.brainysoftware.jdk5.app16;
import javax.swing.JFrame;
import javax.swing.JLabel;
import javax.swing.JTextField;
import javax.swing.SwingUtilities;

public class NoLayoutTest extends JFrame {
    private static void constructGUI() {
        JFrame.setDefaultLookAndFeelDecorated(true);
        JFrame frame = new JFrame("NoLayout Test");
        frame.setDefaultCloseOperation(JFrame.EXIT_ON_CLOSE);
        frame.setLayout(null);
        JLabel label = new JLabel("First Name:");
        label.setBounds(20, 20, 100, 20);
        JTextField textField = new JTextField();
        textField.setBounds(124, 25, 100, 20);
        frame.add(label);
        frame.add(textField);
        frame.setSize(300, 100);
        frame.setVisible(true);
    }

    public static void main(String[] args) {
        SwingUtilities.invokeLater(new Runnable() {
            public void run() {
                constructGUI();
            }
        });
    }
}
```

If you run this class, you'll see something similar to Figure 16.7.

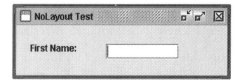

Figure 16.7: Absolute positioning

Event Handling

Swing is event-driven. A component can raise events and you can write code that handles the event. This event-driven-ness is the foundation of user interactivity in Swing applications. Before you jump straight to handling events in Swing, you should first get yourself familiar with Java 2 event model, because Swing event model follows this.

The Java Event Model

In the Java event model any object can notify other objects about a change in its state to other objects interested in that change. In event-driven programming, such change in state is called an event. The information about the event is encapsulated in an event object. In this model, there are three participants involved:

- The event source, which is the object whose state changes
- The event object, which encapsulates the state changes in the event source
- The event listener, which is the object that wants to be notified of the state changes in the event source.

To put it more briefly: When an event occurs, the event source generates an event object and sends it to the event listener.

Let's take a look at each participant in Java 2 event model.

The Event Source

Any object can be an event source. However, an event source class must provide methods for event listeners to register and de-register their interest in receiving events. Also, an event source must maintain a list of interested event listeners. For example, a **JButton** emits an **java.awt.event.ActionEvent** object when the user clicks it. Therefore, the **JButton** is an event source. The **JButton** class has the **addActionListener** and **removeActionListener** methods for action event listeners to register and deregister their interest. In addition, the **JButton** class has a protected field called **listenerList** (inherited from **JComponent**) that helps maintain registered event listeners internally.

> ### Note
> An object can be the source of more than one event. For example, JButton can raise a **java.awt.event.ActionEvent** as well as a **javax.swing.event.Change** events.

The Event Object

An event object encapsulates information about a particular type of event, such as the old and new values of the state that changed. The class for an event object must extends the **java.util.EventObject** class. The **EventObject** class has the **getSource** method that returns the event source. The signature of the **getSource** method is as follows:

```
public java.lang.Object getSource()
```

For example, when a **JButton** is clicked, it emits the action event. Information about the event is encapsulated in a **java.awt.event.ActionEvent** object. The **ActionEvent** class extends **java.awt.AWTEvent**, which in turns extends **java.util.EventObject**.

Event Listeners

An event listener can receive a particular type of event by implementing the appropriate listener interface. All listener interfaces are sub-interfaces of the **java.util.EventListener** interface. This interface does not have any methods and acts as a marker interface. Your event listener interface must then define a method for receiving the appropriate event object.

For example, to receive notification from a **JButton** when it is clicked, you can create a class that implements the **java.awt.event.ActionListener** interface, a subinterface of **java.util.EventListener**. **ActionListener** has one method, **actionPerformed**.

```
public void actionPerformed(ActionEvent event)
```

There are two things to note about the listener. First, you do not call its methods directly. Instead, they are called by the JVM when the event in question gets triggered. Second, the method being called receives an event object. When the action event occurs, for example, the **actionPerformed** method of the registered action listener gets called and passed an **ActionEvent** object.

Note

When handling Swing events, you will spend time on writing event listeners. Really, you do not worry about event sources and event objects because Swing support for event handling is very thorough.

Swing Event Handling

Different Swing components can raise different events. Events can be raised by a user's action (such as a user's clicking a button) or by the application itself (such as when you programmatically add items to a **JList**). In either case, you need to write an event listener if you want some code to be executed when an event occurs.

The API for event handling does not come with Swing. Instead, it is available in the **java.awt.event** package. Therefore, Swing event handling is based on the AWT. The good thing about AWT (and Swing) event handling is the availability of adapters, which are base classes that provide default implementation for event listener interfaces. For example, the **java.awt.event.MouseListener** interface has five methods. When you write a listener class by implementing **MouseListener**, you have to write the implementations for all these five methods, even if you are only interested in one method. The **MyMouseListener** class in Listing 16.7 should make this clear.

Listing 16.7: Writing a listener by implementing an interface

```
import java.awt.event.MouseEvent;
```

```
import java.awt.event.MouseListener;
public class MyMouseListener implements MouseListener {
    public void mouseClicked(MouseEvent e) {
    }
    public void mouseEntered(MouseEvent e) {
    }
    public void mouseExited(MouseEvent e) {
    }
    public void mousePressed(MouseEvent e) {
    }
    public void mouseReleased(MouseEvent e) {
    }
}
```

Fortunately, the **java.awt.event** package also provides the
java.awt.event.MouseAdapter class. This class implements
java.awt.event.MouseListener and provides default implementations of its
five methods. Instead of implementing **MouseListener**, you can extend
MouseAdapter and write override only methods you want to change. The
MyShorterMouseListener class in Listing 16.8 has the same functionality as
the **MyMouseListener** class in Listing 16.7, but is shorter.

Listing 16.8: Writing listener by extending an adapter

```
import java.awt.event.MouseAdapter;
import java.awt.event.MouseEvent;
public class MyShorterMouseListener extends MouseAdapter {
    // override methods here
    public void mouseClicked(MouseEvent e) {
        System.out.println("Mouse clicked");
    }
}
```

In addition to **ActionEvent** and **MouseEvent** described earlier, there are also
other types event you can capture in your Swing applications. Some of these
events are listed in Table 16.1.

Event	Listener/Adapter	Component
ActionEvent	ActionListener	JButton, JCheckBox, JRadioButton, JMenuItem, etc
MouseEvent	MouseListener	JFrame, JDialog, all Swing components
KeyEvent	KeyListener	JFrame, JDialog, all Swing components
WindowEvent	WindowListener	JFrame, JDialog

Table 16.1: Swing events

What events a **JComponent** can trigger are indicated by what listeners you can register. For example, the **JButton** class has the **addActionListener** method. This indicates that a **JButton** can raise an action event.

JButton, **JCheckBox**, and some other components can raise both **ActionEvent** and **MouseEvent**. The difference between the two events are sometimes unclear. However, as a rule, you should use **ActionEvent** if you want to be notified when it is clicked. This is because a **JButton** can be 'pushed' or a **JCheckBox** can be checked by using a keyboard shortcut. Pushing a **JButton** like this will still trigger an action event, but not a mouse event. **MouseEvent**, on the other hand, is captured if you want to know the coordinate of where the mouse pointer is clicked, etc.

AWT Event API

Before I present some event-handling examples, let's review several types in the **java.awt.event** package that are commonly used when writing Swing applications.

The java.awt.event.ActionEvent Class

An **ActionEvent** object encapsulates information about an action event. This event is raised by several components to signal that a **JButton** is pushed or a **JCheckBox** is checked/unchecked, either by clicking the mouse or by pressing the keyboard. Here are the methods defined in **ActionEvent**.

```
public java.lang.String getActionCommand()
```
Returns the command string associated with this action. This is normally the text on a **JButton** or **JCheckBox** that raised the event.

```
public long getWhen()
```
Returns a long that represents the time the action occurred.

```
public int getModifiers()
```
Returns the modifiers keys held down when this event was raised.

```
public java.lang.String paramString()
```
Returns a parameter identifying the event.

The java.awt.event.ActionListener Interface

You implement this interface to capture an action event. There is only one method defined in this interface, **actionPerformed**. Its signature is

```
public void actionPerformed(ActionEvent e)
```

The **actionPerformed** method of a registered action listener is invoked when an action event occurred.

The java.awt.event.MouseEvent Class

A **MouseEvent** object encapsulates information on a mouse event. There are several actions that can raise a mouse event, including clicking a mouse button, pressing and releasing a mouse button, moving the mouse cursor to enter a component area, and moving the mouse cursor to exit a component area.

Here are some of the methods in **MouseEvent**.

```
public int getButton()
```
> Returns an **int** that indicates which button has changed state. The value can be one of the following static final fields: **NOBUTTON**, **BUTTON1**, **BUTTON2**, and **BUTTON3**.

```
public int getClickCount()
```
> Returns the number of times the mouse was clicked.

```
public java.awt.Point getPoint()
```
> Returns the coordinate relative to top-left corner of the component at which the mouse event occurred.

```
public int getX()
```
> Returns the horizontal position relative to the left edge of the component at which the mouse event occurred.

```
public int getY()
```
> Returns the vertical position relative to the top edge of the component at which the mouse event occurred.

The java.awt.event.MouseListener Interface

You implement this interface to capture a mouse event. There are five methods, all self-explanatory, defined in this interface.

```
public void mouseClicked(MouseEvent e)
```

```
public void mousePressed(MouseEvent e)
public void mouseReleased(MouseEvent e)
public void mouseEntered(MouseEvent e)
public void mouseExited(MouseEvent e)
```

For example, the **mouseClicked** method of a registered mouse listener is invoked if a source object is clicked.

The java.awt.event.KeyEvent Class

This class represents a key event as a result of a keystroke on the user's keyboard. There are a good number of static final **int** fields that each represent a keyboard key, such as **VK_A** (representing the A key), **VK_Z** (representing the Z key), **VK_SHIFT**, **VK_SPACE**, **VK_F1**, **VK_ALT**, **VK_AMPERSAND**, etc.

In addition, here are methods that you often invoke on a **KeyEvent** object.

```
public int getKeyCode()
```
    Returns an integer key code associated with the key in the event. For example, if the A key was pressed this method returns **KeyEvent.VK_A**.

```
public char getKeyChar()
```
    Returns the char associated with the key in this event.

The java.awt.event.KeyListener Interface

You implement this interface to handle a key event. This interface defines the following methods.

```
public void keyPressed(KeyEvent e)
public void keyReleased(KeyEvent e)
public void keyTyped(KeyEvent e)
```

The java.awt.event.WindowEvent Class

A **WindowEvent** object encapsulates information on a window event. A window event is triggered when a source object is opened, closed, activated, deactivated, iconified, deiconified, or when it gets focus. The following methods are defined in the **WindowEvent** class.

```
public int getNewState()
```
> Returns the new state of the window. The return value is a bitwise mask of the following static final fields:

- **NORMAL**
- **ICONIFIED**
- **MAZIMIZED_HORIZ**
- **MAXIMIZED_VERT**
- **MAXIMIZED_BOTH**

```
public int getOldState()
```
> Returns the old state of the window. The return value is a bitwise mask of the final fields described under the **getNewState** method.

```
public java.awt.Window getWindow()
```
> Returns the source object.

The java.awt.event.WindowListener Interface

You implement this interface to handle a window event. This interface defines the following methods.

```
public void windowActivated(WindowEvent e)
public void windowClosed(WindowEvent e)
public void windowClosing(WindowEvent e)
public void windowDeactivated(WindowEvent e)
public void windowDeiconified(WindowEvent e)
public void windowIconified(WindowEvent e)
public void windowOpened(WindowEvent e)
```

Handling ActionEvent

Let's now look at an example of how we can handle an action event that originates from a **JButton**. Please read the **MyActionListener** class and **ActionListenerTest1** class in Listing 16.9.

Listing 16.9: Handling an action listener

```
package com.brainysoftware.jdk5.app16;
import java.awt.event.ActionEvent;
import java.awt.event.ActionListener;
import javax.swing.JButton;
import javax.swing.JDialog;
import javax.swing.JFrame;
```

```
import javax.swing.JOptionPane;
import javax.swing.SwingUtilities;

class MyActionListener implements ActionListener {
    public void actionPerformed(ActionEvent e) {
        JButton source = (JButton) e.getSource();
        String buttonText = source.getText();
        JOptionPane.showMessageDialog(null,
                "You clicked " + buttonText);
    }
}

public class ActionListenerTest1 {
    private static void constructGUI() {
        JFrame.setDefaultLookAndFeelDecorated(true);
        JDialog.setDefaultLookAndFeelDecorated(true);
        JFrame frame = new JFrame("ActionListener Test 1");
        frame.setDefaultCloseOperation(JFrame.EXIT_ON_CLOSE);
        JButton button = new JButton("Register");
        button.addActionListener(new MyActionListener());
        frame.getContentPane().add(button);
        frame.pack();
        frame.setVisible(true);
    }

    public static void main(String[] args) {
        SwingUtilities.invokeLater(new Runnable() {
            public void run() {
                constructGUI();
            }
        });
    }
}
```

The **MyActionListener** class is an action listener that captures an action event of a **JButton**. Here is its **actionPerformed** method.

```
    public void actionPerformed(ActionEvent e) {
        JButton source = (JButton) e.getSource();
        String buttonText = source.getText();
        JOptionPane.showMessageDialog(null,
                "You clicked " + buttonText);
    }
```

It downcasts the source object to a **JButton** and displays its text in a **JOptionPane**.

The ActionListenerTest1 class constructs a **JFrame** with a **JButton**. Pay attention to the code in bold in the **constructGUI** method:

```
button.addActionListener(new MyActionListener());
```

This line of code creates an instance of **MyActionListener** and passes it to the **addActionListener** method. This in effect registers the **MyActionListener** object as an interested party for the **JButton**'s action event.

To test this example, run the ActionListenerTest1 class. You'll see a **JFrame** like the one in Figure 16.8:

Figure 16.8: The result of running the ActionListenerTest1 class

Now, click the Register button. You will see a **JOptionPane** like that in Figure 16.9.

Figure 16.9: A JOptionPane that gets displayed on clicking a JButton

Handling MouseEvent

This example shows how you can handle a mouse event. There are two classes in this example, **MouseClickListener** and **MouseListenerTest1**. The **MouseClickListener** class is a mouse listener that extends the **java.awt.event.MouseAdapter**. The **MouseListenerTest1** displays an area you can click on. Both classes are shown in Listing 16.10.

Listing 16.10: Handling a mouse event

```
package com.brainysoftware.jdk5.app16;
import java.awt.event.MouseAdapter;
```

```java
import java.awt.event.MouseEvent;
import javax.swing.JFrame;
import javax.swing.SwingUtilities;

class MouseClickListener extends MouseAdapter {
    public void mouseClicked(MouseEvent e) {
        if (SwingUtilities.isLeftMouseButton(e)) {
            System.out.print("The mouse left button was clicked ");
        } else if (SwingUtilities.isRightMouseButton(e)) {
            System.out.print("The mouse right button was clicked ");
        } else if (SwingUtilities.isMiddleMouseButton(e)) {
            System.out.print(
                    "The mouse middle button was clicked ");
        }
        System.out.print(e.getClickCount() + " time(s)");
        int x = e.getX();
        int y = e.getY();
        System.out.println(" at (" + x + "," + y + ")");
    }
}

public class MouseListenerTest1 {
    private static void constructGUI() {
        JFrame.setDefaultLookAndFeelDecorated(true);
        JFrame frame = new JFrame("MouseListener Test 1");
        frame.setDefaultCloseOperation(JFrame.EXIT_ON_CLOSE);
        frame.addMouseListener(new MouseClickListener());
        frame.setSize(200, 200);
        frame.setVisible(true);
    }

    public static void main(String[] args) {
        SwingUtilities.invokeLater(new Runnable() {
            public void run() {
                constructGUI();
            }
        });
    }
}
```

If you run the MouseListenerTest1 class, you will see a JFrame like the one shown in Figure 16.10.

Figure 16.10: Handling mouse events

Now click on the area, you will see a message printed on your console. For example:

```
The mouse right button was clicked 1 time(s) at (110,165)
```

Writing a Listener as an Anonymous Class

In the last two examples, you created a different class for each listener. While this works well, you can reduce the number of classes in your Swing application by using anonymous classes. (Anonymous classes were explained in Chapter 14, "Nested and Inner Classes.")

First, let's review the code in Listing 16.11 which features an action listener written as a nested class.

Listing 16.11: Writing a listener as a nested class

```java
package com.brainysoftware.jdk5.app16;
import java.awt.event.ActionEvent;
import java.awt.event.ActionListener;
import javax.swing.JButton;
import javax.swing.JFileChooser;
import javax.swing.JFrame;
import javax.swing.SwingUtilities;

public class ActionListenerTest2 extends JFrame {
    String fileSelected;
    public ActionListenerTest2(String title) {
        super(title);
    }

    public void init() {
```

```java
        JButton button = new JButton("Select File");
        button.addActionListener(new MyActionListener());
        this.getContentPane().add(button);
    }

    private static void constructGUI() {
        JFrame.setDefaultLookAndFeelDecorated(true);
        ActionListenerTest2 frame = new ActionListenerTest2(
                "ActionListener Test 2");
        frame.setDefaultCloseOperation(JFrame.EXIT_ON_CLOSE);
        frame.init();
        frame.pack();
        frame.setVisible(true);
    }

    public static void main(String[] args) {
        SwingUtilities.invokeLater(new Runnable() {
            public void run() {
                constructGUI();
            }
        });
    }

    class MyActionListener implements ActionListener {
        public void actionPerformed(ActionEvent e) {
            JFileChooser fileChooser = new JFileChooser();
            int returnVal = fileChooser.showOpenDialog(null);
            if (returnVal == JFileChooser.APPROVE_OPTION) {
                fileSelected =
                        fileChooser.getSelectedFile().getName();
                System.out.print(fileSelected);
            }
        }
    }
}
```

The **MyActionListener** nested class is an action listener that listens on a **JButton**. If the source object is clicked, it will displays a **JFileChooser** and printed the name of the user selected file.

Running the **ActionListenerTest2** class will give you the **JFrame** in Figure 16.11.

Figure 16.11: A listener as a nested class

When you click the **JButton**, a **JFileChooser** like the one in Figure 16.12 will be displayed.

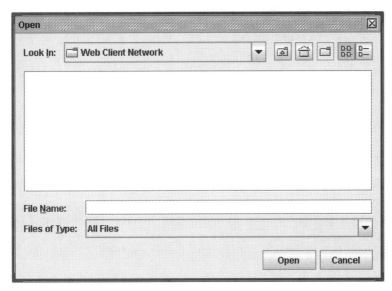

Figure 16.12: A JFileChooser that gets displayed on the user clicking a JButton

Now, examine the code in Listing 16.12.

Listing 16.12: An anonymous listener class

```
package com.brainysoftware.jdk5.app16;
import java.awt.event.ActionEvent;
import java.awt.event.ActionListener;
import javax.swing.JButton;
import javax.swing.JFileChooser;
import javax.swing.JFrame;
import javax.swing.SwingUtilities;

public class ActionListenerTest3 extends JFrame {
    String fileSelected;
```

```
    public ActionListenerTest3(String title) {
        super(title);
    }

    public void init() {
        JButton button = new JButton("Select File");
        button.addActionListener(new ActionListener() {
            public void actionPerformed(ActionEvent e) {
                JFileChooser fileChooser = new JFileChooser();
                int returnVal = fileChooser.showOpenDialog(null);
                if (returnVal == JFileChooser.APPROVE_OPTION) {
                    fileSelected =
                            fileChooser.getSelectedFile().getName();
                    System.out.print(fileSelected);
                }
            }
        });
        this.getContentPane().add(button);
    }

    private static void constructGUI() {
        JFrame.setDefaultLookAndFeelDecorated(true);
        ActionListenerTest3 frame = new ActionListenerTest3(
                "ActionListener Test 3");
        frame.setDefaultCloseOperation(JFrame.EXIT_ON_CLOSE);
        frame.init();
        frame.pack();
        frame.setVisible(true);
    }

    public static void main(String[] args) {
        SwingUtilities.invokeLater(new Runnable() {
            public void run() {
                constructGUI();
            }
        });
    }
}
```

The code in bold shows the anonymous class. If a listener is only used to listen on a single component, then it may be a good candidate to be written as an anonymous class.

Note
If the anonymous class eludes you, go back to Chapter 14, "Nested and Inner Classes."

Handling ActionEvent of JRadioButton

As another example, let's see how you can handle action events raised by a **JRadioButton**. There are three **JRadioButton** used in this example and they share the same listener. As such, you cannot write your listener as an anonymous class. This example writes it as a nested class.

The code is given in Listing 16.13.

Listing 16.13: Handling JRadioButtons' action event

```java
package com.brainysoftware.jdk5.app16;
import java.awt.FlowLayout;
import java.awt.event.ActionEvent;
import java.awt.event.ActionListener;
import javax.swing.ButtonGroup;
import javax.swing.JFrame;
import javax.swing.JLabel;
import javax.swing.JRadioButton;
import javax.swing.SwingUtilities;

public class ActionListenerTest4 extends JFrame {
    class RadioClickListener implements ActionListener {
        public void actionPerformed(ActionEvent e) {
            String command = e.getActionCommand();
            ActionListenerTest4.this.setTitle(command);
        }
    }

    public ActionListenerTest4(String title) {
        super(title);
        init();
    }

    private void init() {
        this.setLayout(new FlowLayout());
        this.setDefaultCloseOperation(JFrame.EXIT_ON_CLOSE);
        JRadioButton button1 = new JRadioButton("Red");
        JRadioButton button2 = new JRadioButton("Green");
        JRadioButton button3 = new JRadioButton("Blue");
```

```
        RadioClickListener listener = new RadioClickListener();
        button1.addActionListener(listener);
        button2.addActionListener(listener);
        button3.addActionListener(listener);
        ButtonGroup colorButtonGroup = new ButtonGroup();
        colorButtonGroup.add(button1);
        colorButtonGroup.add(button2);
        colorButtonGroup.add(button3);
        button1.setSelected(true);
        this.add(new JLabel("Color:"));
        this.add(button1);
        this.add(button2);
        this.add(button3);
    }

    private static void constructGUI() {
        JFrame.setDefaultLookAndFeelDecorated(true);
        ActionListenerTest4 frame = new ActionListenerTest4(
                "ActionListener Test 4");
        frame.pack();
        frame.setVisible(true);
    }

    public static void main(String[] args) {
        SwingUtilities.invokeLater(new Runnable() {
            public void run() {
                constructGUI();
            }
        });
    }
}
```

If you run the **ActionListenerTest4** class, you'll see a **JFrame** like the one displayed in Figure 16.13.

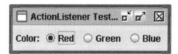

Figure 16.13: Capturing JRadioButtons' action event

The **actionPerformed** method in the **RadioClickListener** class reads the return value of the **getActionCommand** method and assigns it as the **JFrame**'s title.

Handling KeyEvent

The following example shows to handle a key event. The listener captures the user's keyboard input and capitalizes it. The code is shown in Listing 16.14.

Listing 16.14: Key event listener

```java
package com.brainysoftware.jdk5.app16;
import java.awt.BorderLayout;
import java.awt.event.KeyEvent;
import java.awt.event.KeyListener;
import javax.swing.JFrame;
import javax.swing.JTextField;

public class KeyListenerTest1 extends JFrame
        implements KeyListener {
    public KeyListenerTest1(String title) {
        super(title);
        this.getContentPane().setLayout(new BorderLayout());
        JTextField textField = new JTextField(20);
        textField.addKeyListener(this);
        this.getContentPane().add(textField);
    }

    public void keyTyped(KeyEvent e) {
        e.setKeyChar(Character.toUpperCase(e.getKeyChar()));
    }

    public void keyPressed(KeyEvent e) {
    }

    public void keyReleased(KeyEvent e) {
    }

    private static void constructGUI() {
        // Make sure we have nice window decorations.
        JFrame.setDefaultLookAndFeelDecorated(true);
        KeyListenerTest1 frame =
                new KeyListenerTest1("KeyListener Test 1");
        frame.setDefaultCloseOperation(JFrame.EXIT_ON_CLOSE);
        frame.pack();
        frame.setVisible(true);
    }

    public static void main(String[] args) {
        javax.swing.SwingUtilities.invokeLater(new Runnable() {
```

```
        public void run() {
            constructGUI();
        }
    });
}
}
```

What's special in this example is that the listener interface is implemented by the main class itself. As a result, you override the **KeyListener** interface methods within the class itself.

If you run the **KeyListenerTest1** class, you will see a **JFrame** with a **JTextField** control like the one in Figure 16.14.

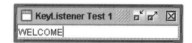

Figure 16.14: Using KeyListener

Handling WindowListener

This example demonstrates how you can write a window listener. The listener is implemented as an anonymous class that overrides the **windowIconified** method and sets the window state to normal. As a result, you cannot minimize the window.

The code is given in Listing 16.15.

Listing 16.15: A window listener

```
package com.brainysoftware.jdk5.app16;
import java.awt.Frame;
import java.awt.event.WindowAdapter;
import java.awt.event.WindowEvent;
import javax.swing.JFrame;

public class WindowListenerTest1 extends JFrame {
    public WindowListenerTest1(String title) {
        super(title);
        this.addWindowListener(new WindowAdapter() {
            public void windowIconified(WindowEvent e) {
                WindowListenerTest1.this.setState(Frame.NORMAL);
            }
```

```
            });
        }

        private static void constructGUI() {
            JFrame.setDefaultLookAndFeelDecorated(true);
            WindowListenerTest1 frame =
                    new WindowListenerTest1("WindowEventDemo");
            frame.setDefaultCloseOperation(JFrame.EXIT_ON_CLOSE);
            frame.setSize(100, 100);
            frame.setVisible(true);
        }

        public static void main(String[] args) {
            javax.swing.SwingUtilities.invokeLater(new Runnable() {
                public void run() {
                    constructGUI();
                }
            });
        }
    }
```

Working with Menus

Rarely a serious Swing application go by without menus. Menus are handy because they only take little space out of the screen real estate. Also, only a menu bar needs to appear at all times. Most menu items are in fact hidden and do not take space at all. To use menus, first add a menu bar to the container and add menus to the menu bar. Then, add menu items to a menu. To support hierarchical menus, you can add menu items to a menu item.

In Swing, a menu bar is represented by the **javax.swing.JMenuBar** class, a menu by **javax.swing.JMenu**, and a menu item by **javax.swing.JMenuItem**, which is a child class of **JAbstractButton**. **JMenuItem** has the following subclasses: **JMenu**, **JCheckboxMenuItem**, and **JRadioButtonMenuItem**

Clicking a menu on the menu bar displays the menu. This happens automatically without you having to write a listener. A menu item acts more like a **JButton**, you can add an action listener to handles a mouse click.

The **JMenuTest1** class in Listing 16.16 displays a **JFrame** with menus.

Listing 16.16: Using JMenu

```
package com.brainysoftware.jdk5.app16;
import java.awt.event.ActionEvent;
import java.awt.event.ActionListener;
import javax.swing.JFrame;
import javax.swing.JMenu;
import javax.swing.JMenuBar;
import javax.swing.JMenuItem;
import javax.swing.SwingUtilities;

class MyMenuActionListener implements ActionListener {
    public void actionPerformed(ActionEvent e) {
        System.out.println(e.getActionCommand());
    }
}

public class JMenuTest1 {
    private static void constructGUI() {
        JFrame.setDefaultLookAndFeelDecorated(true);
        JFrame frame = new JFrame("JMenu Test 1");
        frame.setDefaultCloseOperation(JFrame.EXIT_ON_CLOSE);
        MyMenuActionListener actionListener =
                new MyMenuActionListener();
        JMenuBar menuBar = new JMenuBar();
        JMenu fileMenu = new JMenu("File");
        JMenu editMenu = new JMenu("Edit");
        JMenu helpMenu = new JMenu("Help");
        menuBar.add(fileMenu);
        menuBar.add(editMenu);
        menuBar.add(helpMenu);
        JMenuItem fileNewMI = new JMenuItem("New");
        JMenuItem fileOpenMI = new JMenuItem("Open");
        JMenuItem fileSaveMI = new JMenuItem("Save");
        JMenuItem fileExitMI = new JMenuItem("Exit");
        fileMenu.add(fileNewMI);
        fileNewMI.addActionListener(actionListener);
        fileMenu.add(fileOpenMI);
        fileOpenMI.addActionListener(actionListener);
        fileMenu.add(fileSaveMI);
        fileSaveMI.addActionListener(actionListener);
        fileMenu.addSeparator();
        fileMenu.add(fileExitMI);
        fileExitMI.addActionListener(actionListener);

        JMenuItem editCopyMI = new JMenuItem("Copy");
```

```
        JMenuItem editPasteMI = new JMenuItem("Paste");
        editMenu.add(editCopyMI);
        editMenu.add(editPasteMI);

        JMenuItem helpAboutMI = new JMenuItem("About");
        helpMenu.add(helpAboutMI);

        frame.setJMenuBar(menuBar);
        frame.setSize(200, 100);
        frame.setVisible(true);
    }

    public static void main(String[] args) {
        SwingUtilities.invokeLater(new Runnable() {
            public void run() {
                constructGUI();
            }
        });
    }
}
```

Running the **JMenuTest1** class produces a **JFrame** like the one in Figure 16.15.

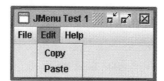

Figure 16.15: Using JMenu

The Look and Feel

The look and feel of a GUI application is very important. Swing is a GUI technology where you can expect uniformity of the look and feel of your GUI, regardless the operating system the application is run on. This is in contrast to AWT or Eclipse SWT (the GUI technology used and developed by the Eclipse community) whereby the look and feel of your application depends on the platform. However, it does not mean Swing only supports one type of look and feel. In fact, there are several. Once you choose a look and feel, your application looks the same everywhere. Figures 16.16 to 16.18 show some of the look and feels available in Swing.

Figure 16.16: Swing on GTK

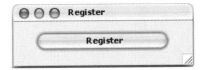

Figure 16.17: Swing on Macintosh, and Windows

Figure 16.18: Swing on Windows

Changing look and feels is also easy because each look and feel is governed by a **javax.swing.LookAndFeel** object. Changing the **LookAndFeel** class of an application results in a different look and feel.

Choosing Look and Feels

Unless instructed otherwise, Java uses the default look and feel. To change the look and feel, you use the **javax.swing.UIManager** class's **setLookAndFeel** method to select a look and feel. Here is its signature:

```
public static void setLookAndFeel(java.lang.String className)
        throws java.lang.ClassNotFoundException,
        java.lang.InstantiationException,
        java.lang.IllegalAccessException,
        UnsupportedLookAndFeelException
```

The default JDK has provided a few subclass of LookAndFeel that you can use as the argument to **setLookAndFeel**. They are as follows:

- **com.sun.java.swing.plaf.gtk.GTKLookAndFeel**
- **javax.swing.plaf.metal.MetalLookAndFeel**
- **com.sun.java.swing.plaf.windows.WindowsLookAndFeel**
- **com.sun.java.swing.plaf.motif.MotifLookAndFeel**

For instance, the following code forces the application to use the Motif look and feel.

```
UIManager.setLookAndFeel(
        "com.sun.java.swing.plaf.motif.MotifLookAndFeel");
```

In addition, you can pass the return value of the following methods as an argument to **setLookAndFeel**:

```
UIManager.getCrossPlatformLookAndFeelClassName().
```
Returns the look and feel tat works on all platforms (the Java look and feel).

```
UIManager.getSystemLookAndFeelClassName().
```
Returns the look and feel for the current platform, that is, if the application is running on Windows the Windows look and feel will be used, etc.

You must call the **setLookAndFeel** method before constructing your GUI. Normally, you do this before calling the **constructGUI** method in your application. Here is an example of using the current system's look and feel:

```
public static void main(String[] args) {
    try {
        UIManager.setLookAndFeel(
                UIManager.getSystemLookAndFeelClassName());
    } catch (Exception e) {
        e.printStackTrace();
    }
    SwingUtilities.invokeLater(new Runnable() {
        public void run() {
            constructGUI();
        }
    });
}
```

Alternatively, you can select a look and feel by using the –D flag when invoking the application. This way, you do not have to hardcode it in your class. For example, the following command invokes the **MySwingApp** application and tells the JVM to use the **com.sun.java.swing.plaf.gtk.GTKLookAndFeel** class:

```
java -Dswing.defaultlaf=com.sun.java.swing.plaf.gtk.GTKLookAndFeel
```

Summary

Chapter 15, "Swing Basics" discussed simple Swing components. This chapter covered more advanced topics such as layout management, event handling, working with menus, and look and feels.

Questions

1. What is a layout manager?
2. Name at least four types of layout managers.
3. What is a source object in event-handling?
4. Name at least four Swing events.
5. What is the advantage of writing your listener as an anonymous class?

Chapter 17
Polymorphism

Polymorphism is the hardest concept to explain to those new to object-oriented programming (OOP). In fact, most of the time its definition would not make sense without an example or two. Well, try this. Here is the definition in many programming books: Polymorphism is an OOP feature that enables an object to determine which method implementation to invoke upon receiving a method call. If you find this hard to digest, do not worry. Polymorphism is hard to explain in simple language, but it does not mean the concept is hard to understand.

This chapter starts with a simple example that should make polymorphism crystal clear. It then proceeds with another example that demonstrates the use of polymorphism with reflection.

Note
In other programming languages, polymorphism is also called late-binding or runtime-binding or dynamic binding.

Defining Polymorphism

In Java and other OOP languages, it is legal to assign to a reference variable an object whose type is different from the variable type, if certain conditions are met. In essence, if you have a reference variable **a** whose type is **A**, it is legal to assign an object of type **B**, such as this.

```
A a = new B();
```

if one of the following conditions is met.

- **A** is a class and **B** is a subclass of **A**.
- **A** is an interface and **B** or its parent implements **A**.

As you have learned in Chapter 6, "Inheritance," this is called upcasting.

When you assign **a** an instance of **B** like in the code above, **a** is of type **A**. This means, you cannot call a method in **B** that is not defined in A. However, if you print the value of **a.getClass().getName()**, you'll get "B" and not "A." So, what does this mean? At compile time, the type of **a** is **A**, so the compiler will not allow you to call a method in **B** that is not defined in **A**. On the other hand, at runtime the type of a is B, as proven by the return value of **a.getClass().getName()**.

Now, here comes the essence of polymorphism. If **B** overrides a method (say, a method named **play**) in **A**, calling **a.play()** will cause the implementation of **play** in **B** (and not in **A**) to be invoked. Polymorphism enables an object (in this example, the one referenced by **a**) to determine which method implementation to choose (either the one in **A** or the one in **B**) when a method is called. Polymorphism dictates that the implementation in the runtime object is invoked. But, polymorphism does not stop here.

What if you call another method in **a** (say, a method called **stop**) and the method is not implemented in **B**? The JVM will be smart enough to know this and look into the inheritance hierarchy of **B**. **B**, as it happens, must be a subclass of **A** or, if **A** is an interface, a subclass of another class that implements **A**. Otherwise, the code would not have compiled. Having figured this out, the JVM will climb the ladder of the hierarchy and find the implementation of **stop** and run it.

Now, there is more sense in the definition of polymorphism: Polymorphism is an OOP feature that enables an object to determine which method implementation to invoke upon receiving a method call.

Technically, though, how does Java achieve this? The Java compiler, as it turns out, upon encountering a method call such as **a.play()**, checks if the class/interface represented by **a** defines such a method (a **play** method) and if the correct set of parameters are passed to the method. But, that is the farthest the compiler goes. With the exception of static and final methods, it does not connect (or bind) a method call with a method body. The JVM determines how to bind a method call with the method body at runtime. In other words, except for static and final methods, method binding in Java happens at runtime and not at compile time. Runtime binding is also called late binding or dynamic binding. The opposite is early binding, in which binding occurs at compile time or link time. Early binding happens in other languages, such as C.

Therefore, polymorphism is made possible by the late binding mechanism in Java. Because of this, polymorphism is rather inaccurately also called late-binding or dynamic binding or runtime binding.

Let's now visit the Java code in Listing 17.1 that demonstrates polymorphism.

Listing 17.1: An example of polymorphism

```
package com.brainysoftware.jdk5.app17;

class Employee {
    public void work() {
        System.out.println("I am an employee.");
    }
}

class Manager extends Employee {
    public void work() {
        System.out.println("I am a manager.");
    }

    public void manage() {
        System.out.println("Managing ...");
    }
}

public class PolymorphismTest1 {
    public static void main(String[] args) {
        Employee employee;
        employee = new Manager();
        System.out.println(employee.getClass().getName());
        employee.work();
        Manager manager = (Manager) employee;
        manager.manage();
    }
}
```

Listing 17.1 defines two non-public classes: **Employee** and **Manager**. **Employee** has a method called **work**, and **Manager** extends **Employee** and adds a new method called **manage**.

The **main** method in the **PolymorphismTest1** class defines an object variable called **employee** of type **Employee**:

```
Employee employee;
```

However, **employee** is assigned an instance of **Manager**, as in:

```
employee = new Manager();
```

This is legal because **Manager** is a subclass of **Employee**, so a **Manager** "is an" **Employee**. Because **employee** is assigned an instance of **Manager**, what is the outcome of **employee.getClass().getName()**? You're right. It's "Manager," not "Employee."

Then, the **work** method is called.

```
employee.work();
```

Guess what is written on the console?

```
I am a manager.
```

This means that it is the **work** method in the **Manager** class that gets called, which is polymorphism in action.

Note
Polymorphism does not work with static methods because they are early-bound. For example, if the **work** method in both the **Employee** and **Manager** classes were static, a call to **employee.work()** would print "I am an employee."
Also, since you cannot extend final methods, polymorphism will not work with final methods either.

Now, because the runtime type of **a** is **Manager**, you can downcast a to **Manager**, as the code shows:

```
Manager manager = (Manager) employee;
manager.manage();
```

After seeing the code, you might ask, why would you declare **employee** as **Employee** in the first place? Why didn't you declare **employee** as type **Manager**, such as this?

```
Manager employee;
employee = new Manager();
```

You do this to ensure flexibility in cases where you don't know whether the object reference (**employee**) will be assigned an instance of **Manager** or something else. For the same reason, in your programming career you would see something like this a lot of time:

```
List list = new ArrayList();
```

However, the power of polymorphism is not really apparent here, because you can always write

```
Manager employee = new Manager();
```

or

```
ArrayList list = new ArrayList();
```

You are right. But I guarantee you will acknowledge that polymorphism is very useful after you see the next examples.

Polymorphism in Action

Suppose you have a Swing application and you have a method that changes the foreground color of a control. You want to be able to pass to the method a **JButton**, a **JLabel**, or any other control that may be added to a **JFrame**. For this example, such a method is called **brightenForegroundColor** and is given in Listing 17.2.

Listing 17.2: The brightenForegroundColor method

```
public static void brightenForegroundColor(Component component) {
    Color oldColor = component.getForeground();
    int red = oldColor.getRed();
    int green = oldColor.getGreen();
    int blue = oldColor.getBlue();
    if (red < 245) {
        red += 10;
    }
    if (green < 245) {
        green += 10;
    }
    if (blue < 245) {
        blue += 10;
    }
    Color newColor = new Color(red, green, blue);
    component.setForeground(newColor);
}
```

The **brightenForegroundColor** method takes a **java.awt.Component** object. Because the **Component** class is the parent class of all Swing controls, thanks to polymorphism you can pass any Swing component to **brightenForegroundColor**. This way, you only need one method for all components. Without polymorphism, you need a method for each type of component. You would have **brightenJLabelForegroundColor**, **brightenJButtonForegroundColor**, and so forth.

Note
The **com.brainysoftware.jdk5.app17.MyFrame** class allows you to test the **brightenForegroundColor** method.

Polymorphism in a Drawing Application

The strength of polymorphism is in situations where the programmer does not know in advance the type of the object that will be created. For example, consider the Simple Draw application in Figure 17.1. This applications lets you draw three types of objects: rectangles, lines, and ovals.

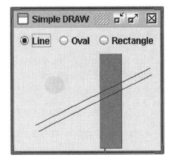

Figure 17.1: The Simple Draw application

To draw a line, for example, first click the Line radio, and then click and drag on the drawing area, and release the mouse button. The position you first click on the drawing area will become the start point (x1, y1). The coordinate on which you release your mouse button will be the end point (x2, y2).

Now let's figure out how the application works.

First, look at the **Shape** interface and its implementation classes (**Rectangle**, **Line**, and **Oval**) in Listing 17.3.

Listing 17.3: The Shape interface and its implementations

```java
package com.brainysoftware.jdk5.app17.simpledraw;
import java.awt.Color;
import java.awt.Graphics;

interface Shape {
    public void draw(Graphics g);
}

class Rectangle implements Shape {
    // (x1,y1) = mouse press coordinate
    public int x1, y1, x2, y2;

    public Rectangle(int x1, int y1, int x2, int y2) {
        this.x1 = x1 < x2 ? x1 : x2;
        this.y1 = y1 < y2 ? y1 : y2;
        this.x2 = x1 < x2 ? x2 : x1;
        this.y2 = y1 < y2 ? y2 : y1;
    }

    public void draw(Graphics g) {
        g.setColor(Color.green);
        g.fill3DRect(x1, y1, x2 - x1, y2 - y1, true);
    }
} // end of class Rectangle

class Line implements Shape {
    int x1, y1, x2, y2;

    public Line(int x1, int y1, int x2, int y2) {
        this.x1 = x1;
        this.y1 = y1;
        this.x2 = x2;
        this.y2 = y2;
    }

    public void draw(Graphics g) {
        g.setColor(Color.red);
        g.drawLine(x1, y1, x2, y2);
    }
} // end of class Line

class Oval implements Shape {
    int x1, y1, x2, y2;
```

```
    public Oval(int x1, int y1, int x2, int y2) {
        this.x1 = x1 < x2 ? x1 : x2;
        this.y1 = y1 < y2 ? y1 : y2;
        this.x2 = x1 < x2 ? x2 : x1;
        this.y2 = y1 < y2 ? y2 : y1;
    }

    public void draw(Graphics g) {
        g.setColor(Color.yellow);
        g.fillOval(x1, y1, x2 - x1, y2 - y1);
    }
} // end of class Oval
```

There is only one method in the **Shape** interface, **draw**. It is meant to be overridden by implementation classes to draw the appropriate shape. In the **Rectangle** class, for example, the **draw** method has been overridden to draw the shape of a rectangle.

Now, let's check the Swing application in Listing 17.4.

Listing 17.4: The SimpleDraw application

```
package com.brainysoftware.jdk5.app17.simpledraw;
import java.awt.BorderLayout;
import java.awt.Color;
import java.awt.FlowLayout;
import java.awt.Graphics;
import java.awt.event.ActionEvent;
import java.awt.event.ActionListener;
import java.awt.event.MouseEvent;
import java.awt.event.MouseListener;
import java.util.ArrayList;
import javax.swing.ButtonGroup;
import javax.swing.JFrame;
import javax.swing.JPanel;
import javax.swing.JRadioButton;
import javax.swing.SwingUtilities;

public class SimpleDraw extends JFrame
        implements ActionListener, MouseListener {
    // (x1,y1) = coordinate of mouse pressed
    // (x2,y2) = coordinate of mouse released
    int x1;
    int y1;
    int x2;
```

```
    int y2;

    ArrayList<Shape> shapes = new ArrayList<Shape>();

    String shapeType = "Rectangle";

    public SimpleDraw() {
        this.setTitle("Simple DRAW");
        this.setDefaultCloseOperation(JFrame.EXIT_ON_CLOSE);
        // add check box group
        ButtonGroup cbg = new ButtonGroup();
        JRadioButton lineButton = new JRadioButton("Line");
        JRadioButton ovalButton = new JRadioButton("Oval");
        JRadioButton rectangleButton =
                new JRadioButton("Rectangle");
        cbg.add(lineButton);
        cbg.add(ovalButton);
        cbg.add(rectangleButton);
        lineButton.addActionListener(this);
        ovalButton.addActionListener(this);
        rectangleButton.addActionListener(this);
        rectangleButton.setSelected(true);
        JPanel radioPanel = new JPanel(new FlowLayout());
        radioPanel.add(lineButton);
        radioPanel.add(ovalButton);
        radioPanel.add(rectangleButton);
        this.addMouseListener(this);
        this.setLayout(new BorderLayout());
        this.add(radioPanel, BorderLayout.NORTH);
    }

    public void paint(Graphics g) {
        paintComponents(g);
        for (Shape shape : shapes) {
            shape.draw(g);
        }
    }

    public void actionPerformed(ActionEvent ae) {
        shapeType = ae.getActionCommand().toString();
    }

    public void mouseClicked(MouseEvent me) {
    }

    public void mouseEntered(MouseEvent me) {
```

```
        }

        public void mouseExited(MouseEvent me) {
        }

        public void mousePressed(MouseEvent me) {
            x1 = me.getX();
            y1 = me.getY();
        }

        public void mouseReleased(MouseEvent me) {
            x2 = me.getX();
            y2 = me.getY();
            Shape shape = null;
            if (shapeType.equals("Rectangle")) {
                // a Rectangle cannot have a zero width or height
                if (x1 != x2 || y1 != y2) {
                    shape = new Rectangle(x1, y1, x2, y2);
                }
            } else if (shapeType.equals("Line")) {
                // a Line cannot have a zero width or height
                if (x1 != x2 && y1 != y2) {
                    shape = new Line(x1, y1, x2, y2);
                }
            } else if (shapeType.equals("Oval")) {
                // an Oval cannot have a zero width or height
                if (x1 != x2 || y1 != y2) {
                    shape = new Oval(x1, y1, x2, y2);
                }
            }
            if (shape != null) {
                this.shapes.add(shape);
                this.repaint();
            }
        }

        private static void constructGUI() {
            JFrame.setDefaultLookAndFeelDecorated(true);
            SimpleDraw frame = new SimpleDraw();
            frame.pack();
            frame.setVisible(true);
        }
        public static void main(String[] args) {
            SwingUtilities.invokeLater(new Runnable() {
                public void run() {
                    constructGUI();
```

```
            }
        });
    }
}
```

The **SimpleDraw** class, a subclass of **JFrame**, employs three **JRadioButton** controls for the user to select a shape to draw and has several class variables. The first are four **int**s **x1, y1, x2, y2**. **(x1, y1)** indicates the mouse press coordinate on the drawing area. **(x2, y2)** denotes the mouse release coordinate. Then, there is an **ArrayList** that stores all the **Shape** objects drawn. The **paint** method in **SimpleDraw** class iterates over the **ArrayList** to draw the shapes. Lastly, there is the **shapeType String** variable that stores the value of user selected shape.

The **SimpleDraw** class implements the **java.awt.event.ActionListener** and **java.awt.event.MouseListener** interfaces. The **ActionListener** is used to detect a click on the **JRadioButtons**.

```
public void actionPerformed(ActionEvent ae) {
    shapeType = ae.getActionCommand().toString();
}
```

The **getActionCommand** method will return either "Rectangle," "Line," or "Oval," depending on which **JRadioButton** is clicked. The value returned by **getActionCommand** is stored in the **shapeType** class variable.

The **MouseListener** is used to detect the mouse press and mouse release events on the drawing **JPanel**. Here is the **mousePressed** method:

```
public void mousePressed(MouseEvent me) {
    x1 = me.getX();
    y1 = me.getY();
}
```

It retrieves the position relative to the top-left hand corner of the **JPanel** and stores the coordinate in **x1** and **y1** class variables.

And, here is the implementation of the **mouseReleased** method

```
public void mouseReleased(MouseEvent me) {
    x2 = me.getX();
    y2 = me.getY();
    Shape shape = null;
    if (shapeType.equals("Rectangle")) {
        // a Rectangle cannot have a zero width or height
```

```
            if (x1 != x2 || y1 != y2) {
                shape = new Rectangle(x1, y1, x2, y2);
            }
        } else if (shapeType.equals("Line")) {
            // a Line cannot have a zero width or height
            if (x1 != x2 && y1 != y2) {
                shape = new Line(x1, y1, x2, y2);
            }
        } else if (shapeType.equals("Oval")) {
            // an Oval cannot have a zero width or height
            if (x1 != x2 || y1 != y2) {
                shape = new Oval(x1, y1, x2, y2);
            }
        }
        if (shape != null) {
            this.shapes.add(shape);
            this.repaint();
        }
    }
```

This is where polymorphism takes place. First, the **mouseReleased** method obtains the values for **(x2, y2)**, then it declares the **shape** variable of type **Shape**. The object assigned to **shape** depends on the value of **shapeType**. In this case, you see that what object to create is not known at the time the class was written. Nor was it known at compile-time.

Another trace of polymorphism can be found in the **paint** method.

```
public void paint(Graphics g) {
    paintComponents(g);
    for (Shape shape : shapes) {
        shape.draw(g);
    }
}
```

The **paint** method uses the enhance **for** to iterate over the **ArrayList** referenced by **shapes**. Each iteration may deal with a **Rectangle**, a **Line**, or an **Oval**. However, that does not really matter because a call on **draw(g)** will invoke the correct **draw** method, that is if at the current iteration **shape** is referencing an **Oval**, the **draw** method in the **Oval** class will be executed.

Polymorphism and Reflection

Polymorphism is often used along with reflection. Consider this scenario.

The Order Processing application is a business application for handling purchase orders. It can store orders in various databases (Oracle, MySQL, etc) and retrieve orders for display. The **Order** class represents purchase orders. Orders are stored in a database and an **OrderAccessObject** object handles the storing and retrieval of **Order** objects.

The **OrderAccessObject** class acts as an interface between the application and the database. All purchase order manipulations are done through an instance of this class. The OrderAccessObject interface is given in Listing 17.5.

Listing 17.5: The OrderAccessObject Interface

```
public interface OrderAccessObject {
    public void addOrder(Order order);
    public void getOrder(int orderId);
}
```

The **OrderAccessObject** interface needs an implementation class that provides the code for the two methods in it. The application may have many implementation classes for **OrderAccessObject**, each of which caters to a specific type of database. For example, the implementation class that connects to an Oracle database is called **OracleOrderAccessObject** class and the one for MySQL is **MySQLOrderAccessObject**. Figure 17.2 shows the UML diagram for **OrderAccessObject** and its implementing classes.

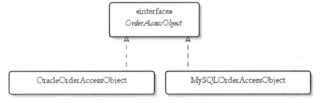

Figure 17.2: The OrderAccessObject interface and implementing classes

The need for multiple implementing classes arises from the fact that each database could have a specific command for performing certain function. For example, autonumbers are common in MySQL, but do not exist in Oracle.

The Order Processing application needs to be flexible enough that it can work with a different database without recompilation. It should also be possible to add support for a new database in the future without recompilation. In fact, you just need to specify the implementing class of **OrderAccessObject** when invoking the application. For example, to use an Oracle database you specify this

```
java OrderProcessing com.mycompany.OracleOrderAccessObject
```

And to work with MySQL, you call it using this command:

```
java OrderProcessing com.mycompany.MySqlOrderAccessObject
```

Now, here is the part of the code that instantiates an **OrderAccessObject** in the database:

```
public static void main (String[] args) {
    OrderAccessObject accessObject = null;
    Class klass = null;
    try {
        klass = Class.forName(args[0]);
        accessObject = (OrderAccessObject) klass.newInstance();
    } catch (ClassNotFoundException e) {
    } catch (Exception e) {
    }

    // continue here
}
```

This is polymorphism because the **accessObject** reference variable can be assigned a different object type each time.

Note
The forName and newInstance methods are explained in the section "java.lang.Class" in Chapter 5, "Core Classes."

Summary

Polymorphism is one of the main pillars in object-oriented programming. It is useful in circumstances where the type of an object is not known at compile time. This chapter has demonstrated polymorphism through several examples.

Questions

1. In your own words, describe polymorphism.
2. In what situations is polymorphism most useful?

Chapter 18
Annotations

A new feature in Java 5, annotations are notes in Java programs to instruct the Java compiler to do something. You can annotate any program elements, including Java packages, classes, constructors, fields, methods, parameters, and local variables. Java annotations are defined in JSR 175 (http://www.jcp.org/en/jsr/detail?id=175). Java provides three standard annotations and four standard meta-annotations. In addition, you can create custom annotations.

This chapter starts with an overview of annotations, and then teaches you how to use the standard annotations. It concludes with a discussion of custom annotations.

An Overview of Annotations

Annotations are notes for the Java compiler. When you annotate a program element in a source file, you add notes to the Java program elements in that source file. You can annotate Java packages, types (classes, interfaces, enumerated types), constructors, methods, fields, parameters, and local variables. For example, you can annotate a Java class so that any warnings that the **javac** program would otherwise issue will be suppressed. Or, you can annotate a method that you want to override to ask the compiler to verify that you are really overriding the method, not overloading it. Additionally, you can annotate a Java class with the name of the developer. In a large project, annotating every Java class can be useful for the project manager or architect to measure the productivity of developers. For example, if all classes are annotated this way, it is easy to find out who is the most or the least productive programmer.

The Java compiler can be instructed to interpret annotations and discard them (so those annotations only live in source files) or include them in resulting Java classes. Those that are included in Java classes may be ignored by the Java virtual machine, or they may be loaded into the virtual machine. The latter type is called runtime-visible and you can use reflection to inquire about them.

Annotations and Annotation Types

When studying annotations, you will come across these two terms very often: annotations and annotation types. To understand their meanings, it is useful to first bear in mind that an annotation type is a special interface type. An annotation is an instance of an annotation type. Just like an interface, an annotation type has a name and members. The information contained in an annotation takes the form of key/value pairs. There can be zero or multiple pairs and each key has a specific type. It can be a **String**, **int**, or other Java types. Annotation types with no key/value pairs are called marker annotation types. Those with one key/value pair are often referred to single-value annotation types.

There are three annotation types in Java 5: **Deprecated, Override,** and **SuppressWarnings**. They are part of the **java.lang** package and you will learn to use them in the section "Built-in Annotations." On top of that, there are four other annotation types that are part of the **java.lang.annotation** package: **Documented, Inherited, Retention,** and **Target**. These four annotation types are used to annotate annotations, and you will learn about them in the section "Custom Annotation Types" later in this chapter.

Annotation Syntax

In your code, you use an annotation differently from using an ordinary interface. You declare an annotation type by using this syntax.

```
@AnnotationType
```

or

```
@AnnotationType(elementValuePairs)
```

The first syntax is for marker annotation types and the second for single-value and multi-value types. It is legal to put white spaces between the at sign (@) and annotation type, but this is not recommended.

For example, here is how you use the marker annotation type **Deprecated**:

```
@Deprecated
```

And, this is how you use the second element for multi-value annotation type Author:

```
@Author(firstName="Ted",lastName="Diong")
```

There is an exception to this rule. If an annotation type has a single key/value pair and the name of the key is **value**, then you can omit the key from the bracket. Therefore, if the fictitious annotation type **Stage** has a single key named **value**, you can write

```
@Stage(value=1)
```

or

```
@Stage(1)
```

The Annotation Interface

Know that an annotation type is a Java interface. All annotation types are subinterfaces of the **java.lang.annotation.Annotation** interface. It has one method, **annotationType**, that returns an **java.lang.Class** object.

```
java.lang.Class<? extends Annotation> annotationType()
```

In addition, any implementation of **Annotation** will override the **equals**, **hashCode**, and **toString** methods from the **java.lang.Object** class. Here are their default implementations.

```
public boolean equals(Object object)
```
> Returns **true** if *object* is an instance of the same annotation type as this one and all members of *object* are equal to the corresponding members of this annotation.

```
public int hashCode()
```
> Returns the hash code of this annotation, which is the sum of the hash codes of its members

```
public String toString()
```
Returns a string representation of this annotation, which typically lists all the key/value pairs of this annotation.

You will use this class when learning custom annotation types later in this chapter.

Standard Annotations

Java 5 comes with three built-in annotations, all of which are in the **java.lang** package: **Override**, **Deprecated**, and **SuppressWarnings**. They are discussed in this section.

Override

Override is a marker annotation type that can be applied to a method to indicate to the compiler that the method overrides a method in a superclass. This annotation type guards the programmer against making a mistake when overriding a method.

For example, consider this class **Parent**:

```
class Parent {
    public float calculate(float a, float b) {
        return a * b;
    }
}
```

Suppose, you want to extend **Parent** and override its **calculate** method. Here is a subclass of **Parent**:

```
public class Child extends Parent {
    public int calculate(int a, int b) {
        return (a + 1) * b;
    }
}
```

The **Child** class compiles. However, the **calculate** method in **Child** does not override the method in **Parent** because it has a different signature, namely it returns and accepts **int**s instead of **float**s. In this example, a programming mistake like this is easy to spot because you can see both the **Parent** and

Child classes. However, you are not always this lucky. Sometimes the parent class is buried somewhere in another package. This seemingly trivial error could be fatal because when a client class calls the **calculate** method on an **Child** object and passes two floats, the method in the **Parent** class will be invoked and a wrong result will be returned.

Using the **Override** annotation type will prevent this kind of mistake. Whenever you want to override a method, declare the **Override** annotation type before the method:

```
public class Child extends Parent {
    @Override
    public int calculate(int a, int b) {
        return (a + 1) * b;
    }
}
```

This time, the compiler will generate a compile error and you'll be notified that the **calculate** method in **Child** is not overriding the method in the parent class.

It is clear that **@Override** is useful to make sure programmers override a method when they intend to override it, and not overload it.

Deprecated

Deprecated is a marker annotation type that can be applied to a method or a type (class/interface) to indicate that the method or type is deprecated. A deprecated method or type is marked so by the programmer to warn the users of his code that they should not use or override the method or use or extend the type. The reason why a method or a type is marked deprecated is usually because there is a better method or type and the method or type is retained in the current software version for backward compatibility.

For example, the **DeprecatedTest** class in Listing 18.1 uses the **Deprecated** annotation type.

Listing 18.1: Deprecating a method

```
package com.brainysoftware.jdk5.app18;
public class DeprecatedTest {
    @Deprecated
    public void serve() {
```

```
        }
}
```

If you use or override a deprecated method, you will get a warning at compile time. For example, Listing 18.2 shows the **DeprecatedTest2** class that uses the **serve** method in **DeprecatedTest**.

Listing 18.2: Using a deprecated method

```
package com.brainysoftware.jdk5.app17;
public class DeprecatedTest2 {
    public static void main(String[] args) {
        DeprecatedTest test = new DeprecatedTest();
        test.serve();
    }
}
```

Compiling **DeprecatedTest2** generates this warning:

```
Note: com/brainysoftware/jdk5/app18/DeprecatedTest2.java uses or
overrides a deprecated API.
Note: Recompile with -Xlint:deprecation for details.
```

Note

In Chapter 27, "Java Doc" you will learn that you can mark a method deprecated by using the **@deprecated** tag in Java Doc. By using the **–deprecation** flag in **javac**, you will be notified if any deprecated method is used.

On top of that, you can use **@Deprecated** to mark a class or an interface, as shown in Listing 18.3.

Listing 18.3: Marking a class deprecated

```
package com.brainysoftware.jdk5.app17;
@Deprecated
public class DeprecatedTest3 {
    public void serve() {
    }
}
```

SuppressWarnings

SuppressWarnings is used, as you must have guessed, to suppress compiler warnings. You can apply **@SuppressWarnings** to types, constructors, methods, fields, parameters, and local variables.

You use it by passing a **String** array that contains warnings that need to be suppressed. Its syntax is as follows.

```
@SuppressWarnings(value={string-1, …, string-n})
```

where *string-1* to *string-n* indicate the set of warnings to be suppressed. Duplicate and unrecognized warnings will be ignored.

The following are valid parameters to **@SuppressWarnings**:

- **unchecked**. Give more detail for unchecked conversion warnings that are mandated by the Java Language Specification.
- **path**. Warn about nonexistent path (classpath, sourcepath, etc) directories.
- **serial**. Warn about missing serialVersionUID definitions on serializable classes.
- **finally**. Warn about finally clauses that cannot complete normally.
- **fallthrough**. Check switch blocks for fall-through cases, namely cases, other than the last case in the block, whose code does not include a **break** statement, allowing code execution to "fall through" from that case to the next case. As an example, the code following the case 2 label in this **switch** block does not contain a **break** statement:

```
switch (i) {
case 1:
    System.out.println("1");
    break;
case 2:
    System.out.println("2");
    //  falling through
case 3:
    System.out.println("3");
}
```

As an example, the **SuppressWarningsTest** class in Listing18.4 uses the **SuppressWarnings** annotation type to prevent the compiler from issuing unchecked and fallthrough warnings.

Listing 18.4 Using @SuppressWarnings

```
package com.brainysoftware.jdk5.app18;
import java.io.File;
import java.io.Serializable;
import java.util.ArrayList;

@SuppressWarnings(value={"unchecked","serial"})
public class SuppressWarningsTest implements Serializable {
    public void openFile() {
        ArrayList a = new ArrayList();
        File file = new File("X:/java/doc.txt");
    }
}
```

Note

@SuppressWarnings has not been implemented in Java 5.0. It will be in Java 5.1.

Standard Meta-Annotations

Meta annotations are annotations that are applied to annotations. There are four meta-annotation types that come standard with Java 5 that are used to annotate annotations; they are **Documented**, **Inherited**, **Retention**, and **Target**. All the four are part of the **java.lang.annotation** package. This section discusses these annotation types.

Documented

Documented is a marker annotation type used to annotate the declaration of an annotation type so that instances of the annotation type will be included in the documentation generated using Javadoc or similar tools.

For example, the **Override** annotation type is not annotated using **Documented**. As a result, if you use Javadoc to generate a class whose method is annotated **@Override**, you will not see any trace of **@Override** in the resulting document.

For instance, Listing 18.5 shows the **OverrideTest2** class that uses **@Override** to annotate the **toString** method.

Listing 18.5: The OverrideTest2 class

```
package com.brainysoftware.jdk5.app17;
public class OverrideTest2 {
    @Override
    public String toString() {
        return "OverrideTest2";
    }
}
```

On the other hand, the **Deprecated** annotation type is annotated **@Documented**. Recall that the **serve** method in the **DeprecatedTest** class in Listing 18.2 is annotated **@Deprecated**. Now, if you use **Javadoc** to generate the documentation for **OverrideTest2** (Javadoc is discussed in Chapter 27, "Java Doc"), the details of the **serve** method in the documentation will also include **@Deprecated**, like this:

```
serve
@Deprecated
public void serve()
```

Inherited

You use **Inherited** to annotate an annotation type so that any instance of the annotation type will be inherited. If you annotate a class using an inherited annotation type, the annotation will be inherited by any subclass of the annotated class. If the user queries the annotation type on a class declaration, and the class declaration has no annotation of this type, then the class's parent class will automatically be queried for the annotation type. This process will be repeated until an annotation of this type is found or the root class is reached.

Check the section "Custom Annotation Types" on how to query an annotation type.

Retention

@Retention indicates how long annotations whose annotated types are annotated @Retention are to be retained. The value of **@Retention** can be one of the members of the **java.lang.annotation.RetentionPolicy** enum:

- **SOURCE**. Annotations are to be discarded by the Java compiler.
- **CLASS**. Annotations are to be recorded in the class file but not be retained by the JVM. This is the default value.
- **RUNTIME**. Annotations are to be retained by the JVM so you can query them using reflection.

For example, the declaration of the **SuppressWarnings** annotation type is annotated **@Retention** with the value of **SOURCE**.

```
@Retention(value=SOURCE)
public @interface SuppressWarnings
```

Target

Target indicates which program element(s) can be annotated using instances of the annotated annotation type. The value of **Target** is one of the members of the **java.lang.annotation.ElementType** enum:

- **ANNOTATION_TYPE**. The annotated annotation type can be used to annotate annotation type declaration.
- **CONSTRUCTOR**. The annotated annotation type can be used to annotate constructor declaration.
- **FIELD**. The annotated annotation type can be used to annotate field declaration.
- **LOCAL_VARIABLE**. The annotated annotation type can be used to annotate local variable declaration.
- **METHOD**. The annotated annotation type can be used to annotate method declaration.
- **PACKAGE**. The annotated annotation type can be used to annotate package declarations.
- **PARAMETER**. The annotated annotation type can be used to annotate parameter declarations.
- **TYPE**. The annotated annotation type can be used to annotate type declarations.

As an example, the **Override** annotation type declaration is annotated the following **Target** annotation, making **Override** can only be applied to method declarations.

```
@Target(value=METHOD)
```

You can have multiple values in the **Target** annotation. For example, this is from the declaration of **SuppressWarnings**:

```
@Target(value={TYPE,FIELD, METHOD, PARAMETER,CONSTRUCTOR,
LOCAL_VARIABLE})
```

Custom Annotation Types

An annotation type is a Java interface, except that you must add an at sign before the **interface** keyword when declaring it.

```
public @interface CustomAnnotation {
}
```

By default, all annotation types implicitly or explicitly extend the **java.lang.annotation.Annotation** interface. In addition, even though you can extend an annotation type, its subtype is not treated as an annotation type.

A Custom Annotation Type

As an example, Listing 18.6 shows a custom annotation type called **Author**.

Listing 18.6: The Author annotation type

```
package com.brainysoftware.jdk5.app18.custom;
import java.lang.annotation.Documented;
import java.lang.annotation.Retention;
import java.lang.annotation.RetentionPolicy;

@Documented
@Retention(RetentionPolicy.RUNTIME)
public @interface Author {
    String firstName();
    String lastName();
    boolean internalEmployee();
}
```

Using Custom Annotation Type

The **Author** annotation type is like any other Java type. Once you import it into a class or an interface, you can use it simply by writing

```
@Author(firstName="firstName",lastName="lastName",
internalEmployee=true|false)
```

For example, the **Test1** class in Listing 18.7 is annotated **Author**.

Listing 18.7: A class annotated Author

```
package com.brainysoftware.jdk5.app18.custom;
@Author(firstName="John",lastName="Guddell",internalEmployee=true)
public class Test1 {
}
```

Is that it? Yes, that's it. Very simple, isn't it?

The next subsection "Using Reflection to Query Annotations" shows how the **Author** annotations can be of good use.

Using Reflection to Query Annotations

In Java 5, the **java.lang.Class** has a few methods related to annotations.

```
public <A extends java.lang.annotation.Annotation> A getAnnotation
      (Class<A> annotationClass)
```
Returns this element's annotation for the specified annotation type, if present. Otherwise, returns **null**.

```
public java.lang.annotation.Annotation[] getAnnotations()
```
Returns all annotations present on this class.

```
public boolean isAnnotation()
```
Returns **true** if this class is an annotation type.

```
public boolean isAnnotationPresent(Class<? extends
        java.lang.annotation.Annotation> annotationClass)
```
Indicates whether an annotation for the specified type is present on this class

The **com.brainysoftware.jdk5.app18.custom** package includes three test classes, **Test1**, **Test2**, and **Test3**, that are annotated Author. Listing 18.8 shows a test class that employs reflection to query the test classes.

Listing 18.8: Using reflection to query annotations

```
package com.brainysoftware.jdk5.app18.custom;
```

```java
public class CustomAnnotationTest {
    public static void printClassInfo(Class c) {
        System.out.print(c.getName() + ". ");
        Author author = (Author) c.getAnnotation(Author.class);
        if (author != null) {
            System.out.println("Author:" + author.firstName()
                    + " " + author.lastName());
        } else {
            System.out.println("Author unknown");
        }
    }

    public static void main(String[] args) {
        CustomAnnotationTest.printClassInfo(Test1.class);
        CustomAnnotationTest.printClassInfo(Test2.class);
        CustomAnnotationTest.printClassInfo(Test3.class);
        CustomAnnotationTest.printClassInfo(
                CustomAnnotationTest.class);
    }
}
```

When run, you will see the following message in your console:

```
com.brainysoftware.jdk5.app17.custom.Test1. Author:John Guddell
com.brainysoftware.jdk5.app17.custom.Test2. Author:John Guddell
com.brainysoftware.jdk5.app17.custom.Test3. Author:Lesley Nielsen
com.brainysoftware.jdk5.app17.custom.CustomAnnotationTest. Author
unknown
```

Summary

Annotations are a new feature in Java 5 used to instruct the Java compiler to do something to an annotated program element. Any program element can be annotated, including Java packages, classes, constructors, fields, methods, parameters, and local variables. This chapter explained standard annotation types and taught how to create custom annotation types.

Questions

1. What is an annotation type?
2. What is a meta-annotation?
3. What are the standard annotation types included in Java 5?

Chapter 19
Internationalization

In this era of globalization, it is now more compelling than before that you are able to write applications that can be deployed in different countries and regions that speak different languages. There are two terms you need to be familiar with in this regard. The first is internationalization, often abbreviated to i18n because the word starts with an i and ends with and n, and there are 18 characters between the first i and the last n. Internationalization is the technique for developing applications that support multiple languages and data formats without rewriting the programming logic. The second term in localization, which is the technique of adapting an internationalized application to support a specific locale. A locale is a specific geographical, political, or cultural region. An operation that takes a locale into consideration is said to be locale-sensitive. For example, displaying a date is locale-sensitive because the date must be in the format used by the country or region of the user. The fifteenth day of November 2006 is written 11/15/2006 in the US, but written as 15/11/2006 in Australia. For the same reason internationalization is abbreviated i18n, localization is abbreviated to l10n.

Java was designed with internationalization in mind, employing Unicode for characters and strings. Making international applications in Java is therefore very easy. How you internationalize your applications depends on how much static data needs to be presented in different languages. There are two approaches.

1. If a large amount of data is static, create a separate version of the resource for each locale. This approach normally applies to Web application with lots of static HTML pages. It is straightforward and will not be discussed in this chapter.
2. If the amount of static data that needs to be internationalized is limited, isolate textual elements such as component labels and error messages into text files. Each text file stores the translations of all textual elements for a locale. The application then retrieves each element dynamically.

The advantage is clear. Each textual element can be edited easily without recompiling the application. This is the technique that will discussed in this chapter.

This chapter starts by explaining what a locale. Next comes the technique for internationalizing your applications, followed by a Swing application example.

Locales

The **java.util.Locale** class represents a locale. There are three main components of a **Locale** object: language, country, and variant. The language is obviously the most important part; however, sometimes the language itself is not sufficient to differentiate a locale. For example, the English language is spoken in countries such as the US and England. However, the English language spoken in the US is not exactly the same as the one used in the UK. Therefore, it is necessary to specify the country of the language. As another example, the Chinese language used in China is not exactly the same as the one used in Taiwan.

The variant argument is a vendor- or browser-specific code. For example, you use WIN for Windows, MAC for Macintosh, and POSIX for POSIX. Where there are two variants, separate them with an underscore, and put the most important one first. For example, a Traditional Spanish collation might construct a locale with parameters for language, country, and variant as es, ES, Traditional_WIN, respectively.

To construct a **Locale** object, use one of the **Locale** class's constructors.

```
public Locale(java.lang.String language)
public Locale(java.lang.String language, java.lang.String country)
public Locale(java.lang.String language, java.lang.String country,
        java.lang.String variant)
```

The language code is a valid ISO language code. Table 19.1 displays examples of language codes.

The country argument is a valid ISO country code, which is a two-letter, uppercase code specified in ISO 3166 (http://userpage.chemie.fu-berlin.de/diverse/doc/ISO_3166.html). Table 19.1 lists some of the country codes in ISO 3166.

Code	Language
de	German
el	Greek
en	English
es	Spanish
fr	French
hi	Hindi
it	Italian
ja	Japanese
nl	Dutch
pt	Portuguese
ru	Russian
zh	Chinese

Table 19.1: Examples of ISO 639 Language Codes

Country	Code
Australia	AU
Brazil	BR
Canada	CA
China	CN
Egypt	EG
France	FR
Germany	DE
India	IN
Mexico	MX
Switzerland	CH
Taiwan	TW
United Kingdom	GB
United States	US

Table 19.2: Examples of ISO 3166 Country Codes

For example, to construct a **Locale** object representing the English language used in Canada, write this.

```
Locale locale = new Locale("en", "CA");
```

In addition, the **Locale** class provides static final fields that return locales for specific countries or languages, such as **CANADA, CANADA_FRENCH, CHINA, CHINESE, ENGLISH, FRANCE, FRENCH, UK, US**, etc. Therefore, you can also construct a **Locale** object by calling its static field:

```
Locale locale = Locale.CANADA_FRENCH;
```

In addition, the static **getDefault** method returns the user computer's locale.

```
Locale locale = Locale.getDefault();
```

Internationalizing Applications

Internationalizing and localizing your applications require you to

1. Isolating textual components into properties files
2. Be able to select and reading the correct properties file

This section elaborates the two steps and provides a simple example. The section "An Internationalized Swing Application" later in this chapter presents another example.

Isolating Textual Components into Properties Files

An internationalized application stores its textual elements in a separate properties file for each locale. Each file contains key/value pairs, and each key uniquely identifies a locale-specific object. Keys are always strings, and values can be strings or any other type of object. For example, to support American English, German, and Chinese you will have three properties files, all of which have the same keys.

The following is the English version of the properties file. Note that it has two keys: **greetings** and **farewell**.

```
greetings = Hello
farewell = Goodbye
```

The German version would be as follows:

```
greetings = Hallo
farewell = Tschüß
```

And the properties file for the Chinese language is as follows:

```
greetings=\u4f60\u597d
farewell=\u518d\u89c1
```

Read the sidebar "Converting Chinese Characters to Unicode" on how we arrived at the previous properties file.

Converting Chinese Characters to Unicode

In the Chinese language, 你好 (meaning hello, represented by the Unicode codes 4f60 and 597d, respectively) and 再见 (meaning good bye and is represented by Unicode codes 518d and 89c1, respectively) are the most common expressions. Of course, no one remembers the Unicode code of each Chinese character. Therefore, you create the .properties file in two steps:

1. Using your favorite Chinese text editor, create a text file like this:

   ```
   greetings=你好
   farewell=再见
   ```

2. Convert the content of the text file into the Unicode representation. Normally, a Chinese text editor has the feature for converting Chinese characters into Unicode codes. You will get the end result:

   ```
   greetings=\u4f60\u597d
   farewell=\u518d\u89c1
   ```

Now, you need to master the **java.util.ResourceBundle** class. It enables you to easily choose and read the properties file specific to the user's locale and look up the values. **ResourceBundle** is an abstract class, but it provides static **getBundle** methods that return an instance of a concrete subclass.

A **ResourceBundle** object has a base name, which can be any name. In order for a **ResourceBundle** object to pick up a properties file, the filename must be composed of the **ResourceBundle** base name, followed by an underscore, followed by the language code, and optionally followed by another underscore and the country code. The format for the properties file name is as follows:

```
basename_languageCode_countryCode
```

For example, suppose the base name is **MyResources** and you define the following three locales:

- US-en

- DE-de
- CN-zh

Then you would have these three properties files:

- **MyResources_en_US.properties**
- **MyResources_de_DE.properties**
- **MyResources_zh_CN.properties**

Reading Properties Files using ResourceBundle

As mentioned previously, **ResourceBundle** is an abstract class. Nonetheless, you can obtain an instance of **ResourceBundle** by calling its static **getBundle** method. The signatures of its overloads are

```
public static ResourceBundle getBundle(java.lang.String baseName)
```

```
public static ResourceBundle getBundle(java.lang.String baseName,
        Locale locale)
```

For example:

```
ResourceBundle rb =
        ResourceBundle.getBundle("MyResources", Locale.US);
```

This will load the **ResourceBundle** object with the values in the corresponding properties file.

If a suitable properties file is not found, the **ResourceBundle** object will use the default properties file, which will be the one whose name equals the base name and has the **properties** extension. In this case, the default file would be **MyResources.properties**. If this file is not found, a **java.util.MissingResourceException** will be thrown.

Then, to read a value, you use the **ResourceBundle** class's **getString** method, passing the key.

```
public java.lang.String getString(java.lang.String key)
```

If the entry with the specified key is not found, a **java.util.MissingResourceException** will be thrown.

An Internationalized Swing Application

The following example illustrates the effort to support internationalization with two languages: English and French. This example uses three properties files:

- **MyResources_en_US.properties**, given in Listing 19.1
- **MyResources_fr_CA.properties**, shown in Listing 19.2
- **MyResources.properties** (the default), presented in Listing 19.3

These files are placed in the directory specified in the class path.

Listing 19.1: The MyResources_en_US.properties File

```
userName=User Name
password=Password
login=Login
```

Listing 19.2: The MyResources_fr_CA.properties File

```
userName=Compte
password=Mot de passe
login=Ouvrir session
```

Listing 19.3: The MyResources.properties File

```
userName=User Name
password=Password
login=Login
```

Note

The properties file should be placed in the working directory, even if the class that uses the **ResourceBundle** class is part of a non-default package.

The **I18NTest** class, shown in Listing 19.4, obtains the **ResourceBundle** object according to the locale of your computer and supplies localized messages for the **JLabel**s and **JButton**.

Listing 19.4: The I18NTest class

```
package com.brainysoftware.jdk5.app19;
import java.awt.GridLayout;
import java.util.Locale;
import java.util.ResourceBundle;
```

```
import javax.swing.JButton;
import javax.swing.JFrame;
import javax.swing.JLabel;
import javax.swing.JPasswordField;
import javax.swing.JTextField;
import javax.swing.SwingUtilities;

public class I18NTest {
    private static void constructGUI() {
        Locale locale = Locale.getDefault();
        ResourceBundle rb =
                ResourceBundle.getBundle("MyResources", locale);
        JFrame.setDefaultLookAndFeelDecorated(true);
        JFrame frame = new JFrame("I18N Test");
        frame.setDefaultCloseOperation(JFrame.EXIT_ON_CLOSE);
        frame.setLayout(new GridLayout(3, 2));
        frame.add(new JLabel(rb.getString("userName")));
        frame.add(new JTextField());
        frame.add(new JLabel(rb.getString("password")));
        frame.add(new JPasswordField());
        frame.add(new JButton(rb.getString("login")));
        frame.pack();
        frame.setVisible(true);
    }

    public static void main(String[] args) {
        SwingUtilities.invokeLater(new Runnable() {
            public void run() {
                constructGUI();
            }
        });
    }
}
```

The English version of the application is shown in Figure 19.1.

Figure 19.1: The English version of the example

To test a different language, change your computer locale setting.

In practice, most internationalized applications will create localized contents that are based on different languages, rather than different locales. This is to say that if an application has provided textual elements in the German language for people from Germany, chances are slim that it will also provide another variant of German for people from Austria or Switzerland. Providing many variants of the same language is expensive and impractical. Any German speaking user will understand any variant of the German language, anyway.

Summary

This chapter explains how to develop an internationalized application. First it explained the **java.util.Locale** class and the **java.utilResourceBundle** class. It then continued with an example of an internationalized application.

Questions

1. What is the approach to internationalizing applications with plenty of static contents?
2. How do you isolate textual elements of a Java application?
3. What are the two classes used in internationalization and localization?

Chapter 20
Applets

An applet is small a Java program that runs inside another application, usually a Web browser or an applet viewer. The JDK includes an applet viewer that makes it easy for you to test your applets. However, most of the time your applets will run inside a Web browser.

This chapter starts with a brief history of applets and by introducing the **java.applet.Applet** class. However, it is easier to write a subclass of **Applet**, **javax.swing.JApplet**, just as it is easier to write Swing applications than using AWT components. Besides, **JApplet** is much more powerful than **Applet** so you should always subclass **JApplet** for your applet classes.

A Brief History of Applets

A couple of years after Java 1.0 was launched in 1995, applets dominated the Web's dynamic content arena. People used applets to achieve what server technologies are good for today as well as to improve interactivity on the client-side. Applets used to be the only widely accepted technology that could read and write to the server, access and manipulate data in the database, take user input, perform interactive animation, play sound files on the browser, and so on.

Then, we saw server-side technologies such as Servlet/JSP, Microsoft's ASP and ASP.NET, PHP, etc, mature and get accepted as the technologies for developing server applications. They can do many things that applets can plus more. The role of applets was diminishing and applets were only used for making the client-side richer than simple HTML. Later on, applets became less appealing. Several factors attributed to the near-demise of applets.

1. The emergence of scripting languages such as JavaScript and VBScript that are interpreted by the Web browser. These scripts are easier to write and do not need to be compiled.
2. The emergence of competing technologies that can add interactivity to the client side, such as Microsoft's ActiveX components and Macromedia's Flash.
3. The lawsuit between Sun Microsystems and Microsoft that resulted in Microsoft's unplugging its Microsoft Java Virtual Machine from Internet Explorer 6. Even though users can download a JVM from Sun's Website to run applets, application developers realized applets would not run automatically in IE 6 (the most commonly used browsers until today) and many started to shy away from applets. Apart from this, Microsoft's winning the browser war also did not make applet developers' lives easier. Microsoft JVM in Internet Explorer was only compliant with JDK 1.1, making it impractical to write **JApplet**s because they would not run automatically in IE. If **JApplet**, which allows you to use the richer Swing components (rather than AWT components) in your applets, had been given all possible supports, it's not impossible that applets would have continued to be the main technology for writing active contents on the browser.

   Later on, top computer makers such as Dell and HP took the initiative of installing a JVM in all boxes they sell, but this did not help applets make a comeback.

However, while JavaScript and DHTML can make Web contents dynamic, it is not powerful enough to bring Web pages to the next level: become more like a desktop application that has very high user-responsiveness. It's not surprising that a technology such as AJAX (asynchronous JavaScript + XML) that can make Web pages more like desktop applications is getting momentum since 2005. Applets are easier to program than AJAX and are more mature, more powerful, and more stable. Will people realize this one day and bring applets back to fame?

The Applet API

The API for writing applets is packaged into the **java.applet** package. There is only one class, **Applet**, in this package and three interfaces: **AppletContext**,

AudioClip, and **AppletStub**. These members of **java.applet** will be discussed in the next sections.

The Applet Class

The **java.applet.Applet** class is a template for all applets. This class is a subclass of **java.awt.Panel**, so to write effective applets, you also need some knowledge of the Abstract Window Toolkit (AWT) discussed in Chapter 15, "Swing Basics."

Because **Applet** is a **Panel**, you can add AWT components to it. As such, writing applets is like writing AWT applications. You use AWT components or draw on its **java.awt.Graphics** object. You can also use AWT layout managers and event listeners described in Chapter 16, "Swinging Higher."

The class diagram in Figure 20.1 shows the **Applet** class with its parent and child.

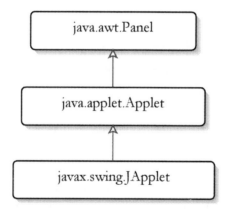

Figure 20.1: The java.applet.Applet class hierarchy

What makes **Applet** different from other AWT controls are the following four lifecycle methods of Applet.

```
public void init()
```
Called by the Web browser or applet viewer right after the applet class is loaded. It is called the before the first invocation of the **start** method.

```
public void start()
```

Called by the Web browser or applet viewer to tell this applet that it can start execution. The **start** method is called each time the applet is revisited in the Web page.

`public void stop()`

Called by the Web browser or applet viewer before the current Web page containing the applet is unloaded, for example when the user navigates to another page. The **stop** method is called before the **destroy** method is called.

`public void destroy()`

Called by the Web browser or applet viewer to tell this applet that it is being reclaimed and it should release all resources it has allocated.

In addition, there are also the following methods in the **Applet** class.

`public boolean isActive()`

Indicates if the current applet is active. An applet is made active just before the **start** method is called and made inactive just before the **stop** method is invoked.

`public void paint(java.awt.Graphics g)`

This method is inherited from the **java.awt.Container** to draw on an applet user interface. The **paint** method is called to draw the content of an applet.

`public void showStatus(java.lang.String message)`

This method displays a method in the status bar of the applet viewer or the Web browser running this applet.

`public String getParameter(java.lang.String parameterName)`

Returns a parameter passed by using the **param** tag in the HTML file. If the specified parameter name is not found, **getParameter** returns **null**.

`public java.net.URL getCodeBase()`

Returns the URL of the directory from which this applet was downloaded. The **java.net.URL** class is discussed in Chapter 21, "Java Networking." **getCodeBase** is different from **getDocumentBase** because the latter returns the URL of the Web page that contains this applet. If the applet and its containing Web page come from the same directory, the **getCodeBase** method and the **getDocumentBase** method return identical URL objects.

`public java.net.URL getDocumentBase()`

Returns the URL of the directory of the Web page containing this applet. The **getDocumentBase** method is different from the **getCodeBase** method. See the description of the **getCodeBase** method.

```
public AudioClip getAudioClip(java.net.URL url)
```
Returns the **AudioClip** object specified by the URL.

```
public AudioClip getAudioClip(java.net.URL url,
     java.lang.String filename)
```
Returns the **AudioClip** object specified by the URL and the *filename* argument.

```
public void play(java.net.URL url)
```
Play the audio clip specified by the URL.

```
public void play(java.net.URL url, java.lang.String filename)
```
Plays the audio clip specified by the URL and *filename*.

```
public static final AudioClip newAudioClip(java.net.URL url)
```
A convenience method that returns an **AudioClip** object specified by the URL. This method can be used in non-applet applications.

```
public java.awt.Image getImage(java.net.URL url)
```
Returns an Image object from the specified URL.

```
public java.awt.Image getImage(java.net.URL url,
     java.lang.String filename)
```
Returns an **Image** object from the specified URL and filename.

```
public AppletContext getAppletContext()
```
The **getAppletContext** method returns the **AppletContext** object. Read the description of the **AppletContext** interface.

The AppletContext Interface

An **AppletContext** object is created by the Web browser or applet viewer and represents the environment in which an applet is running. An applet can obtain the reference to its **AppletContext** object by calling the **getAppletContext** method. Most methods in **AppletContext** are duplicated in **Applet**, except the **showDocument** methods, that you can use to navigate to a different Web page than the current one. Here are the two overloads of **showDocument**.

```
public void showDocument(java.net.URL url)
```

Navigates to the specified URL

```
public void showDocument(java.net.URL url,
       java.lang.String filename)
```
Navigates to the specified URL and filename.

See the NewsTickerApplet applet for an example.

The AudioClip Interface

An **AudioClip** object represents an audio clip. The following audio formats can be played by the **AudioClip** interface's **play** and **loop** methods: .au, .wav, mid, rmf, aif.

The **AudioClip** interface has three methods:

```
public void play()
```
Plays the audio clip.

```
public void loop()
```
Plays the audio clip and keeps repeating indefinitely, until the stop method is called..

```
public void stop()
```
Stop playing this audio clip.

The AppletStub Interface

When a Web browser or an applet viewer creates an applet, it also creates an **AppletStub** object that it passes to the applet by calling the **setStub** method on the **Applet** object. **AppletStub** acts as an interface between an applet and the browser environment or applet viewer environment in which the applet is running. Unless you are writing an applet viewer, you will rarely need to worry about creating an **AppletStub**.

Security Restrictions

For security reasons, applets downloaded from the Internet are restricted. They cannot do the following operations:

- read form and write to files in the client computer
- make network connections other than the originating host.
- define native calls.
- Read system properties other than those listed in Table 20.1.

Property	Description
file.separator	File separator (for example, "/")
java.class.version	Java class version number
java.vendor	Java vendor-specific string
java.vendor.url	Java vendor URL
java.version	Java version number
line.separator	Line separator
os.arch	Operating system architecture
os.name	Operating system name
path.separator	Path separator (for example, ":")

Table 20.1: System properties accessible to applets

To read a system property from within an applet, use the **getProperty** method of the **java.lang.System** class. For example:

```
String newline = System.getProperty("line.separator");
```

To give an applet greater access, you need to digitally sign it. Applet signing is discussed in Chapter 24, "Security."

Writing and Deploying Applets

As an example, the code in Listing 20.1 presents an applet class.

Listing 20.1: LifeCycleApplet

```
package com.brainysoftware.jdk5.app20;
import java.applet.Applet;
import java.awt.Graphics;

public class LifeCycleApplet extends Applet {
    StringBuilder stringBuilder = new StringBuilder();
    public void init() {
        stringBuilder.append("init()... ");
    }
    public void start() {
```

```
            stringBuilder.append("start()... ");
    }
    public void stop() {
        stringBuilder.append("stop()... ");
    }
    public void destroy() {
        stringBuilder.append("destroy()... ");
    }
    public void paint(Graphics g) {
        stringBuilder.append("paint(g)... ");
        g.drawString(stringBuilder.toString(), 4, 10);
    }
}
```

You can compile the applet as you would other Java classes. To run the applet, you first have to write an HTML page that references the applet's class. Listing 20.2 shows the content of **runApplet.html**, the HTML file that references the **LifeCycleApplet** applet.

Listing 20.2: The runApplet.html page

```
<html>
<head>
<title>Testing LifeCycleApplet</title>
</head>
<body>
<applet code="com.brainysoftware.jdk5.app20.LifeCycleApplet.class"
    width="400" height="300">
</applet>
</body>
</html>
```

The HTML file must reside in the same directory as the class's root directory. Figure 20.2 shows the directory structure of the applet and the HTML file (runApplet.html file).

Figure 20.2: The directory structure of the HTML file and the applet class

You can either run the HTML file using a Web browser or by using the **AppletViewer** application that comes with the JDK. The **appletviewer.exe** file can be found in the same directory as the **java.exe** and **javac.exe** programs.

To run your applet using **AppletViewer**, from the directory on which the **runApplet.html** file resides, type

```
appletviewer runApplet.html
```

Figure 20.3 displays the applet in **AppletViewer** and Figure 20.4 in a Web browser.

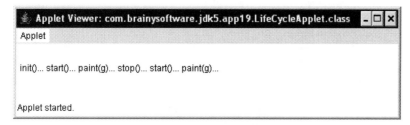

Figure 20.3: Running LifeCycleApplet in AppletViewer

Figure 20.4: Running LifeCycleApplet in a Web browser

There is a difference between running in the applet viewer and the browser. When you minimize the applet viewer, it invokes the **stop** method of the applet. When you restore the applet viewer, it invokes the **start** method and **paint** method again. When you minimize your browser, the applet's **stop** method is not invoked.

How AppletViewer Works

It is not hard to understand how an applet viewer, such as the **AppletViewer** program, works. These are the things you need to bear in mind. An applet is an AWT component that can be added to a container, and an applet viewer needs to call the **init** and **start** methods of the applet it's running.

Listing 20.3 presents a **JFrame** that acts as an applet viewer.

Listing 20.3: A custom applet viewer called AppletRunner

```
package com.brainysoftware.jdk5.app20;
import java.applet.Applet;
import java.awt.BorderLayout;
import javax.swing.JFrame;

public class AppletRunner extends JFrame {
    public void run(String appletClassName) {
        this.setDefaultCloseOperation(JFrame.EXIT_ON_CLOSE);
        this.setLayout(new BorderLayout());
        this.setTitle("Applet Runner");
        Applet applet = null;
        try {
            // use reflection to instantiate the applet
            Class appletClass = Class.forName(appletClassName);
            applet = (Applet) appletClass.newInstance();
        }
        catch (Exception e) {
            e.printStackTrace();
        }
        if (applet!=null) {
            this.add(applet);
            this.pack();
            this.setVisible(true);
            // call the applet's lifecycle methods
            applet.init();
            applet.start();
        }
        else {
            System.exit(-1);
        }
    }

    public static void main(String[] args) {
        if (args.length!=1) {
```

```
        System.out.println(
                "Usage: AppletRunner appletClassName");
        System.exit(0);
    }
    // args[0] should be the fully qualified class name of the
    // applet to be run
    (new AppletRunner()).run(args[0]);
    }
}
```

To use the program, you pass an applet's fully qualified class name as the argument to the **AppletRunner** class:

```
java AppletRunner appletClassName
```

For example, to run the **LifeCycleApplet**, type

```
java AppletRunner com.brainysoftware.jdk5.app20.LifeCycleApplet
```

Figure 20.5 shows the **LifeCycleApplet** in **AppletRunner**.

Figure 20.5: A home-made applet viewer

Passing Parameters to an Applet

To pass parameters to an applet, you use the **param** tag inside the **applet** tag in your HTML file. The **param** tag can have two attributes:

- **name**. Represents the parameter name.
- **value**. Represents the parameter value.

For example:

```
<param name="customer" value="Jane Goddall"/>
```

From inside an applet, you can retrieve a parameter by using the Applet class's getParameter method:

```
public java.lang.String getParameter(java.lang.String paramName)
```

Let's now examine the NewsTickerApplet class in Listing 20.4. The applet can be used to display headlines that you pass as parameters in **param** tags. A headline can be associated with a URL. If a headline is clicked, the applet redirects you the corresponding URL.

Listing 20.4: The NewsTickerApplet class

```java
package com.brainysoftware.jdk5.app20;
import java.applet.Applet;
import java.awt.BorderLayout;
import java.awt.Color;
import java.awt.Label;
import java.awt.event.MouseAdapter;
import java.awt.event.MouseEvent;
import java.net.MalformedURLException;
import java.net.URL;
import java.util.ArrayList;
import java.util.List;

public class NewsTickerApplet extends Applet implements Runnable {
    Label label = new Label();
    String[] headlines;
    String[] urls;
    boolean running = true;
    Thread thread;
    int counter = 0;

    public void run() {
        while (running) {
            label.setText(headlines[counter]);
            try {
                Thread.sleep(1500);
            } catch (InterruptedException e) {
            }
            counter++;
            if (counter == headlines.length)
                counter = 0;
        }
    }

    public void init() {
```

```java
        this.setLayout(new BorderLayout());
        this.add(label);
        label.setBackground(Color.LIGHT_GRAY);
        label.addMouseListener(new MouseAdapter() {
            public void mouseClicked(MouseEvent me) {
                try {
                    URL url = new URL(urls[counter]);
                    getAppletContext().showDocument(url);
                } catch (MalformedURLException e) {
                } catch (Exception e) {
                }
            }
        });
    }

    public void start() {
        List<String> list = new ArrayList<String>();
        for (int i = 1;; i++) {
            String headline = this.getParameter("headline"
                    + Integer.toString(i));
            if (headline != null) {
                list.add(headline);
            } else {
                headlines = new String[list.size()];
                list.toArray(headlines);
                break;
            }
        }
        list.clear();
        for (int i = 1;; i++) {
            String url = this.getParameter("url" +
                    Integer.toString(i));
            if (url != null) {
                list.add(url);
            } else {
                urls = new String[list.size()];
                list.toArray(urls);
                break;
            }
        }
        if (thread == null) {
            thread = new Thread(this);
            thread.start();
        }
    }
```

```
    public void stop() {
        running = false;
    }
}
```

The **NewsTickerApplet** class uses a **java.awt.Label** to display headlines. It also employs two class-level **String** arrays to store headlines and corresponding URLs.

```
Label label = new Label();
String[] headlines;
String[] urls;
```

The **init** method, which is called when the applet is initialized, adds the label to the applet and adds a mouse listener to the label. This listener will redirects the user to the URL corresponding to the headline clicked.

```
public void init() {
    this.setLayout(new BorderLayout());
    this.add(label);
    label.setBackground(Color.LIGHT_GRAY);
    label.addMouseListener(new MouseAdapter() {
        public void mouseClicked(MouseEvent me) {
            try {
                URL url = new URL(urls[counter]);
                getAppletContext().showDocument(url);
            } catch (MalformedURLException e) {
            } catch (Exception e) {
            }
        }
    });
}
```

The listener is implemented as an anonymous class (discussed in Chapter 14, "Nested and Inner Classes").

The start method reads parameters from the param tags. The first headline is stored in the parameter named **headline1** and the first URL by **url1**. Similarly, the second headline is stored in the **headline2** parameter, and so on.

To display the headlines, you use a thread. Java threads are explained in Chapter 23, for now know that the run method in the applet displays the headlines one at a time.

Listing 20.5 shows the HTML file that contains the **NewsTickerApplet** applet.

Listing 20.5: The HTML file that contains NewsTickerApplet

```
<html>
<head>
<title>Testing NewsTickerApplet</title>
</head>
<body>
<applet code="com.brainysoftware.jdk5.app20.NewsTickerApplet.class"
    width="200" height="20">
<param name="headline1" value="Economic Survey"/>
<param name="url1" value="http://www.economist.com"/>
<param name="headline2" value="Business Today"/>
<param name="url2" value="http://news.yahoo.com"/>
<param name="headline3" value="World Live"/>
<param name="url3" value="http://www.cnn.com"/>
</applet>
</body>
</html>
```

Load the HTML file in Listing 20.5 to a Web browser, and you should be able to see the applet in the browser, like the one shown in Figure 20.6.

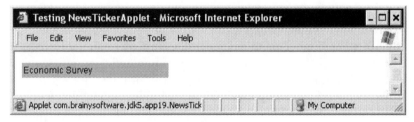

Figure 20.6: Passing parameters to the NewsTickerApplet

SoundPlayerApplet

The following example shows an important feature of the **Applet** class: play audio clips. Playing an audio clip is as easy as composing a URL that points to the location of an audio file. Most of the time, you can simply call the **getCodeBase** and **getDocumentBase** methods to get a URL object.

Listing 20.6 shows the **SoundPlayerApplet** class that play the **quick.au** sound file.

Listing 20.6: SoundPlayerApplet class

```
package com.brainysoftware.jdk5.app20;
import java.applet.Applet;
import java.applet.AudioClip;

public class SoundPlayerApplet extends Applet {
    public void start() {
        AudioClip audioClip = this.getAudioClip(getCodeBase(),
                "quack.au");
        // audioClip.play();
        audioClip.loop();
    }
}
```

Note that calling **play** before **loop** causes the audio clip to be played once only.

JApplet

The Swing API (discussed in Chapter 15, "Swing Basics") includes the **javax.swing.JApplet** class. This class is a direct child of **java.applet.Applet** and allows you to add Swing components on it. When Swing was first released, people shunned **JApplet** because most browsers did not yet support Java 1.2. As such, applets that subclass **JApplet** would not run in many Web browsers. Those awful years have passed, though, because now most browsers that support Java use JDK 1.2 or later. Therefore, **JApplet** is the preferred choice when writing applets today.

JApplet is a Swing component, but it is also a subclass of **java.applet.Applet**. As such, a **JApplet** is still an applet that needs to run on an applet viewer or a Web browser. On the other hand, it behaves much like a **JFrame**. For example, you can add Swing components, respond to events, and use Swing layout management.

Listing 20.7 presents an example of **JApplet**.

Listing 20.7: A JApplet

```
package com.brainysoftware.jdk5.app19;
```

```
import java.awt.BorderLayout;
import javax.swing.JApplet;
import javax.swing.JButton;
import javax.swing.JLabel;
import javax.swing.JTextField;

public class MyJApplet extends JApplet {
    public void start() {
        this.setLayout(new BorderLayout());
        JLabel label1 = new JLabel("Registration Form");
        label1.setHorizontalAlignment(JLabel.CENTER);
        this.add(label1, BorderLayout.NORTH);
        JLabel label2 = new JLabel("Name:");
        this.add(label2, BorderLayout.WEST);
        JTextField textField = new JTextField("<your name>");
        this.add(textField, BorderLayout.CENTER);
        JButton button1 = new JButton("Register");
        this.add(button1, BorderLayout.EAST);
        JButton button2 = new JButton("Clear Form");
        this.add(button2, BorderLayout.SOUTH);
    }
}
```

When run, the **JApplet** looks like a JFrame, but it runs on the applet viewer or the Web browser. Figure 20.7 shows this.

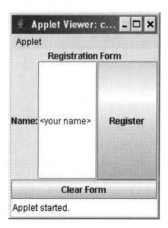

Figure 20.7: A JApplet

Applet Deployment in a JAR File

Applets can also be packaged into a jar file and deployed. The advantage is you can deploy your applet and its resources in one single file. In addition, if your applet needs to access restricted resources, you can digitally sign it. Signing a jar file is discussed in Chapter 24, "Java Security."

To package Java classes and related resources into a jar file, you use the **jar** tool included in the JDK. To create a jar file, use this command.

```
jar cf jarfile inputfiles
```

where *jarfile* is the name of the JAR file to be created and *inputfiles* is a list of files to be included in the JAR file.

For example, to jar all Java classes that belong to the package **com.brainysoftware.jdk5.app20** and all audio files in the working directory into the **MyJar.jar** file, change directory to the working directory of this chapter's application and type this.

```
jar cf MyJar.jar com/brainysoftware/jdk5/app20/*.class *.au
```

Note
A jar file has the same format as a zip file. If you have a zip file viewer, you can change the extension of the jar file to .zip and use the viewer to view the content of the jar file.

The **jar** tool can also be used with options and to update and extract a JAR file. For details see Appendix C, "The Jar Tool."

If you deploy your applet in a jar file, you need to use the **archive** attribute in your **applet** tag to tell Web browsers how to find the jar file. Because a jar file can house more than one Java class, you still need the **code** attribute to tell Web browsers which class to invoke. The following is an example of an applet tag that downloads an applet from a jar file (**MyJar.jar**) and invoke the **MyApplet.class** in the jar file.

```
<applet code="MyApplet.class" archive="MyJar.jar" width="600"
    height="50">
</applet>
```

Summary

Applets are small Java programs that run on an applet viewer or a Web browser. The Applet API is deployed in the **java.applet** package. The **Applet** class represents an applet. The **init**, **start**, and **destroy** methods are life cycle methods of an applet. They get called by the applet viewer.

When the Swing technology was released, it included the **javax.swing.JApplet** class that is a child class of **java.applet.Applet**. JApplet is a Swing component and allows you to add Swing components on it.

Applets are normally downloaded from the Internet. As such, it must be defined using the **applet** tag in the HTML file.

Questions

1. What are the life cycle methods of an applet?
2. How do you pass parameters to an applet?
3. Is **JApplet** an applet or a **JFrame**?

Chapter 21
Java Networking

Computer networking is concerned with communication between computers. Nowadays, this form of interaction is ubiquitous. Whenever you surf the Internet, it is your machine exchanging messages with remote servers. When you transfer a file over an FTP channel, you are also using some kind of networking service. Java comes equipped with the **java.net** package that contains types that make network programming easy. We'll examine some of the types after an overview of networking. Towards the end of the chapter, some examples are presented for you to play with.

An Overview of Networking

A network is a collection of computers that can communicate with each other. Depending on how wide the coverage is, a network can be referred to as a local area network (LAN) or a wide area network (WAN). A LAN is normally confined to a limited geographic area, such as a building, and comprises from as few as three to as many as hundreds of computers. A WAN, by contrast, is a combination of multiple LANs that are geographically separate. The largest network of all is, of course, the Internet.

The communication medium within a network can be cables, telephone lines, high-speed fiber, satellites, and so on. As the wireless technology gets more and more mature and inexpensive, a wireless local area network (WLAN) is becoming more commonplace nowadays.

Just like two people use a common language to converse, two computers communicate by using a common 'language' both agreed on. In computer jargon, this 'language' is referred to as protocol. What's confusing is that there are several layers of protocols. This is because at the physical layer two computer communicate by exchanging bitstreams, which are collections of 1s and 0s. This is too hard to be understood by applications and humans. Therefore, there is another layer that translates bitstreams into something more tangible and vice versa.

The easiest protocols are those at the application layer. Writing applications require you to understand protocols in the application layer. There are several protocols in this layer: HTTP, FTP, telnet, etc.

Application layer protocols use the protocols in the transport layer. Two popular ones at the transport layer are TCP and UDP. In turn transport layer protocols utilize the protocols at the layer below it. The diagram in Figure 21.1 shows some of these layers.

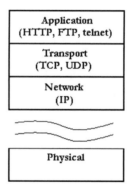

Figure 21.1: Layers of protocol in the computer network

Thanks to this strategy, you don't have to worry about protocols in other layers than the application layer. Java even goes the extra mile to provide classes that encapsulate application layer protocols. For example, with Java, you do not need to understand the HTTP to be able to send a message to an HTTP server. The HTTP, one of the most popular protocols, is covered in detail in this chapter for those who want to know more than the surface.

Another thing that you should know is that a network employs an addressing system to distinguish a computer from another, just like your house has an address so that the mailman can deliver mail. The equivalent of the street address on the Internet is the IP address. Each computer is assigned a unique IP address.

The IP address is not the smallest unit in the network addressing system. The port is. The analogy is an apartment building that share the same street address but has many units, each with its own suite number.

The Hypertext Transfer Protocol (HTTP)

The HTTP is the protocol that allows Web servers and browsers to send and receive data over the Internet. It is a request and response protocol. The client requests a file and the server responds to the request. HTTP uses reliable TCP connections—by default on TCP port 80. The first version of HTTP was HTTP/0.9, which was then overridden by HTTP/1.0. Replacing HTTP/1.0 is the current version of HTTP/1.1, which is defined in Request for Comments (RFC) 2616 and downloadable from http://www.w3.org/Protocols/HTTP/1.1/rfc2616.pdf.

In the HTTP, it is always the client who initiates a transaction by establishing a connection and sending an HTTP request. The Web server is in no position to contact a client or make a callback connection to the client. Either the client or the server can prematurely terminate a connection. For example, when using a Web browser you can click the Stop button on your browser to stop downloading a file, effectively closing the HTTP connection with the Web server.

HTTP Requests

An HTTP request consists of three components:

- Method—Uniform Resource Identifier (URI)—Protocol/Version
- Request headers
- Entity body

The following is an example of an HTTP request:

```
POST /examples/default.jsp HTTP/1.1
Accept: text/plain; text/html
Accept-Language: en-gb
Connection: Keep-Alive
Host: localhost
User-Agent: Mozilla/4.0 (compatible; MSIE 4.01; Windows 98)
Content-Length: 33
Content-Type: application/x-www-form-urlencoded
Accept-Encoding: gzip, deflate

lastName=Franks&firstName=Michael
```

The method—URI—protocol version appears as the first line of the request.

```
POST /examples/default.jsp HTTP/1.1
```

where **POST** is the request method, **/examples/default.jsp** the URI and **HTTP/1.1** the Protocol/Version section.

Each HTTP request can use one of the many request methods as specified in the HTTP standards. The HTTP 1.1 supports seven types of request: GET, POST, HEAD, OPTIONS, PUT, DELETE, and TRACE. GET and POST are the most commonly used in Internet applications.

The URI specifies an Internet resource. It is usually interpreted as being relative to the server's root directory. Thus, it should always begin with a forward slash **/**. A Uniform Resource Locator (URL) is actually a type of URI (See http://www.ietf.org/rfc/rfc2396.txt). The protocol version represents the version of the HTTP protocol being used.

The request header contains useful information about the client environment and the entity body of the request. For example, it could contain the language the browser is set for, the length of the entity body, and so on. Each header is separated by a carriage return/linefeed (CRLF) sequence.

Between the headers and the entity body, there is a blank line (CRLF) that is important to the HTTP request format. The CRLF tells the HTTP server where the entity body begins. In some Internet programming books, this CRLF is considered the fourth component of an HTTP request.

In the previous HTTP request, the entity body is simply the following line:

```
lastName=Franks&firstName=Michael
```

The entity body can easily become much longer in a typical HTTP request.

HTTP Responses

Similar to an HTTP request, an HTTP response also consists of three parts:

- Protocol—Status code—Description
- Response headers
- Entity body

The following is an example of an HTTP response:

```
HTTP/1.1 200 OK
Server: Microsoft-IIS/4.0
Date: Thu, 5 Jan 2006 13:13:33 GMT
Content-Type: text/html
Last-Modified: Thu, 5 Jan 2006 13:13:12 GMT
Content-Length: 112

<html>
<head>
<title>HTTP Response Example</title>
</head>
<body>
Welcome to Brainy Software
</body>
</html>
```

The first line of the response header is similar to the first line of a request header. The first line tells you that the protocol used is HTTP version 1.1, the request succeeded (200 is the success code), and that everything went okay.

The response headers contain useful information similar to the headers in the request. The entity body of the response is the HTML content of the response itself. The headers and the entity body are separated by a sequence of CRLFs.

java.net.URL

A URL is a unique address to an Internet resource. For example, every page on the Internet has a different URL. Here is a URL:

```
http://www.yahoo.com:80/en/index.html
```

A URL has several components. The first component denotes the protocol to use to retrieve the resource. In the preceding example, the protocol is HTTP. The second part, www.yahoo.com, is the host. It tells you where the resource resides. Number 80 after the host is the port number. The last part, /en/index.html, specifies the path of the URL. By default, the HTTP uses port 80.

The HTTP is the most common protocol used in a URL. However, it is not the only one. For example, this URL refers to a jpeg file in the local computer.

```
file://localhost/C:/data/MyPhoto.jpg
```

Detailed information about URLs can be found at this location:

```
http://www.ietf.org/rfc/rfc2396.txt
```

In Java, a URL is represented by a **java.net.URL** object. You construct a URL object by invoking one of the URL class's constructors. Here are some easier constructors:

```
public URL(java.lang.String spec)
public URL(java.lang.String protocol, java.lang.String host,
        java.lang.String file)
public URL(java.lang.String protocol, java.lang.String host,
        int port, java.lang.String file)
public URL(URL context, String spec)
```

Here is an example.

```
URL myUrl = new URL("http://www.brainysoftware.com/");
```

Because no page is specified, the default page is assumed.

As another example, the following lines of code create identical URL objects.

```
URL yahoo1 = new URL("http://www.yahoo.com/index.html");
URL yahoo2 = new URL("http", "www.yahoo.com", "/index.html");
URL yahoo3 = new URL("http", "www.yahoo.com", 80, "/index.html");
```

Parsing a URL

You can retrieve the various components of a URL object by using these methods:

```
public java.lang.String getFile()
public java.lang.String getHost()
public java.lang.String getPath()
public int getPort()
public java.lang.String getProtocol()
public java.lang.String getQuery()
```

For example, the code in Listing 21.1 creates a URL then prints its various parts.

Listing 21.1: Parsing a URL

```
package com.brainysoftware.jdk5.app21;
import java.net.URL;

public class URLTest1 {
    public static void main(String[] args) throws Exception {
        URL url = new URL(
            "http://www.yahoo.com:80/en/index.html?name=john#first");
        System.out.println("protocol:" + url.getProtocol());
        System.out.println("port:" + url.getPort());
        System.out.println("host:" + url.getHost());
        System.out.println("path:" + url.getPath());
        System.out.println("file:" + url.getFile());
        System.out.println("query:" + url.getQuery());
        System.out.println("ref:" + url.getRef());
    }
}
```

The result of running the **URLTest1** class is as follows.

```
protocol:http
port:80
host:www.yahoo.com
path:/en/index.html
file:/en/index.html?name=john
query:name=john
ref:first
```

Reading A Web Resource

You can use the URL class's **openStream** method to read a Web resource. Here is the signature of this method.

```
public final java.io.InputStream openStream()
        throws java.io.IOException
```

For example, the **URLTest2** class in Listing 21.2 prints the content of http://www.google.com.

Listing 21.2: Opening a URL's stream

```
package com.brainysoftware.jdk5.app21;
import java.io.BufferedReader;
```

```
import java.io.IOException;
import java.io.InputStream;
import java.io.InputStreamReader;
import java.net.MalformedURLException;
import java.net.URL;

public class URLTest2 {
    public static void main(String[] args) {
        try {
            URL url = new URL("http://www.google.com/");
            InputStream inputStream = url.openStream();
            BufferedReader bufferedReader = new BufferedReader(
                        new InputStreamReader(inputStream));
            String line = bufferedReader.readLine();
            while (line!= null) {
                System.out.println(line);
                line = bufferedReader.readLine();
            }
            bufferedReader.close();
        }
        catch (MalformedURLException e) {
            e.printStackTrace();
        }
        catch (IOException e) {
            e.printStackTrace();
        }
    }
}
```

Note

You can use a URL object only to read a Web resource. To write to a server, use a **java.net.URLConnection** object.

java.net.URLConnection

A **URLConnection** object represents a connection to a remote machine. You use it to read a resource from and write to a remote machine. The **URLConnection** class does not have a public constructor, so you cannot construct a **URLConnection** object using the new keyword. To obtain an instance of **URLConnection**, call the **openConnection** method on a **URL** object.

The **URLConnection** class has two **boolean** fields, **doInput** and **doOutput**, that indicate whether the **URLConnection** can be used for reading and writing, respectively. The default value of **doInput** is **true**, indicating you can always use a **URLConnection** to read a Web resource. The default value of **doOutput** is **false**, meaning a **URLConnection** is not for writing. To use a **URLConnection** object to write, you need to set the value of **doOutput** to **true**. Setting the values of **doInput** and **doOutput** can be done using the **setDoInput** and **setDoOutput** methods:

```
public void setDoInput(boolean value)
public void setDoOutput(boolean value)
```

You can use the following methods to get the values of **doInput** and **doOutput**:

```
public boolean getDoInput()
public boolean getDoOutput()
```

To read using a **URLConnection** object, call its **getInputStream** method. This method returns a **java.io.InputStream** object. This method is similar to the **openStream** method in the **URL** class. This is to say that

```
URL url = new URL("http://www.google.com/");
InputStream inputStream = url.openStream();
```

has the same effect as

```
URL url = new URL("http://www.google.com/");
URLConnection urlConnection = url.openConnection();
InputStream inputStream = urlConnection.getInputStream();
```

However, **URLConnection** is more powerful than **URL.openStream** because you can also read the response headers and write to the server. Here are some methods you can use to read the response headers:

```
public java.lang.String getHeaderField(int n)
```
  Returns the value of the nth header.

```
public java.lang.String getHeaderField(java.lang.String headerName)
```
  Returns the value of the named header.

```
public long getHeaderFieldDate(java.lang.String headerName,
        long default)
```

Returns the value of the named field as a date. The result is the number of milliseconds that has lapsed since January 1, 1970 GMT. If the field is missing, *default* is returned.

```
public java.util.Map getHeaderFields()
```
Returns a **java.util.Map** containing the response headers.

And, here are some other useful methods:

```
public java.lang.String getContentEncoding()
```
Returns the value of the content-encoding header

```
public int getContentLength()
```
Returns the value of the **content-length** header.

```
public java.lang.String getContentType()
```
Returns the value of the **content-type** header.

```
public long getDate()
```
Returns the value of the **date** header.

```
public long getExpiration()
```
Returns the value of the expires header.

Reading Web Resources

As an example, Listing 21.3 shows a class that reads from a server and displays the response headers.

Listing 21.3: Reading a Web resource's headers and content

```
package com.brainysoftware.jdk5.app21;
import java.io.BufferedReader;
import java.io.IOException;
import java.io.InputStream;
import java.io.InputStreamReader;
import java.net.MalformedURLException;
import java.net.URL;
import java.net.URLConnection;
import java.util.List;
import java.util.Map;
import java.util.Set;

public class URLConnectionTest1 {
    public static void main(String[] args) {
        try {
```

```
URL url = new URL("http://www.java.com/");
URLConnection urlConnection = url.openConnection();
Map<String, List<String>> headers =
        urlConnection.getHeaderFields();
Set<Map.Entry<String, List<String>>> entrySet =
        headers.entrySet();
for (Map.Entry<String, List<String>> entry : entrySet) {
    String headerName = entry.getKey();
    System.out.println("Header Name:" + headerName);
    List<String> headerValues = entry.getValue();
    for (String value : headerValues) {
        System.out.print("Header value:" + value);
    }
    System.out.println();
    System.out.println();
}
InputStream inputStream =
        urlConnection.getInputStream();
BufferedReader bufferedReader = new BufferedReader(
        new InputStreamReader(inputStream));
String line = bufferedReader.readLine();
while (line != null) {
    System.out.println(line);
    line = bufferedReader.readLine();
}
bufferedReader.close();
} catch (MalformedURLException e) {
    e.printStackTrace();
} catch (IOException e) {
    e.printStackTrace();
}
    }
}
```

The first few lines of the response are the headers: (you might get different ones)

```
Header Name:Set-cookie
Header value:JSESSIONID=92B6E51AD28EE79182924C33E7A3AE85;Path=/

Header Name:Transfer-encoding
Header value:chunked

Header Name:Date
Header value:Wed, 21 Dec 2005 01:01:26 GMT
```

```
Header Name:Server
Header value:Sun-Java-System-Web-Server/6.1

Header Name:Content-type
Header value:text/html; charset=UTF-8

Header Name:null
Header value:HTTP/1.1 200 OK
```

The headers are followed by the resource content (not displayed here to save space).

Writing to a Web server

You can use a **URLConnection** object to send an HTTP request. For example, the snippet here sends a form to http://www.mydomain.com/form.jsp page.

```
URL url = new URL("http://www.mydomain.com/form.jsp");
URLConnection connection = url.openConnection();
connection.setDoOutput(true);
PrintWriter out = new PrintWriter(connection.getOutputStream());
out.println("firstName=Joe");
out.println("lastName=Average");
out.close();
```

While you can use a **URLConnection** to post messages, you don't normally use it for this purpose. Instead, you use the more powerful **java.net.Socket** and **java.net.ServerSocket** classes discussed in the next sections.

java.net.Socket

A socket is an endpoint of a network connection. A socket enables an application to read from and write to the network. Two software applications residing on two different computers can communicate with each other by sending and receiving byte streams over a connection. To send a message from your application to another application, you need to know the IP address as well as the port number of the socket of the other application. In Java, a socket is represented by a **java.net.Socket** object.

To create a socket, you can use one of the many constructors of the **Socket** class. One of these constructors accepts the host name and the port number:

```
public Socket(java.lang.String host, int port)
```

where *host* is the remote machine name or IP address and *port* is the port number of the remote application. For example, to connect to yahoo.com at port 80, you would construct the following **Socket** object:

```
new Socket("yahoo.com", 80)
```

Once you create an instance of the **Socket** class successfully, you can use it to send and receive streams of bytes. To send byte streams, you must first call the **Socket** class's **getOutputStream** method to obtain a **java.io.OutputStream** object. To send text to a remote application, you often want to construct a **java.io.PrintWriter** object from the **OutputStream** object returned. To receive byte streams from the other end of the connection, you call the **Socket** class's **getInputStream** method that returns a **java.io.InputStream**.

The code in Listing 21.4 simulates an HTTP client using a socket. It sends an HTTP request to the host and displays the response from the server.

Listing 21.4: A simple HTTP client

```java
package com.brainysoftware.jdk5.app21;
import java.io.BufferedReader;
import java.io.IOException;
import java.io.InputStreamReader;
import java.io.OutputStream;
import java.io.PrintWriter;
import java.net.Socket;

public class SocketTest1 {
    public static void main(String[] args) {
        String host = "books.brainysoftware.com";
        String protocol = "http";
        try {
            Socket socket = new Socket(protocol + "://" + host, 80);
            OutputStream os = socket.getOutputStream();
            boolean autoflush = true;
            PrintWriter out = new
                    PrintWriter(socket.getOutputStream(),
                    autoflush);
            BufferedReader in = new BufferedReader(
```

```
                    new InputStreamReader(socket.getInputStream()));

            // send an HTTP request to the web server
            out.println("GET / HTTP/1.1");
            out.println("Host: " + host + ":80");
            out.println("Connection: Close");
            out.println();

            // read the response
            boolean loop = true;
            StringBuilder sb = new StringBuilder(8096);
            while (loop) {
                if (in.ready()) {
                    int i = 0;
                    while (i != -1) {
                        i = in.read();
                        sb.append((char) i);
                    }
                    loop = false;
                }
            }

            // display the response to the out console
            System.out.println(sb.toString());
            socket.close();
        } catch (IOException e) {
            e.printStackTrace();
        }
    }
}
```

To get a proper response from the Web server, you need to send an HTTP request that complies with the HTTP protocol. If you have read the previous section, "The Hypertext Transfer Protocol (HTTP)," you should be able to understand the HTTP request in the code above.

Note

The HttpClient library from the Apache Jakarta's Commons project (http://jakarta.apache.org/commons/httpclient) provides classes that can be used as a more sophisticated HTTP client.

java.net.ServerSocket

The **Socket** class represents a "client" socket, i.e. a socket that you construct whenever you want to connect to a remote server application. Now, if you want to implement a server application, such as an HTTP server or an FTP server, you need a different approach. Your server must stand by all the time as it does not know when a client application will try to connect to it. In order for your application to be able to do this, you need to use the **java.net.ServerSocket** class. This is an implementation of a server socket.

ServerSocket is different from **Socket**. The role of a server socket is to wait for connection requests from clients. Once the server socket gets a connection request, it creates a **Socket** instance to handle the communication with the client.

To create a server socket, you need to use one of the four constructors the **ServerSocket** class provides. You need to specify the IP address and port number the server socket will be listening on. Typically, the IP address will be 127.0.0.1, meaning that the server socket will be listening on the local machine. The IP address the server socket is listening on is referred to as the binding address. Another important property of a server socket is its backlog, which is the maximum queue length of incoming connection requests before the server socket starts to refuse the incoming requests.

One of the constructors of the **ServerSocket** class has the following signature:

```
public ServerSocket(int port, int backLog,
        InetAddress bindingAddress);
```

Notice that for this constructor, the binding address must be an instance of **java.net.InetAddress**. An easy way to construct an **InetAddress** object is by calling its **getByName** static method, passing a **String** containing the host name, such as in the following code.

```
InetAddress.getByName("127.0.0.1");
```

The following line of code constructs a **ServerSocket** that listens on port 8080 of the local machine. The **ServerSocket** has a backlog of 1.

```
new ServerSocket(8080, 1, InetAddress.getByName("127.0.0.1"));
```

Once you have a **ServerSocket** instance, you can tell it to wait for an incoming connection request to the binding address at the port the server socket is listening on. You do this by calling the **ServerSocket** class's **accept** method. This method will only return when there is a connection request and its return value is an instance of the **Socket** class. This **Socket** object can then be used to send and receive byte streams from the client application, as explained in the previous section, "java.net.Socket." Practically, the **accept** method is the only method used in the application accompanying this chapter.

The Web server application in the next section, "A Web Server Application" illustrates the use of **ServerSocket**.

A Web Server Application

This application illustrates the use of the **ServerSocket** and **Socket** classes to communicate with remote computers. The Web server application contains the following three classes that belong to the **com.brainysoftware.jdk5.app21.webserver** package:

- **HttpServer**
- **Request**
- **Response**

The entry point of this application is the **main** method in the **HttpServer** class. The method creates an instance of **HttpServer** and calls its **await** method. The **await** method, as the name implies, waits for HTTP requests on a designated port, processes them, and sends responses back to the clients. It keeps waiting until a shutdown command is received.

The application cannot do more than sending static resources, such as HTML files and image files, residing in a certain directory. It also displays the incoming HTTP request byte streams on the console. However, it does not send any header, such as dates or cookies, to the browser.

We will now look at the three classes in the following subsections.

The HttpServer Class

The **HttpServer** class represents a Web server and is presented in Listing 21.5.
Note that the **await** method is given in Listing 21.6 and is not included in
Listing 21.5 to save space.

Listing 21.5: The HttpServer class

```
package com.brainysoftware.jdk5.app21.webserver;
import java.net.Socket;
import java.net.ServerSocket;
import java.net.InetAddress;
import java.io.InputStream;
import java.io.OutputStream;
import java.io.IOException;
import java.io.File;

public class HttpServer {
    /**
     * WEB_ROOT is the directory where our HTML and
     * other files reside. For this package, WEB_ROOT is
     * the "webroot" directory under the working directory.
     * The working directory is the location in the file system
     * from where the java command was invoked.
     */
    public static final String WEB_ROOT =
            System.getProperty("user.dir") + File.separator
            + "webroot";

    // shutdown command
    private static final String SHUTDOWN_COMMAND = "/SHUTDOWN";

    // the shutdown command received
    private boolean shutdown = false;

    public static void main(String[] args) {
        HttpServer server = new HttpServer();
        server.await();
    }

    public void await() {
        ...
    }
}
```

This Web server can serve static resources found in the directory indicated by the public static final **WEB_ROOT** and all subdirectories under it. **WEB_ROOT** is initialized as follows:

```
public static final String WEB_ROOT =
        System.getProperty("user.dir") + File.separator + "webroot";
```

The code listings include a directory called **webroot** that contains some static resources that you can use for testing this application.

To request for a static resource, you type the following URL in your browser's Address or URL box:

```
http://machineName:port/staticResource
```

If you are sending a request from a different machine from the one running your application, *machineName* is the name or IP address of the computer running this application. If your browser is on the same machine, you can use **localhost** as the machine name. *port* is 8080 and *staticResource* is the name of the file requested and must reside in WEB_ROOT.

For instance, if you are using the same computer to test the application and you want to ask the **HttpServer** object to send the index.html file, you use the following URL:

```
http://localhost:8080/index.html
```

To stop the server, you send a shutdown command from a web browser by typing the pre-defined string in the browser's Address or URL box, after the **host:port** section of the URL. The shutdown command is defined by the SHUTDOWN static final variable in the **HttpServer** class:

```
private static final String SHUTDOWN_COMMAND = "/SHUTDOWN";
```

Therefore, to stop the server, you use the following URL:

```
http://localhost:8080/SHUTDOWN
```

Now, let's look at the **await** method printed in Listing 21.6.

Listing 21.6: The HttpServer class's await method

```
public void await() {
    ServerSocket serverSocket = null;
    int port = 8081;
    try {
```

```
        serverSocket = new ServerSocket(port, 1, InetAddress
                .getByName("127.0.0.1"));
    } catch (IOException e) {
        e.printStackTrace();
        System.exit(1);
    }
    // Loop waiting for a request
    while (!shutdown) {
        Socket socket = null;
        InputStream input = null;
        OutputStream output = null;
        try {
            socket = serverSocket.accept();
            input = socket.getInputStream();
            output = socket.getOutputStream();
            // create Request object and parse
            Request request = new Request(input);
            request.parse();

            // create Response object
            Response response = new Response(output);
            response.setRequest(request);
            response.sendStaticResource();

            // Close the socket
            socket.close();

            // check if the previous URI is a shutdown command
            shutdown = request.getUri().equals(SHUTDOWN_COMMAND);
        } catch (Exception e) {
            e.printStackTrace();
            continue;
        }
    }
}
```

The method name **await** is used instead of **wait** because the latter is the name of an important method in the **java.lang.Object** class that is frequently used in multithreaded programming.

The **await** method starts by creating an instance of **ServerSocket** and then entering a **while** loop.

```
serverSocket =  new ServerSocket(port, 1,
        InetAddress.getByName("127.0.0.1"));
    ...
```

```
// Loop waiting for a request
while (!shutdown) {
    ...
}
```

The code inside the **while** loop stops at the **accept** method of **ServerSocket**, that blocks until an HTTP request is received on port 8080:

```
socket = serverSocket.accept();
```

Upon receiving a request, the **await** method obtains a **java.io.InputStream** and a **java.io.OutputStream** objects from the **Socket** instance returned by the **accept** method.

```
input = socket.getInputStream();
output = socket.getOutputStream();
```

The **await** method then creates a **Request** object and calls its **parse** method to parse the HTTP request raw data.

```
// create Request object and parse
Request request = new Request(input);
request.parse();
```

Afterwards, the **await** method creates a **Response** object, assigns the **Request** object to it, and calls its **sendStaticResource** method.

```
// create Response object
Response response = new Response(output);
response.setRequest(request);
response.sendStaticResource();
```

Finally, the **await** method closes the **Socket** and calls the **getUri** method of **Request** to check if the URI of the HTTP request is a shutdown command. If it is, the **shutdown** variable is set to **true** and the program exits the **while** loop.

```
// Close the socket
socket.close();

//check if the previous URI is a shutdown command
shutdown = request.getUri().equals(SHUTDOWN_COMMAND);
```

The Request Class

The **Request** class represents an HTTP request. An instance of this class is constructed by passing the **java.io.InputStream** object obtained from the **Socket** object that handles communication with the client. You call one of the **read** methods on the **InputStream** object to obtain the HTTP request raw data.

The **Request** class is offered in Listing 21.7. It has two public methods, **parse** and **getUri**, which are given in Listings 21.8 and 21.9, respectively.

Listing 21.7: The Request class

```
package com.brainysoftware.jdk5.app21.webserver;
import java.io.InputStream;
import java.io.IOException;

public class Request {
    private InputStream input;
    private String uri;

    public Request(InputStream input) {
        this.input = input;
    }

    public void parse() {
        ...
    }

    private String parseUri(String requestString) {
        ...
    }

    public String getUri() {
        return uri;
    }
}
```

The **parse** method parses the raw data in the HTTP request. Not much is done by this method. The only information it makes available is the URI of the HTTP request that it obtains by calling the private method **parseUri**. **parseUri** stores the URI in the **uri** variable. The public **getUri** method is invoked to return the URI of the HTTP request.

To understand how the **parse** and **parseUri** methods work, you need to know the structure of an HTTP request, discussed in the previous section, "The Hypertext Transfer Protocol (HTTP)." In this section, we are only interested in the first part of the HTTP request, the request line. A request line begins with a method token, followed by the request URI and the protocol version, and ends with carriage-return linefeed (CRLF) characters. Elements in a request line are separated by a space character. For instance, the request line for a request for the index.html file using the GET method is as follows.

```
GET /index.html HTTP/1.1
```

The **parse** method reads the whole byte stream from the socket's **InputStream** that is passed to the **Request** object and stores the byte array in a buffer. It then populates a **StringBuffer** object called **request** using the bytes in the buffer byte array, and passes the string representation of the **StringBuffer** to the **parseUri** method.

The **parse** method is given in Listing 21.8.

Listing 21.8: The Request class's parse method

```
public void parse() {
    // Read a set of characters from the socket
    StringBuffer request = new StringBuffer(2048);
    int i;
    byte[] buffer = new byte[2048];
    try {
        i = input.read(buffer);
    } catch (IOException e) {
        e.printStackTrace();
        i = -1;
    }
    for (int j = 0; j < i; j++) {
        request.append((char) buffer[j]);
    }
    System.out.print(request.toString());
    uri = parseUri(request.toString());
}
```

The **parseUri** method then obtains the URI from the request line. Listing 21.9 presents the **parseUri** method. This method searches for the first and the second spaces in the request and obtains the URI from it.

Listing 21.9: the Request class's parseUri method

```java
private String parseUri(String requestString) {
    index1 = requestString.indexOf(' ');
    int index2;
    if (index1 != -1) {
        index2 = requestString.indexOf(' ', index1 + 1);
        if (index2 > index1) {
            return requestString.substring(index1 + 1, index2);
        }
    }
    return null;
}
```

The Response Class

The **Response** class represents an HTTP response and is given in Listing 21.10.

Listing 21.10: The Response class

```java
package com.brainysoftware.jdk5.app21.webserver;
import java.io.OutputStream;
import java.io.IOException;
import java.io.FileInputStream;
import java.io.File;

public class Response {

    private static final int BUFFER_SIZE = 1024;
    Request request;
    OutputStream output;

    public Response(OutputStream output) {
        this.output = output;
    }

    public void setRequest(Request request) {
        this.request = request;
    }

    public void sendStaticResource() throws IOException {
        byte[] bytes = new byte[BUFFER_SIZE];
        FileInputStream fis = null;
        try {
```

```
            File file = new File(HttpServer.WEB_ROOT,
                    request.getUri());
            if (file.exists()) {
                fis = new FileInputStream(file);
                int ch = fis.read(bytes, 0, BUFFER_SIZE);
                while (ch!=-1) {
                    output.write(bytes, 0, ch);
                    ch = fis.read(bytes, 0, BUFFER_SIZE);
                }
            }
            else {
                // file not found
                String errorMessage =
                        "HTTP/1.1 404 File Not Found\r\n" +
                        "Content-Type: text/html\r\n" +
                        "Content-Length: 23\r\n" +
                        "\r\n" +
                        "<h1>File Not Found</h1>";
                output.write(errorMessage.getBytes());
            }
        } catch (Exception e) {
            // thrown if cannot instantiate a File object
            System.out.println(e.toString() );
        } finally {
            if (fis != null) {
                fis.close();
            }
        }
    }
}
```

First note that the **Response** class's constructor accepts a
java.io.OutputStream object:

```
public Response(OutputStream output) {
    this.output = output;
}
```

A **Response** object is constructed by the **HttpServer** class's **await** method by passing the **OutputStream** object obtained from the socket.

The **Response** class has two public methods: **setRequest** and **sendStaticResource** method. The **setRequest** method is used to pass a **Request** object to the **Response** object.

The **sendStaticResource** method is used to send a static resource, such as an HTML file. It first instantiates the **java.io.File** class by passing the parent path and child path to the **File** class's constructor.

```
File file = new File(HttpServer.WEB_ROOT, request.getUri());
```

It then tests if the file exists. If the file exists, **sendStaticResource** constructs a **java.io.FileInputStream** object by passing the **File** object. Then, it invokes the **read** method of the **FileInputStream** and writes the byte array to the **OutputStream** output. Note that in this case the content of the static resource is sent to the browser as raw data.

```
if (file.exists()) {
    fis = new FileInputStream(file);
    int ch = fis.read(bytes, 0, BUFFER_SIZE);
    while (ch != -1) {
        output.write(bytes, 0, ch);
        ch = fis.read(bytes, 0, BUFFER_SIZE);
    }
}
```

If the file does not exist, the **sendStaticResource** method sends an error message to the browser.

```
String errorMessage = "HTTP/1.1 404 File Not Found\r\n" +
    "Content-Type: text/html\r\n" +
    "Content-Length: 23\r\n" +
    "\r\n" +
    "<h1>File Not Found</h1>";
output.write(errorMessage.getBytes());
```

Running the Application

To run the application, from the working directory, type the following:

```
java com.brainysoftware.jdk5.app21.webserver.HttpServer
```

To test the application, open your browser and type the following in the URL or Address box:

```
http://localhost:8080/index.html
```

You will see the index.html page displayed in your browser, as in Figure 21.2.

On the console, you can see the HTTP request similar to the following:

```
GET /index.html HTTP/1.1
Accept: image/gif, image/x-xbitmap, image/jpeg, image/pjpeg,
        application/vnd.ms-excel, application/msword,
        application/vnd.ms-powerpoint, application/x-shockwave-flash,
        application/pdf, */*
Accept-Language: en-us
Accept-Encoding: gzip, deflate
User-Agent: Mozilla/4.0 (compatible; MSIE 6.0; Windows NT 5.1; .NET
        CLR 1.1.4322)
Host: localhost:8080
Connection: Keep-Alive

GET /images/logo.gif HTTP/1.1
Accept: */*
Referer: http://localhost:8080/index.html
Accept-Language: en-us
Accept-Encoding: gzip, deflate
User-Agent: Mozilla/4.0 (compatible; MSIE 6.0; Windows NT 5.1; .NET
        CLR 1.1.4322)
Host: localhost:8080
Connection: Keep-Alive
```

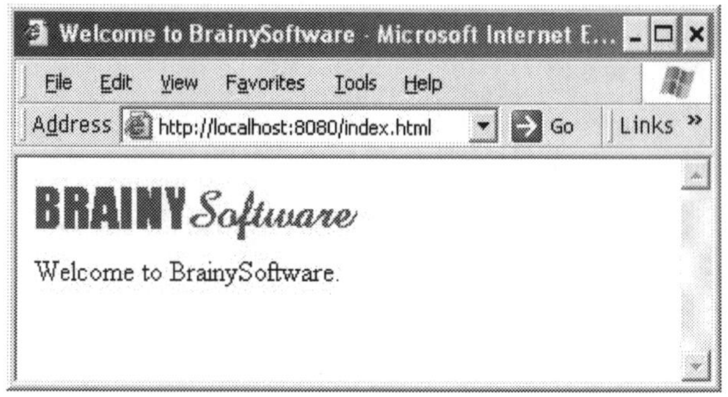

Figure 21.2: The output from the web server

Note

This simple Web server application was taken from my other book,
"How Tomcat Works: A Guide to Developing Your Own Java Servlet
Container." Consult this book for more detailed discussion on how
Web servers and servlet containers work.

Summary

With the emergence of the Internet, computer networking has become an integral part of life today. Java, with its java.net package, makes network programming easy. This chapter discussed the more important types of the **java.net** package, including **URL**, **URLConnection**, **Socket**, and **ServerSocket**. The last section of the chapter presented a simple Web application that illustrates the use of **Socket** and **ServerSocket**.

Questions

1. Why are there several layers of protocols in computer networking?
2. What are the components of a URL?
3. What is the class that represents URLs?
4. What is a socket?
5. What is the difference between a socket and a server socket?

Chapter 22
Java Database Connectivity

Even though Java is an object-oriented programming language, data and object state are commonly stored in relational databases. Accessing the database and manipulating data in it therefore is a very important topic of discussion.

There are many brands of databases. To name a few: Oracle, Sybase, Microsoft SQL Server, Microsoft Access, PostgreSQL, and MySQL. Every database server allows access through a proprietary protocol. As such, accessing different databases require different skills. Fortunately for Java programmers, Java Database Connectivity (JDBC) is available to enable easy database and data manipulation. JDBC provides a uniform way of accessing different databases. http://java.sun.com/products/jdbc/index.html is the official Web site for the JDBC technology.

Java 5 includes the version 3.0 of the JDBC. At the time of writing version 4.0 was in the making. The JDBC Application Programming Interface (API) has two parts: the JDBC Core API and the JDBC Optional Package API. The Core part is good for basic database programming, such as creating tables, retrieving data from single and multiple tables, storing data in a table, updating and deleting data, and others. The classes and interfaces in the Core part are members of the **java.sql** package. The JDBC Optional Package API is specified in the **javax.sql** package and supports advanced features such as connection pooling, support for Java Naming and Directory Interface (JNDI), distributed transactions, etc. This book only deals with the Core part.

Note
The discussion of JDBC in this book assumes you have basic knowledge of SQL.

Introduction to JDBC

JDBC enables Java programmers to use the same code to access different databases. This is achieved through the use of JDBC drivers that act as translators between Java code and relational databases. Imagine a general assembly in the United Nations headquarters in New York. When the Prime Minister of Thailand delivers a speech in the Thai language, every delegate from any country can understand what he is saying because there is a translator for every language. A JDBC driver is basically a translator.

Every database needs a different JDBC driver. Fortunately, there are JDBC drivers for virtually all database drivers in the market today. Because Java is so popular, any database manufacturer has the interest in making available the JDBC driver for their product. However, JDBC drivers can also come from a third party. Popular databases even come with multiple versions of JDBC drivers. Take Oracle as an example. There is an Oracle JDBC driver for server-side applications, there is one optimized for working with stored procedures, etc.

Java distributions also include a default JDBC-ODBC driver to connect to any database where an ODBC connection to the database is available. This proved to be a clever strategy to make Java widely accepted when it first came out. At that time virtually all databases could be connected through ODBC. By providing the JDBC-ODBC driver, Java programmers could connect to those databases without waiting for the database manufacturers to write a JDBC driver for their own database.

The following site contains a comprehensive list of JDBC drivers:

```
http://developers.sun.com/product/jdbc/drivers
```

Technically, there are four types of JDBC drivers. They are simply called Type 1, Type 2, Type 3, and Type 4. Here are some brief descriptions of each type.

- Type 1. Type 1 is a JDBC-ODBC bridge that provides access to a database through an ODBC driver. This type of driver is slow and only appropriate for situations where no other JDBC driver is available.
- Type 2. This type is written partly in native-API and partly in Java. This type of driver uses the client API of the database to connect to the database.

- Type 3. This type of driver translates JDBC calls into the middleware vendor's protocol, which is then translated to the database access protocol by the middleware server.
- Type 4. This type of driver is written in Java and connects to the database directly.

You can find the architecture for each driver type here.

```
http://java.sun.com/products/jdbc/overview.html
```

Four Steps to Data Access

Database access and data manipulation through JDBC require four steps.

1. Loading the JDBC driver of the database to connect to.
2. Obtaining a database connection.
3. Creating a SQL statement object that represents an SQL statement.
4. Optionally creating a **java.sql.ResultSet** object to store data returned from the database.

These steps are detailed in the following subsections.

Loading the JDBC Driver

A JDBC driver is represented by the **java.sql.Driver** interface, which define a contract between a JDBC driver and any Java class that needs to connect to the database. A JDBC driver is often deployed as a jar or zip file. You need to make sure that the driver file is included in the class path when running your Java application.

You load a JDBC driver by using the **java.lang.Class** class's **forName** static method:

```
class.forName(driverClass)
```

where *driverClass* is the fully qualified name of the driver. For example, here is code for loading Sun's JDBC-ODBC driver, MySQL driver, and PostgreSQL driver:

```
Class.forName("sun.jdbc.odbc.JdbcOdbcDriver");
```

```
Class.forName("com.mysql.jdbc.Driver");
Class.forName("org.postgresql.Driver");
```

The **forName** method may throw a **java.lang.ClassNotFoundException**, therefore you must enclose it in a **try** block, such as:

```
try {
    Class.forName("org.postgresql.Driver");
} catch (ClassNotFoundException e) {
}
```

When you load a JDBC driver, you automatically register it with the **java.sql.DriverManager** object so that the latter can find the driver to create a connection.

Obtaining a Database Connection

A database connection facilitates communication between Java code and a relational database. The **java.sql.Connection** interface is the template for connection objects. You use the **java.sql.DriverManager** class's **getConnection** static method to obtain a **Connection** instance. This method searches the loaded JDBC drivers in memory and returns a **java.sql.Connection** object.

Here are the signatures of the most commonly used **getConnection** method overloads.

```
public static Connection getConnection(java.lang.String url)
        throws SQLException
```

```
public static Connection getConnection(java.lang.String url,
        java.lang.String userName, java.lang.String password)
        throws SQLException
```

The first overload is suitable for connecting to a database that requires no user authentication. The second is for connecting to one that requires user authentication. You can still use the first overload to pass user credentials. When using the second overload to connect to a database that requires no authentication, pass **null** to both the second and third arguments.

The *url* argument specifies the location of the database server and the database to connect. The database server can reside in the same computer as the running Java code or in a computer in the network. In addition to the location, you must also pass your user name and password to prove to the database you are an authorized user. Most database servers require this before they grant you a connection. As such, the second **getConnection** method overload is easier to use. If you use the first overload, you can append the user name and password to the database URL. Here is the format of the *url* argument.

```
jdbc:subprotocol:subname
```

The *subprotocol* part specifies the database type. The JDBC driver documentation should tell you the value of the subprotocol. Here are some examples:

- **postgresql**: Connecting to a PostgreSQL database.
- **mysql**: Connecting to a My SQL database.
- **oracle:thin**. Connecting to an Oracle database using the thin driver (there are several types of Oracle JDBC drivers).
- **odbc**. Specify this if you are connecting to a database through ODBC.

The *subname* part specifies the name of the machine running the database server, the port the database is servicing connections, and the database name. For example, the following is the URL for accessing a PostgreSQL database named **PurchasingDB** on **localhost**:

```
jdbc:postgresql://localhost/PurchasingDB
```

As another example, the following URL is used to connect to an Oracle database named **Customers** residing on the machine called **Production01**. Note that by default Oracle works on port 1521.

```
jdbc:oracle:thin:@Production01:1521:Customers
```

The following is the URL to connect to a MySQL database named **CustomerDB** on the computer named **PC2**.

```
jdbc:mysql://PC2/CustomerDB
```

The following is the URL to connect to an ODBC database whose data source name is **Legacy**:

```
jdbc:odbc:Legacy
```

The user name and password are best passed-in as separate arguments using the second **getConnection** overload. However, if you must use the first overload, use the following syntax:

```
url?user=username&password=password
```

Assuming that the user name is **Ray** and the password is **Pwd**, the previous three database URLs can be rewritten as follows.

```
jdbc:postgresql://localhost/PurchasingDB?user=Ray&password=Pwd

jdbc:oracle:thin:@Production01:1521:Customers?user=Ray&password=Pwd

jdbc:mysql://PC2/CustomerDB?user=Ray&password=Pwd

jdbc:odbc:Legacy?user=Ray&password=Pwd
```

The **Connection** interface has the **close** method to close the connection once you're finished with it.

Creating an SQL Statement Object

A **java.sql.Statement** object represents an SQL statement. You can get a **Statement** object by calling the **createStatement** method on a **java.sql.Connection** object.

```
Statement statement = connection.createStatement();
```

Next, you need to call a method on the **Statement** object, passing a SQL statement. If your SQL statement retrieves data, you use the **executeQuery** method. Otherwise, use **executeUpdate**.

```
public ResultSet executeQuery(java.lang.String sql)
        throws SQLException
public int executeUpdate(java.lang.String sql) throws SQLException
```

Both **executeUpdate** and **executeQuery** methods accept a **String** containing an SQL statement. The SQL statement does not end with the database statement terminator, which can vary from one database to another. For example, Oracle uses a semicolon (;) to indicate the end of a statement, and Sybase uses the word **go**. The driver will automatically supply the appropriate statement terminator, and you will not need to include it in your JDBC code.

The **executeUpdate** method executes an SQL INSERT, UPDATE, or DELETE statement as well as data definition language (DDL) statements to create, drop, and alter tables. This method returns the row count for INSERT, UPDATE, or DELETE statements or returns 0 for SQL statements that return nothing.

The **executeQuery** method executes an SQL SELECT statement that returns data. This method returns a **java.sql.ResultSet** object that contains the data produced by the given query. If there is no data returned, **executeQuery** returns an empty **ResultSet**. It never returns **null**.

Once you're finished with a **Statement** object, call its **close** method immediately to free resources.

Note that the SQL statement is executed on the server. Therefore, though not recommended, you could pass database-specific instructions.

Creating a ResultSet Object

A **ResultSet** is the representation of a database table that is returned from a **Statement** object. A **ResultSet** object maintains a cursor pointing to its current row of data. When the cursor is first returned, it is positioned before the first row. To access the first row of the **ResultSet**, you need to call the **next** method on the **ResultSet** instance.

The **next** method moves the cursor to the next row and can return either **true** or **false**. It returns **true** if the new current row is valid; it returns **false** if there are no more rows. Normally, you use this method in a **while** loop to iterate through the **ResultSet** object.

To get data from a **ResultSet**, you can use one of the many **getXXX** methods of the **ResultSet** interface, such as **getInt**, **getLong**, getShort, and so forth. You use the **getInt** method, for example, to obtain the value of the designated column in the current row of this **ResultSet** object as an **int** in the Java programming language. The **getLong** method obtains the cell data as a **long**, etc. The most commonly used method is **getString**, which returns the cell data as a String. Using **getString** is preferable in many cases because you don't need to worry about the data type of the table field in the database.

The **getString** method, similar to other **getXXX** methods, has two overloads that allow you to retrieve a cell's data by passing either the column index or the column name. The signatures of the two overloads of **getString** are as follows:

```
public java.lang.String getString(int columnIndex)
      throws SQLException
```

```
public java.lang.String getString(java.lang.String columnName)
      throws SQLException
```

Like other JDBC interfaces, **ResultSet** also provides the **close** method that you should call as soon as you are done with a **ResultSet** object.

Reading Metadata

In few cases, you also want to read the metadata of a **ResultSet** object. Metadata includes the number of columns in the **ResultSet**, the name and type of each individual column, and so on.

Metadata is encapsulated by a **java.sql.ResultSetMetaData** object and you can get it by calling the **getMetaData** method of the **ResultSet** interface.

```
public ResultSetMetaData getMetaData() throws SQLException
```

Some of the methods in **ResultSetMetaData** are given below.

```
public int getColumnCount() throws SQLException
```
> Returns the number of columns in the **ResultSet**

```
public java.lang.String getColumnName(int columnIndex)
      throws SQLException
```
> Returns the name of the specified column. The index is 1-based, **getColumnName(1)** returns the first column name.

```
public int getColumnType(int columnIndex) throws SQLException
```
> Returns the type of the column. The value is one of the static final fields in the **java.sql.Types** class, such as **ARRAY, BIGINT, BINARY, BLOB, CHAR, DATE, DECIMAL, TINYINT, VARCHAR**, etc.

The SQLTool Example

The following example presents an application that you can use to input an SQL statement and display the result. It uses a MySQL database, but can be modified to support other databases as well. It demonstrates how you can use JDBC to access a database and manipulate its data. It also shows how to deal with metadata.

Note
The reason for choosing MySQL for this example is because it is free, popular, available in many platforms, and very easy to install. PostgreSQL is also free but it is harder to install, especially on Windows. For cost-effective production however, PostgreSQL is worth considering because its license is more relaxed than that of MySQL.

Preparing MySQL

This section includes downloading the MySQL and its JDBC driver.

Downloading the Software

Download the latest version of MySQL for your platform from www.mysql.com. The JDBC driver can be downloaded from the Connector section at the same Web site. The MySQL folks named their JDBC driver **Connector/J**. The driver is distributed in a gz or zip file that also includes the source and documentation. You need to extract the jar file from it. The name of the jar file containing the JDBC driver is something like

```
mysql-connector-java-x.y.z-bin.jar
```

where x.y.z is the version number. The version number of the driver is not the same as the database version number.

Installing and Running MySQL

Installation is very straightforward. For Windows it's even easier because the software is distributed as the msi format, so you can double-click the file and simply follow the instructions.

When you finish installing MySQL, you will see the data directory under your installation directory. The **bin** directory contains programs to run and configure MySQL. There two databases created: mysql and test. There is one user called **root** also created with a blank password.

To run the server, change directory to the **bin** directory, and then type:

```
mysqld --console
```

You will see messages that tell you the version number and that MySQL is now running on port 3306.

Creating the Customers table

For testing the application, you need to create a table named Employees. Let's just use the test database, which is one of the default databases created when you install MySQL. (The other default database is named mysql.). Let's also use the root user.

Note
The documentation at www.mysql.com provides documentation for adding new users, changing passwords, etc.

You can create a table by passing an SQL statement to the server, using the MySQL client application. You can launch the client application by opening a console, changing directory to the **bin** directory under your MySQL installation directory, and typing this command and pressing Enter:

```
mysql -u root
```

The **-u root** option indicates that the root user is being used to login to the MySQL server. The default password for root is an empty string.

To select the test database, type this on the console and press Enter.

```
mysql> use test
```

To create the Employees table, type this on the console in a single line and Press Enter.

```
CREATE TABLE Employees (employeeId INT NOT NULL AUTO_INCREMENT,
        firstName varchar(30), lastName varchar(30),
        PRIMARY KEY(employeeId));
```

Note that you terminate the command with a semicolon.

Then, run the following two commands to inserts to records to the Employees table.

```
INSERT INTO Employees (firstName, lastName) VALUES
        ('John', 'Average');

INSERT INTO Employees (firstName, lastName) VALUES
        ('Anne', 'Frank');
```

The SQLTool Class

Listing 21.1 shows the SQLTool class that you can use to pass SQL statements to the MySQL server running on the local machine.

Listing 21.1: The SQLTool class

```java
package com.brainysoftware.jdk5.app22;
import java.sql.Connection;
import java.sql.DriverManager;
import java.sql.ResultSet;
import java.sql.ResultSetMetaData;
import java.sql.SQLException;
import java.sql.Statement;
import java.util.Scanner;
import javax.swing.JOptionPane;

public class SQLTool {
    private String dbDriverClass;
    private String dbUrl;
    private String dbUserName;
    private String dbPassword;
    private static final int COLUMN_WIDTH = 25;

    public SQLTool(String dbDriverClass, String dbUrl,
            String dbUserName, String dbPassword) {
        this.dbDriverClass = dbDriverClass;
        this.dbUrl = dbUrl;
        this.dbUserName = dbUserName;
        this.dbPassword = dbPassword;
    }

    public void executeSQL(String sql) {
        if (sql == null) {
```

```java
            return;
        }
        sql = sql.trim();
        try {
            Class.forName(dbDriverClass);
            Connection connection = DriverManager.getConnection(
                    dbUrl, dbUserName, dbPassword);
            Statement statement = connection.createStatement();
            if (sql.toUpperCase().startsWith("SELECT")) {
                ResultSet resultSet = statement.executeQuery(sql);
                ResultSetMetaData metaData =
                        resultSet.getMetaData();
                int columnCount = metaData.getColumnCount();
                for (int i = 0; i < columnCount; i++) {
                    System.out.print(pad(metaData.getColumnName(i
                            + 1)));
                }
                // draw line
                int length = columnCount * COLUMN_WIDTH;
                StringBuilder sb = new StringBuilder(length);
                for (int i = 0; i < length; i++) {
                    sb.append('=');
                }
                System.out.println();
                System.out.println(sb.toString());

                while (resultSet.next()) {
                    String[] row = new String[columnCount];
                    for (int i = 0; i < columnCount; i++) {
                        row[i] = resultSet.getString(i + 1);
                        System.out.print(pad(row[i]));
                    }
                    System.out.println();
                }
                resultSet.close();

            } else {
                int recordsUpdated = statement.executeUpdate(sql);
                System.out.println(recordsUpdated +
                        " record(s) updated");
            }
            statement.close();
            connection.close();
        } catch (ClassNotFoundException e1) {
            System.out.println(e1.toString());
        } catch (SQLException e2) {
```

```
            System.out.println(e2.toString());
        } catch (Exception e3) {
            System.out.println(e3.toString());
        }
    }

    // appends s with spaces so that the length is 25
    private String pad(String s) {
        int padCount = COLUMN_WIDTH - s.length();
        StringBuilder sb = new StringBuilder(25);
        sb.append(s);
        for (int i = 0; i < padCount; i++) {
            sb.append(" ");
        }
        return sb.toString();
    }

    public static void main(String[] args) {
        String dbDriverClass = "com.mysql.jdbc.Driver";
        String dbUrl = "jdbc:mysql://localhost:3306/test";
        String dbUserName = "root";
        String dbPassword = "";
        SQLTool sqlTool = new SQLTool(dbDriverClass, dbUrl,
                dbUserName, dbPassword);
        Scanner scanner = new Scanner(System.in);
        String sql = JOptionPane.showInputDialog(null,
                "Enter an SQL Statement");
        sqlTool.executeSQL(sql);
    }
}
```

If you run the **SQLTool** class in Listing 22.1, a **javax.swing.JOptionPane** will be displayed to take your SQL statement:

```
        SQLTool sqlTool = new SQLTool(dbDriverClass, dbUrl,
                dbUserName, dbPassword);
        Scanner scanner = new Scanner(System.in);
        String sql = JOptionPane.showInputDialog(null,
                "Enter an SQL Statement");
```

The **JOptionPane** is shown in Figure 21.1:

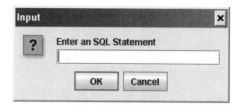

Figure 21.1: JOptionPane that takes an SQL statement

If you enter an SQL statement and click the OK button on the **JOptionPane**, the SQL statement will be passed to the **executeSQL** method:

```
sqlTool.executeSQL(sql);
```

The **executeSQL** method will load the MySQL JDBC driver and establish a connection to the **test** database in the MySQL server on the local machine:

```
Class.forName(dbDriverClass);
Connection connection = DriverManager.getConnection(
        dbUrl, dbUserName, dbPassword);
Statement statement = connection.createStatement();
```

It then checks if the SQL statement is a SELECT statement or something else. If it is a SELECT statement, the **executeQuery** method of the **Statement** object is called and a **ResultSet** is returned.

```
if (sql.toUpperCase().startsWith("SELECT")) {
    ResultSet resultSet = statement.executeQuery(sql);
```

The **executeSQL** method will first displays the ResultSet's column names:

```
ResultSetMetaData metaData =
        resultSet.getMetaData();
int columnCount = metaData.getColumnCount();
for (int i = 0; i < columnCount; i++) {
    System.out.print(pad(metaData.getColumnName(i
            + 1)));
}
// draw line
int length = columnCount * COLUMN_WIDTH;
StringBuilder sb = new StringBuilder(length);
for (int i = 0; i < length; i++) {
    sb.append('=');
}
System.out.println();
System.out.println(sb.toString());
```

It then uses a **while** loop to iterate the **ResultSet** and prints the columns to the console.

```
while (resultSet.next()) {
    String[] row = new String[columnCount];
    for (int i = 0; i < columnCount; i++) {
        row[i] = resultSet.getString(i + 1);
        System.out.print(pad(row[i]));
    }
    System.out.println();
}
resultSet.close();
```

If the SQL statement passed is not a select statement, the **executeSQL** method displays the number of records affected by the statement.

```
} else {
    int recordsUpdated = statement.executeUpdate(sql);
    System.out.println(recordsUpdated +
        " record(s) updated");
}
```

Passing the SQL statement "SELECT * FROM Employees" on my machine prints the following output on the console.

```
employeeId              firstName              lastName
======================================================================
1                       John                   Average
2                       Anne                   Frank
```

Summary

Java has its own technology for database access and data manipulation called JDBC. Its functionality is wrapped in the **java.sql** package. In this chapter, you have seen various members of this package and learned how to use them. You also have learned how to create a tool that takes any SQL statement and pass it to a MySQL database.

Questions

1. Name the four steps to accessing a database and manipulating the data in it.
2. Name the five most important types in the **java.sql** package.

Chapter 23
Java Threads

One of the most appealing features in Java is the support for easy thread programming. Prior to 1995, the year Java was released, threads were the domain of programming experts. With Java, even beginners can write multi-threaded applications.

This chapter introduces what threads are and why they are important. It also talks about problems thread synchronization and thread coordination. Towards the end of the chapter, an overview of two classes, **java.util.Timer** and **javax.swing.Timer**, is given.

Introduction to Java Threads

The next time you play a computer game, ask yourself this question: I am not using a multi-processor computer, how come there seems to be two processors running at the same time, one moving the asteroids and one moving the spaceships? Well, the simultaneous movements are possible thanks to multi-threaded programming.

A program can allocate processor time to units in its body. Each unit is then given a portion of the processor time. Even if your computer only has one processor, it can have multiple units that work at the same time. The trick for single-processor computers is to slice processor time and give each slice to each processing unit. The smallest unit that can take processor time is called a thread. A program that has multiple threads is referred to as a multi-threaded application. Therefore, a computer game is often multi-threaded. If you have two threads, you can use one thread to move the kungfu fighter and another thread to move the karate master.

The formal definition of a thread is this. A thread is a basic processing unit to which an operating system allocates processor time, and more than one thread can be executing code inside a process. A thread is sometimes called an lightweight process or an execution context.

A word of caution, though, threads consume resources. You should be aware of this and not be overgenerous with using more threads than necessary. In addition, keeping track with many threads is a complex programming task.

Every Java program has at least one thread, the thread that executes the Java program. It is created when you invoke the static **main** method of your Java class. Many Java programs have more than one thread without you realizing it. For example, a Swing application dedicates a thread to handle the painting of components, one that handles user input, etc.

Multi-threaded programming is not only for games. Non-game applications can use multithreads to improve user responsiveness. For example, with only one single thread executing, an application may seem to be 'hanging' when writing a large file to the hard disk, with the mouse cursor unable to move and buttons refusing to be clicked. By dedicating a thread to save a file and another to receive user input, your application can be more responsive.

There are several ways to create a thread. Most prominently, by extending the **java.lang.Thread** class or by implementing the **java.lang.Runnable** interface. However, for more high level programming, you can use the **java.util.Timer** class to schedule tasks that need to be performed repeatedly or some time in the future. In addition, for Swing programming you can use the **javax.swing.Timer** class. You will learn these classes in the next sections.

Creating a Thread

There are two ways to create a thread.

1. Extend the **java.lang.Thread** class
2. Implement the **java.lang.Runnable** interface.

If you choose the first, you need to override its **run** method and write in it code that you want executed by the thread. Once you have a **Thread** object, you call its **start** method to start the thread. When a thread is started, its **run** method is executed. Once the **run** method returns or throws an exception, the thread dies and will be garbage-collected.

In Java you can give a **Thread** object a name, which is a common practice when you're working with multiple **Thread** objects. In addition, every **Thread** has a state and a **Thread** can be in one of these six states.

- new. A state in which a thread has not been started.
- runnable. A state in which a thread is executing.
- blocked. A state in which a thread is waiting for a lock to access an object.
- waiting. A state in which a thread is waiting indefinitely for another thread to perform an action.
- timed_waiting. A state in which a thread is waiting for up to a specified period of time for another thread to perform an action.
- terminated. A state in which a thread has exited.

The values that represent these states are encapsulated in the **java.lang.Thread.State** enum. The members of this enum are **NEW**, **RUNNABLE**, **BLOCKED**, **WAITING**, **TIMED_WAITING**, and **TERMINATED**.

The **Thread** class provides public constructors you can use to create **Thread** objects. Here are some of them.

```
public Thread()
public Thread(String name)
public Thread(Runnable target)
public Thread(Runnable target, String name)
```

Note
I will explain the third and fourth constructors later after the discussion of the **Runnable** interface.

Here are some useful methods in the **Thread** class.

```
public String getName()
```
Returns the thread's name.

```
public Thread.State getState()
```
Returns the state the thread is currently in.

```
public void interrupt()
```
Interrupts this thread.

```
public void start()
```
Starts this thread.

```
public static void sleep(long millis)
```
Stops the current thread for the specified number of milliseconds.

In addition, the **Thread** class provides the static **currentThread** method that returns the current working thread.

```
public static Thread currentThread()
```

Extending Thread

The code in Listing 22.1 shows how you can create a thread by extending **java.lang.Thread**.

Listing 22.1: A simple multi-threaded program

```
package com.brainysoftware.jdk5.app23;
public class ThreadTest1 extends Thread {
    public void run() {
        for (int i = 1; i <= 10; i++) {
            System.out.println(i);
            try {
                sleep(1000);
            } catch (InterruptedException e) {
            }
        }
    }
    public static void main(String[] args) {
        (new ThreadTest1()).start();
    }
}
```

The **ThreadTest1** class extends the **Thread** class and overrides its **run** method. The **ThreadTest1** class begins by instantiating itself. A newly created **Thread** will be in the NEW state. Calling the **start** method will make the thread move from the NEW state to RUNNABLE, which causes the **run** method to be called. This method prints number 1 to 10 and between two numbers the thread sleeps for a second. When the **run** method returns the thread dies and will be garbage collected. You do not need to do anything to free the resource taken by the **Thread** object. There is nothing fancy about this class, but it gives you a general idea of how to work with **Thread**.

Of course, you cannot always have the luxury of extending **Thread** from the main class. For example, if your class extends **javax.swing.JFrame**, then you cannot extend **Thread** because Java does not allow you to extend multiple classes. However, you can always create a new class and extend **Thread** from there, as given in the code in Listing 22.2. Or, if you need to access members of the main class, you can write a nested class that extends **Thread**.

Listing 22.2: Using a separate class that extends Thread

```
package com.brainysoftware.jdk5.app23;
class MyThread extends Thread {
    public void run() {
        for (int i = 1; i <= 10; i++) {
            System.out.println(i);
            try {
                sleep(1000);
            } catch (InterruptedException e) {
            }
        }
    }
}

public class ThreadTest2 {
    public static void main(String[] args) {
        MyThread thread = new MyThread();
        thread.start();
    }
}
```

The **ThreadTest2** class in Listing 22.2 does exactly the same thing as the **ThreadTest1** class in Listing 22.1. The difference is the **ThreadTest2** class is free to extend another class.

Implementing Runnable

Another way to create a thread is by implementing **java.lang.Runnable**. This interface has the **run** method that you need to implement. The **run** method in **Runnable** is the same as the **run** method in the **Thread** class. In fact, **Thread** itself implements **Runnable**.

If you use **Runnable**, you have to instantiate the **Thread** class and pass a **Runnable** object. Listing 22.3 shows how to work with **Runnable**. It does the same thing as Listings 22.1 and 22.2.

Listing 22.3: Using Runnable

```
package com.brainysoftware.jdk5.app23;
```

```
public class RunnableTest1 implements Runnable {
    public void run() {
        for (int i = 1; i <= 10; i++) {
            System.out.println(i);
            try {
                Thread.sleep(1000);
            } catch (InterruptedException e) {
            }
        }
    }

    public static void main(String[] args) {
        RunnableTest1 test = new RunnableTest1();
        Thread thread = new Thread(test);
        thread.start();
    }
}
```

Working with Multiple Threads

You can work with multiple threads. The following example is a Swing application that creates two **Thread** objects. The first is responsible for incrementing a counter and the second for decrementing another counter. Listing 22.4 shows it.

Listing 22.4: Using two threads

```
package com.brainysoftware.jdk5.app23;
import java.awt.FlowLayout;
import javax.swing.JFrame;
import javax.swing.JLabel;

public class ThreadTest3 extends JFrame {
    JLabel countUpLabel = new JLabel("Count Up");
    JLabel countDownLabel = new JLabel("Count Down");

    class CountUpThread extends Thread {
        public void run() {
            int count = 1000;
            while (true) {
                try {
                    sleep(100);
                } catch (InterruptedException e) {
                }
```

```
                if (count == 0)
                    count = 1000;
                countUpLabel.setText(Integer.toString(count--));
            }
        }
    }

    class CountDownThread extends Thread {
        public void run() {
            int count = 0;
            while (true) {
                try {
                    sleep(50);
                } catch (InterruptedException e) {
                }
                if (count == 1000)
                    count = 0;
                countDownLabel.setText(Integer.toString(count++));
            }
        }
    }
    public ThreadTest3(String title) {
        super(title);
        init();
    }

    private void init() {
        this.setDefaultCloseOperation(JFrame.EXIT_ON_CLOSE);
        this.getContentPane().setLayout(new FlowLayout());
        this.add(countUpLabel);
        this.add(countDownLabel);
        this.pack();
        this.setVisible(true);
        new CountUpThread().start();
        new CountDownThread().start();
    }

    private static void constructGUI() {
        JFrame.setDefaultLookAndFeelDecorated(true);
        ThreadTest3 frame = new ThreadTest3("Thread Test 3");
    }

    public static void main(String[] args) {
        javax.swing.SwingUtilities.invokeLater(new Runnable() {
            public void run() {
                constructGUI();
```

```
                    }
             });
        }
}
```

The **ThreadTest3** class defines two nested classes that extends Thread, **CountUpThread** and **CountDownThread**. Both are implemented as nested classes so that they can access the **JLabel** controls. Running the code, you will see something similar to Figure 23.1.

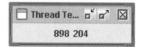

Figure 22.1: Using two threads

Thread Priority

When dealing with multiple threads, you need to think of thread scheduling. In other words, you need to make sure each thread gets a fair chance to run. This is achieved by calling sleep from a thread's run method. A long processing thread should always calls the sleep method to give other threads a slice of the CPU processing time. A thread that calls the sleep method is said to yield.

Now, if there are more than one thread waiting, which one gets to run when the processing thread yields? The thread with the highest priority. To set a thread priority, call its **setPriority** method. Its signature is as follows.

```
public final void setPriority(int priority)
```

The following example is a Swing application that has two counters. The counter on the left is powered by a thread that has a priority of 10 and another by a thread whose priority is 1. Run the code and see how the thread with the higher priority runs faster.

Listing 22.5: Testing thread priority

```
package com.brainysoftware.jdk5.app23;
import java.awt.FlowLayout;
import javax.swing.JFrame;
import javax.swing.JLabel;
```

```java
public class ThreadPriorityTest extends JFrame {
    JLabel counter1Label = new JLabel("Priority 10");
    JLabel counter2Label = new JLabel("Priority 1");

    class CounterThread extends Thread {
        JLabel counterLabel;
        public CounterThread(JLabel counterLabel) {
            super();
            this.counterLabel = counterLabel;
        }

        public void run() {
            int count = 0;
            while (true) {
                try {
                    sleep(1);
                } catch (InterruptedException e) {
                }
                if (count == 50000)
                    count = 0;
                counterLabel.setText(Integer.toString(count++));
            }
        }
    }

    public ThreadPriorityTest(String title) {
        super(title);
        init();
    }

    private void init() {
        this.setDefaultCloseOperation(JFrame.EXIT_ON_CLOSE);
        this.setLayout(new FlowLayout());
        this.add(counter1Label);
        this.add(counter2Label);
        this.pack();
        this.setVisible(true);
        CounterThread thread1 = new CounterThread(counter1Label);
        thread1.setPriority(10);
        CounterThread thread2 = new CounterThread(counter2Label);
        thread2.setPriority(1);
        thread2.start();
        thread1.start();
    }

    private static void constructGUI() {
```

```
        JFrame.setDefaultLookAndFeelDecorated(true);
        ThreadPriorityTest frame = new ThreadPriorityTest(
                "Thread Priority Test");
    }

    public static void main(String[] args) {
        javax.swing.SwingUtilities.invokeLater(new Runnable() {
            public void run() {
                constructGUI();
            }
        });
    }
}
```

The two threads running are instances of the same class (**CounterThread**). The first thread has the priority of 10, and the second 1. Figure 23.2 shows that even though the second thread starts first, the first thread runs faster.

Figure 23.2: Threads with different priorities

Stopping a Thread

The **Thread** class has the **stop** method to stop a thread. However, you should not use this method because it is unsafe. Instead, you should arrange so that the **run** method exits naturally when you want to stop a thread. A common technique used is to employ a while loop with a condition. When you want to stop the thread, simply make the condition evaluates to false. For example:

```
boolean condition = true;
public void run {
    while (condition) {
        // do something here
    }
}
```

In your class, you also need to provide a method to change the value of **condition**.

```
public synchronized void stopThread() {
```

```
        condition = false;
    }
```

Note

The keyword **synchronized** is explained in the section, "Synchronizing Threads."

Stopping a thread is illustrated in the example in Listing 23.6.

Listing 23.6: Stopping a thread

```
package com.brainysoftware.jdk5.app23;
import java.awt.FlowLayout;
import java.awt.event.ActionEvent;
import java.awt.event.ActionListener;
import javax.swing.JButton;
import javax.swing.JFrame;
import javax.swing.JLabel;

public class StopThreadTest extends JFrame {
    JLabel counterLabel = new JLabel("Counter");
    JButton startButton = new JButton("Start");
    JButton stopButton = new JButton("Stop");
    CounterThread thread = null;
    boolean stopped = false;
    int count = 1;

    class CounterThread extends Thread {
        public void run() {
            while (!stopped) {
                try {
                    sleep(10);
                } catch (InterruptedException e) {
                }
                if (count == 1000) {
                    count = 1;
                }
                counterLabel.setText(Integer.toString(count++));
            }
        }
    }

    public StopThreadTest(String title) {
        super(title);
        init();
    }
```

```java
private void init() {
    this.setDefaultCloseOperation(JFrame.EXIT_ON_CLOSE);
    this.getContentPane().setLayout(new FlowLayout());
    this.stopButton.setEnabled(false);
    startButton.addActionListener(new ActionListener() {
        public void actionPerformed(ActionEvent e) {
            StopThreadTest.this.startButton.setEnabled(false);
            StopThreadTest.this.stopButton.setEnabled(true);
            startThread();
        }
    });
    stopButton.addActionListener(new ActionListener() {
        public void actionPerformed(ActionEvent e) {
            StopThreadTest.this.startButton.setEnabled(true);
            StopThreadTest.this.stopButton.setEnabled(false);
            stopThread();
        }
    });
    this.getContentPane().add(counterLabel);
    this.getContentPane().add(startButton);
    this.getContentPane().add(stopButton);
    this.pack();
    this.setVisible(true);
}

public synchronized void startThread() {
    stopped = false;
    thread = new CounterThread();
    thread.start();
}

public synchronized void stopThread() {
    stopped = true;
}

private static void constructGUI() {
    JFrame.setDefaultLookAndFeelDecorated(true);
    StopThreadTest frame = new StopThreadTest("Stop Thread
Test");
}

public static void main(String[] args) {
    javax.swing.SwingUtilities.invokeLater(new Runnable() {
        public void run() {
            constructGUI();
```

```
            }
        });
    }
}
```

The **StopThreadTest** class uses a **JLabel** to display the counter and two **JButtons** to start and stop the counter, respectively. An action listener is added to each **JButton**. The action listener in the Start button calls the **startThread** method and the one in the Stop button invokes the **stopThread** method.

```
public synchronized void startThread() {
    stopped = false;
    thread = new CounterThread();
    thread.start();
}
public synchronized void stopThread() {
    stopped = true;
}
```

To stop the counter, simply change the **stopped** variable to true. This will cause the **while** loop in the **run** method to stop. To start or restart the counter, you must create a new **Thread** object. Once the **run** method of a thread exits, the thread is dead and you cannot re-call the thread's **start** method.

Figure 23.3 shows the counter from the **StopThreadTest** class. It can be stopped and restarted.

Figure 23.3: Stopping and restarting a thread

Synchronizing Threads

So far you've seen threads that run independently from each other. In real life, there are situations whereby multiple threads need to access the same resource or data. Problems might arise if you cannot guarantee that no two threads will simultaneously try to access the same object.

For example, consider the **UserStat** class in Listing 23.7.

Listing 23.7: The UserStat class

```
package com.brainysoftware.jdk5.app23;
public class UserStat {
    int userCount;

    public int getUserCount() {
        return userCount;
    }

    public void increment() {
        userCount++;
    }

    public void decrement() {
        userCount--;
    }
}
```

What happens if a thread attempts to read the **userCount** variable by calling **getUserCount** while another thread is incrementing it? Bear in mind that the statement **userCount++** is actually a shortcut for:

```
int temp = userCount + 1;
userCount = temp;
```

If the thread that reads the variable accesses the **UserStat** object when the second thread has just executed the first line of code, the first thread will get the old data, which is incorrect. On the other hand, if the first thread accesses it after the second line (**userCount = temp**) is executed, then it gets a different result. This is called a race condition. It is a situation in which multiple threads are reading or writing some shared data simultaneously, and the result are unpredictable. Race conditions can lead to subtle or severe bugs that are hard to find.

To avoid race conditions, Java provides you with a feature that allows a thread to lock an object during its accessing the object. During this time, other threads that try to access the same object will have to wait until the first thread is finished. Back to the **UserStat** example, the first thread can acquire the lock of the **UserStat** object and increments the **userCount** value. When the second thread attempts to access the **UserStat** object to read the value of **userCount**, it will find the object is locked. The second thread has to wait until the first thread is finished updating the value. This way, the second thread is guaranteed to get the correct result.

Java provides the **synchronized** modifier to lock an object. When a thread calls a non-static synchronized method, it will always attempts to acquire the method's object lock before the method can execute. The thread holds the lock until the method returns. Once a thread locks an object, other threads cannot call the same method or other synchronized methods on the same object. The other threads will have to wait until the lock becomes available again. The lock is reentrant, which means the thread holding the lock can invoke other synchronized methods. This ensures that you can call another synchronized method from a synchronized method.

Note

You can also synchronize a static method, in which case the lock of the Class object associated with the method's class will be used.

The **UserStat** class can be written into **SafeUserStat** in Listing 23.8.

Listing 23.8: The SafeUserStat class

```
package com.brainysoftware.jdk5.app23;
public class SafeUserStat {
    int userCount;

    public synchronized int getUserCount() {
        return userCount;
    }

    public synchronized void increment() {
        userCount++;
    }

    public synchronized void decrement() {
        userCount--;
    }
}
```

Within a program, the code segments that guarantee only one thread at a time have access to a shared resource are called critical sections. In Java critical sections are achieved using the synchronized keyword. In the **SafeUserStat** class, the **increment**, **decrement**, and **getUserCount** methods are critical sections. Access to **userCount** is only permitted through a synchronized method. This ensures race conditions will not happen.

Synchronizing methods are not always possible. Imagine writing a multi-threaded application with multiple threads accessing a shared object, but the object class was not written with thread safety in mind. Worse still, you do not have access to the source code of the shared object. Just say, you have to work with the **UserStat** class and its source code is not available.

A simple solution would be to synchronize code blocks that access the instance of UserStat, as demonstrated by this code..

```
UserStat userStat = new UserStat();
...
synchronized(userStat) {
    // statements to be synchronized, such as calls to
    // the increment, decrement, and getUserCount methods
    // on userStat

}
```

Thread Coordination

There are even more complex situations where the timing of a thread accessing an object affects other threads that need to access the same object. Such situations compel you to coordinate the threads. The following example illustrates this situation and presents a solution.

You have a courier service company that picks up and delivers goods. You employ a dispatcher and several truck drivers. The dispatcher's job is to prepare delivery notes and place them in a delivery note holder. Any free driver checks the note holder. If a delivery note is found, the driver should perform a pick up and delivery service. If no delivery note is found, he/she should wait until there is one. In addition, you want to make sure that the first delivery note is executed first. Therefore, you only allow one delivery note to be in the holder at a time. The dispatcher will notify any waiting driver if a new note is available in the holder.

The **java.lang.Object** class provides several methods that are useful in thread coordination:

```
public final void wait() throws InterruptedException
```
Causes the current thread to wait until another thread invokes the **notify** or **notifyAll** method. **wait** normally occurs in a synchronized method

and causes the calling thread that is accessing the synchronized method to place itself in the wait state and relinquish the object lock.

```
public final void wait(long timeout) throws InterruptedException
```
Cause the current thread to wait until another thread invokes the **notify** or **notifyAll** method for this object, or the specified amount of time has elapsed. **wait** normally occurs in a synchronized method and causes the calling thread that is accessing the synchronized method to place itself in the wait state and relinquish the object lock.

```
public final void notify()
```
Notifies a single thread that is waiting on this object's lock. If there are multiple waiting threads, one of them is chosen to be notified and the choice is arbitrary.

```
pubic final void notifyAll()
```
Notifies all threads that are waiting on this object's lock.

Let's see how we can implement the delivery service business model in Java using **wait**, **notify**, and **notifyAll**. There are three types of objects involved:

- **DeliveryNoteHolder**. Represents the note holder. It is accessed by the **DispatcherThread** and **DriverThread**. Presented in Listing 23.9.
- **DispatcherThread**. Represents the dispatcher and is given in Listing 23.10.
- **DriverThread**. Represents a driver, shown in Listing 23.11.

Listing 23.9: The DeliveryNoteHolder class

```
package com.brainysoftware.jdk5.app23;
public class DeliveryNoteHolder {
    private String deliveryNote;
    private boolean available = false;

    public synchronized String get() {
        while (available == false) {
            try {
                wait();
            } catch (InterruptedException e) { }
        }
        available = false;
        System.out.println(System.currentTimeMillis()
                + ": got " + deliveryNote);
        notifyAll();
        return deliveryNote;
```

```
        }

    public synchronized void put(String deliveryNote) {
        while (available == true) {
            try {
                wait();
            } catch (InterruptedException e) { }
        }
        this.deliveryNote = deliveryNote;
        available = true;
        System.out.println(System.currentTimeMillis() +
                ": Put " + deliveryNote);
        notifyAll();
    }
}
```

There are two synchronized methods in the **DeliveryNoteHolder** class, **get** and **put**. The **DispatcherThread** object calls the **put** method and the **DriverThread** object calls the **get** method. A delivery note is simply a **String** (**deliveryNote**) that contains the delivery information. The **available** variable indicates if a delivery note is available in this holder. The initial value of **available** is **false**, denoting that the **DeliveryNoteHolder** object is empty. Note that only one thread at a time can call any of the synchronized methods.

If the **DriverThread** is the first thread that accesses **DeliveryNoteHolder**, it will encounter the following **while** loop in the **get** method:

```
    while (available == false) {
        try {
            wait();
        } catch (InterruptedException e) {
        }
    }
```

Since **available** is **false**, the thread will invoke **wait** that causes the thread to lie dormant and relinquish the lock. Now, other threads can access the **DeliveryNoteHolder** object.

If the DispatcherThread is the first thread that accesses DeliveryNoteHolder, it will see the following code:

```
    while (available == true) {
        try {
            wait();
```

```
        } catch (InterruptedException e) {
        }
    }
    this.deliveryNote = deliveryNote;
    available = true;
    notifyAll();
```

Because the value of available is false, it will skip the while loop and causes the **DeliveryNoteHolder** object's **deliveryNote** to be assigned a value. The thread will also set available to **true** and notify all waiting threads.

On the invocation of **notifyAll**, if the **DriverThread** is waiting on the **DeliveryNoteHolder** object, it will awaken, reacquire the **DeliveryNoteHolder** object lock, escape from the **while** loop, and execute the rest of the **get** method:

```
    available = false;
    notifyAll();
    return deliveryNote;
```

The **available boolean** will be switched back to **false**, the **notifyAll** method called, and the **deliveryNote** returned.

Now, let's examine the **DispatcherThread** class in Listing 23.10.

Listing 23.10: The DispatcherThread class

```
package com.brainysoftware.jdk5.app23;

public class DispatcherThread extends Thread {
    private DeliveryNoteHolder deliveryNoteHolder;

    String[] deliveryNotes = { "XY23. 1234 Arnie Rd.",
            "XY24. 3330 Quebec St.",
            "XY25. 909 Swenson Ave.",
            "XY26. 4830 Davidson Blvd.",
            "XY27. 9900 Old York Dr." };

    public DispatcherThread(DeliveryNoteHolder holder) {
        deliveryNoteHolder = holder;
    }

    public void run() {
        for (int i = 0; i < deliveryNotes.length; i++) {
            String deliveryNote = deliveryNotes[i];
            deliveryNoteHolder.put(deliveryNote);
```

```
        try {
            sleep(100);
        } catch (InterruptedException e) {
        }
    }
}
}
```

The **DispatcherThread** class extends **java.lang.Thread** and declares a **String** array that contain delivery notes to be put in the **DeliveryNoteHolder** object. It gets access to the **DeliveryNoteHolder** object from its constructor. Its **run** method contains a **for** loop that attempts to call the **put** method on the DeliveryNoteHolder object.

The **DriverThread** class also extends **java.lang.Thread** and is given in Listing 23.11.

Listing 23.11: The DriverThread class

```
package com.brainysoftware.jdk5.app23;
public class DriverThread extends Thread {
    DeliveryNoteHolder deliveryNoteHolder;
    boolean stopped = false;
    String driverName;

    public DriverThread(DeliveryNoteHolder holder, String
        driverName) {
        deliveryNoteHolder = holder;
        this.driverName = driverName;
    }

    public void run() {
        while (!stopped) {
            String deliveryNote = deliveryNoteHolder.get();
            try {
                sleep(300);
            } catch (InterruptedException e) {
            }
        }
    }
}
```

The **DriverThread** method tries to obtain delivery notes by calling the **get** method on the **DeliveryNoteHolder** object. The **run** method employs a

while loop that is controlled by the **stopped** variable. A method to change **stopped** is not given here to keep this example simple.

Finally, the **ThreadCoordinationTest** class in Listing 23.12 puts everything together.

Listing 23.12: ThreadCoordinationTest class

```
package com.brainysoftware.jdk5.app23;
public class ThreadCoordinationTest {
    public static void main(String[] args) {
        DeliveryNoteHolder c = new DeliveryNoteHolder();
        DispatcherThread dispatcherThread = new DispatcherThread(c);
        DriverThread driverThread1 = new DriverThread(c, "Eddie");
        dispatcherThread.start();
        driverThread1.start();
    }
}
```

Here is the output from running **ThreadCoordinationTest** class.:

```
1135212236001: Put XY23. 1234 Arnie Rd.
1135212236001: got XY23. 1234 Arnie Rd.
1135212236102: Put XY24. 3330 Quebec St.
1135212236302: got XY24. 3330 Quebec St.
1135212236302: Put XY25. 909 Swenson Ave.
1135212236602: got XY25. 909 Swenson Ave.
1135212236602: Put XY26. 4830 Davidson Blvd.
1135212236903: got XY26. 4830 Davidson Blvd.
1135212236903: Put XY27. 9900 Old York Dr.
1135212237203: got XY27. 9900 Old York Dr.
```

Using Timers

The **java.util.Timer** class provides an alternative way to perform scheduled or recurrent tasks. It is easy to use too. After you create a Timer instance, you call the schedule method on the instance passing a **java.util.TimerTask** object. The latter contains code that needs to be executed by the Timer object.

The easiest constructor to use is the no-argument one.

```
public Timer()
```

The **Timer** class's **schedule** method has several overloads:

```
public void schedule(TimerTask task, Date time)
```
Schedules the specified task to be executed once at the specified time.

```
public void schedule(TimerTask task, Date firstTime, long period)
```
Schedules the specified task to be executed for the first time at the specified time and then recurrently at an interval specified by the period argument (in milliseconds)

```
public void schedule(TimerTask task, long delay, long period)
```
Schedules the specified task to be executed for the first time after the specified delay and then recurrently at an interval specified by the period argument (in milliseconds).

To cancel the scheduled task, call the Timer class's cancel method:

```
public void cancel()
```

The **TimerTask** class has the run method that you need to override in your task class. Unlike the **run** method in **java.lang.Runnable**, you do not need to enclose the scheduled or recurrent task code in a loop.

The **TimerTest** class in Listing 23.13 shows an Swing application that uses **Timer** and **TimerTask** to conduct a quiz. There are five questions in the quiz and each question is displayed in a **JLabel** for ten seconds, giving the user enough time to answer. Any answer will be inserted into a **JComboBox** control.

Listing 23.13: Using Timer

```java
package com.brainysoftware.jdk5.app23;
import java.awt.BorderLayout;
import java.awt.Dimension;
import java.awt.Toolkit;
import java.awt.event.ActionEvent;
import java.awt.event.ActionListener;
import java.util.Timer;
import java.util.TimerTask;
import javax.swing.JButton;
import javax.swing.JComboBox;
import javax.swing.JFrame;
import javax.swing.JLabel;
import javax.swing.JTextField;

public class TimerTest extends JFrame {
    String[] questions = { "What is the largest mammal?",
            "Who is the current Japanese prime minister?",
```

```
                "Who invented the Internet?",
                "What is the smallest country in the world?",
                "What is the biggest city in America?",
                "Finished. Please remain seated" };

    JLabel questionLabel = new JLabel("Click Start to begin");
    JTextField answer = new JTextField();
    JButton startButton = new JButton("Start");
    JComboBox answerBox = new JComboBox();
    int counter = 0;
    Timer timer = new Timer();

    public TimerTest(String title) {
        super(title);
        init();
    }

    private void init() {
        this.setDefaultCloseOperation(JFrame.EXIT_ON_CLOSE);
        this.getContentPane().setLayout(new BorderLayout());
        this.getContentPane().add(questionLabel, BorderLayout.WEST);
        questionLabel.setPreferredSize(new Dimension(300, 15));
        answer.setPreferredSize(new Dimension(100, 15));
        this.getContentPane().add(answer, BorderLayout.CENTER);
        this.getContentPane().add(startButton, BorderLayout.EAST);
        startButton.addActionListener(new ActionListener() {
            public void actionPerformed(ActionEvent e) {
                ((JButton) e.getSource()).setEnabled(false);
                timer.schedule(
                        new DisplayQuestionTask(), 0, 10 * 1000);
            }
        });
        this.getContentPane().add(answerBox, BorderLayout.SOUTH);
        this.startButton.setFocusable(true);
        this.pack();
        this.setVisible(true);
    }

    private String getNextQuestion() {
        return questions[counter++];
    }

    private static void constructGUI() {
        JFrame.setDefaultLookAndFeelDecorated(true);
        TimerTest frame = new TimerTest("Timer Test");
    }
```

```
public static void main(String[] args) {
    javax.swing.SwingUtilities.invokeLater(new Runnable() {
        public void run() {
            constructGUI();
        }
    });
}

class DisplayQuestionTask extends TimerTask {
    public void run() {
        Toolkit.getDefaultToolkit().beep();
        if (counter > 0) {
            answerBox.addItem(answer.getText());
            answer.setText("");
        }
        String nextQuestion = getNextQuestion();
        questionLabel.setText(nextQuestion);
        if (counter == questions.length) {
            timer.cancel();
        }
    }
}
}
```

The questions are stored in the String array questions. It contains six members, the first five being questions and the last one being an instruction for the user to remain seated.

The **DisplayQuestionTimerTask** nested class extends **java.util.TimerTask** and provides the code to be executed. Each task begins with a beep and continues with displaying the next question in the array. When all the array members have been displayed, the cancel method of the **Timer** object is called.

Figure 23.4 shows the application.

Figure 23.4: A Timer application

Swing Timers

Similar to the **java.util.Timer** class, the **javax.swing.Timer** class can only be used in Swing applications. **javax.swing.Timer** is not as powerful as **java.util.Timer** but it gives you the familiar feeling of working with Swing and is a more appropriate choice over **java.util.Timer** for Swing applications because **javax.swing.Timer** handles thread sharing. Instead of putting scheduled tasks in the **run** method of a **TimerTask** subclass, you implement the **java.awt.event.ActionListener** interface and write your task code in its **actionPerformed** method. In addition, to cancel a task, you use the javax.swing.Timer class's **stop** method.

The **javax.swing.Timer** class only has one constructor:

```
public Timer(int delay, java.awt.event.ActionListener listener)
```

where *delay* specifies the number of milliseconds from the time the **start** method is invoked to the first invocation of the task and *listener* is an **ActionListener** instance that contains code to be called.

The quiz application in Listing 23.13 is rewritten in Listing 23.14 to use **javax.swing.Timer**.

Listing 23.14: Using Swing Timer.

```
package com.brainysoftware.jdk5.app23;
import java.awt.BorderLayout;
import java.awt.Dimension;
import java.awt.Toolkit;
import java.awt.event.ActionEvent;
import java.awt.event.ActionListener;
import javax.swing.JButton;
import javax.swing.JComboBox;
import javax.swing.JFrame;
import javax.swing.JLabel;
import javax.swing.JTextField;
import javax.swing.Timer;

public class SwingTimerTest extends JFrame {
    String[] questions = { "What is the largest mammal?",
            "Who is the current Japanese prime minister?",
            "Who invented the Internet?",
            "What is the smallest country in the world?",
            "What is the biggest city in America?",
```

```
                    "Finished. Please remain seated" };

    JLabel questionLabel = new JLabel("Click Start to begin");
    JTextField answer = new JTextField();
    JButton startButton = new JButton("Start");
    JComboBox answerBox = new JComboBox();
    int counter = 0;
    Timer timer = new Timer(10000, new MyTimerActionListener());

    public SwingTimerTest(String title) {
        super(title);
        init();
    }

    private void init() {
        this.setDefaultCloseOperation(JFrame.EXIT_ON_CLOSE);
        this.getContentPane().setLayout(new BorderLayout());
        this.getContentPane().add(questionLabel, BorderLayout.WEST);
        questionLabel.setPreferredSize(new Dimension(300, 15));
        answer.setPreferredSize(new Dimension(100, 15));
        this.getContentPane().add(answer, BorderLayout.CENTER);
        this.getContentPane().add(startButton, BorderLayout.EAST);
        startButton.addActionListener(new ActionListener() {
            public void actionPerformed(ActionEvent e) {
                ((JButton) e.getSource()).setEnabled(false);
                timer.start();
            }
        });
        this.getContentPane().add(answerBox, BorderLayout.SOUTH);
        this.startButton.setFocusable(true);
        this.pack();
        this.setVisible(true);
    }

    private String getNextQuestion() {
        return questions[counter++];
    }

    private static void constructGUI() {
        JFrame.setDefaultLookAndFeelDecorated(true);
        SwingTimerTest frame = new SwingTimerTest("Swing Timer
    Test");
    }

    public static void main(String[] args) {
        javax.swing.SwingUtilities.invokeLater(new Runnable() {
```

```
        public void run() {
            constructGUI();
        }
    });
}

class MyTimerActionListener implements ActionListener {
    public void actionPerformed(ActionEvent e) {
        Toolkit.getDefaultToolkit().beep();
        if (counter > 0) {
            answerBox.addItem(answer.getText());
            answer.setText("");
        }
        String nextQuestion = getNextQuestion();
        questionLabel.setText(nextQuestion);
        if (counter == questions.length) {
            timer.stop();
        }
    }
}
}
```

Summary

Multi-threaded application development in Java is very easy, thanks to Java support for threads. To create a thread, you can extends the **java.lang.Thread** class or implement the **java.lang.Runnable** interface. In this chapter you have learned how to write programs that manipulate threads and synchronize threads. You have also learned how to use thread-safe methods. In the last two sections of this chapter, you have learned how to use the **java.util.Timer** and **javax.swing.Timer** classes to run scheduled tasks.

Questions

1. What is a thread?
2. What does the **synchronized** modifier do?
3. What are critical sections?
4. Where do you write the scheduled task for a **java.util.Timer**?

5. What is the difference between **java.util.Timer** and **javax.swing.Timer**.

Chapter 24
Security

Along with a bag of goodies, the Internet brings with it a box full of viruses, spyware, and other malevolent programs. You've been warned too many times to always watch what you run on your PC. A malicious program, once run, can do anything, including send your confidential files over the Internet and mercilessly wipe your hard disk. If only all applications were written in Java, then you wouldn't need to worry so much.

Java was designed with security in mind and Java security was designed for:

- Java users, i.e. people running Java applications. With Java, at least, there is ease of mind. However, as you will see later, Java users need to understand Java's security feature in order to configure security settings.
- Java developers. You can use Java APIs to incorporate fine-grained security features into your applications, such as security checks and cryptography.

There are two main topics of Java security in this chapter:

- Restricting running Java applications. Unlike applets that by default run in a restricted environment, Java applications are unrestricted.
- Cryptography, namely encrypting and decrypting your message and Java code.

This chapter starts with an overview of the security feature in Java. This section explains how you can secure a Java application and how it works in general. Then, it will discuss cryptography with emphasis on asymmetric cryptography, the type of cryptography used extensively over the Internet. The immediate and practical use of cryptography is to digitally sign your code, an example of which is also given in at the end of this chapter.

A Java Security Overview

When people say that Java is secure, it does not mean security comes automatically. Generally, running a Java application is not secure because it runs in an unrestricted environment. This means, a malicious Java program can do anything to its environment, including making you cry when it deletes all your precious data. It can do anything because by default, when you run an application, you give it permissions to do anything.

To impose restrictions, you must run the application with the security manager, which is a Java component responsible for restricting access to system resources. When the security manager is on, all the permissions are revoked.

Web browsers install a security manager that imposes security restrictions on applets. This is why applets by default run in a restricted environment. Java applications, on the other hand, by default run with the security manager turned off.

The security model in Java is traditionally called the sandbox model. The idea of a sandbox is that you, the user of a Java application, may restrict the application you're running within a certain "playing ground." This means, you may dictate what the application can and cannot do, especially with regard to file reading/writing, network access, etc.

With the security manager on, a Java application is pretty limited because no access to system resources is allowed. For example, it cannot read/write to a file, it cannot establish connection to a network, it cannot read system properties, etc. I mean, you can still write methods that do those things, however when your application is run with the security manager on, the application will be paralyzed.

Most applications cannot run properly in this very restricted situation, so you need to relax some of the restrictions by giving the application some permissions. For example, you might give an application the permission to read files but not to delete them. Or, you might grant an application access to the network but ban input output operations. The way to tell the security manager what permissions are allowed is by passing a policy file. A policy file is a text file, so no programming is necessary to configure security settings for the security manager.

Using the Security Manager

The security manager is often used in a Java program that executes other Java classes written by other people. Here are some examples:

- An applet viewer. An applet viewer is a Java application that runs applets. Applets can be written by other parties and it is in the interest of the applet viewer to make sure those applets do not attack the host.
- A servlet container is a Java application that runs servlets. Servlets are like applets but run on the server side. A servlet container is normally written in Java, and when run, it can be set to restrict access of the servlets it is running. For example, if you are an ISP, you want to make sure other servlets you are hosting do not breach security.

However, any Java application can be run with the security manager. To use the security manager, you invoke the java program using the following **–D** flag.

```
java -Djava.security.manager MyClass arguments
```

Applications invoked this way will run under the scrutiny of the security manager and will have none of the permissions discussed in the previous section. In other words, the application will not have access to a file, will not be able to open a socket connection, and so on. In many cases, this is too restrictive.

You can give an application permissions to perform otherwise restricted operations by telling the security manager which permissions you are willing to relax. You do this by writing a policy file. It is a text file with the **policy** extension and lists all the permissions granted to the application.

Note

You can use a text editor to create or edit a policy file or you can use the Policy Tool, which is included in the JDK. The Policy Tool is discussed in the section "The Policy Tool."

Here is the syntax for passing a policy file to the **java** tool.

```
java -Djava.security.manager -Djava.security.policy=policyFile
        MyClass arguments
```

where *policyFile* is the path to a policy file, *MyClass* is the Java class to invoke, and *arguments* is the list of arguments for the Java class.

If the **java** program is invoked with the **–Djava.security.manager** but no **-Djava.security.policy** is used, the default policy files will be used. The default policy files are specified in the security properties file (**java.security** file) under the **${java.home}/lib/security** directory, where **${java.home}** is the installation directory of your JRE.

The security properties file specifies security-related settings, such as policy files, provider package names, whether property file expansion is allowed, etc.

To add a policy file into the security properties file, use the property name **policy.url.*n***, where ***n*** is a number. For instance, the following sets a policy file called **myApp.policy** located in **C:\user** directory (in Windows):

```
policy.url.3=file:/C:/user/myApp.policy
```

And, this one sets the policy file **myApp.policy** in **/home/userX** directory:

```
policy.url.3=file:/home/userX/myApp.policy
```

I will not discuss the security file further, but will explain more about the policy file in the next section.

Policy Files

A policy configuration file, or a policy file for short, contains a list of entries. It can contain an optional **keystore** entry and any number of **grant** entries. Listing 24.1 shows the the content of the default policy file **java.policy** that can be found under **${java.home}/lib/security**. It has two **grant** entries and no **keystore** entry. Note that the line starting with // is a comment.

Listing 24.1: The default policy file

```
// Standard extensions get all permissions by default
grant codeBase "file:${{java.ext.dirs}}/*" {
  permission java.security.AllPermission;
};
// default permissions granted to all domains
grant {
  // Allows any thread to stop itself using the
  //java.lang.Thread.stop() method that takes no argument.
```

```
// Note that this permission is granted by default only to remain
// backwards compatible.
// It is strongly recommended that you either remove this
// permission from this policy file or further restrict it to code
// sources that you specify, because Thread.stop() is potentially
// unsafe.
// See "http://java.sun.com/notes" for more information.
permission java.lang.RuntimePermission "stopThread";

// allows anyone to listen on un-privileged ports
permission java.net.SocketPermission "localhost:1024-", "listen";

// "standard" properies that can be read by anyone
permission java.util.PropertyPermission "java.version", "read";
permission java.util.PropertyPermission "java.vendor", "read";
permission java.util.PropertyPermission "java.vendor.url", "read";
permission java.util.PropertyPermission "java.class.version",
  "read";
permission java.util.PropertyPermission "os.name", "read";
permission java.util.PropertyPermission "os.version", "read";
permission java.util.PropertyPermission "os.arch", "read";
permission java.util.PropertyPermission "file.separator", "read";
permission java.util.PropertyPermission "path.separator", "read";
permission java.util.PropertyPermission "line.separator", "read";
permission java.util.PropertyPermission
  "java.specification.version", "read";
permission java.util.PropertyPermission
  "java.specification.vendor", "read";
permission java.util.PropertyPermission "java.specification.name",
  "read";
permission java.util.PropertyPermission
  "java.vm.specification.version", "read";
permission java.util.PropertyPermission
  "java.vm.specification.vendor", "read";
permission java.util.PropertyPermission
  "java.vm.specification.name", "read";
permission java.util.PropertyPermission "java.vm.version", "read";
permission java.util.PropertyPermission "java.vm.vendor", "read";
permission java.util.PropertyPermission "java.vm.name", "read";
};
```

The default policy file lists the activities that are permitted when running the
security manager using this file. For example, the last few lines specify the
permission to read system properties. The **java.version**, and **java.vendor**
system properties are allowed to be read. But, reading other system properties,

such as **user.dir** is not allowed. Therefore, the default policy is very restricted. In most cases you want to write a policy file that gives the application more room for maneuver.

The rest of this section discusses the keystore and grant entries. It teaches you how to write your own policy file.

Note
Policy file syntax can be found at
http://java.sun.com/j2se/1.5.0/docs/guide/security/PolicyFiles.html.

keystore

This entry specifies a keystore that stores private keys and related certificates. Keystores are discussed in the section "Java Cryptography."

grant

A grant entry includes one or more permission entries, preceded by optional **codeBase**, **signedBy**, and **principal** name/value pairs that specify which code to be granted permissions. The syntax of the grant entry is as follows.

```
grant [signedBy "signerNames"], [codeBase "URL"],
  [ principal principal_class_name_1 "principal_name_1",
    principal principal_class_name_2 "principal_name_2",
    ...
    principal principal_class_name_n principal_name_n
  ]
{
  permission permission_class_name_1 "target_name_1", "action_1",
    signedBy "signer_name_1"
  permission permission_class_name_2 "target_name_2", "action_2",
    signedBy "signer_name_2"
  ...
  permission permission_class_name_n "target_name_n", "action_n",
    signedBy "signer_name_n"
}
```

The order of **signedBy**, **codeBase**, and **principal** values is not important.

A **codeBase** value indicates the URL of the source code you are granting permission(s) to. An empty **codeBase** means any code. For example, the following **grant** entry grants the permission associated with the **java.security.AllPermission** class to the directory denoted by the value of **java.ext.dirs** directory:

```
grant codeBase "file:${{java.ext.dirs}}/*" {
    permission java.security.AllPermission;
};
```

The **signedBy** entry indicates the alias for a certificate stored in the keystore. This explanation probably does not make sense unless you have read and understood the section on Java cryptography. Therefore, feel free to revisit this section after you read the whole chapter.

A **principal** value specifies a className/principalName pair which must be present within the executing threads principal set. Again, revisit this section after you've understood the concept of Java cryptography.

For now, note that a **grant** entry consists of one or more **permission** entry. Each entry specifies a permission type that the application is allowed to perform. For instance, the following permission entry specifies that the application may read the value of the **java.vm.name** system property.

```
permission java.util.PropertyPermission "java.vm.name", "read";
```

The permission entry is discussed in the next section "Permissions."

Permissions

A permission is represented by the **java.security.Permission** class, which is an abstract class. Its subclasses represent permissions to access different types of access to system resources. For example, the **java.io.FilePermission** class represents a permission to read and write to a file.

The permission entry in a policy file has the following syntax:

```
permission permissionClassName target action
```

The *permissionClassName* argument specifies a permission type that corresponds to a specific permission. For example, the **java.io.FilePermission** class refers to file manipulation operations.

The *target* argument specifies the target of the permission. Some permission types require a target, some don't.

The *action* argument specifies the type of action associated with this permission.

For example, consider the following **permission** entry.

```
permission java.util.PropertyPermission "os.name", "read";
```

The permission class **java.util.PropertyPermission** concerns with reading and writing system properties. The "os.name" target specifies the system property **os.name**, and "read" specifies the action. The permission entry says that the application is permitted to read the system property **os.name**.

The following subsections describe each of the standard permission classes in Java.

java.io.FilePermission

This class represents permissions for file reading, writing, deletion, and execution. The constructor of this class accept two arguments, a target and an action.

```
public FilePermission(java.lang.String path,
        java.lang.String actions)
```

The *target* argument contains the name of a file or a directory. There must be no white spaces in the string. You can use an asterisk to represent all files in a directory and a hyphen to represent the contents of a directory recursively. Table 24.1 lists some examples and their descriptions.

The *action* argument describe a possible action. Its value is one of the following: **read, write, delete**, and **execute**. You can use the combination of the four. For example, "read,write" means that the permission concerns the reading and writing of the target file or directory.

Target	Description
myFile	the myFile file in the current directory
myDirectory	the myDirectory directory in the current directory
myDirectory/	the myDirectory directory in the current directory
myDirectory/*	all files in the myDirectory directory
myDirectory/-	all files under myDirectory and under direct and indirect subdirectories of myDirectory
*	all files in the current directory
-	all files under the current directory
<<ALL FILES>>	a special string that denotes all files in the system.

Table 24.1: Examples of targets of FilePermission

Note

Use \ as the directory separator in Windows. Therefore,
C:\\temp* denotes all files under **C:\temp**. You need to escape
the \ character.

java.security.BasicPermission

The **BasicPermission** class is a subclass of **Permission**. It is used as the base
class for "named" permissions, i.e. ones that contain no actions. Subclasses of
this class include **java.lang.RuntimePermission,
java.security.SecurityPermission, java.util.PropertyPermission**, and
java.net.NetPermission.

java.util.PropertyPermission

The **PropertyPermission** class represents the permissions to read the
specified system property (by using the **getProperty** method on
java.lang.System) and to alter the value of the specified property (by invoking
the **setProperty** method on **java.lang.System**). The targets for this
permission are the names of Java properties, such as "java.home" and
"user.dir". You can use an asterisk to denote any property or to substitute part
of the name of a property. In other words, "user.*" denotes all properties
whose names have the prefix "user.".

java.net.SocketPermission

This permission represents access to a network via sockets. The target for this permission has the following syntax.

```
hostName:portRange
```

where *hostname* can be expressed as a single host, an IP address, localhost, an empty string (the same as localhost), hostname.domain, hostname.subDomain.domain, *.domain (all hosts in the specified domain), *.subDomain.domain, and * (all hosts).

portRange can be expressed as a single port, **N-** (all ports numbered N and above), **-N** (all ports numbered N and below), and **N1-N2** (all ports between N1 and N2, inclusive). A port number must be between 0 and 65535 (inclusive).

The possible values for actions are **accept**, **connect**, **listen**, and **resolve**. Note that the first three values imply **resolve** as well.

java.security.UnresolvedPermission

This class represents permissions that were unresolved when the Policy was initialized, i.e. permissions whose classes do not yet exist at the time the policy is initialized.

java.lang.RuntimePermission

The **RuntimePermission** class represent a runtime permission. It is used without an action and the target can be one of the following (all self-explanatory)

```
createClassLoader
getClassLoader
setContextClassLoader
setSecurityManager
createSecurityManager
exitVM
setFactory
setIO
modifyThread
modifyThreadGroup
```

```
stopThread
getProtectionDomain
readFileDescriptor
writeFileDescriptor
loadLibrary.{libraryName}
accessClassInPackage.{packageName}
defineClassInPackage.{packageName}
accessDeclaredMembers.{className}
queuePrintJob
```

java.awt.AWTPermission

AWTPermission represents permissions related to the AWT package. It has no actions and its possible targets are

```
accessClipboard
accessEventQueue
listenToAllAWTEvents
showWindowWithoutWarningBanner
```

java.net.NetPermission

This permission is also used without actions, and its possible targets are

```
requestPasswordAuthentication
setDefaultAuthenticator
specifyStreamHandler
```

java.lang.reflect.ReflectPermission

This permission is related to reflective operations and has no actions. There is only one name defined: **suppressAccessChecks**, which is used to denote the permission to suppress the standard Java language access checks for public, default, protected, or private members.

java.io.SerializablePermission

This permission has no action and its target is one of the following.

```
enableSubclassImplementation
enableSubstitution
```

java.security.SecurityPermission

The **SecurityPermission** class represents a permission to access security-related objects, such as Identity, Policy, Provider, Security, and Signer. This permission is used with no actions and here are its possible targets.

```
setIdentityPublicKey
setIdentityInfo
printIdentity
addIdentityCertificate
removeIdentityCertificate
getPolicy
setPolicy
getProperty.{key}
setProperty.{key}
insertProvider.{providerName}
removeProvider.{providerName}
setSystemScope
clearProviderProperties.{providerName}
putProviderProperty.{providerName}
removeProviderProperty.{providerName}
getSignerPrivateKey
setSignerKeyPair
```

java.security.AllPermission

This permission is used as a shortcut to denote all permissions.

javax.security.auth.AuthPermission

This permission represents authentication permissions and authentication-related objects, such as Configuration, LoginContext, Subject, and SubjectDomainCombiner. This class is used without actions and can have one of the following as its target.

```
doAs
doAsPrivileged
getSubject
getSubjectFromDomainCombiner
setReadOnly
modifyPrincipals
modifyPublicCredentials
```

```
modifyPrivateCredentials
refreshCredential
destroyCredential
createLoginContext.{name}
getLoginConfiguration
setLoginConfiguration
```
refreshLoginConfiguration

Using the Policy Tool

Using a text editor to create and edit a policy file is error-prone. Besides, you will have to remember a number of things, including the permission classes and the syntax of each entry. Java comes with a tool named Policy Tool that you can invoke by typing **policytool**.

Figure 24.1 shows the Policy Tool window. When it opens it always attempts to open the **.java.policy** file (note, the filename starts with a .) in the user's home directory. If it cannot find one it will report it as an error.

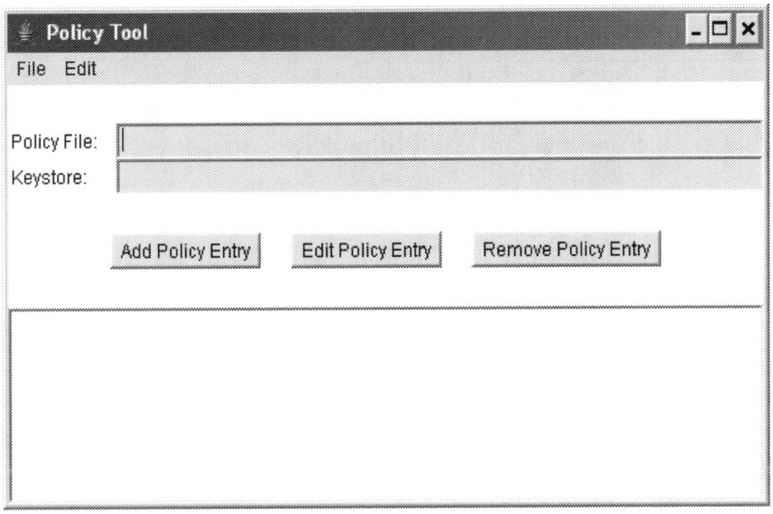

Figure 24.1: The Policy Tool window

If the default policy file is not found, you can create a new one by clicking **New** from the **File** menu or open an existing one by clicking **Open** from the

File menu. The **File** menu also contains the **Save** menu item that you can click to save the policy file.

You can now proceed with adding a policy entry by clicking the **Add Policy Entry** button, that will open the Policy Entry window as shown in Figure 24.2.

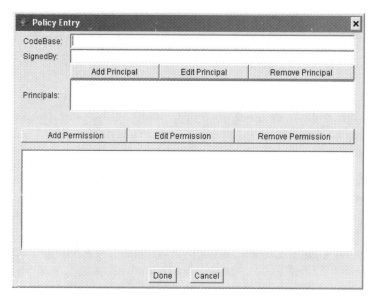

Figure 24.2: The Policy Entry window

You can add a permission by clicking the **Add Permission** button in the Policy Entry window. This will bring up the Permissions window, shown in Figure 24.3.

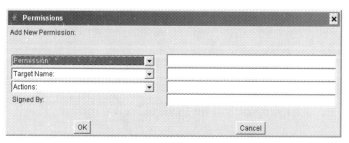

Figure 24.3: The Permission window

From the Permission window, you can select a permission class name, specify a target, and select an action. After you're finished, click the OK button, the new permission will be added to the lower box on the Policy Entry window. You can continue adding permissions and then save the policy file when you are done.

Applet Security

By default, Web browsers run applets with the security manager on. In fact, an applet is very restricted because most of the time you run one written by someone else. Applets downloaded from the Net are untrusted applets and are prohibited from doing the following:

- Reading and writing to files in the client computer
- Making network connections other than the originating host.
- Defining native calls.

An applet can be made trusted by doing one of these.

- Installing the applet class on the local hard disk.
- Digitally sign the applet.

The first one is normally not an option because this means you cannot distribute your applet on the Internet. This leaves us with the second option, which is fortunately is easy enough to do using the JarSigner tool, one of the tools included in the JDK. In fact, the section "The JarSigner Tool" later in this chapter presents an example of how to sign an applet. However, digital signing requires you to understand cryptography, therefore you should read the section "Cryptography Overview" before starting to sign your code.

Note
More information on applet security can be found at
http://java.sun.com/sfaq/

Programming with Security

By now you should be aware that your users may run your application with the security manager on. If nothing is done to check this in your code, your application could throw a security exception and exit unexpectedly.

To make your application security manager aware, watch out for methods that can throw a **java.lang.SecurityException**. For example, the delete method of the **java.io.File**, which you can use to delete a file, has the following signature:

```
public boolean delete()
```

However, if you read the description for the method in the Java Doc more carefully , you will see the following entry:

Throws:
```
SecurityException - If a security manager exists and its
SecurityManager.checkDelete(java.lang.String) method denies delete
access to the file.
```

This indicates that the **File.delete** method can be restricted by a security manager. If the user runs your application that performs **File.delete** with a security manager that does not allow this operation, your program will crash. To avoid such an abrupt exit, enclose your code with a try block that catches a **SecurityException**. For example:

```
try {
    File file = new File(filename);
    file.delete();
} catch (IOException e) {
} catch (SecurityException e) {
    System.err.println("You do not have permission to " +
            "delete the file.");
}
```

Cryptography Overview

From time to time there has always been a need for secure communication channels, i.e. where messages are safe and other parties cannot understand and tamper with the messages even if they can get access to them.

Historically, cryptography was only concerned with encryption and decryption, where two parties exchanging messages can be rest assured that only they can read the messages. In the beginning, people encrypt and decrypt messages using symmetric cryptography. In symmetric cryptography, you use the same key to encrypt and decrypt messages. Here is a very simple encryption/decryption technique. Today, of course, encryption techniques are more advanced than the example.

Suppose, the encryption method uses a secret number to shift forward each character in the alphabet. Therefore, if the secret number is 2 the encrypted version of "ThisFriday" is "VjkuHtkfca". When you reach the end of the alphabet, you start from the beginning, therefore y becomes a. The receiver, knowing the key is 2, can easily decrypt the message.

However, symmetric cryptography requires both parties know in advance the key for encryption/decryption. Symmetric cryptography is not suitable for the Internet for the following reasons

- Two people exchanging messages often do not know each other. For example, when buying a book at Amazon.com you need to send your particulars and credit card details. If symmetric cryptography was to be used, you would have to call Amazon.com prior to the transaction to agree on a key.
- Each person wants to be able to communicate with many other parties. If symmetric cryptography was used, each person would have to maintain different unique keys, each for a different party.
- Since you do not know the entity you are going to communicate with, you need to be sure that they are really who they claim to be.
- Messages over the Internet pass through many different computers. It is fairly trivial to tap other people's messages. Symmetric cryptography does not guarantee that a third party may not tamper with the data.

Therefore, today secure communication over the Internet uses asymmetric cryptography that offers the following three features:

- encryption/decryption. Messages are encrypted to hide the messages from third parties. Only the intended receiver can decrypt them.
- authentication. Authentication verifies that an entity is who it claims to be.

- data integrity. Messages sent over the Internet pass many computers. It must be ensured that the data sent is unchanged and intact.

In asymmetric cryptography, public key encryption is used. With this type of encryption, data encryption and decryption is achieved through the use of a pair of asymmetric keys: a public key and a private key. A private key is private. The owner must keep it in a secure place and it must not fall into the possession of any other party. A public key is to be distributed to the public, usually downloadable by anyone who would like to communicate with the owner of the keys. You can use tools to generate pairs of public keys and private keys. These tools will be discussed later in this chapter.

The beauty of public key encryption is this: data encrypted using a public key can only be decrypted using the corresponding private key; at the same token data encrypted using a private key can only be decrypted using the corresponding public key. This elegant algorithm is based on very large prime numbers and was invented by Ron **R**ivest, Adi **S**hamir, and Len **A**dleman at Massachusetts Institute of Technology (MIT) in 1977. They simply called the algorithm RSA, based on the initials of their last names.

The RSA algorithm proves to be practical for use on the Internet, especially for e-commerce, because only a vendor is required to have one single pair of keys for communications with all its buyers and purchasers do not need to have a key at all.

An illustration of how public key encryption works normally use two figures called Bob and Alice, so we'll use them too here.

Encryption/Decryption

One of the two parties who want to exchange messages must have a pair of keys. Suppose Alice wants to communicate with Bob and Bob has a public key and a private key. Bob will send Alice his public key and Alice can use it to encrypt messages sent to Bob. Only Bob can decrypt them because he owns the corresponding private key. To send a message to Alice, Bob encrypts it using his private key and Alice can decrypt it using Bob's public key.

However, unless Bob can meet with Alice in person to hand over his public key, this method is far from perfect. Anybody with a pair of keys can claim to be Bob and there is no way Alice can find out. On the Internet, where two parties exchanging messages often live half a globe away, meeting in person is often not possible.

Authentication

In SSL authentication is addressed by introducing certificates. A certificate contains the following:

- a public key
- information about the subject, i.e. the owner of the public key.
- the certificate issuer's name.
- some timestamp to make the certificate expire after a certain period of time.

The crucial thing about a certificate is that it must be digitally signed by a trusted certificate issuer, such as VeriSign or Thawte. To digitally sign an electronic file (a document, a Java jar file, etc) is to add your signature to your document/file. The original file is not encrypted, and the real purpose of signing is to guarantee that the document/file is has not been tampered with. Signing a document involves creating the digest of the document and encrypted the digest using the signer's private key. To check if the document is still in its still original condition, you do these two steps.

1. Decrypt the digest accompanying the document using the signer's public key. You will soon learn that the public key of a trusted certificate issuer is widely available.
2. Create a digest of the document.
3. Compare the result of Step 1 and the result of Step 2. If the two match, then the file is original.

Such authentication method works because only the holder of the private key can encrypt the document digest, and this digest can only be decrypted using the associated public key. Assuming you trust that you hold the original public key, then you know that the file has not been changed.

Note
Because certificates can be digitally signed by a trusted certificate issuer, people make their certificates publicly available, instead of their public keys.

There are a number of certificate issuers, including VeriSign and Thawte. A certificate issuer has a pair of public key and private key. To apply for a certificate, Bob has to generate a pair of keys and send his public key to a certificate issuer, who would later authenticate Bob by asking him to send a copy of his passport or other types of identification. Having verified Bob, a certificate issuer will sign the certificate using its private key. By 'signing' it means encrypting. Therefore, the certificate can only be read by using the certificate issuer's public key. The public key of a certificate issuer is normally distributed widely. For example, Internet Explorer, Netscape, FireFox and other browsers by default include several certificate issuers' public keys.

For example, in IE, click Tools --> Internet Options --> Content --> Certificates --> Trusted Root Certification Authorities tab to see the list of certificates. (See Figure 24.4).

Figure 24.4: Several certificate issuers whose public keys are embedded in Internet Explorer

Now, having a certificate, Bob will distribute the certificate instead of his public key before exchanging messages with another party.

Here is how it works.

A->B   Hi Bob, I'd like to speak with you, but first of all I need to know that you're really Bob.

B->A   Understandable, here is my certificate

A->B   This is not sufficient, I need something else from you

B->A   Alice, it's really me + [message digest encrypted using Bob's private key]

In the last message from Bob to Alice, the message has been signed using Bob's private key, to convince Alice that the message is authentic. This is how authentication is proved. Alice contacts Bob and Bob sends his certificate. However, a certificate alone is not sufficient because anyone can get Bob's certificate. Remember that Bob sends his certificate to anyone who wants to exchange messages with him. Therefore, Bob sends her a message ("Alice, it's really me") and the digest of the same message encrypted using his private key.

Alice gets Bob's public key from the certificate. She can do it because the certificate is signed using the certificate issuer's private key and Alice has access to the certificate issuer's public key (her browser keeps a copy of it). Now, she also gets a message and the digest encrypted using Bob's private key. All Alice needs to do is digest the message and compare it with the decrypted digest send by Bob. Alice can decrypt it because it has been encrypted using Bob's private key, and Alice has Bob's public key. If the two match, Alice can be sure that the other party is really Bob.

The first thing Alice does after authenticating Bob is to send a secret key that will be used in subsequent message exchange. That's right, once a secure channel is established, SSL uses symmetric encryption because it is much faster than asymmetric one.

Now, there is still one thing missing from this picture. Messages over the Internet pass many computers. How do you make sure the integrity of those messages because anyone could intercept those messages on the way?

Data Integrity

Mallet, a malicious party, could be sitting between Alice and Bob, trying to decipher the messages being sent. Unfortunately, even though he could copy the messages, they are encrypted and Mallet does not know the key. However, Mallet could still destroy the messages or not relay some of them. To overcome this, SSL introduces a message authentication code (MAC). A MAC is a piece of data that is computed by using a secret key and some transmitted data. Because Mallet does not know the secret key, he cannot compute the right value for the digest. The message receiver can and therefore will discover if there is an attempt to tamper with the data, or if the data is not complete. If this happens, both parties can stop communicating.

One of such message digest algorithm is MD5. It is invented by RSA and is very secure. If 128-bit MAC values are employed, for example, the chance of a malicious party's of guessing the right value is about 1 in 18,446,744,073,709,551,616, or practically never.

How SSL Works

Now you know how SSL addresses the issues of encryption/decryption, authentication, and data integration, let's review how SSL works. This time, let's take Amazon as an example (in lieu of Bob) and a buyer (instead of Alice). Amazon.com, like any other bona fide e-commerce vendor has applied for a certificate from a trusted certificate issuer. The buyer is using Internet Explorer, that embeds the public keys of trusted certificate issuers. The buyer does not really need to know about how SSL works and does not need to have a public key or a private key. One thing he needs to ensure is that when entering important details, such as a credit card number, the protocol being used is HTTPS, instead of HTTP. This has to appear on the URL box. Therefore, instead of http://www.amazon.com, it has to start with https. For instance: https://secure.amazon.com. Some browsers also display a secure icon on its status bar. Figure 24.5 shows a secure sign in IE.

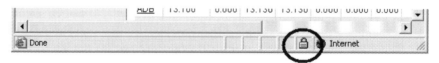

Figure 24.5: The secure sign in IE

When the buyer enters a secure page (when he finishes shopping), this is the sequence of events that happens in the background, between his browser and Amazon's server.

browser: Are you really Amazon.com?

server: Yes, here is my certificate.

The browser then checks the validity of the certificate using the certificate issuer's public key to decrypt it. If something is wrong, such as if the certificate has expired, the browser warns the user. If the user agrees to continue despite the certificate being expired, the browser will continue.

browser: A certificate alone is not sufficient, please send something else.

server: I'm really Amazon.com + [the digest of the same message encrypted using Amazon.com's private key].

The browser decrypted the digest using Amazon's public key and create a digest of "I'm Really Amazon.com". If the two match, authentication is successful. The browser will then generate a random key, encrypt it using Amazon's public key. This random key is to encrypt and decrypt subsequent messages. In other words, once Amazon is authenticated, symmetric encryption is used because it is faster then asymmetric cryptography. In addition to messages, both parties also send message digests for making sure that the messages are intact and unchanged.

Let's now examine how you can create a digital certificate of your own.

Creating Certificates

You can use a Java tool called Keytool, discussed in the section "The Keytool Program," to generate pairs of public and private keys. A public key is normally wrapped in a certificate since a certificate is a more trusted way of distributing a public key. The certificate is signed using the private key that corresponds to the public key contained in the certificate. It is called a self-signed certificate. In other words, a self-signed certificate is one for which the signer is the same as the subject described in the certificate.

A self-signed certificate is good enough for people to authenticate the sender of a signed document if those people already know the sender. For better acceptance, you need a certificate signed by a Certificate Authority, such as VeriSign and Thawte. You need to send them your self-signed certificate.

After a CA authenticates you, they will issue you a certificate that replaces the self-signed certificate. This new certificate may also be a chain of certificates. At the top of the chain is the 'root', which is the self-signed certificate. Next in the chain is the certificate from a CA that authenticates you. If the CA is not well known, they will send it to a bigger CA that will authenticate the first CA's public key. The last CA will also send the certificate, hence forming a chain of certificates. This bigger CA normally has their public keys widely distributed so people can easily authenticate certificates they sign.

Java provides a set of tools and APIs that can be used to work with asymmetric cryptography explained in the previous section. With them you can do the following:

- Generate pairs of public and private keys. You can then send the public key generated to a certificate issuer to obtain your own certificate. There is fee, of course.
- Store your private and public keys to a database called a keystore. A keystore has a name and is password protected.
- Store other people's certificates in the same keystore.
- Create your own certificate by signing it with your own private key. However, such certificates will have limited use. For practice, self-signed certificates are good enough.
- Digitally sign a file. This is particularly important because browsers will only allow applets access to resources if the applets are stored in a jar file that has been signed. Signed Java code guarantee the user that you are really the developer of the class. If they trust you they may have less doubt in running the Java class.

Let's now review the tools first, then let's see how to do it programmatically.

The KeyTool Program

The KeyTool program is a utility to create and maintain public and private keys and certificates. It comes with the JDK and is located in the **bin** directory of the JDK. Keytool is a command-line program. To check the correct syntax, simply type keytool at the command prompt. The following will provide examples of some important functions.

Generating Key Pairs

Before you start, there are a few things to notice with regard to key generation in Java.

1. Keytool will generate a pair of public key and private key and create a certificate signed using the private key (self-signed certificate). Among others, the certificate contains the public key and the identity of the entity whose key it is. Therefore, you need to supply your name and other information. This name is called a distinguished name and contains the following information:

```
CN= common name, e.g. Joe Sample
OU=organizational unit, e.g. Information Technology
O=organization name, e.g. Brainy Software Corp
L=locality name, e.g. Vancouver
S=state name, e.g. BC
C=country, (two letter country code) e.g. CA
```

2. Your keys will be stored in a database called a keystore. A keystore is file-based and password-protected so that no unauthorized persons can access the private keys stored in it.

3. If no keystore is specified when generating keys or when performing other functions, the default keystore is assumed. The default keystore is named **.keystore** in the user's home directory (i.e. in the directory defined by the **user.home** system property. For example, for Windows XP the default keystore is located under C:\Documents and Settings*userName* directory in Windows.

4. There are two types of entries in a keystore:
   a. Key entries, each of which is a private key accompanies by the certificate chain of the corresponding public key.
   b. Trusted certificate entries, each of which contains the public key of an entity you trust.
   Each entry is also password-protected, therefore there are two types of passwords, the one that protects the keystore and one that protects an entry.

5. Each entry in a keystore is identified by a unique name or an alias. You must specify an alias when generating a key pair or doing other activities with keytool.

6. If when generating a key pair you don't specify an alias, **mykey** is used as an alias.

The shortest command to generate a key pair is this.

```
keytool -genkey
```

Using this command, the default keystore will be used or one will be created if none exists in the user's home directory. The generated key will have the alias **mykey**. You will then be prompted to enter the password for the keystore and supply information for your distinguished name. Finally, you will be prompted for the entry's password.

Invoking **keytool –genkey** again will result in an error because it will attempt to create a pair key and use the alias **mykey** again.

To specify an alias, use the –alias argument. For example, the following command creates a key pair identified using the keyword email.

```
keytool -genkey -alias email
```

Again, the default keystore is used.

To specify a keystore, use the **–keystore** argument. For example, this command generate a key pair and store it in the keystore named **myKeystore** in the C:\javakeys directory.

```
keytool -genkey -keystore C:\javakeys\myKeyStore
```

After you invoke the program, you will be asked to enter mission information.

A complete command for generating a key pair is one that uses the genkey, alias, keypass, storepass and dname arguments. For example.

```
keytool -genkey -alias email4 -keypass myPassword -dname
"CN=JoeSample, OU=IT, O=Brain Software Corp, L=Surrey, S=BC, C=CA"
-storepass myPassword
```

Getting Certified

While you can use Keytool to generate pairs of public and private keys and self-signed certificates, your certificates will only be trusted by people who already know you. To get more acceptance, you need your certificates to be signed by a certificate authority (CA), such as VeriSign or Entrust or Thawte.

If you intend to do this, you need to generate a Certificate Signing Request (CSR) by using the –certreq argument of Keytool. Here is the syntax:

```
keytool -certreg -alias alias -file certregFile
```

The input of this command is the certificate referenced by *alias* and the output is a CSR, which is the file whose path is specified by *certregFile*. Send the CSR to a CA and they will authenticate you offline, normally by asking you to provide valid identification details, such as a copy of your passport or driver's license.

If the CA is satisfied with your credentials, they will send you a new certificate or a certificate chain that contains your public key. This new certificate is used to replace the existing certificate chain you sent (which was self-signed). Once you receive the reply, you can import your new certificate into a keystore by using the –import argument of Keytool.

Importing a Certificate into the Keystore

If you receive a signed document from a third party or a reply from a CA, you can store it in a keystore. You need to assign an alias you can easily remember to this certificate.

To import or store a certificate into a keystore, use the import argument. Here is the syntax.

```
keytool -import -alias anAlias -file filename
```

As an example, to import the certificate in the file joeCertificate.cer into the keystore and give it the alias brotherJoe, you use this:

```
keytool -import -alias brotherJoe -file joeCertificate.cer
```

The advantages of storing a certificate in a keystore is twofold. First, you have a centralized store that is password protected. Second, you can easily authenticate a signed document from a third party if you have imported their certificate in a keystore.

Exporting a Certificate from the Keystore

With your private key you can sign a document. When you sign the document, you make a digest of the document and then encrypt the digest with your private key. You then distribute the document as well as the encrypted digest.

For others to authenticate the document, they must have your public key. For security, your public key needs to be signed too. You can self-sign it or you can send it to a trusted certificate issuer to sign it.

The first step to take is extract your certificate from a keystore and save it as a file. Then, you can easily distribute the file. To extract a certificate from a keystore, you need to use the –export argument and cite (?) the alias and define the name of the file to contain your certificate. Here is the syntax:

```
keytool -export -alias anAlias -file filename
```

A file containing a certificate is typically (?) given the .cer extension. For example, to extract a certificate whose alias is Meredith and save it to the meredithcertificate.cer file, you use this command:

```
keytool -export -alias Meredith -file meredithcertificate.cer
```

Listing Keystore Entries

Now that you have a keystore to store your private keys and the certificates of parties you trust, you can enquiry its content by listing it using the keytool program. You do it by using the **list** argument.

```
keytool -list -keystore myKeyStore -storepass myPassword
```

Again, the default keystore is assumed if the keystore argument is missing.

Note
More information on Keytool can be found here:
http://java.sun.com/j2se/1.5.0/docs/tooldocs/windows/keytool.html

The JarSigner Tool

As you have seen, Keytool is a great tool for generating keys and maintaining them. To sign documents or Java classes, you need another tool: JarSigner. In addition to sign documents, JarSigner can also be used to verify the signatures and integrity of signed jar files from third parties.

Using JarSigner, you must first save your file(s) in a jar file. You can do this using the **jar** tool, which was explained in Appendix C, "jar." In addition to signing a jar file, JarSigner can also be used to verify the signature and integrity of a signed jar file. Let's review these two functions below.

Signing JAR Files

As the name implies, JarSigner can only be used to sign jar files, one at a time. Therefore, if you have a document you want to sign, you need to first package it using the **jar** tool (explained in Appendix C, "jar").

```
jarsigner [options] -signedJar newJarFile jarFile alias
```

where *jarFile* is the path to the jar file to be signed, and *newJarFile* is the resulting output. The new jar file is exactly the same as the signed jar, except that it has two extra files under the META-INF directory. The two extra files are a signature file (with a .SF extension) and a signature block file (with a .DSA extension).

You can sign a jar file multiple times, each using a different alias.

Verifying Signed JAR Files

Verifying a signed jar file includes checking that the signature in the jar file is valid and the documents signed have not been tampered with. You use the **jarsigner** program with the –verify argument to verify a signed jar file. Its syntax is as follows:

```
jarsigner -verify [options] jarFile
```

where *jarFile* is the path to the jar file to be verified.

The **jarsigner** program verifies a jar file by examining the signature in the .SF file and the digest listed in each entry in the .SF file with each corresponding section in the manifest.

Note
More information on **jarsigner** can be found here:
http://java.sun.com/j2se/1.5.0/docs/tooldocs/windows/jarsigner.ht
ml

An Example: Signing an Applet

The following example shows how to use Java cryptography to sign an applet.
The applet class (**MyApplet**) is given in Listing 24.2.

Listing 24.2: MyApplet.java

```java
import java.applet.Applet;
import java.awt.Graphics;
import java.io.File;
import java.io.FileNotFoundException;
import java.io.PrintWriter;

public class MyApplet extends Applet {
    StringBuffer buffer = new StringBuffer();

    public void start() {
        buffer.append("Trying to create Test.txt " +
                "in the browser's installation directory.");
        File file = new File("Test.txt");
        try {
            PrintWriter pw = new PrintWriter(file);
            pw.write("Hello");
            pw.close();
            buffer.append(" Writing successful");
        } catch (FileNotFoundException e) {
            buffer.append(e.toString()  );
        } catch (SecurityException e) {
            buffer.append(e.toString()  );
        }
        repaint();
    }
    public void paint(Graphics g) {
        //Draw a Rectangle around the applet's display area.
        g.drawRect(0, 0, getSize().width - 1, getSize().height - 1);
        g.drawString(buffer.toString(), 10, 20);
    }
}
```

The **MyApplet** applet attempts to write to a file and of course it will throw a
SecurityException if run in a browser because the browser will impose a
security restriction against access to the client's file system. Signing the applet
would persuade the browser to relax security restriction. The browser will
check if the applet has been signed by a trusted party. If it has, the applet will

be granted access. If the signer is not trusted, the browser will ask the user to either grant or reject permissions.

Before you can sign the applet, you must first package it in a jar file. This is very easy to achieve by using the jar program discussed in Appendix C, "jar." Basically, all you need is run this command in the directory the applet class resides.

```
jar -cf MyJar.jar MyApplet.class
```

You'll get a jar file named **MyJar.jar**.

Now, sign the jar file using jarsigner:

```
jarsigner -verbose -signedJar MySignedJar.jar MyJar.jar mykey
```

where **mykey** is a key in your keystore. you'll be prompted to enter the password for the keystore. The result will be the **MySignedJar.jar** file. We're ready to test it to run in a browser. The HTML file in Listing 24.3 is needed to call the applet.

Listing 24.3: The HTML that calls the applet.

```html
<html>
<head>
<title>Testing Signed Applet</title>
</head>
<body>
<applet code="MyApplet.class" archive="MySignedJar.jar" width="600"
        height="50">
</applet>
</body>
</html>
```

Now, when you invoke the HTML page containing the applet, the browser will ask you the permission to run the applet, because the applet has not been signed by a trusted CA. Figure 24.6 shows the security warning.

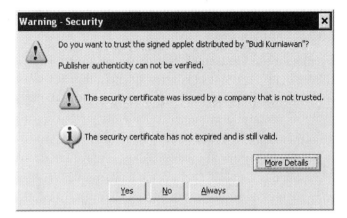

**Figure 24.6: The security warning asking the user whether to grant
permissions to an applet**

The More Details button reveals the details of the signature in the signed
applet. Figure 24.7 shows these details.

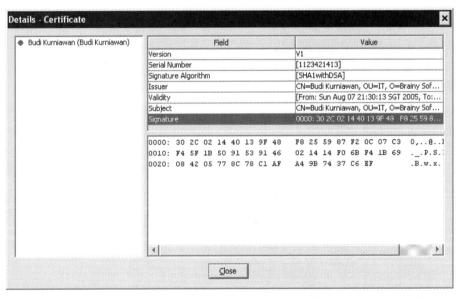

Figure 24.7: The details of the signature used to sign the applet

If you grant it access, the applet will have access to create a file and write to
the file. You will see something like Figure 24.8.

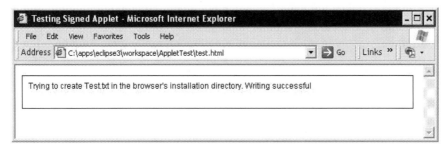

Figure 24.8: The applet has successfully access the file system

Note
The application that accompanies this chapter include the
MySignedJar.jar file that has been signed using my signature. Included
for your convenience.

Java Cryptography API

For a beginner, it is sufficient if you understand the concept of public key
encryption and know how to generate key pairs and sign a jar file. Java offers
more, however. You can do what you can do with keytool programmatically by
using the Java Cryptography API. You are recommended to look into the
javax.crypto package if you are interested in knowing more about Java
cryptography.

Summary

This chapter explained how the security manager restricts a Java application
and how to write a policy file to grant permissions to the application. It also
discussed asymmetric cryptography and how Java implements it. Towards the
end of the chapter you have seen how to digitally sign an applet so it could
write to the user's file system.

Questions

1. What is a policy file?
2. Why is symmetric cryptography not suitable for use on the Internet?
3. What is a keystore?
4. What are the steps to digitally sign an applet?

Chapter 25
Java Web Applications

There are three technologies for developing Web applications in Java: Servlet, JavaServer Pages (JSP), and JavaServer Faces (JSF). They are not part of the Java SE but members of the Java EE. However, considering that Web applications are the most popular applications today, they are also covered in this chapter. Each technology is complex enough to require a book of its own, therefore I can only promise an introduction here.

Of the three, the Servlet technology is the core technology on which JSP and JSF are based. The emergence of JSP after servlets did not make the Servlet technology obsolete. Rather, they are used together in modern Java Web applications.

This chapter explores the Servlet API and presents a few servlet applications as examples. Chapter 26, "JavaServer Pages" covers JSP.

The Architecture of a Servlet Application

A servlet application consists of one or more servlets. A servlet application must run in a servlet container. A servlet container, also known as a servlet engine, passes requests from the user to the servlet application and response from the servlet application back to the user. Web users use browsers to access servlet applications. Figure 25.1 shows the architecture of a servlet application.

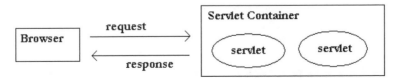

Figure 25.1: The architecture of a Web application

The Web server and the browser use the Hypertext Transfer Protocol (HTTP) to communicate with each other. The HTTP was discussed in Chapter 21, "Java Networking."

A Web client must know the URL the Web server hosting the Web application on the Internet. The URL is only useful in delivering a request to the server, but does not tell the Web application which servlet to invoke. For this, you need to append the name of the servlet to the URL. When a request comes without a servlet name, the request will be forwarded to the default servlet, if one has been specified.

Servlet Containers and J2EE Containers

A J2EE container is an engine to run J2EE applications. It supports all J2EE technologies, such as Servlet, JSP, Enterprise JavaBeans (EJB), etc. Examples of J2EE containers include BEA WebLogic, IBM WebSphere, Oracle 10g Application Server, JBoss, etc. A servlet container is an engine that can run a servlet/JSP application but does not normally support other J2EE technologies. All J2EE containers can also run servlet/JSP applications. The most popular servlet container available is Apache Tomcat.

Servlet API Overview

The Servlet API, which at the time of writing is at version 2.4, comes in two packages, **javax.servlet** and **javax.servlet.http**. The **javax.servlet** package contains classes and interfaces that define the contract between a servlet class and a servlet container. The **javax.servlet.http** package contains classes and interfaces that define the contract between a servlet class running under the HTTP protocol and a servlet container. Many of the members of the **javax.servlet.http** package are descendants of the members of the **javax.servlet** package. In addition, the **javax.servlet.http** package features classes and interfaces that encapsulate functionality specific to the HTTP protocol.

The javax.servlet Package

Figure 25.2 shows the main types in the **javax.servlet** package.

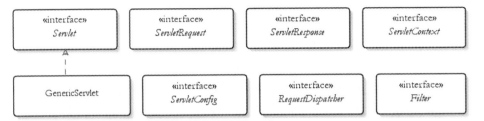

Figure 25.2: The members of the javax.servlet package

The center of the Servlet technology is the **Servlet** interface, which defines the contract between a servlet and a servlet container. All servlets must implement this interface either directly or indirectly.

The contract between the servlet container and a servlet boils down to the promise by the servlet container to load the servlet class into memory and call specific methods on the servlet instance. There is only one instance of each servlet type, which is shared by all requests for the servlet. See the section "Servlet" for details.

A user request causes the servlet container to call the servlet's **service** method, passing an instance of **ServletRequest** and an instance of **ServletResponse**. The **ServletRequest** object encapsulates the current HTTP request so that servlet developers do not have to parse and manipulate raw HTTP data. The **ServletResponse** object represents the HTTP response for the current user and makes sending response to the user easy.

In addition, the servlet container creates an instance of **ServletContext** that encapsulates the environment all servlets in the same application are running on. For each servlet, there is also a **ServletConfig** object that encapsulates the servlet configuration.

Let's continue with a look at these interfaces in detail.

Servlet

All servlets must implement the **javax.servlet.Servlet** interface, either directly or indirectly. The **Servlet** interface defines five methods:

```
public void init(ServletConfig config) throws ServletException
public void service(ServletRequest req, ServletResponse res)
```

```
       throws ServletException, java.io.IOException
public void destroy()
public java.lang.String getServletInfo()
public ServletConfig getServletConfig()
```

The **init**, **service**, and **destroy** methods are life cycle methods. The servlet container invokes these three methods by following these rules.

- **init**. The servlet container invokes this method the first time the servlet is requested. This method is not called at subsequent requests. You use this method to write initialization code. When invoking this method, the servlet container passes a **ServletConfig** object. Normally, you will assign the **ServletConfig** object to a class level variable so that this object can be used from other points in the servlet class.
- **service**. The servlet container invokes this method each time the servlet is requested. You write the code that the servlet is supposed to do here. The first time the servlet is requested, the servlet container calls the **init** method and, if the **init** method finishes successfully, the **service** method. For subsequent requests, only the **service** method is invoked. When invoking the **service** method, the servlet container passes two objects: a **ServletRequest** object and a **ServletResponse** object.
- **destroy**. The servlet container invokes this method when the servlet is about to be destroyed. A servlet container destroys a servlet when the application is unloaded or when the servlet container is being shut down. Normally, you write clean-up code in this method.
- **getServletInfo**. This method returns the description of the servlet. You can return any string that might be useful or even **null**.
- **getServletConfig**. This method returns the **ServletConfig** object passed by the servlet container to the **init** method. However, for the **getServletConfig** method to be able to do so, you must have assigned the **ServletConfig** object to a class level variable in the **init** method.

A very important point to note is thread safety. Your servlet container creates an instance of a servlet which is shared among all users, so class-level variables are not recommended, unless they are read-only.

The next section, "Writing A Basic Servlet Application," shows how you can implement **Servlet** to write your first servlet and deploy the application.

Writing a Basic Servlet Application

This section will present an example of a servlet application named **app25a**. You need a servlet container to run your servlets. Tomcat, an open source servlet container, is available free of charge and runs on any platform where Java is available. The first step in this example therefore discusses how to install and run Tomcat. Afterwards, the servlet code is given.

Installing Tomcat

You can download Tomcat 5.5, the latest version at the time of writing, from http://tomcat.apache.org/download-55.cgi. You should get the latest binary distribution in either zip or gz.

If you downloaded a zip or gz file, extract the file. You will see several directories under the installation directory, as shown in Figure 25.3.

Figure 25.3: Tomcat installation directory

Of special interest are the **bin** and **webapps** directories. In the **bin** directory, you will find programs to start and stop Tomcat. The **webapps** directory is important because you store servlet applications you write there.

After the extraction, set the **JAVA_HOME** environment variable to the JDK installation directory. If you encounter a problem, consult this site:

`http://tomcat.apache.org/tomcat-5.5-doc/setup.html`.

For Windows users, it is a good idea to download the Windows installer for easier installation.

Once you're finished, you can start Tomcat by running the **startup.bat** (on Windows) or the **startup.sh** file (in Unix/Linux). By default, Tomcat runs on port 8080, so you can test Tomcat by directing your Web browser to this address:

```
http://localhost:8080
```

Writing and Compiling the Servlet Class

The next step is to write and compile a servlet class. This servlet class must implement the **javax.servlet.Servlet** interface. The servlet class for this example, **MyServlet**, is given in Listing 25.1. By convention, the names of servlet classes are suffixed **Servlet**.

Listing 25.1: The MyServlet class

```java
package com.brainysoftware.jdk5.app25a;
import java.io.IOException;
import javax.servlet.Servlet;
import javax.servlet.ServletConfig;
import javax.servlet.ServletException;
import javax.servlet.ServletRequest;
import javax.servlet.ServletResponse;

public class MyServlet implements Servlet {
    public void init(ServletConfig config) throws ServletException {
        System.out.println("init");
    }

    public void service(ServletRequest request,
            ServletResponse response)
            throws ServletException, IOException {
        response.getWriter().print("Welcome");
    }

    public void destroy() {
        System.out.println("destroy");
    }

    public String getServletInfo() {
        return null;
    }

    public ServletConfig getServletConfig() {
```

```
        return null;
    }
}
```

To compile the servlet, you must include the types in the Servlet API used in the class. Tomcat includes the **servlet-api.jar** file that packages members of the **javax.servlet** and **javax.servlet.http** packages. The jar file is located in the **common/lib** directory under the installation directory.

Note
The sample applications accompanying this chapter include the Java class files for the examples.

Deployment Descriptor

Every servlet application has a deployment descriptor. This is an XML document named **web.xml** that is deployed with the application and can contain configuration settings for the application. There is a bunch of information that can go to the document descriptor. For this example, the **web.xml** file is given in Listing 25.2.

Note
As a Web developer, you need to be familiar with the basics of XML.

Listing 25.2: The web.xml File

```xml
<?xml version="1.0" encoding="ISO-8859-1"?>
<web-app xmlns="http://java.sun.com/xml/ns/j2ee"
    xmlns:xsi="http://www.w3.org/2001/XMLSchema-instance"
    xsi:schemaLocation="http://java.sun.com/xml/ns/j2ee
http://java.sun.com/xml/ns/j2ee/web-app_2_4.xsd"
    version="2.4">

    <servlet>
        <servlet-name>FirstServlet</servlet-name>
        <servlet-class>
            com.brainysoftware.jdk5.app25a.MyServlet
        </servlet-class>
    </servlet>
    <servlet-mapping>
        <servlet-name>FirstServlet</servlet-name>
        <url-pattern>/first</url-pattern>
    </servlet-mapping>
```

```
</web-app>
```

The root element of the deployment descriptor is **web-app**. Inside **web-app** are the **servlet** and **servlet-mapping** elements.

The **servlet** element registers the servlet to the servlet container. There are two elements inside **<servlet>**, **servlet-name** and **servlet-class**. The **servlet-name** element specifies the name by which the servlet will be known as. The **servlet-class** specifies the fully qualified name of the servlet class.

The **servlet-mapping** element tells the servlet container the URL that has to be used to invoke the servlet. The **servlet-mapping** element has two elements, **servlet-name** and **url-pattern**. The **servlet-name** element specifies the servlet name and the **url-pattern** element specifies a relative URL. The value of the **url-pattern** element must start with a **/**.

In the deployment descriptor in Listing 25.2, the servlet is called **FirstServlet** and the URL pattern to invoke it is **/first**.

Preparing the Application Directory

A servlet application must be deployed in a certain directory structure. Figure 25.4 shows the directory structure for this application.

Figure 25.4: The application directory

The **app25a** directory at the top is the application directory. The application directory need to reside under the **webapps** directory of Tomcat.

Under the application directory is the **WEB-INF** directory. It has two subdirectories.

- **classes**. Your servlet classes and other Java classes must reside here. The directories under classes reflect the class package. In Figure 25.4 there is one class deployed, **com.brainysoftware.jdk5.app25a.MyServlet**.
- **lib**. Deploy jar files required by your servlet application here. The Servlet API jar file does not need to be deployed here because the servlet container already has a copy of it. In this application, the **lib** directory is empty. An empty lib directory may be deleted.

Inside **WEB-INF** you also have the deployment descriptor (**web.xml** file). Also, if you are including the source code with your application, you should put them under **WEB-INF** or a directory under **WEB-INF**. Anything you put under **WEB-INF** is not directly accessible to the client.

A servlet/JSP application normally has JSPs, HTML files, image files, and other resources. These should go under the application directories. They are often organized in subdirectories. For instance, all image files should go to the **images** directory, all JSPs to **jsp**, etc.

Deploying the Application to Tomcat

With Tomcat, you deploy your application by copying the application directory to the **webapps** directory under Tomcat installation. Other servlet containers have different ways of deploying applications.

Alternatively, you can deploy your application as a war file. A war file is a jar file with the **war** extension. You create a war file using the **jar** program that comes with the JDK (discussed in Appendix C, "jar"). Once you get a war file, copy it to Tomcat's **webapps** directory, restart Tomcat, and Tomcat will extract the WAR file automatically when it starts.

Invoking the Servlet

Now, start or restart Tomcat and direct your browser to the following URL.

```
http://localhost:8080/app25a/first
```

The output should be similar to Figure 25.5.

Figure 25.5: Response from MyServlet

ServletResponse

The **javax.servlet.ServletResponse** interface represents a servlet response. Prior to invoking a servlet's **service** method, the servlet container creates a **ServletResponse** object and pass it as the second argument to the **service** method. The **ServletResponse** object hides the complexity of sending response to the client's browser.

The most important method of **ServletResponse** is the **getWriter** method, which returns a **java.io.PrintWriter** object that can send character text to the client. By default, the **PrintWriter** object uses the ISO-8859-1 encoding.

When sending response to the client, you send it as HTML. You are therefore assumed to be familiar with HTML.

Note
There is also another method that you can use to send output to the browser: **getOutputStream**. However, this method is for sending binary data, so in most cases you will use **getWriter** and not **getOutputStream**.

Before sending any HTML tag, you also want to set the content type of the response by calling the **setContentType** method, passing "text/html" as the argument. This is how you tell the browser that the content type is HTML. Most browsers by default render a response as HTML. However, some browsers will display HTML tags as they are if you do not set the response content type instead of rendering them.

The **app25b** application shows how to use the **ServletResponse** object. The servlet class in Listing 25.3 presents the **ResponseTestServlet** class.

Listing 25.3: The ResponseTestServlet class

```
package com.brainysoftware.jdk5.app25b;
import java.io.IOException;
import java.io.PrintWriter;
import javax.servlet.Servlet;
import javax.servlet.ServletConfig;
import javax.servlet.ServletException;
import javax.servlet.ServletRequest;
import javax.servlet.ServletResponse;

public class ResponseTestServlet implements Servlet {
    public void init(ServletConfig config) throws ServletException {
    }

    public void service(ServletRequest request,
        ServletResponse response)
        throws ServletException, IOException {
        response.setContentType("text/html");
        PrintWriter writer = response.getWriter();
        writer.println("<html>");
        writer.println("<head><title>Welcome</title></head>");
        writer.println("<body>Thank you for coming</body>");
        writer.println("</html>");
    }

    public void destroy() {
    }

    public String getServletInfo() {
        return null;
    }

    public ServletConfig getServletConfig() {
        return null;
    }
}
```

The deployment descriptor of this application is given in Listing 25.4.

Listing 25.4: The deployment descriptor of app25b

```
<?xml version="1.0" encoding="ISO-8859-1"?>
<web-app xmlns="http://java.sun.com/xml/ns/j2ee"
```

```
    xmlns:xsi="http://www.w3.org/2001/XMLSchema-instance"
    xsi:schemaLocation="http://java.sun.com/xml/ns/j2ee
http://java.sun.com/xml/ns/j2ee/web-app_2_4.xsd"
    version="2.4">
    <servlet>
        <servlet-name>MainServlet</servlet-name>
        <servlet-class>
            com.brainysoftware.jdk5.app25b.ResponseTestServlet
        </servlet-class>
    </servlet>

    <servlet-mapping>
        <servlet-name>MainServlet</servlet-name>
        <url-pattern>/main</url-pattern>
    </servlet-mapping>
</web-app>
```

Now you need to compile the servlet class, create a directory structure like the one in app25a, and restart Tomcat. You can then use the following URL to invoke the servlet.

```
http://localhost:8080/app25b/main
```

You will see the response like the screenshot in Figure 25.6.

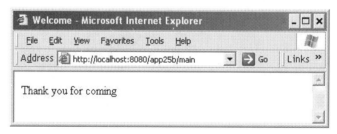

Figure 25.6: The response of ResponseTestServlet

ServletRequest

The next subject is the **javax.servlet.ServletRequest** interface. For every HTTP request, the servlet container creates an instance of **ServletRequest** that encapsulates the information about the request and passes the object to the servlet's **service** method.

These are some of the methods in the **ServletRequest** interface.

```
public int getContentLength()
```
Returns the number of bytes of the request body. If the length is now known, this method returns -1.

```
public java.lang.String getContentType()
```
Returns the MIME type of the body of the request, or null if the type is not known.

```
public java.lang.String getParameter(java.lang.String name)
```
Returns the value of the specified request parameter.

```
public java.lang.String getProtocol()
```
Returns the name and version of the protocol of this HTTP request.

The most important method is **getParameter**. A common use of this method is to return the value of an HTML form field.

The **app25c** application illustrates the use of the **ServletRequest** object passed-in to the servlet's **service** method to retrieve the values of HTML form fields on the client side. The application has two servlets, the SendFormServlet class (in Listing 25.5) that sends a Login form to the browser and the **LoginServlet** (in Listing 25.6) that displays the value the user enters.

Listing 25.5: The SendFormServlet class

```java
package com.brainysoftware.jdk5.app25c;
import java.io.IOException;
import java.io.PrintWriter;
import javax.servlet.Servlet;
import javax.servlet.ServletConfig;
import javax.servlet.ServletException;
import javax.servlet.ServletRequest;
import javax.servlet.ServletResponse;

public class SendFormServlet implements Servlet {
    public void init(ServletConfig config) throws ServletException {
    }

    public void service(ServletRequest request,
            ServletResponse response)
            throws ServletException, IOException {
        response.setContentType("text/html");
        PrintWriter writer = response.getWriter();
        writer.println("<html>");
```

```
        writer.println("<head><title>Login Form</title></head>");
        writer.println("<body>");
        writer.println("<form method=\"post\" action=\"login\">");
        writer.println("
            User Name: <input type=\"text\" name=\"userName\"/>");
        writer.println("<br/>");
        writer.println(
        "Password: <input type=\"password\" name=\"password\"/>");
        writer.println("<br/>");
        writer.println("<input type=\"submit\" value=\"Login\"/>");
        writer.println("</form>");
        writer.println("</body>");
        writer.println("</html>");
    }

    public void destroy() {
    }

    public String getServletInfo() {
        return null;
    }

    public ServletConfig getServletConfig() {
        return null;
    }
}
```

Listing 25.6: The LoginServlet class

```
package com.brainysoftware.jdk5.app25c;
import java.io.IOException;
import java.io.PrintWriter;
import javax.servlet.Servlet;
import javax.servlet.ServletConfig;
import javax.servlet.ServletException;
import javax.servlet.ServletRequest;
import javax.servlet.ServletResponse;

public class LoginServlet implements Servlet {
    public void init(ServletConfig config) throws ServletException {
    }

    public void service(ServletRequest request,
            ServletResponse response)
            throws ServletException, IOException {
        String userName = request.getParameter("userName");
        response.setContentType("text/html");
```

```
        PrintWriter writer = response.getWriter();
        writer.println("<html>");
        writer.println("<head><title>Welcome</title></head>");
        writer.println("<body>Welcome " + userName + "</body>");
        writer.println("</html>");
    }

    public void destroy() {
    }

    public String getServletInfo() {
        return null;
    }

    public ServletConfig getServletConfig() {
        return null;
    }
}
```

Both servlets must be registered in the deployment descriptor. The deployment descriptor for the **app25c** application is given in Listing 25.7.

Listing 25.7: The deployment descriptor of app25c

```
<?xml version="1.0" encoding="ISO-8859-1"?>
<web-app xmlns="http://java.sun.com/xml/ns/j2ee"
    xmlns:xsi="http://www.w3.org/2001/XMLSchema-instance"
    xsi:schemaLocation="http://java.sun.com/xml/ns/j2ee ¬
        http://java.sun.com/xml/ns/j2ee/web-app_2_4.xsd"
    version="2.4">
    <servlet>
        <servlet-name>FormServlet</servlet-name>
        <servlet-class>
            com.brainysoftware.jdk5.app25c.SendFormServlet
        </servlet-class>
    </servlet>
    <servlet>
        <servlet-name>LoginServlet</servlet-name>
        <servlet-class>
            com.brainysoftware.jdk5.app25c.LoginServlet
        </servlet-class>
    </servlet>

    <servlet-mapping>
        <servlet-name>FormServlet</servlet-name>
        <url-pattern>/getForm</url-pattern>
```

```
    </servlet-mapping>
    <servlet-mapping>
        <servlet-name>LoginServlet</servlet-name>
        <url-pattern>/login</url-pattern>
    </servlet-mapping>
</web-app>
```

After you deploy the application, you can invoke it by using this URL:

```
http://localhost:8080/app25c/getForm
```

This will display a Login form like that in Figure 25.7.

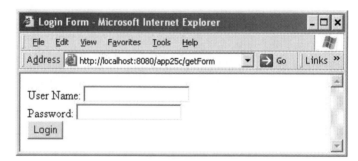

Figure 25.7: The Login form in app25c

If you type in a user name and a password and click Login, you will see the user name is displayed on the browser.

ServletConfig

You've seen that the servlet container passes a **ServletConfig** object to the servlet's **init** method when the servlet container initializes the servlet. The **ServletConfig** object encapsulates configuration information that you can pass to a servlet through the deployment descriptor. This could be useful if you want to pass dynamic information that may be different from one deployment to another to the application. Changing the information would be as easy as editing a text file and no recompilation would be needed. For the changes to be reflected, however, you still need to reload the application.

Every piece of information for the **ServletConfig** object is called an initial parameter. An initial parameter has two components: key and value. To pass an initial parameter to a servlet, use the **init-param** element within the servlet element. Inside the **init-param** element, you use the **param-name** element to specify the initial parameter name and the **param-value** element to specify the initial parameter value. There can be any number of **init-param** elements for a servlet.

For example, the following is a **servlet** element that includes two **init-param** elements.

```
<servlet>
    <servlet-name>ConfigTestServlet</servlet-name>
    <servlet-class>
        com.brainysoftware.jdk5.app25d.ConfigTestServlet
    </servlet-class>
    <init-param>
        <param-name>contactName</param-name>
        <param-value>Jonathan Lucas</param-value>
    </init-param>
    <init-param>
        <param-name>contactEmail</param-name>
        <param-value>contactus@brainysoftware.com</param-value>
    </init-param>
</servlet>
```

To retrieve initial parameters from inside the servlet, call the **getInitParameter** method on the **ServletConfig** object passed by the servlet container to the servlet's **init** method. The signature of **getInitParameter** is as follows.

```
public java.lang.String getInitParameter(java.lang.String name)
```

In addition, the **getInitParameterNames** method return an **Enumeration** of all initial parameter names:

```
public java.util.Enumeration getInitParameterNames()
```

For example, to retrieve the value of the **contactName** parameter, use this.

```
String contactName = servletConfig.getInitParameter("contactName");
```

The **app25d** application shows a servlet that uses the **ServletConfig** object.

GenericServlet

The preceding examples showed how you could write servlets by implementing the **Servlet** interface. However, did you notice that you had to provide the implementations for all the methods in **Servlet**, even though often some of the methods did not contain code? In addition, you needed to preserve the **ServletConfig** object into a class level variable.

Fortunately, the **GenericServlet** abstract class comes to rescue. In keeping with the spirit of easier code writing in OOP, **GenericServlet** implements both **Servlet** and **ServletConfig** (as well as **java.io.Serializable**) and perform the following tasks:

- Assign the **ServletConfig** object in the **init** method to a class level variable so that it can be retrieved by calling **getServletConfig**.
- Provide default implementations of all methods in the **Servlet** interface.
- Provide methods that wrap the methods in the **ServletConfig** objects.

The **GenericServlet** class is shown in Listing 25.8.

Listing 25.8: The GenericServlet class

```
package javax.servlet;
import java.io.IOException;
import java.util.Enumeration;

public abstract class GenericServlet
        implements Servlet, ServletConfig, java.io.Serializable {

    private transient ServletConfig servletConfig;
    public void init(ServletConfig servletConfig)
            throws ServletException {
        this.servletConfig = servletConfig;
        this.init();
    }
    public void init() throws ServletException {
    }
    public abstract void service(ServletRequest request,
            ServletResponse response)
            throws ServletException, IOException;
    public void destroy() {
    }
    public ServletConfig getServletConfig() {
        return servletConfig;
```

```
    }
    public String getInitParameter(String name) {
        return getServletConfig().getInitParameter(name);
    }
    public Enumeration getInitParameterNames() {
        return getServletConfig().getInitParameterNames();
    }
    public ServletContext getServletContext() {
        return getServletConfig().getServletContext();
    }
    public String getServletInfo() {
        return "";
    }
    public void log(String msg) {
        getServletContext().log(getServletName() + ": "+ msg);
    }
    public void log(String message, Throwable t) {
        getServletContext().log(getServletName() + ": "
                + message, t);
    }
    public String getServletName() {
        return config.getServletName();
    }
}
```

GenericServlet preserves the **ServletConfig** object by assigning it to a class level variable **servletConfig**. However, there is a slight problem. If you need to override this method, you must call **super.init(servletConfig)** before your initialization code. To save you from having to do so, **GenericServlet** provides a second **init** method that does not take arguments. This method is called by the first **init** method after **ServletConfig** is assigned to **servletConfig**:

```
public void init(ServletConfig servletConfig)
        throws ServletException {
    this.servletConfig = servletConfig;
    this.init();
}
```

This means, you can write initialization code by overriding the no-argument **init** method and the **ServletConfig** object will still be preserved by the **GenericServlet** instance.

The **ConfigTestServlet** class in Listing 25.9 is a servlet class that extends **GenericServlet** instead of implementing **Servlet**.

Listing 25.9: Extending GenericServlet

```java
package com.brainysoftware.jdk5.app25d;
import java.io.IOException;
import java.io.PrintWriter;
import javax.servlet.GenericServlet;
import javax.servlet.ServletException;
import javax.servlet.ServletRequest;
import javax.servlet.ServletResponse;

public class ConfigTestServlet extends GenericServlet {
    public void service(ServletRequest request,
            ServletResponse response)
            throws ServletException, IOException {
        response.setContentType("text/html");
        PrintWriter writer = response.getWriter();
        writer.println("<html>");
        writer.println("<head><title>" +
                "Servlet Config Test</title></head>");
        writer.println("<body>");
        writer.println("<b>Emergency contact details:</b><br/>");
        writer.print(getServletConfig().
                getInitParameter("contactName"));
        writer.println(" (" + getServletConfig().getInitParameter
                ("contactEmail") + ")");
        writer.println("</body>");
        writer.println("</html>");
    }
}
```

As you can see, by extending **GenericServlet**, you do not need to override methods that you don't want to change. As a result, you have cleaner code. In Listing 25.9, the only method being overridden is the **service** method. Also, there is no need to preserve the **ServletConfig** object yourself. **GenericServlet** does this for you. If you need to access the **ServletConfig** object, you can simply call the **getServletConfig** method.

ServletContext

The **ServletContext** object represents the servlet application. There is only one context per Web application. In the case of distributed environment, where the same application is deployed simultaneously to multi containers, there is one **ServletContext** object per Java Virtual Machine.

You can obtain the **ServletContext** object by calling the **getServletContext** method of the **ServletConfig** object. If you are extending **GenericServlet**, you can call its **getServletContext** method more easily.

The main reason for the existence of **ServletContext** is to share common information among resources in the same application. This is done by storing objects in an internal **Map** within the **ServletContext**. Objects stored in **ServletContext** are called attributes, and objects stored by a servlet can be retrieved by other servlets in the same application. The following methods are provided to work with attributes:

```
public java.lang.Object getAttribute(java.lang.String name)
public java.util.Enumeration getAttributeNames()
public void setAttribute(java.lang.String name,
        java.lang.Object object)
public void removeAttribute(java.lang.String name)
```

HTTP Servlets

Most, if not all, servlet applications you write will work with HTTP. This means, you can make use of the features offered by HTTP. The **javax.servlet.http** package is the second package in the Servlet API and contains classes and interfaces you can use to write servlet applications. Many of the members in **javax.servlet.http** override those in **javax.servlet**. Most of the time, you will use the members in **javax.servlet.http**.

Figure 25.8 shows the main types in **javax.servlet.http**.

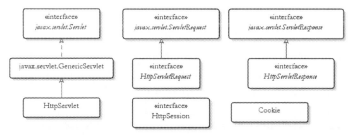

Figure 25.8: The main members of javax.servlet.http

HttpServlet

The **HttpServlet** class overrides the **javax.servlet.GenericServlet** class. When using **HttpServlet**, you will also work with the **HttpServletRequest** and **HttpServletResponse** objects that represent the servlet request and the servlet response, respectively. The **HttpServletRequest** interface extends **javax.servlet.ServletRequest** and **HttpServletResponse** extends **javax.servlet.ServletResponse**.

Most servlets extends **HttpServlet**. **HttpServlet** overrides the **service** method in **GenericServlet** and adds another **service** method with the following signature:

```
protected void service(HttpServletRequest request,
      HttpServletResponse response)
         throws ServletException, java.io.IOException
```

The difference between the new **service** method and the one in **javax.servlet.Servlet** is that the former accepts an **HttpServletRequest** and an **HttpServletResponse**, instead of a **ServletRequest** and a **ServletResponse**.

The servlet container, as usual, calls the original **service** method in **javax.servlet.Servlet**, which in **HttpServlet** is written as follows:

```
public void service(ServletRequest req, ServletResponse res)
      throws ServletException, IOException {
   HttpServletRequest request;
   HttpServletResponse response;
   try {
       request = (HttpServletRequest) req;
       response = (HttpServletResponse) res;
   } catch (ClassCastException e) {
       throw new ServletException("non-HTTP request or response");
   }
   service(request, response);
}
```

The original **service** method downcasts the request and response objects from the servlet container to **HttpServletRequest** and **HttpServletResponse**, respectively, and call the new **service** method. The **downcasting** is always successful because the servlet containers always passes an **HttpServletRequest** and an **HttpServletResponse** objects when calling a servlet's **service** method, to anticipate the use of HTTP. Even if you are implementing **javax.servlet.Servlet** or extending **javax.servlet.GenericServlet**, you can downcast the servlet request and servlet response passed to the **service** method to **HttpServletRequest** and **HttpServletResponse**.

The new **service** method in **HttpServlet** then examine the HTTP method used to send the request (by calling **request.getMethod**) and call one of the following methods: **doGet**, **doPost**, **doHead**, **doPut**, **doTrace**, **doOptions**, and **doDelete**. Each of the seven methods represents an HTTP method. **doGet** and **doPost** are the most often used. In addition, you rarely override the **service** methods anymore. Instead, you override **doGet** or **doPost** or both **doGet** and **doPost**.

To summarize, there are two features in **HttpServlet** that you do not find in **GenericServlet**:

- Instead of the **service** method, you will override **doGet**, **doPost**, or both of them. In rare cases, you will also override either of these: **doHead**, **doPut**, **doTrace**, **doOptions**, **doDelete**.
- You will work with **HttpServletRequest** and **HttpServletResponse**, instead of **ServletRequest** and **ServletResponse**.

HttpServletRequest

HttpServletRequest represents the servlet request in the HTTP environment. It extends the **javax.servlet.ServletRequest** interface and adds several methods. Some of the methods are:

```
public java.lang.String getContextPath()
```
Returns the portion of the request URI that indicates the context of the request.

```
public Cookie[] getCookies()
```
Returns an array of Cookie objects.

```
public java.lang.String getHeader(java.lang.String name)
```
Returns the value of the specified HTTP header.

```
public java.lang.String getMethod()
```
Returns the name of the HTTP method with which this request was made.

```
public java.lang.String getQueryString()
```
Returns the query string in the request URL.

```
public HttpSession getSession()
```
Returns the session object associated with this request. If none is found, creates a new session object.

```
public HttpSession getSession(boolean create)
```
Returns the current session object associated with this request. If none is found and the create argument is **true**, create a new session object.

HttpServletResponse

HttpServletResponse represents the servlet response in the HTTP environment. Here are some of the methods defined in it.

```
public void addCookie(Cookie cookie)
```
Adds a cookie to this response object.

```
public void addHeader(java.lang.String name, java.lang.String value)
```
Adds a header to this response object.

```
public void sendRedirect(java.lang.String location)
```
Sends a response code that redirects the browser to the specified location.

Writing an Http Servlet

Extending the **HttpServlet** class is similar to subclassing **GenericServlet**. However, instead of overriding the **service** method, with you override the **doGet** and **doPost** methods in a **HttpServlet** subclass.

The **app25f** application that accompanies this chapter comes with two servlets, **SendFormServlet** (given in Listing 25.10) and **RegistrationServlet** (given in Listing 25.11). Both servlets extends **HttpServlet** but override different methods. The **SendFormServlet** sends an HTML form to the browser and must be invoked using the HTTP GET method. When the HTML form sent by **SendFormServlet** is submitted, the POST method is used and this invokes the **doPost** method in **RegistrationServlet**.

Listing 25.10: The SendFormServlet class

```
package com.brainysoftware.jdk5.app25f;
```

```
import java.io.IOException;
import java.io.PrintWriter;
import javax.servlet.ServletException;
import javax.servlet.http.HttpServlet;
import javax.servlet.http.HttpServletRequest;
import javax.servlet.http.HttpServletResponse;

public class SendFormServlet extends HttpServlet {
    public void doGet(HttpServletRequest request,
            HttpServletResponse response)
            throws ServletException, IOException {
        response.setContentType("text/html");
        PrintWriter writer = response.getWriter();
        writer.println("<html>");
        writer.println("<head><title>Registration Form" +
                ""</title></head>");
        writer.println("<body>");
        writer.println("Please fill in your details<br/>");
        writer.println("<form method=\"post\"" +
                "action=\"register\">");
        writer.println("First Name: <input type=\"text\" +" +
                "name=\"firstName\"/>");
        writer.println("<br/>");
        writer.println("Last Name: <input type=\"text\" +" +
                "name=\"lastName\"/>");
        writer.println("<br/>");
        writer.println("<input type=\"submit\" " +
                "value=\"Register\"/>");
        writer.println("</form>");
        writer.println("</body>");
        writer.println("</html>");
    }
}
```

Listing 25.11: The RegistrationServlet class

```
package com.brainysoftware.jdk5.app25f;
import java.io.IOException;
import java.io.PrintWriter;
import javax.servlet.ServletException;
import javax.servlet.http.HttpServlet;
import javax.servlet.http.HttpServletRequest;
import javax.servlet.http.HttpServletResponse;

public class RegistrationServlet extends HttpServlet {
    public void doPost(HttpServletRequest request,
            HttpServletResponse response)
```

```
        throws ServletException, IOException {
    String firstName = request.getParameter("firstName");
    String lastName = request.getParameter("lastName");
    response.setContentType("text/html");
    PrintWriter writer = response.getWriter();
    writer.println("<html>");
    writer.println("<head><title>Thank you</title></head>");
    writer.println("<body>" + firstName + " " + lastName
            + ", thank you for registering with us.</body>");
    writer.println("</html>");
    }
}
```

You can invoke the **app25f** application using this URL:

```
http://localhost:8080/app25f/getForm
```

Summary

The Servlet technology is part of the Java EE, and is covered here because of its popularity and importance. There are two packages that wrap the Servlet API: **javax.servlet** and **javax.servlet.http**. All servlets run in a servlet container, and the contract between the container and the servlets takes the form of the **javax.servlet.Servlet** interface. The **javax.servlet** package also provides the **GenericServlet** abstract class that implements **Servlet**. This is a convenient class that you can extend to create a servlet. However, most modern servlets will work in the HTTP environment. As such, subclassing the **javax.servlet.http.HttpServlet** class is more appropriate. The **HttpServlet** class itself is a subclass of **GenericServlet**.

Questions

1. What are the three life cycle methods of the **javax.servlet.Servlet** interface?
2. What's the main difference between the **getWriter** method and the **getOutputStream** method in the **javax.servlet.ServletResponse** interface? Which one of the two do you use more often?
3. Name four interfaces in **javax.servlet** and three interfaces in **javax.servlet.http**.

Chapter 26
JavaServer Pages

As evidenced in Chapter 25, there are two drawbacks servlets are not capable of overcoming. First, when sending a response, all HTML tags must be enclosed in strings, making sending HTTP response a tedious effort. Second, all text and HTML tags are hardcoded, and, as a result, minor changes to an application presentation part, such as changing a page background color, requires recompilation.

JavaServer Pages (JSP) comes to the rescue and solves the two problems in servlets. JSP does not replace Servlet, however, but complements it. Modern Java Web applications use servlets and JSP pages at the same time. The latest version of JSP at the time of writing is 2.0, but 2.1 is on the way.

A JSP Overview

A JSP page is essentially a servlet. However, working with JSP pages is easier than with servlets because of two reasons. First, you do not have to compile JSP pages. Second, JSP pages are basically text files with the **jsp** extension and you can use any text editor to write them.

JSP pages run on a JSP container. A servlet container is normally also a JSP container. Tomcat, for instance, is a servlet/JSP container. The first time a JSP page is requested, the JSP container does two things:

1. Translate the JSP page into a JSP page implementation class. This class must implement the **javax.servlet.Servlet** interface. The result of the translation is dependent on the JSP container. The class name is also JSP container-specific. You do not have to worry about this implementation class or its name because you never need to work with it directly. If there is a translation error, an error message will be sent to the client.

2. If the translation was successful, the JSP container compiles the implementation class, and then loads and instantiate it and perform the normal lifecycle operations it does for a servlet.

For subsequent requests for the same JSP page, the JSP container checks if the JSP page has been modified since the last time it was translated. If so, it was retranslated, recompiled, and executed. If not, the JSP servlet already in memory is executed. This way, the first invocation of a JSP page is always much longer than subsequent requests because it involves translation and compilation. To get around this problem, you can do one of the following:

- Configure the application so that all JSP pages will be called (so that they will be translated and compiled) when the application starts, rather than wait for the first requests.
- Precompiled the JSP pages and deploy them as servlets.

JSP comes with an API that comprises three packages. However, when working with JSP, you do not often work directly with this API. Instead, you will work with classes and interfaces in the Servlet API. In addition, you need to familiarize yourself with the syntax of a JSP page.

A JSP page can contain template data and syntactic elements. An element is something that has a special meaning to the JSP translator. For example, **<%** is an element because it denotes the start of a Java code block within a JSP page. **%>** is also an element because it ends a Java code block. Anything else that is not an element is template data. Template data is sent as is to the browser. For instance, HTML tags and text in a JSP page are template data.

Listing 26.1 presents a JSP page named **welcome.jsp** that sends "Welcome" to the client. Notice how simple it is compared to the servlet in Listing 25.1 that does the same thing?

Listing 26.1: The welcome.jsp page

```
<html>
<head><title>Welcome</title></head>
<body>
Welcome
</body>
</html>
```

In addition, JSP application deployment is simpler too. A JSP page is compiled into a servlet class, but a JSP does not need to be registered in the deployment descriptor or mapped. Every JSP page deployed in an application directory can be invoked by typing the name of the page. Figure 26.1 shows the directory structure of **app26**, the JSP application accompanying this chapter..

Figure 26.1: The application directory of the app26 JSP application

With only a JSP page, the structure of the **app26** application is very simple. It only has the **WEB-INF** directory and the **welcome.jsp** page. The WEB-INF directory is empty. You don't even need a deployment descriptor.

You can invoke the **welcome.jsp** page using this URL:

```
http://localhost:8080/app26/welcome.jsp
```

Note
You do not need to restart Tomcat when adding a new JSP page.

Listing 26.1 is a simple HTML file. Listing 26.2 shows how to use Java code to produce a dynamic page. The **todayDate.jsp** page in Listing 24.2 shows today's date.

Listing 26.2: The todayDate.jsp page

```
<%@page import="java.util.Date"%>
<%@page import="java.text.DateFormat"%>
<html>
<head><title>Today's date</title></head>
<body>
<%
    DateFormat dateFormat =
            DateFormat.getDateInstance(DateFormat.LONG);
    String s = dateFormat.format(new Date());
    out.println("Today is " + s);
%>
</body>
</html>
```

The **todayDate.jsp** page sends the string "Today is" followed by today's date (in the long format, such as June 30, 2006) to the browser.

There are two things to note. First, Java code can appear anywhere in a page and is enclosed by **<%** and **%>**. Second, to import a type to be used from Java code, you use the **import** attribute of the **page** directive. Both the **<% ... %>** block and the page directive will be discussed much later in this chapter.

You can invoke the **todayDate.jsp** page using this URL:

```
http://localhost:8080/app26/todayDate.jsp
```

jspInit, jspDestroy, and Other Methods

As mentioned before, a JSP is translated into a servlet source file and then compiled into a servlet class. A JSP page body more or less translates into the **service** method of **Servlet**. However, in a servlet you have the **init** and **destroy** methods for writing initialization and cleaning up code. How do you override the methods in a JSP page?

In a JSP page you have two similar methods:

- **jspInit**. This method is similar to the **init** method in **Servlet**. **jspInit** is invoked when the JSP page is initialized. One difference is **jspInit** does not take an argument. You can still obtain the **ServletConfig** object through the **config** implicit object. (See the next section, "Implicit Objects.")
- **jspDestroy**. This method is similar to the **destroy** method in **Servlet** and is invoked when the JSP page is about to be destroyed.

A method definition in a JSP page is enclosed with **<%!** and **%>**. Listing 26.3 presents the **lifeCycle.jsp** page that demonstrates how you can override **jspInit** and **jspDestroy**.

Listing 26.3: The lifeCycle.jsp page

```
<%!
    public void jspInit() {
        System.out.println("jspInit ...");
    }
    public void jspDestroy() {
        System.out.println("jspDestroy ...");
    }
%>
<html>
```

```
<head><title>jspInit and jspDestroy</title></head>
<body>
Overriding jspInit and jspDestroy
</body>
</html>
```

You can invoke the JSP page by using this URL:

```
http://localhost:8080/app26/lifeCycle.jsp
```

You will see "jspInit ..." on your console when you first invoke the JSP page, and "jspDestroy ..." if you shut down Tomcat.

A **<%! ... %>** block can appear anywhere in a JSP page, and there can be more than one **<%! ... %>** block in a single page.

You can also write other methods using the **<%! ... %>** block. These methods can be invoked from inside the JSP page.

Implicit Objects

With the **service** method in **javax.servlet.Servlet**, you get an **HttpServletRequest** and an **HttpServletResponse** objects. You also get a **ServletConfig** object (passed to the **init** method) and the **ServletContext** object. In addition, you can obtain an **HttpSession** object by calling the **getSession** method on the **HttpServletRequest** object.

In JSP, you retrieve those objects using JSP implicit objects. The implicit objects are listed in Table 26.1.

For example, the **request** implicit object represents the **HttpServletRequest** object passed by the servlet/JSP container to the servlet's **service** method. You can use **request** as if it was a variable reference to the **HttpServletRequest** object. For instance, the following code retrieves the **userName** parameter from the **HttpServletRequest** object.

```
<%
    String userName = request.getParameter("userName");
%>
```

Object	Type
request	javax.servlet.http.HttpServletRequest
response	javax.servlet.http.HttpServletResponse
out	javax.servlet.jsp.JspWriter
session	javax.servlet.http.HttpSession
application	javax.servlet.ServletContext
config	javax.servlet.ServletConfig
pageContext	javax.servlet.jsp.PageContext
page	javax.servlet.jsp.HttpJspPage
exception	java.lang.Throwable

Table 26.1: JSP Implicit Objects

The **out** implicit object references a **JspWriter** object, which is similar to the **java.io.PrintWriter** object you obtain from the **getWriter** method of the **HttpServletResponse** object. You can call its **print** method overloads just as you would a **PrintWriter** object, to send messages to the browser.

```
out.println("Welcome");
```

The **implicitObjects.jsp** page in Listing 26.4 demonstrates the use of some of the implicit objects.

Listing 26.4: The implicitObjects.jsp page

```
<%@page import="java.util.Enumeration"%>
<html>
<head><title>JSP Implicit Objects</title></head>
<body>
<b>Http headers:</b><br/>
<%
    for (Enumeration e = request.getHeaderNames();
            e.hasMoreElements(); ) {
        String header = (String) e.nextElement();
        out.println(header + ": " + request.getHeader(header) +
            "<br/>");
    }
%>
<hr/>
<%
    out.println("Buffer size: " + response.getBufferSize() +
        "<br/>");
    out.println("Session id: " + session.getId() + "<br/>");
    out.println("Servlet name: " + config.getServletName() +
        "<br/>");
```

```
        out.println("Server info: " + application.getServerInfo());
%>
</body>
</html>
```

Even though you can have retrieve the **HttpServletResponse** object through the **response** implicit object, you do not need to set the content type. By default, the JSP compiler sets the content type of every JSP to **text/html**.

The **page** implicit object represents the current JSP page and is not normally used by JSP page authors.

JSP Syntactic Elements

To write JSP pages, you need to be familiar with the JSP syntax, more than with the JSP API. There are three types of JSP syntactic elements: directives, scripting elements, and actions. Directives and scripting elements are discussed in this chapter.

Directives

Directives are instructions for the JSP translator on how a JSP page should be translated into a servlet implementation class. There are several directives defined in JSP 2.0, but only the two most important ones, **page** and **include**, are discussed in this chapter. The other directives that are not covered are **taglib**, **tag**, **attribute**, and **variable**.

The page Directive

You use the **page** directive to instruct the JSP translator on certain aspects of the current JSP page. For example, you can tell the JSP translator the size of the buffer that should be used for the **out** implicit object, what content type to use, what Java types to import, and so on.

You use the **page** directive using this syntax:

```
<%@ page attribute1="value1" attribute2="value2" ... %>
```

where the space between **@** and **page** is optional and *attribute1*, *attribute2*, and so on are the **page** directive's attributes. There are 13 attributes of the **page** directive.

- **import**. Specifies the type that will be imported and useable by the Java code in this page. For example, specifying **import="java.util.ArrayList"** will import the **ArrayList** class. You can use the wildcard * to import the whole package, such as in **import="java.util.*"**. To import multiple types you can separate two types with a comma, such as in **import="java.util.ArrayList, java.io.File, java.io.PrintWriter"**. All types in the following packages are implicitly imported: **java.lang**, **javax.servlet**, **javax.servlet.http**, **javax.servlet.jsp**.

- **session**. A value of **true** indicates that this page participates in session management, and a value of **false** indicates otherwise. By default, the value is **true**, which means the invocation of this page will cause a **javax.servlet.http.HttpSession** instance to be created, if one does not yet exist.

- **buffer**. Specifies the buffer size of the **out JspWriter** object in kilobytes. The suffix **kb** is mandatory. The default buffer size is 8kb or more, depending on the JSP container. It is also possible to assign **none** to this attribute to indicate that no buffering should be used, which will cause all output is written directly through to the corresponding **PrintWriter** object.

- **autoFlush**. A value of **true**, the default value, indicates that the buffered output should be flushed automatically when the buffer becomes full. A value of **false** indicates that buffer is only flushed if the **flush** method of the response object is called. Consequently, an exception will be thrown in the case of buffer overflow.

- **isThreadSafe**. Indicates the level of thread safety implemented in the page. JSP authors are advised against using this attribute as it could result in the generated servlet containing deprecated code.

- **info**. Specifies the return value of the **getServletInfo** method of the generated servlet.

- **errorPage**. Indicates the page that will handler errors in this page.

- **isErrorPage**. Indicates if this page is an error page handler.

- **contentType**. Specifies the content type of the response object of this page. By default, the value is **text/html**.

- **pageEncoding**. Specifies the character encoding for this page. By default, the value is **ISO-8859-1**.
- **isELIgnored**. Indicates whether EL expressions are ignored. EL, which is short for expression language, is not discussed in this chapter.
- **language**. Specifies the scripting language used in this page. By default, its value is **java** and this is the only valid value in JSP 2.0.
- **extends**. Specifies the superclass that this JSP page's implementation class must extend. This attribute is rarely used and should only be used with extra caution.

The **page** directive can appear anywhere in a page, except if it contains the **contentType** attribute or the **pageEncoding** attribute, because the content type and the character encoding must be set prior to sending any content.

The **page** directive can also appear multiple times. However, an attribute that appears in multiple **page** directives must have the same value. An exception to this is the **import** attribute. The effect of the **import** attribute appearing in multiple **page** directives is cumulative. For example, the following page directives import both **java.util.ArrayList** and **java.io.File**.

```
<%@page import="java.util.ArrayList"%>
<%@page import="java.io.File"%>
```

This is the same as

```
<%@page import="java.util.ArrayList, java.io.File"%>
```

As another example, here is another **page** directive:

```
<%@page session="false" buffer="16kb"%>
```

The include Directive

You use the **include** directive to include the content of another file in the current JSP page. You can use multiple **include** directives in a JSP page. Modularizing a particular content into an include file is useful if that content is used by different pages or used by a page in different places.

The syntax of the include directive is as follows:

```
<%@ include file="url"%>
```

where the space between **@** and **include** is optional and *url* represents the relative path to an include file. If *url* begins with a forward slash (/), it is interpreted as an absolute path on the server. If it does not, it is interpreted as relative to the current JSP page.

The JSP translator translates the **include** directive by replacing the directive with the content of the include file. In other words, if you have written the **copyright.html** file in Listing 26.5.

Listing 26.5: The copyright.html include file

```
<hr/>
&copy;2005 BrainySoftware
<hr/>
```

And, you have the **main.jsp** page in Listing 26.6.

Listing 26.6: The main.jsp page

```
<html>
<head><title>Including a file</title></head>
<body>
This is the included content: <hr/>
<%@ include file="copyright.html"%>
</body>
</html>
```

Using the **include** directive in the **main.jsp** page has the same effect as writing the following JSP page.

```
<html>
<head><title>Including a file</title></head>
<body>
This is the included content: <hr/>
<hr/>
&copy;2005 BrainySoftware
<hr/>
</body>
</html>
```

For the above **include** directive to work, the **copyright.html** file must reside in the same directory as the including page.

Scripting Elements

You use scripting elements to insert Java code into a JSP page. There are three types of scripting elements: scriptlets, declarations, and expressions. They are discussed in the following subsections.

Scriptlets

A scriptlet is a block of Java code. A scriptlet starts with the **<%** tag and ends with the **%>** tag. You have seen the use of scriplets throughout this chapter. As another example, consider the JSP page in Listing 26.7.

Listing 26.7: Using a scriplet

```
<%@page import="java.util.Enumeration"%>
<html>
<head><title>Scriptlet example</title></head>
<body>
<b>Http headers:</b><br/>
<%
    for (Enumeration e = request.getHeaderNames();
            e.hasMoreElements(); ) {
        String header = (String) e.nextElement();
        out.println(header + ": " + request.getHeader(header) +
                "<br/>");
    }
    String message = "Thank you.";
%>
<hr/>
<%
    out.println(message);
%>
</body>
</html>
```

There are two scriptlets in the JSP page in Listing 26.7. Note that variables defined in a scriptlet is visible to other scriptlets below it.

It is legal for the first line of code in a scriptlet to be in the same line as the <% tag and for the %> tag to be in the same line as the last line of code. However, this would result in a less readable page.

Expressions

An expression is evaluated and its result is fed to the **print** method of the **out** implicit object. An expression starts with **<%=** and ends with **%>**. For example, here is an expression:

```
Today is <%=java.util.Calendar.getInstance().getTime()%>
```

Note that there is no semicolon after the expression. With this expression, the JSP container first evaluates **java.util.Calendar.getInstance().getTime()**, and then passes the result to **out.print()**. This is the same as writing the following scriptlet:

```
Today is
<%
    out.print(java.util.Calendar.getInstance().getTime());
%>
```

Declarations

You can declare variables and methods that can be used in a JSP page. You enclose a declaration with <%! and %>. For example, Listing 26.8 shows a JSP page that declares a method named **getTodayDate**.

Listing 26.8: Using a declaration

```
<%!
    public String getTodayDate() {
        return new java.util.Date();
    }
%>
<html>
<head><title>Declarations</title></head>
<body>
Today is <%=getTodayDate()%>
</body>
</html>
```

Handling Errors

Error handling well supported in JSP. Java code can be handled using the try statement, however you can also specify a page that will be displayed should any of the pages in the application encounter an uncaught exception. In such events, the user will see a well designed page that explains what happened, and not an error message that makes them frown.

You make a JSP page an error page by using the attribute **isErrorPage** attribute of the **page** directive. The value of the attribute must be **true**. Listing 26.9 shows such an error handler.

Listing 26.9: The errorHandler.jsp page

```
<%@page isErrorPage="true"%>
<html>
<head><title>Error</title></head>
<body>
An error has occurred. <br/>
Error message:
<%
  out.println(exception.toString());
%>
</body>
</html>
```

Other pages that need protection against uncaught exception will have to use the **errorPage** attribute of the **page** directive, citing the path to the error handling page as the value. For example, the **buggy.jsp** page in Listing 26.10 uses the error handler in Listing 26.9.

Listing 26.10: The buggy.jsp page

```
<%@page errorPage="errorHandler.jsp"%>
Deliberately throw an exception
<%
  Integer.parseInt("Throw me");
%>
```

If you run the **buggy.jsp** page, it will throw an exception. However, you will not see the error message produced by the servlet/JSP container. Instead, the content of the **errorHandler.jsp** page is displayed.

Summary

JSP is the second technology for building Web applications. JSP was invented after Servlet to complement it, not to replace it. Well designed Java Web applications use both servlets and JSP.

This chapter presented a brief introduction to JSP.

Questions

1. What are the two problems in the Servlet technology that JSP solves?
2. Why is it easier to program JSP than to write servlets?

Chapter 27
Javadoc

You already know how to write comments in your classes, by using the // and /* ... */ notations. These comments serve as documentation that is good mostly for the developer who is writing the class or new developers who will continue work on the class. There is another type of documentation in Java. This type is suitable if you are writing API that will be used by other people. You use the **javadoc** program that comes with the JDK and can be found under the bin directory of your JDK installation. By default, Javadoc generates HTML files that describe packages and types. Every single HTML file generated describes either a package or a type. Within a description of a type you can also describe methods and fields of the type, plus constructors of the type if the type is a class.

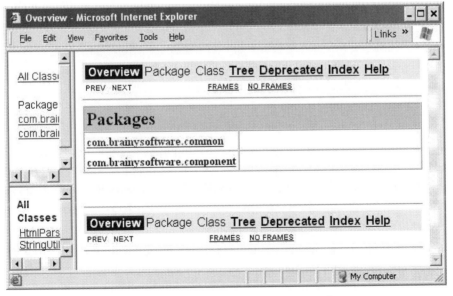

Figure 27.1: Java API documentation

The input to Javadoc is Java source files. Javadoc will be happy to overlook any compiler errors that may be present in the classes. This means, you can generate documentation even before the project is complete. The output by default is a set of HTML files, however you can customize **javadoc** to format output differently.

The chapters provides three topics of discussions.

- How to write documentation in your Java class,
- How to use **javadoc** to generate HTML files.

Writing Documentation in Java Classes

This section teaches you how to embed documentation comments, or doc comments for short, in your source code. You can write doc comments for a class, an interface, a method, constructor, and a field.

A doc comment begins with a /* sequence (or /* * in pre-5 JDKs) and ends with */. It can contains one or more lines of text, which is called the main description, and each line can be preceded by a *. When parsed, any leading * and tabs are ignored. A doc comment must appear right before the declaration of a class, an interface, a constructor, a method, or a field.

For example, here is a doc comment with a description "This is a comment".

```
/**
 * This is a comment
 */
```

Because by default doc comments will be generated as HTML files, be careful when part of the text in a comment contains what looks like an HTML tag, such as **<b>** or **<i>**. These will be interpreted by the browser as HTML tags. Therefore, a < has to be written as its entity code (<) and > as >, and ampersand & as **&**.

A doc comment can also contain tags, which are special keywords that can be processed. Tags must appear after the description of a doc comment. There can be many tags in a comment and it is possible to have tags and no description.

There are two types of tags:

- Block tags or standalone tags. Appear as *@*tag
- In-line tags. Appear within curly braces, as {*@*tag}.

To be processed, a tag must appear at the beginning of a line, ignoring leading asterisks, white spaces, and the separator (/**). A *@*tag that appears elsewhere will not be translated as a tag. If part of the description starts a line with *@*, you need to escape it using the HTML entity @.

For example, the following doc comment contains an **author** tag that specifies the name of the developer writing the class.

```
/**
 * This is a comment
 * @author Brian Softwood
 */
```

The following sections list tags that can be used in doc comments.

*@*author

You use the **author** tag to specify the author of the commented class or method. You can have multiple **author** tags in a doc comment, in which case two names will be separated by a comma in the resulting HTML.

You specify the **author** tag by using this syntax:

```
@author name
```

For example:

```
@author John Blank
```

or

```
@author John Blank; Cindy Rella
```

Note that the **author** tag will only be included in documentation if the **-author** option is used when using javadoc.

{@code}

You use the **code** tag to display text in code font, the same as using the HTML **code** tag. For example, the following doc comment results in **StringParser** printed in font code:

```
This method creates a {@code StringParser} object.
```

This is similar to:

```
This method creates a <code>StringParser</code> object.
```

The difference is HTML tags within a {@code} will be printed literally. For example, **{@code StringUtil}** will be printed as **StringUtil**, whereas **<code>StringUtil</code>** will be printed as **StringUtil** in bold face.

{@docRoot}

You use **{@docRoot}** to specify the generated document's root directory. This tag is useful when you need to include an external file in all generated pages. **{@docRoot}** can appear in any doc comment, including the text portion of another tag.

For example, the following **{@docRoot}** specifies the location of the **help.html** file.

```
Details can be found in <a href="{@docRoot}/help.html">here</a>
```

@deprecated

Use **@deprecated** to indicate that a type or a method is deprecated. See also the **Deprecated** annotation in Chapter 18, "Annotations."

@exception

You use **@exception** in a doc comment for a method or a constructor to indicate that the method or constructor may throw an exception. For example, the **openFile** method below may throw a **java.io.FileNotFoundException**.

```
/**
```

```
 * @throws java.io.FileNotFoundException. If the specified file is
 * not found.
 */
public void openFile(String filename) {
  // code
}
```

@exception and **@throws** are synonyms.

{@inheritDoc}

This tag explicitly inserts a description in a method main description or **@return**, **@param**, or **@throws** tag comment from the nearest superclass or implemented interface.

Note that if a main description, or **@return**, **@param**, or **@throws** tag is missing from a method comment, **javadoc** automatically copies the corresponding main description or tag comment from the method it overrides or implements.

{@link}

Inserts an HTML hyperlink that references the documentation for the specified package, class, or member name of a referenced class. The syntax of this tag is

```
{@link package.class#member label}
```

where *label* denotes the text that will appear as the link in code font. If one of the *package*, *class*, or *member* elements is missing, the same package or class as the documented type is assumed.

For example, if you have the **com.brainysoftware.common.StringUtil** class in your API, and it possesses the **convertString** method whose signature is as follows:

```
public java.lang.String convertString(java.lang.String s)
```

From another class you can reference the **convertString** method by using this **link** tag:

```
Use the {@link
```

```
com.brainysoftware.common.StringUtil#toMixedCase(java.lang.String)
StringUtil.toMixedCase} method.
```

The link will be translated into this HTML tag in the generated HTML document:

```
Use the
<A HREF="../../../com/brainysoftware/common/StringUtil.html#
toMixedCase(java.lang.String)"><CODE>StringUtil.toMixedCase</CODE>
</A> method.
```

{@linkplain}

This tag is very similar to **{@link}**, except that the label is not shown in code font.

{@literal}

You use this tag if you want to display text and escape all special characters in the text. This means, **<i>** does not mean italicizing the text. The syntax for this tag is

```
{@literal text}
```

@param

You use this tag to describe a parameter of a method or a constructor. The syntax of the **param** tag is as follows.

```
@param parameterName description
```

For example, the following method is described using the **param** tag.

```
/**
 * Convert the specified string according to Rule A
 * @param s the String to be converted
 */
public String convertString(String s) {
  // code
}
```

@return

Use this tag to describe the return value of a method. The syntax is

```
@return description
```

For example, the return value of the **convertString** method below is described.

```
/**
 * Convert the specified string according to Rule A.
 * @param s the String to be converted
 * @return A new String object converted according to Rule A.
 */
public String convertString(String s) {
  // code
}
```

@see

Use this tag to add a "See Also" section, which may be followed by a text entry or a link that references a resource. The syntax has three forms:

```
@see text
@see link
@see package.class#member label
```

The first form does not generate a hyperlink. For example:

```
@see "The Specification Guide"
```

The second form is followed by an HTML hyperlink. For instance:

```
@see <a href="guide.html">Specification Guide</a>
```

The third form is most common and is similar to a {@link}. For example:

```
* @see com.brainysoftware.common.StringUtil#toMixedCase(
java.lang.String) StringUtil.toMixedCase method
```

@serial

This tag is used to describe a default serializable field. Its syntax is

```
@serial fieldDescription | include | exclude
```

The optional *fieldDescription* argument explains the meaning of the field and list acceptable values. The *include* and *exclude* arguments indicate whether a class or package should be included or excluded from the serialized form page. The rule is as follows.

- A public or protected class that implements java.io.Serializable is included unless that class or its package is marked **@serial exclude**.
- A private or package-private class implementing java.io.Serializable is excluded unless that class or its package is marked **@serial include**.

@serialData

Describes the types and order of data in the serialized form.

@serialField

Describes an **ObjectStreamField** component of a **Serializable** class's **serialPersistentFields** member.

@since

Adds a "Since" heading with the specified argument. The syntax is

```
@since text
```

Normally, the text argument contains the software version since which a class or a class member became available. For example:

```
@since 1.5
```

@throws

This tag is a synonym for **@exception**.

{@value}

The syntax of **{@value}** has two forms:

```
{@value}
{@value package.class#field}
```

When used without an argument, this tag describes a static field and displays the value of that constant. For example:

```
/**
 * The default value is {@value}.
 */
public static final int FIELD_COUNT = 5;
```

When used with the argument *package.class#field*, this tag can be used to described any program element and displays the value of the specified constant. For example, the following value tag is used in a doc comment for a method.

```
/**
 * Insert {@value #FIELD_COUNT} columns.
 */
public void insertColumns() {
    // code
}
```

@version

Use this tag to add a "Version" subheading with the specified text argument. Its syntax is

```
@version text
```

This tag will only appear in the documentation if javadoc is invoked using the **–version** option.

Javadoc Syntax

The **javadoc** tool (**javadoc.exe**) is an application to generate API documentation. It reads Java source files and generate output based on doc comments found in the source files. Javadoc formulates its output based on the standard doclet that generates HTML pages. Doclets are Java programs that use the Doclet API to specify the content and format of the output of the Javadoc tool. Java doclets are explained here:

```
http://java.sun.com/j2se/1.5.0/docs/guide/javadoc/doclet/
overview.html
```

You can use Javadoc to generate documentation for a single Java source file, multiple source files, or the whole package. Just like other Java tools, Javadoc can be used with options. Among others, there are options to specify the location of the source files and the location of generated output. The rule for specifying these locations are similar to that used by **java** and **javac**.

One way to generate documentation for a single source file is to run Javadoc from the directory containing the source file. For example, to generate documentation for the **com.brainysoftware.component.HtmlParser.java** file, run javadoc from the directory containing the **com** folder.

```
javadoc com/brainysoftware/component/HtmlParser.java
```

To generate documentation from multiple sources, separate two filenames with a space. For example, the following javadoc command reads two sources:

```
javadoc com/domain/Parent.java com/domain/Child.java
```

To generate a documentation for a package, use the asterisk wild character:

```
javadoc com/domain/*.java
```

Of course, you can generate from multiple packages by separating two packages with a space:

```
javadoc packageA/*.java packageB/*.java packageC/*.java
```

However, it is also easy to generate documentation for a whole package and recursively traverse subpackages in it. For example, the following javadoc command documents the contents of the com package and all its subpackages:

```
javadoc -subpackages com
```

Or, you can specify multiple packages too, by separating two package names with a space or a colon:

```
javadoc -subpackages com:org
```

If you don't specify an output location, the generated documentation will be stored in the same folder as the source, using the same directory structure. However, often you want to separate source files from documentation, and for this purpose you can use the -d option provided by the standard doclet. For example, the following javadoc command saves the generated documents in the doc folder under the current directory:

```
javadoc -subpackages com -d ./doc
```

Alternatively, you can use an absolute path such as this:

```
javadoc -subpackages com -d C:/documents/java/doc
```

or

```
javadoc -subpackages com -d /home/user1/doco
```

Javadoc options are discussed in the subsection "Javadoc Options" and standard doclet options in the subsection "Standard Doclet Options." The last subsection "Generated Documents" discuss the types of documents that Javadoc and the standard doclet generates.

Javadoc Options

You can pass options to Javadoc. To use an option, you use a hyphen right before the option name. An option may take arguments. The syntax is as follows:

```
javadoc -optionA argumentA ... -optionN argumentN
```

Here are some of the more important options. The complete list can be found here:

```
http://java.sun.com/j2se/1.5.0/docs/tooldocs/windows/javadoc.html#
javadocoptions
```

`-classpath classPathList`
> Specifies the paths where javadoc will look for referenced classes.

`-doclet class`
> Uses the specified doclet class in generating the documentation.

`-exclude packageName1:packageName2:...`
> Excludes the specified packages and their subpackages.

`-help`
> Displays the online help that lists all javadoc command line options.

Instructs javadoc to obtain the text for the overview documentation from the file specified by *path/filename* and place it on the **overview-summary.html** file.

`-overview path/filename`

Instructs javadoc to obtain the text for the overview documentation from the file specified by *path/filename* and place it on the overview-summary.htm file.

`-package`

Documents only package, protected, and public classes and members.

`-private`

Documents all classes and members.

`-protected`

Documents only public and protected classes and members. This is the default.

`-public`

Documents only public classes and members.

`-source javaVersion`

Specifies the version of source code accepted. The default is **1.5**, which refers to JDK 5. Other possible values are **1.4** and **1.3**.

`-sourcepath sourcePathList`

Specifies the search paths for finding Java source files to be documented.

`-subpackages package1:package2:...`

Indicates that javadoc should traverse the specified packages recursively.

Standard Doclet Options

Unless explicitly ordered otherwise, javadoc uses the standard doclet to generate HTML files that document an API. You can pass options to the standard doclet too, the same way as passing arguments to the javadoc. Also, options for the standard doclet can be interspersed with options for javadoc.

Here is the list of the more important options for the standard doclet. The complete list of options can be found here:

```
http://java.sun.com/j2se/1.5.0/docs/tooldocs/windows/javadoc.html#
standard
```

`-author`
> Includes @author text in the generated documents.

`-d directory`
> Specifies the target directory to which generated HTML files will be saved.

`-doctitle title`
> Specifies the title for the overview summary file.

`-footer text`
> Specifies the footer that will be place in the end of every generated file.

`-header text`
> Specifies the header that will be placed at the beginning of every generated file.

`-nodeprecated`
> Excludes any deprecated API.

`-nodeprecatedlist`
> Indicates to the standard doclet to not generate the deprecated-list.html file.

`-noindex`
> Omits the index from the generated documents.

`-nosince`
> Ignore all @since tags.

`-notree`
> Omits the class/interface hierarchy pages from the generated documents.

`-stylesheetfile path/filename`
> Specifies the path of a stylesheet file other than the standard one.

`-windowtitle title`
> Specifies the value for the HTML title tag in the generated documents. The *title* argument should not contain any HTML tags.

Generated Documents

Javadoc generates an HTML file for each Java class. The location of this HTML file is in accordance with the package the class belonging in. If a Java class belongs to the **com.domain** package, the corresponding HTML file will be located in the **com/domain** directory.

In addition, there are three other HTML files generated for each package:

- **package-frame.html**. Lists the members of a package.
- **package-summary.html**. Provides a brief description of each package member.
- **package-tree.html**. Contains the package class hierarchy.

By default, there is no description in the **package-summary.html** file. You can provide a description by creating either a **package-info.java** file or a **package.html** file in the package directory. The **package-info.java** option is new to JDK 5 and preferred. For example, here is a **package-info.java** file.

```
/**
 * The com.brainysoftware.common package contains classes
 * that are shared by all other packages.
 */
package com.brainysoftware.common;
```

Note that you must have the package declaration in the Java source.

On top of package-specific files, Javadoc creates files that summarize all packages in the document. These files are located at the root of the destination directory and are as follows.

- **allclasses-frame.html**. List all classes and interfaces. Interfaces are printed in italic. This file is to be one of the frames contained by the **index.html** file.
- **allclasses-noframe.html**. Similar to **allclasses-frame.html** but to be used when the user browser does not support frames.
- **constant-values.html**. List constant field values.
- **deprecated-list.html**. List all deprecated members.
- **help-doc.html**. A general file explaining the organization of the API document.
- **index.html**. The main page that conveniently acts as the entry point to the whole documentation. It contains framesets that reference the

overview-frame.html, allclasses-frame.html, and overview-summary.html files. Figure 27.1 shows a typical **index.html** file.

- **index-all.html**. An index of all package names and package member names.
- **overview-frame.html**. Provides an overview of the document.
- **overview-summary.html**. Provides descriptions of all packages in the document. The descriptions are taken from the **package-info.java** or **package.html file** for each package.
- **overview-tree.html**. Contains the hierarchy of each package in the document.
- **package-list**. Lists all packages.
- **stylesheet.css**. The stylesheet for the generated HTML files.

Summary

One secret to successful API is the availability of documentation that explains how to safely use the members of the API and its class hierarchies. Java supports this by allowing you to provide comments for each package, type, and type member of your API. Each doc comment can contain a description and tags.

Javadoc is a tool that comes with the JDK to generate the document based on comments found in source files. Javadoc works by reading source files and generates document based on a doclet. The standard doclet in Javadoc generates HTML files.

Question

1. What is the difference between doc comments and Java comments in code?

:

Chapter 28
Application Deployment

After you finish developing and testing your application, you now need to think about deploying it to the end user. The technology for Java application deployment is Java Web Start (JWS). It is a tool that runs on the Java Network Launching Protocol (JNLP). This chapter starts with an overview of JWS and proceeds with JNLP. At the end of this chapter, an example is given.

JWS Overview

JWS is a sophisticated deployment tool that allows you to deploy Java applications over the Internet, a local network, or from a CD. The most common is through Internet deployment, however. You can also configure JWS to automatically download the correct version of JRE if the user's computer does not have the right JRE installed. Caching is also supported. If you decide you will allow JWS to cache your application, JWS can run it even though the user computer is not connected to the Internet.

Note
A complete guide to JWS can be found at
http://java.sun.com/j2se/1.5.0/docs/guide/javaws/.

In short, for deployment of an application, you need to package your application in a jar file and create a JNLP file that describes the jar file. The JNLP file can also give the user instructions on what to do to download and install the application. In addition, you may need to configure your Web server to add a MIME type for the **jnlp** extension, if the MIME type has not been added. Optionally, you can create an HTML page that provides a link to the JNLP file and uses JavaScript to check the versions of the JDK in the user's computer.

Typically, here are what you tell JWS to do using a JNLP file.

1. If there is no JRE installed on the user's computer, Java Web Start can download the latest version of JRE and installs it.
2. If there is a JRE with the correct version, JWS simply runs the application.
3. If the JRE on the user's machine is older than that required to run the application, JWS installs the appropriate JRE and runs the application using the downloaded JRE. The new JRE is only used to run this application and will not affect the old JRE.

JWS is installed as part of the JDK. If the user computer does not have a JDK yet, then no JWS is available. Therefore, you need to detect if JWS is already installed and download it automatically if it has not.

If JWS is not installed, then you have these options:

1. Install it silently (only works if the user is using IE, in other words on Windows only)
2. Direct the user to a page that provides links to download JREs.(in Linux/Unix)

In the example that illustrates the use of JWS in this chapter, you can use a JavaScript script to detect if JWS is available and either installs it silently or redirects the user to a JRE download area.

JNLP File Syntax

You need a JNLP file that guides JWS to run your application smoothly. A JNLP is an XML document, and in it you can specify the following:

- What version of JWS can handle this JNLP file.
- What version of JRE is required to run the described application
- The name and the location of the jar file containing Java classes, icons, and other resources.
- The name of the main Java class to invoke.
- The permission the application required
- Whether or not the user will be allowed to run the application offline.

- Whether or not a shortcut should be created on the desktop that points to this application for the user to run it after the first time.

The root element of a JNLP file if **jnlp**. Nested within <jnlp> are the following:

- **information**
- **security**
- **resources**
- **application-desc**
- **applet-desc**

All the tags are discussed in these sections.

The jnlp Element

The **jnlp** element is the root element in a JNLP document. It can have three attributes:

- **spec**. Specifies the version of JWS required to handle this JNLP file. The default is "1.0+", which means all JWS can handle this. Another valid values are "1.5" or "1.5+", which means only JWS that comes with JRE 5 or later can handle it. In most cases, you may want to use the default value so users with older versions of JWS can still run your application.
- **codebase**. Specifies a base URL to which all URL specified in this JNLP file will be relative.
- **href**. The URL of this JNLP file. The value can be an absolute URL or a relative URL to the value of the **codebase** attribute.

For example, the following **jnlp** element specifies that this JNLP file can be handled by any version of JWS and that this JNLP file can be found at http://books.brainysoftware.com/jdk5/deploy/myApp.jnlp.

```
<jnlp
    spec="1.0+"
    codebase="http://books.brainysoftware.com/jdk5/deploy"
    href="myApp.jnlp">
```

The **jnlp** element also implies that the name of this JNLP file is **myApp.jnlp**.

The information Element

This element specifies informational details of the application. It can have the following subelements, some of which are required.

- **title**. The name of the application. This is a required element.
- **vendor**. Specifies the application vendor. This is a required element.
- **homepage**. You use its **href** attribute to point to a Web site that provides more information about the application. The user can get this information from the Java Application Cache Viewer.
- **description**. A short description about the application. And, more than one **description** element can appear in the same JNLP file. Which one to use depends on the situation and on the value of the **kind** attribute. The value of the kind attribute is one of the following:
  - **one-line**. Use this description if the application is going to display a description in a list or a table.
  - **short**. Use this description if the application is going to display a description in a paragraph and there is enough room for it.
  - **tooltip**. Use this description if the application is going to display a description as a tooltip.

    Only one description element of each kind can be specified.
  - **icon**. Its **href** attribute specifies the URL of an image (in gif or jpeg) used to represent the application during the application launch, in the Java Application Cache Viewer, and as a desktop shortcut. For example:

    ```
    <icon href="images/splash.gif"/>
    ```

    If an **icon** element has a **kind="splash"** attribute, the icon specified will be used as a splash screen during the application launch.

- **offline-allowed**. If present, indicates that the application can be launched offline. If JWS launches an application offline, it will still check for updates but will not wait long. This means, if the user connection is slow the cached version of the application will be launched. If the connection is fast, there is a chance that the more up to date version will be downloaded and launched.
  - **shortcut**. Creates a shortcut on the desktop. It may nest the **desktop** and **menu** subelements. For example, the following **shortcut** element causes a shortcut to the application is created both on the desktop and in the menu. The sub menu is My Swing Apps.

```
<shortcut online="false">
    <desktop/>
    <menu submenu="My Swing Apps"/>
</shortcut>
```

- **association**. Tells the client computer to register the application with the operating system as the primary handler of certain extensions and a certain mime-type. If present, the **association** element must have the extensions and mime-type attributes. For example, this **association** element begs the operating system to associate the extension SwingApp with the MIME type application-x/swing-app.

```
<association mime-type="application-x/swing-app"
    extensions="swingApp"/>
```

The security Element

By default, applications deployed using JWS will have restricted access which is effectively the same as an applet in the Web browser. You can use the **security** element if you want to have unrestricted access. However, for unrestricted access your jar file must be signed. See Chapter 24, "Security" for information on how to digitally sign a jar file.

For example, the following **security** element requests unrestricted access for the application.

```
<security>
  <all-permissions/>
</security>
```

The resources Element

You use the resources element to specify the location of your resources, such as your jar file(s), system properties, and images. Here are some of the subelements that can reside inside the **resources** element.

- **jar**. Specifies a jar file that is part of the application's classpath.
- **nativelib**. Specifies a jar file containing native libraries.
- **j2se**. This element specifies what JRE version is required to run the application.

- **property**. Defines a system property that will be available to the application. This property has two attributes, **name** and **value**, to specify the attribute key and value, respectively.

The application-desc Element

Use this element to describe the application, such as the main class to invoke through the **main-class** attribute. The presence of this element also indicates to JWS that the JNLP file is launching a Java application (and not an applet). You can pass arguments through the use of the **argument** subelement. For example, the following **application-desc** element specifies the Java class to launch and passes two arguments.

```
<application-desc
    main-class="com.brainysoftware.jdk5.app27.SwingApp">
    <argument>Simple App</argument>
    <argument>400</argument>
</application-desc>
```

The applet-desc Element

Use this element if the JNLP file is used to launch a Java applet. The applet itself must be contained in the jar file specified using the **resources** element. The **applet-desc** element has the following attributes:

- **documentBase**. The document base of the applet. This must be specified explicitly since applets launched using JWS are not embedded in an HTML page.
- **name**. The name of the applet
- **main-class**. Specifies the fully qualified name of the applet.
- **width**. The width of the applet.
- **height**. The height of the applet.

The **applet-desc** element can have the **param** subelement that has two attributes, **name** and **value**.

For example, the following **applet-desc** element launches the **AnimationApplet** applet.

```
<applet-desc documentBase="http://www.brainysoftware.com/applet/"
```

```
        name="Animation Applet Demo"
        main-class="com.brainysoftware.jdk5.app27.AnimationApplet"
        width="400"
        height="400">
        <param name="interval" value="100"/>
</applet-desc>
```

A Deployment Example

The following is an example of how to deploy a Java Swing application.

Configure the Web server to use the Java Web Start MIME type

The browser needs to know what it needs to do when it downloads a jnlp file, just as it knows that it has to start Microsoft Word when the user clicks on a **doc** file. You need to configure your Web server so that for the **jnlp** file extension, the content type **application/x-java-jnlp-file** will be used. How to configure depends on the type of the Web server. You should consult the documentation provided by the Web server.

For example, for the Apache Web server you must add the following line to the **httpd.conf** configuration file:

```
application/x-java-jnlp-file JNLP
```

Create a jnlp file

The jnlp file for this example is given in Listing 28.1.

Listing 28.1: myApp.jnlp file

```
<?xml version="1.0" encoding="utf-8"?>
<jnlp
    spec="1.0+"
    codebase="http://books.brainysoftware.com/jdk5/deploy"
    href="myApp.jnlp">
    <information>
        <title>A Demo Swing Application</title>
        <vendor>Crouching Panda Software, Inc.</vendor>
```

```
      <description>A little app that swings</description>
      <description kind="short">Swing JMenu</description>
      <icon kind="splash" href="images/splash.gif"/>
      <offline-allowed/>
      <shortcut online="false">
          <desktop/>
          <menu submenu="My Downloaded Apps"/>
      </shortcut>
  </information>
  <resources>
      <j2se version="1.5+"/>
      <jar href="MySwingApp.jar"/>
  </resources>
  <application-desc main-class="JMenuTest1"/>
</jnlp>
```

3. Create an HTML File

An optional HTML file named **download.html** (given in Listing 28.2) is
provided. This HTML file uses JavaScript to detect the browser type (IE or
Netscape) and whether or not JWS can be found, and act based on those
situations.

Listing 28.2: The HTML file

```
<script type="text/javascript">
  var jnlpUrl =
    "http://books.brainysoftware.com/jdk5/deploy/myApp.jnlp";
  var isIE = (navigator.userAgent.indexOf("MSIE")!=-1);
  var jwsFound = false;
  if (isIE) {
    try {
      if (new ActiveXObject("JavaWebStart.isInstalled"))
        jwsFound = true;
    }
    catch(e) {}
  }
  else { // is not IE
    // a Netscape/FireFox
    if (navigator.mimeTypes && navigator.mimeTypes.length) {
      if (navigator.mimeTypes['application/x-java-jnlp-file'])
        jwsFound = true;
    }
  }
```

```
  if (jwsFound) {
    // redirect to JNLP file
    location=jnlpUrl;
  }
  else {
    if (isIE) {
      // use ActiveX component to automatically download
      document.write('<object codebase=' +
        '"http://java.sun.com/update/1.5.0/' +
        'jinstall-1_5_0-windows-i586.cab" ' +
        'classid="clsid:5852F5ED-8BF4-11D4-A245-0080C6F74284" ' +
        'height="0" width="0">' +
        '<param name="app" value="' + jnlpUrl + '">' +
        '<param name="back" value="true">' +
        '<a href="http://java.sun.com/j2se/1.5.0/download.html">' +
        'Download Java Web Start</a>"' +
        '</object>');
    }
    else { //no JWS and not IE
      // provide a link to download
      document.write('You do not have a Java Runtime Environment ' +
        'to run the application. ' +
        'Please download JRE 5.0 from ' +
        '<a href="http://java.sun.com/j2se/1.5.0/download.html">' +
        'here</a>');
    }
  }
</script>
```

4. Test the deployment

You can try this example by directing your browser to

`http://books.brainysoftware.com/jdk5/deploy/download.html`

If the correct JRE can be found on the user computer, the user will see a
dialog similar to the one in Figure 28.1.

Figure 28.1: A dialog that tells the user that the correct JRE was found

If you click Yes, you will see the JMenuTest1 application shown in Figure 28.2.

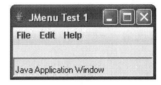

Figure 28.2: The deployed application

If the correct JRE cannot be found, the user will see a dialog like that in Figure 28.3.

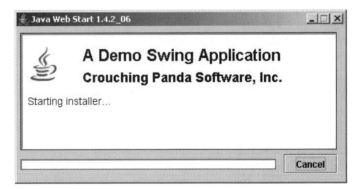

Figure 28.3: A dialog that tells the user that the correct JRE could not be found

In the case whereby the correct JRE cannot be found, JWS will offer to download the correct one. If you agree to download, it will show the license agreement that you must agree on. Figure 28.4 shows the window that displays the license agreement.

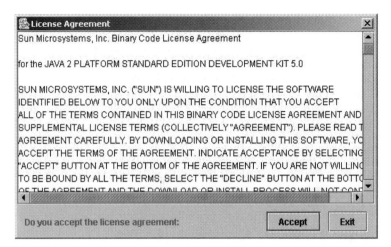

Figure 28.4: The license agreement that you must agree on to download the JRE

Figure 28.5 shows how the window looks like if you agree to install the JRE.

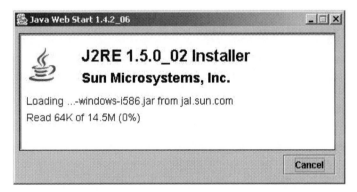

Figure 28.5: JWS downloads the correct JRE

Security Concerns

Chapter 24, "Security" explained the difference between an applet and an ordinary Java application in terms of security. Because applets may come from untrusted resources, the JRE impose security restrictions that cause applets not to be able to access the file system, etc. Unless the applets are signed.

Likewise, applications that are deployed over the Internet are more like applets and the JRE will impose the same restrictions as it does applets. If you are deploying your applications over the Internet and want to have access to resources, then you must deploy your applications in a jar file and sign it. See Chapter 24, "Security" on how to digitally sign a jar file.

Summary

In this chapter you have seen how you can deploy Java applications. JWS is the main tool for deployment and using it you can deploy applications over the Internet or a local network. Also, you can do it from a CD. JWS is also smart enough to detect if the user computer has the correct version of JRE and acts accordingly.

Questions

1. What does JWS stand for
2. What are the steps required to deploy a Java application via JNLP?
3. Why does the JRE restrict Java applications downloaded from the Internet?

Appendix A
javac

javac is the Java compiler to compile Java programs into bytecode. Source files must have the **java** extension and be organized in a directory structure that reflect the package tree. The output are **class** file that are organized in a directory structure reflecting the package tree.

javac has the following syntax.

```
javac [options] [sourceFiles] [@argFiles]
```

where *options* are command-line options, *sourceFiles* one or more Java source files, and *@argFiles* one or more files that list options and source files.

You can pass source code file names to **javac** in one of two ways:

- List the file names on the command line. This method is suitable if the number of source files is small.
- List the file names in a file, separated by blanks or line breaks, then pass the path to the list file to the **javac** command line prefixed by an **@** character. This is appropriate for a large number of source files.

Options

Options are used to pass instructions to **javac**. For example, you can tell **javac** where to find classes referenced in the source files, where to put the generated class files, etc. There are two types of options, standard and nonstandard. Nonstandard options start with -X.

Here are the lists of standard and nonstandard options.

Standard Options

-classpath *classpath*

> If in your source files you reference other Java types than those packaged in the Java standard libraries, you need to tell **javac** how to find these external types by using the **–classpath** option. The value should be the path to a directory containing referenced Java types or a jar file containing them. The path can be absolute or relative to the current directory. Two paths are separated by a semicolon in Windows and by a colon in Unix/Linux.
>
> For example, the following Windows command line compiles **MyClass.java** that references the **primer.FileObject** class located in the **C:\program\classes** directory.

```
javac -classpath C:/program/classes/ MyClass.java
```

> Note that the **FileObject** class is in the **primer** package, so you pass the directory containing the package.
>
> The following Linux command line compiles **MyClass.java** that references the **primer.FileObject** class located in the **/home/user1/classes** directory.

```
javac -classpath /home/user1/classes/ MyClass.java
```

> To reference class files packaged in a jar file, pass the full path to the jar file. For instance, here is how you compile **MyClass.java** that reference **primer.FileObject** in the **MyLib.jar** file located in **C:\temp** in a Windows system.

```
javac -classpath C:/temp/MyLib.jar MyClass.java
```

> This example compiles **MyClass.java** that references classes located in the **/home/user1/lib** directory and packaged in the **Exercises.jar** file located in the **/home/jars** directory in Linux:

```
javac -classpath /home/user1/lib/:/home/user1/Exercises.jar
MyClass.java
```

> If you are referencing a class whose root is the same as the class being compiled, you can pass **./** as the value for the classpath. For example, the following command line compiles **MyClass.java** that references both **C:\temp** and the current directory:

```
javac -classpath C:/temp/;./ MyClass.java
```

The alternative to the **classpath** option is to assign the value to the **CLASSPATH** environment variable. However, if the **classpath** option is present, the value of the **CLASSPATH** environment variable will be overridden.

If the **-sourcepath** option is not specified, the user class path is searched for both source files and class files.

`-Djava.ext.dirs=`*`directories`*

Override the location of installed extensions.

`-Djava.endorsed.dirs=`*`directories`*

Override the location of endorsed standards path.

`-d `*`directory`*

Specify the target directory for class files. The target directory must already exist. **javac** puts the class files in a directory structure that reflects the package name, creating directories as needed.

By default, **javac** creates class files in the same directory as the source file.

`-deprecation`

List each use or override of a deprecated member or class. Without this option, **javac** shows the names of source files that use or override deprecated members or classes. **-deprecation** is shorthand for **-Xlint:deprecation**.

`-encoding `*`encoding`*

Specify the source file encoding name, such as UTF-8. By default, **javac** uses the platform default converter.

`-g`

Print debugging information, including local variables. By default, only line number and source file information is generated.

`-g:none`

Prevent **javac** from generating any debugging information.

`-g:`*`{keyword list}`*

Generate only some kinds of debugging information, specified by a comma separated list of keywords. Valid keywords are:

- **source**. Source file debugging information
- **lines**. Line number debugging information
- **vars**. Local variable debugging information

`-help`

> Print a description of standard options.

`-nowarn`

> Disable warning messages. This has the same effect as **-Xlint:none**.

`-source release`

> Specifies the version of source code accepted. The values allowed are **1.3**, **1.4**, **1.5**, and **5**.

`-sourcepath sourcePath`

> Set the source code path to search for class or interface definitions. As with the user class path, source path entries are separated by semicolons (in Windows) or colons (in Linux/Unix) and can be directories, jar archives, or zip archives. If packages are used, the local path name within the directory or archive must reflect the package name.
> Note: Classes found through the classpath are subject to automatic recompilation if their sources are found.

`-verbose`

> Include information about each class loaded and each source file compiled.

`-X`

> Display information about nonstandard options.

Nonstandard Options

`-Xbootclasspath/p:path`

> Prepend to the bootstrap class path.

`-Xbootclasspath/a:path`

> Append to the bootstrap class path.

`-Xbootclasspath/:path`

> Override location of bootstrap class files.

`-Xlint`

> Enable all recommended warnings.

`-Xlint:none`

> Disable all warnings not mandated by the Java Language Specification.

`-Xlint:-xxx`

> Disables warning *xxx*, where *xxx* is one of the warning names supported for **-Xlint:xxx**.

`Xlint:unchecked`
> Provide more detail for unchecked conversion warnings that are mandated by the Java Language Specification.

`-Xlint:path`
> Warn about nonexistent path directories specified in the **classpath**, **sourcepath**, or other option.

`-Xlint:serial`
> Warn about missing serialVersionUID definitions on serializable classes.

`-Xlint:finally`
> Warn about **finally** clauses that cannot complete normally.

`-Xlint:fallthrough`
> Check switch blocks for fall-through cases and provide a warning message for any that are found. Fall-through cases are cases in a **switch** block, other than the last case in the block, whose code does not include a **break** statement.

`-Xmaxerrors number`
> Specify the maximum number of errors that will be reported

`-Xmaxwarns number`
> Specify the maximum number of warnings to be reported.

`-Xstdout filename`
> Send compiler messages to the named file. By default, compiler messages go to System.err.

The -J Option

`-Joption`
> Pass option to the java launcher called by javac. For example, **-J-Xms48m** sets the startup memory to 48 megabytes. Although it does not begin with **-X**, it is not a `standard option' of **javac**. It is a common convention for -J to pass options to the underlying VM executing applications written in Java.

Command Line Argument Files

If you have to pass long arguments to **javac** again and again, you will save a lot typing if you save those arguments in a file and pass the file to **javac** instead. An argument file can include both **javac** options and source filenames in any combination. Within an argument file, you can separate arguments using a space or separate them as new lines. The **javac** tool even allows multiple argument files.

For example, the following command line invokes **javac** and passes the file **MyArguments** to it:

```
javac @MyArguments
```

The following passes two argument files, **Args1** and **Args2**:

```
javac @Args1 @Args2
```

Appendix B
java

The **java** program is a tool to launch a Java program. Its syntax has two forms.

```
java [options] class [argument ...]
java [options] -jar jarFile [argument ...]
```

where *options* represents command-line options, *class* the name of the class to be invoked, *jarFile* the name of the jar file to be invoked, and *argument* the argument passed to the invoked class's **main** method

Options

There are two types of options you can pass to **java**, standard and nonstandard.

Standard Options

`-client`
> Select the Java HotSpot Client VM.

`-server`
> Select the Java HotSpot Server VM.

`-agentlib:libraryName[=options]`
> Load native agent library libraryName. Example values of *libraryName* are **hprof**, **jdwp=help**, and **hprof=help**.

`-agentpath:pathname[=options]`
> Load a native agent library by full pathname.

`-classpath classpath`
> The same as the **-cp** option.

`-cp classpath`

Specify a list of directories, jar archives, and zip archives to search for class files. Two class paths are separated by a colon in Unix/Linux and by a semicolon in Windows. For examples on using -cp and –classpath, see the description of the **javac** tool's **classpath** option in Appendix A.

`-Dproperty=value`

Set a system property value.

`-d32`

See the description of the **–d64** option.

`-d64`

Specify whether the program is to be run in a 32-bit or a 64-bit environment if available.

Currently only the Java HotSpot Server VM supports 64-bit operation, and the **-server** option is implicit with the use of -d64. This is subject to change in a future release.

If neither **-d32** nor **-d64** is specified, the default is to run in a 32-bit environment, except for 64-bit only systems. This is subject to change in a future release.

`-enableassertions[:<package name>"..." | :<class name> ]`

See the description for the **–ea** option.

`-ea[:<package name>"..." | :<class name> ]`

Enable assertions. Assertions are disabled by default.

`-disableassertions[:<package name>"..." | :<class name> ]`

See the description for the **–da** option.

`-da[:<package name>"..." | :<class name> ]`

Disable assertions. This is the default.

`-enablesystemassertions`

See the description for the **–esa** option.

`-esa`

Enable asserts in all system classes (set the default assertion status for system classes to **true**).

`-disablesystemassertions`

See the description for the **–dsa** option.

`-dsa`

Disables asserts in all system classes.

`-jar`

> Execute a Java class in a jar file. The first argument is the name of the jar file instead of a startup class name. To tell **java** the class to invoke, the manifest of the jar file must contain a line of the form **Main-Class: classname**, where *classname* identifies the class having the public static void **main(String[] args)** method that serves as your application's starting point.

`-javaagent:jarpath[=options]`

> Load a Java programming language agent.

`-verbose`

> See the description for the **–verbose:class** option.

`-verbose:class`

> Display information about each class loaded.

`-verbose:gc`

> Report on each garbage collection event.

`-verbose:jni`

> Report information about use of native methods and other Java Native Interface activity.

`-version`

> Display the JRE version information and exit.

`-showversion`

> Display the version information and continue.

`-?`

> See the description for the **–help** option.

`-help`

> Display usage information and exit.

`-X`

> Display information about nonstandard options and exit.

Nonstandard Options

`-Xint`

> Operate in interpreted-only mode. Compilation to native code is disabled, and all bytecodes are executed by the interpreter. You will not be able to enjoy the performance benefits offered by the Java HotSpot VMs' adaptive compiler.

`-Xbatch`

>   Disable background compilation so that compilation of all methods
>   proceeds as a foreground task until it completes. Without this option,
>   the VM will compile the method as a background task, running the
>   method in interpreter mode until the background compilation is
>   finished.

`-Xdebug`

>   Start with support for JVMDI enabled. JVMDI has been deprecated and
>   is not used for debugging in Java SE 5, so this option isn't needed for
>   debugging in Java SE 5.

`-Xbootclasspath:bootclasspath`

>   Specify a list of directories, jar archives, and zip archives to search for
>   boot class files. Entries are separated by colons (in Linux/Unix) or by
>   semicolons (in Windows). These are used in place of the boot class files
>   included in Java 5.

`-Xbootclasspath/a:path`

>   Specify a list of directories, jar archives, and zip archives to append to
>   the default bootstrap class path. Entries are separated by colons (in
>   Linux/Unix) or by semicolons (in Windows).

`-Xbootclasspath/p:path`

>   Specify a list of directories, jar archives, and zip archives to prepend in
>   front of the default bootstrap class path. Entries are separated by colons
>   (in Linux/Unix) or by semicolons (in Windows).

`-Xcheck:jni`

>   Perform additional checks for Java Native Interface (JNI) functions.
>   Specifically, the Java Virtual Machine validates the parameters passed to
>   the JNI function as well as the runtime environment data before
>   processing the JNI request. Any invalid data encountered indicates a
>   problem in the native code, and the JVM will terminate with a fatal error
>   in such cases. Using this option imposes a performance penalty.

`-Xfuture`

>   Perform strict class-file format checks. For backwards compatibility, the
>   default format checks performed by the Java 2 SDK's virtual machine
>   are no stricter than the checks performed by 1.1.x versions of the JDK
>   software. This flag turns on stricter class-file format checks that enforce

closer conformance to the class-file format specification. Developers are encouraged to use this flag when developing new code because the stricter checks will become the default in future releases of the Java application launcher.

`-Xnoclassgc`

Disable class garbage collection.

`-Xincgc`

Enable the incremental garbage collector. The incremental garbage collector, which is off by default, will reduce the occasional long garbage-collection pauses during program execution. The incremental garbage collector will at times execute concurrently with the program and during such times will reduce the processor capacity available to the program.

`-Xloggc:file`

Report on each garbage collection event, as with **-verbose:gc**, but record this data to file. In addition to the information **-verbose:gc** gives, each reported event will be preceeded by the time (in seconds) since the first garbage-collection event.

Always use a local file system for storage of this file to avoid stalling the JVM due to network latency. The file may be truncated in the case of a full file system and logging will continue on the truncated file. This option overrides the **-verbose:gc** option if both are present.

`-Xmsn`

Specify the initial size of the memory allocation pool in bytes. The value must be a multiple of 1024 greater than 1MB. Append the letter **k** or **K** to indicate kilobytes, or **m** or **M** to indicate megabytes. The default value is 2MB. For example:

```
-Xms6291456
-Xms6144k
-Xms6m
```

`-Xmxn`

Specify the maximum size of the memory allocation pool in bytes. The value must a multiple of 1024 greater than 2MB. Append **k** or **K** to indicate kilobytes, or **m** or **M** to indicate megabytes. The default value is 64MB. For instance:

```
-Xmx83880000
-Xmx8192k
```

```
-Xmx86M
```

`-Xprof`

> Profile the running program and send profiling data to standard output. This option is provided as a utility that is useful in program development and should not be used in production.

`-Xrunhprof[:help][:<suboption>=<value>,...]`

> Enable cpu, heap, or monitor profiling. This option is typically followed by a list of comma-separated "<suboption>=<value>" pairs. You can display the list of suboption and their default values by running the command **java -Xrunhprof:help**.

`-Xrs`

> Reduce the use of operating-system signals by the Java virtual machine (JVM).

`-Xss`*n*

> Set thread stack size.

`-XX:+UseAltSigs`

> The JVM uses SIGUSR1 and SIGUSR2 by default, which can sometimes conflict with applications that signal-chain SIGUSR1 and SIGUSR2. This option will cause the JVM to use signals other than SIGUSR1 and SIGUSR2 as the default.

Appendix C
jar

jar, short for Java archive, is a tool to package Java class files and other related resources into a jar file. The **jar** tool is included in the JDK and initially the reason for its creation was so that an applet class and its related resources could be downloaded with a single HTTP request. Over time, **jar** became the preferred way of packaging any Java classes, not only applets.

The jar format is based on the zip format. As such, you can change the extension of a jar file to **.zip** and view it using a ZIP viewer, such as WinZip. A jar file can also include the META-INF directory for storing package and extension configuration data, including security, versioning, extension and services. jar is also the only format that allows you to digitally sign your code.

Note
More information on the jar file can be found at
http://java.sun.com/j2se/1.5.0/docs/guide/jar/jar.html

This appendix provides the syntax of the **jar** tool and examples of how to use it.

Syntax

You can use **jar** to create, update, extract, and list the content of a jar file. A **jar** command can be used with options, which are explained in the section "Options." Here is the syntax of the **jar** program commands.

To create a jar file, use this syntax.

```
jar c[vOM]f jarFile [-C dir] inputFiles [-Joption]
jar c[vO]mf manifest jarFile [-C dir] inputFiles [-Joption]
jar c[vOM] [-C dir] inputFiles [-Joption]
jar c[vO]m manifest [-C dir] inputFiles [-Joption]
```

To update a jar file, use this syntax.

```
jar u[v0M]f jarFile [-C dir] inputFiles [-Joption]
jar u[v0]mf manifest jarFile [-C dir] inputFiles [-Joption]
jar u[v0M] [-C dir] inputFiles [-Joption]
jar u[v0]m manifest [-C dir] inputFiles [-Joption]
```

To extract a jar file, use this.

```
jar x[v]f jarFile [inputFiles] [-Joption]
jar x[v] [inputFiles] [-Joption]
```

To list the contents of a jar file, use the following syntax.

```
jar t[v]f jarFile [inputFiles] [-Joption]
jar t[v] [inputFiles] [-Joption]
```

And, to add index to a jar file, use this syntax.

```
jar i jarFile [-Joption]
```

The arguments are as follows.

`cuxtiv0Mmf`

> Options that control the **jar** command. These will be detailed in the section "Options."

`jarFile`

> The jar file to be created, updated, extracted, have its contents viewed, or add index to. The absence of the **f** option and *jarFile* indicates that we are accepting input from the standard input (when extracting and viewing the contents) or sending output to the standard output (for creating and updating).

`inputFiles`

> Files or directories, separated by spaces, to be packaged into a jar file (when creating and updating), or to be extracted or listed from *jarFile*. All directories are processed recursively. The files are compressed unless option O (zero) is used.

`manifest`

> Pre-existing manifest file whose **name: value** pairs are to be included in **MANIFEST.MF** in the jar file. The options **m** and **f** must appear in the same order that manifest and jarFile appear.

`-C dir`

> Temporarily changes directories to dir while processing the following *inputFiles* argument. Multiple -C *dir inputFiles* sets are allowed.

`-Joption`

> Option to be passed into the Java runtime environment. (There must be no space between -J and *option*).

Options

The options that can be used in a jar command is as follows.

`c`

> Indicates that the **jar** command is invoked to create a new jar file.

`u`

> Indicates that the **jar** command is invoked to update the specified jar file.

`x`

> Indicates that the **jar** command is invoked to extract the specified jar file. If *inputFiles* is present, only those specified files and directories are extracted. Otherwise, all files and directories are extracted.

`t`

> Indicates that the **jar** command is invoked to list the contents of the specified jar file. If *inputFiles* is present, only those specified files and directories are listed. Otherwise, all files and directories are listed.

`i`

> Generate index information for the specified *jarFile* and its dependent jar files.

`f`

> Specifies the file *jarFile* to be created, updated, extracted, indexed, or viewed.

`v`

> Generates verbose output to standard output.

`0`

> This is a zero that indicates that files should be stored without being compressed.

M

Indicates that a manifest file entry should not be created for creation and update. This option also instructs the **jar** tool to delete any manifest during update.

m

Includes **name: value** attribute pairs from the specified manifest file manifest in the file at **META-INF/MANIFEST.MF**. A **name: value** pair is added unless one with the same name already exists, in which case its value is updated.

-C   *dir*

Temporarily changes directories (cd dir) during execution of the **jar** command while processing the following *inputFiles* argument.

-Joption

Pass option to the Java runtime environment, where option is one of the options described on the reference page for the java application launcher. For example, **-J-Xmx32M** sets the maximum memory to 32 megabytes.

Examples

The following are examples of how to use **jar**.

Create

This **jar** command packages all directories and files in the current directory into a jar file named **MyJar.jar**.

```
jar cf MyJar.jar *
```

The following, with the **v** option, does the same but outputs all messages to the console:

```
jar cvf MyJar.jar *
```

The following packages all class files in the **com/brainysoftware/jdk/** directory into the **MyJar.jar** file.

```
jar cvf MyJar.jar com/brainysoftware/jdk/*.class
```

Update

This command adds **MathUtil.class** to **MyJar.jar**.

```
jar uf MyJar.jar MathUtil.class
```

This command updates the **MyJar.jar** manifest with the name: value pairs in manifest.

```
jar umf manifest MyJar.jar
```

The following command adds **MathUtil.class** in the **classes** directory to **MyJar.jar**.

```
jar uf MyJar.jar -C classes MathUtil.class
```

List

The following command lists the contents of **MyJar.jar**:

```
jar tf MyJar.jar
```

Extract

The following command extracts all files in **MyJar.jar** to the current directory.

```
jar xf MyJar.jar
```

Index

This command generates in **MyJar.jar** an **INDEX.LIST** file that contains location information for each package in **MyJar.jar** and all the jar files specified in the **Class-Path** attribute of **MyJar.jar**.

```
jar i MyJar.jar
```

Setting an Application's Entry Point

The **java** tool, explained in Appendix B, allows you to invoke a class in a jar file. Here is the syntax:

```
java -jar jarFile
```

For **java** to be able to invoke the correct class, you need to include in the jar file a manifest that has the following entry:

```
Main-Class: className
```

Appendix D
NetBeans

Sun Microsystems launched the NetBeans open source project in 2000. The name NetBeans came from Netbeans Ceska Republika, a Czech company that Sun bought over. You guessed right that the new project was based on the code Sun acquired as the result of the purchase.

This appendix provides a quick tutorial to using NetBeans to build Java applications. NetBeans requires the JDK to work.

Download and Installation

You can download NetBeans free from http://www.netbeans.org. The latest version at the time of writing is 5. NetBeans is written in Java and, as such, it can run on any platform where Java is available. Each distribution includes an installer for easy installation. Make sure you download the correct version for your operating system. The installer guides you through step-by-step instructions that are easy to follow. You will be prompted to agree on the terms and conditions of use, specify the installation directory, and select the JDK version to use if your computer has more than one.

Once installed, you can run the NetBeans IDE just like you would other applications. Figure D.1 shows the Welcome page, the page that you will see the first time you launch NetBeans.

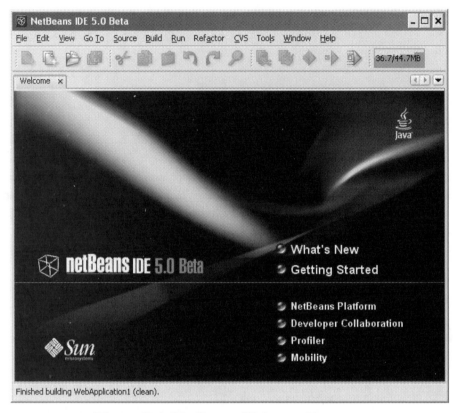

Figure D.1: NetBeans Welcome Page

There are icons that help you navigate NetBeans, but you can safely close this Welcome page by clicking the X button to the right of the pane title.

Creating a Project

NetBeans organizes resources in projects. Therefore, before you can create a Java class, you must first create a project. To do so, follow these steps.

    1. Click **File**, **New Project**. The **New Project** dialog will be displayed (See Figure D.2).

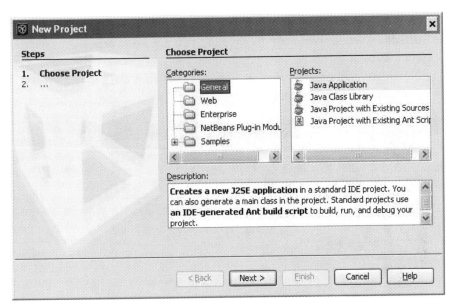

Figure D.2: The New Project dialog

2. Click **General** from the **Categories** box and **Java Application** from the **Projects** box. And then, click **Next**. The next screen will be displayed, as shown in Figure D.3.

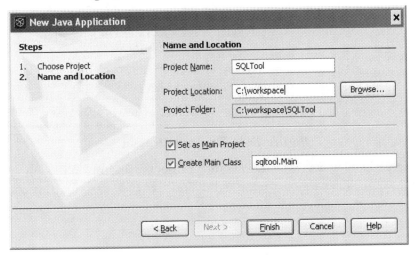

Figure D.3: Select a project name

3. Enter a project name in the **Project Name** box and browse to the directory where you want to save the project's resources. Afterwards, click **Finish**.

NetBeans will create a new project plus the first class in the project. This is depicted in Figure D.4.

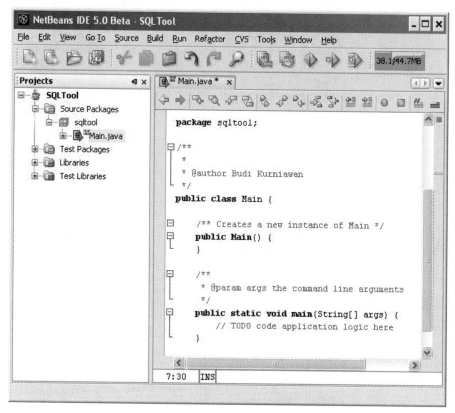

Figure D.4: The Java Project

Figure D.4 shows two windows, the **Projects** window on the left and the source file window on the right. You are ready to write your code.

Creating a Class

To create a class other than that created by default by NetBeans, right-click the project icon in the **Projects** window, then click **New, Java Class**. You will see the **New Java Class** dialog like that in Figure D.5.

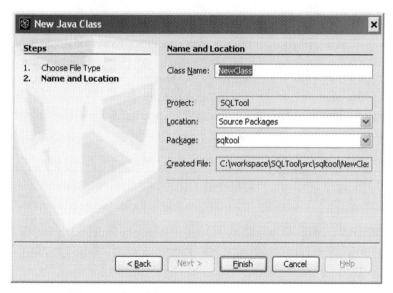

Figure D.5: The New Java Class dialog

Type in the class name and the package for this class, then click **Finish**. A new Java class will be created for you. You can see the new class listed on the **Projects** window.

You can now write your code. As you type, NetBeans will check and correct the syntax of your Java code. You can save your code by clicking **Ctrl+S** and NetBeans automatically compiles it as you save.

Running a Java Class

Once you are finished with a class, you can run it to test it. To run a class, click **Run, Run File**, then select the Java class you want to run. Any result will be displayed in the Console window. Another way to run a Java class is to right-click on the source code and click **Run File**.

Also, to run the last run class, press **Shift+F6**.

Adding Libraries

Oftentimes your classes or interfaces reference types in other projects or in a jar file. To compile these classes/interfaces, you need to tell NetBeans where to find the referenced library by adding a reference to it. You do this by right-clicking the **Libraries** icon in the **Projects** window, and then clicking **Add JAR/Folder**. A navigation window will then appear that lets you select your library file.

Debugging Code

A powerful feature offered by many IDE's is support for debugging. In NetBeans, you can step through a program line by line. The steps for debugging a program are as follows.

1. Add a breakpoint. You do this by clicking on the line on your code and click **Toggle Breakpoint**.
2. Execute the program by clicking **Run**, **Run File**, and then select the Java class to debug.

After selecting a class to debug in Step 2, these windows will open: **Watches**, **Call Stack**, and **Local Variables**. They allow you to monitor the progress of your code. The **Local Variables** window, for instance, allows you to inspect the value of a local variable.

To continue, click the **Run** menu and select whether to step into, step over, continue, or pause the program.

Appendix E
Eclipse

IBM launched Eclipse in 2001 after buying Object Technology International, a Canadian company. Including the purchase, IBM spent $40 million on the code that it finally released as an open source project. Written in Java, Eclipse ships with its own compiler, so it does not rely on Sun's Java compiler. As a result, you don't need a JDK to run Eclipse, just a JRE. In fact, Eclipse comes with compilers for other languages as well, such as C++ and C# because the developers have the ambition to make Eclipse the ultimate IDE.

Another thing to note, even though Eclipse is written in Java, it does not use the Swing technology. It created its own graphics library called the Standard Widget Toolkit in order to make Eclipse look and feel more like native applications. You can still use Eclipse to write Swing applications, though.

This appendix provides a quick tutorial to using Eclipse to build Java applications.

Download and Installation

You can download Eclipse free from http://www.eclipse.org. Version 3.1 and above support Java 5, the latest version at the time of writing is 3.2. You should download the latest **release** version. Release versions tend to be more bug-free, even though stable versions offer more new features. Make sure you download the version that will run on your operating system. Currently Eclipse is available on Windows, Linux, Solaris, AIX, Mac OSX, and HP-UX. You can even download the source code.

Eclipse distributions are packaged in a zip or gz file. In addition, if your Internet connection is slow, you can download Eclipse in torrent format.

Installation is a matter of extracting the distribution zip or gz file into a directory. No other steps are necessary. Once you extract, you can run it right away. Windows users can simply double click the **eclipse.exe** program icon. After a window that asks you where you want to store your work, you will see the Eclipse welcome page as shown in Figure E.1.

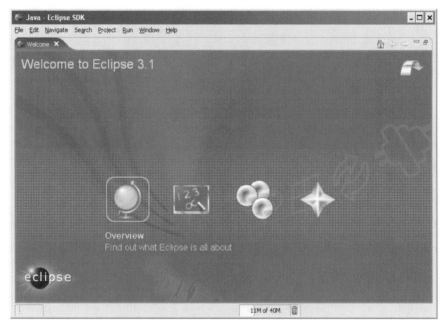

Figure E.1: Eclipse Welcome Page

There are icons that can help you navigate Eclipse, but you can safely close this Welcome page by clicking the X button to the right of the pane title. Figure E.2 shows the main page after you close the Welcome page.

Creating a Project

Eclipse organizes resources in projects. Therefore, before you can create a Java class, you must first create a project. To do so, follow these steps.

1. Click **File**, **New**, and Project. The New Project dialog will be displayed (See Figure E.3).

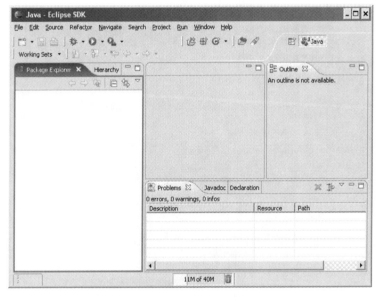

Figure E.2: Eclipse Main Page

Figure E.3: The New Project dialog

2. Make sure **Java Project** is highlighted in the **New Project** dialog, then click **Next**. You will see the next screen that prompts you for a project name. This screen is shown in Figure E.4.

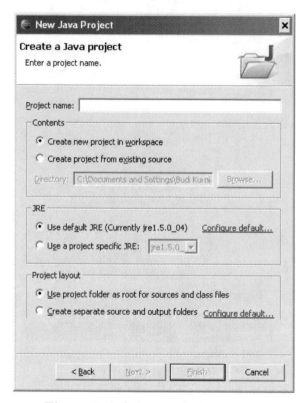

Figure E.4: Select a project name

3. Supply a name for your project. Once you type something in the **Project name** box, the **Next** and **Finish** buttons will become active. Note that by default your project will be created in the default workspace. However, you can choose a different location by clicking the **Create project from existing source** radio button and browsing to a directory in your file system.

4. To proceed you can either click **Next** or **Finish**. Clicking **Finish** uses default settings to create the project, and clicking **Next** allows you to select directories for your source and class files. For now, simply click **Finish**. A project will be created for you. Figure E.5 shows a project named **SQL Tool**.

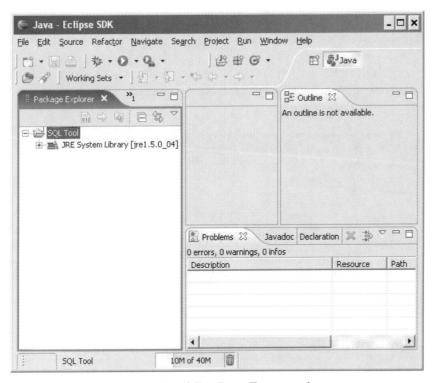

Figure E.5: The Java Perspective

What you see in Figure E.5 is called the Java perspective. A perspective is the combination of views that are suitable for performing a certain task. The Java perspective is used for writing Java code. It consists of the Package Explorer View on the left, the Outline view on the right, and the Problems view at the bottom. The location of each view is changeable by dragging the header of the view. Figure E.5 shows the default position of each view. There are many other views, all of which can be seen by clicking **Window, Show View**.

The other perspectives are Java browsing and Debug. You can select a perspective by clicking **Window, Open Perspective**.

Creating a Class

To create a class, right-click the project icon in the Package Explorer view, then click **New**, **Class**. You will see the **New Java Class** dialog like the one in Figure E.6.

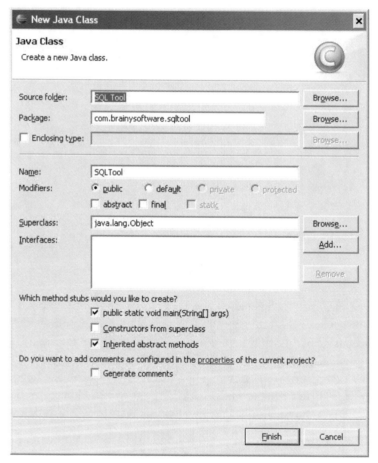

Figure E.6: The New Java Class dialog

Enter the package and the class name, then click **Finish** to create a class. The Java perspective will display the class code in a new pane, as shown in Figure E.7.

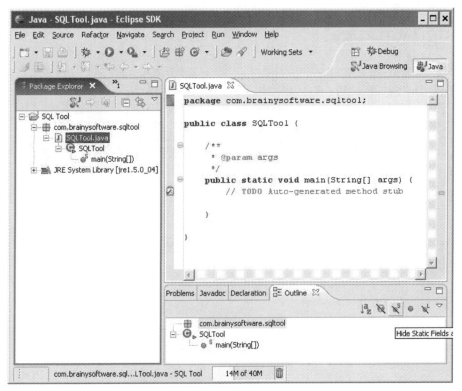

Figure E.7: Editing the Java class

You can now write your code. As you type, Eclipse will check and correct the syntax of your Java code. You can save by clicking **Ctrl+S** and Eclipse automatically compiles it as you save.

Running a Java Class

Once you are finished with a class, you can run it to test it. To run a class, click **Run**, **Run As**, **Java Application**. Any result will be displayed in the Console view. Another way to run a Java class is to right-click on the class pane and click **Run As**, **Java Application**.

Also, to run the last run class, press **Ctrl+F11**.

Adding Libraries

Oftentimes your classes or interfaces reference types in a jar file or in another project. To compile these classes/interfaces, you need to tell Eclipse where to find the library by adding a reference to it. You do this by clicking **Project**, **Properties**. The Properties window, shown in Figure E.8, will appear.

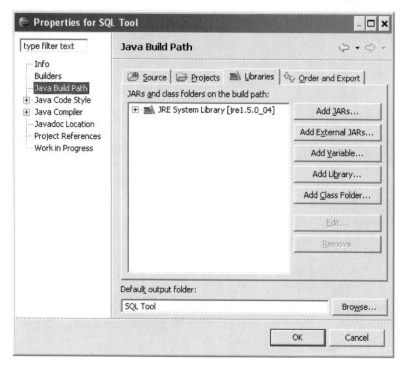

Figure E.8: The Properties Window

Click **Java Build Path** on the right pane and then click the **Libraries** tab on the left. Then, click **Add External JARs** and navigate to select the jar file. If the referenced types are in another project, click the **Projects** tab and add the required project.

Debugging Code

A powerful feature offered by many IDE's is support for debugging. In Eclipse, you can step through a program line by line. The steps for debugging a program are as follows.

1. Add a breakpoint. You do this by clicking on the line on your code and click **Run**, **Toggle Line Breakpoint**.
2. Execute the program by clicking **Run**, **Debug As**, **Java Application**.

Debugging requires the Debug perspective be open. After clicking **Java Application** in Step 2, a window will appear that asks you if you want to switch to the Debug perspective. Click **Yes**, and you will see the Debug perspective like that in Figure E.9.

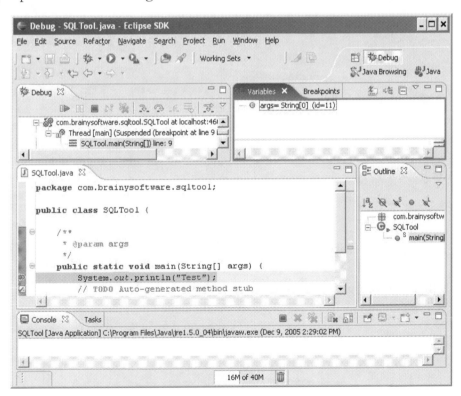

Figure E.9: The Debug Perspective

A useful view that appears is the **Variables** view. It displays the list of variables in your program and lets you inspect their values.

To continue, click the **Run** menu and select whether to step into, step over, resume, or terminate the program.

Index

Struts Design and Programming

A TUTORIAL
by Budi Kurniawan
Published by BrainySoftware.com
448 pages, April 2005
ISBN: 0-9752128-1-8
US $44.99

The first book on both design and programming of Apache Struts. The first part provides a complete reference on the latest version of Struts and teaches how a beginner can start coding with Struts. The second chapter discusses best practices and popular design patterns and teaches how Struts developers/architects should design their applications.

Here are some of the programming and design issues this book addresses:

- Action forms and how to choose the type of an action form's property
- How Struts processes action forms
- Input validation and the Validator plug-in
- Data conversion with Jakarta Commons BeanUtil class
- HTML, Bean, Logic tag libraries
- The Expression Language and JSTL
- The Data Access Object design pattern
- Earlier session invalidation
- Caching, paging, and sorting
- Request wrappers

How Tomcat Works:

A Guide to Developing Your Own Java Servlet Container
by Budi Kurniawan and Paul Deck
Published by BrainySoftware.com
464 pages, April 2004
ISBN: 0-9752128-0-X
US$49.99/C$77.99

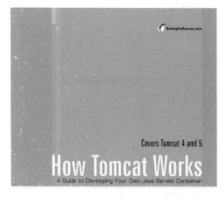

How Tomcat Works is the only book that explains the internal workings of Tomcat, the open source project used by millions of Java developers. Unlike other Tomcat titles, it is unique because it does not simply covers the configuration or servlet development with Tomcat. Listed on the official Tomcat website (http://jakarta.apache.org/tomcat/resources.html) and featured on Java Pro online (the most prestigious Java magazine), this book is meant for advanced readers interested in writing their own Tomcat modules or in understanding more beyond servlet/JSP programming. The publication of this book has generated tremendous interest as indicated by the fact that more than 3,000 people have downloaded the accompanying applications.

The authors of this book have cracked open Tomcat 4 and 5 and revealed the internal workings of each component. Upon understanding the contents of this book, you will be able to develop your own Tomcat components or extend the existing ones

Flash Development with OpenLaszlo

A Tutorial
by Chris Coremans
Published by BrainySoftware.com
500 pages, May 2006
ISBN: 0-9752128-6-9
US$44.95

Introducing developers to OpenLaszlo—a new technology for developing Flash that is based on XML and JavaScript—this guide provides developers with all the information about this free and open-source tool, including how to code within the OpenLaszlo development environment and the OpenLaszlo development suite as it applies to rapid development time. How and why OpenLaszlo is used and supported by industry leaders such as IBM and Yahoo! is also discussed.